IN THE
REALMS
of
GOLD

Pioneering in African History
Roland Oliver

In the Realms of Gold

Roland Oliver at the gateway of the acropolis at Great Zimbabwe, 1993

In the Realms of Gold

Pioneering in African History

Roland Oliver

THE UNIVERSITY OF WISCONSIN PRESS

The University of Wisconsin Press
2537 Daniels Street
Madison, Wisconsin 53718

Printed in the United States of America

Library of Congress Cataloging-in-Publication Data
Oliver, Roland Anthony.
In the realms of gold: pioneering in African history /
Roland Oliver.
440 pp.   cm.
Includes bibliographical references and index.
ISBN 0-299-15650-8 (cloth: alk. paper).
ISBN 0-299-15654-0 (pbk. : alk. paper).
1. Oliver, Roland Anthony.   2. Africanists—United States—Biography.
3. Historians—United States—Biography.   I. Title.
DT 19.7.045A3   1997
960'.07202—dc21
[B]   97-7217

*In Loving Memory
of Caroline Oliver
Faithful Companion
and Fellow Africanist
1909–1983*

Much have I travelled in the realms of gold
And many goodly states and empires seen
—John Keats

Contents

Illustrations

Maps

Preface

This book is presented with only a few references, all to published work. Nevertheless, except for the first four chapters, memory has played its part only under the strict control of the hard evidence of contemporary documents surviving in my private papers. First and foremost I have kept all my engagement books since 1950, and therefore I can see at a glance where I was and whom I met almost every day of my professional life. My first wife Caroline kept careful daily diaries of our two yearlong journeys in Africa in 1949–50 and 1957–58. When in later years I travelled alone, I wrote to her most days about my doings, and she kept all of these letters. During my travels as president of the British Institute in Eastern Africa I kept detailed diaries and wrote careful reports. I habitually preserved most of the personal letters written to me by other people–relations, friends, colleagues, and students—especially those written by my research students engaged on fieldwork in different parts of Africa. I have the texts of articles, reviews, broadcast talks, lecture notes, and conference papers to remind me of what was preoccupying me at different times. What I do not have, and have not tried to search for, is the routine correspondence concerning my teaching and administrative work at the School of Oriental and African Studies. To the extent that it still exists, much of this would be of a confidential or privileged nature and much more would be of merely parochial interest. Academic autobiography, it seems to me, should steer well clear of the classroom, even if it creates the misleading impression that dons spend little time doing what they are mainly paid to do.

My special thanks go to Peter Calvocoressi, Philip Curtin, John Fage, David Henige, Joseph Miller, Leonard Thompson, and Jan Vansina, who have spared the time to read the book in typescript and contributed valuable advice, to Jennifer Henderson, who so kindly helped me to correct the final proofs, and to my wife Suzanne, who has so cheerfully sustained its long gestation.

British titles, especially knighthoods, which are usually conferred late in life, are confusing to non-British people. For the sake of simplicity I have omitted most of them and refer to the holders of titles as I do other people, by first and surnames only. No disrespect is intended. In a few cases of inherited peerages in which the family names are less well known than the title, these have been retained.

In the Realms of Gold

1

A Child of the Raj

(1923–30)

I suppose that my attraction to far-off things can be traced in part to the first seven years of my life, spent in surroundings of legendary beauty in the valley of Kashmir. My father, at the time of his engagement to my mother in 1920, had worked for some twenty years in the Indian Political Service, mostly as a frontier commissioner in remote Himalayan outposts such as Leh and Gilgit. They had met on board ship when he was returning to India from home leave and she was accompanying her mother on a visit to Australia. There were twenty years between them and she hesitated over his proposal. He landed at Bombay and returned to his post with nothing decided, but six months later he made the long journey (about two thousand miles, which would have taken ten days by various modes of transportation) from Kashmir to meet her on her return voyage at Colombo. This time she accepted, and they were married in Bombay the following year. Soon afterwards he took early retirement, and they settled for some years in the capital city of Srinagar, where I was born in March 1923. I was their only child.

For nine months of each year my parents inhabited a string of house-boats, moored on the left bank of the Jhelum, a mile or two upstream from the old Kashmiri town. There was the "drawing-room boat" in which my parents sat, ate, and slept; the "nursery boat" where I lived with my nanny; and the "cook boat" where the servants had their headquarters and from which they approached the other two boats along outside gangplanks. My earliest visual memories are of the view from the nursery boat, which looked across the wide river with its incessant traffic of long thatch-roofed market boats called *dungas*, which either floated gently downstream guided by a single paddler in the stern or were laboriously propelled against the current by grunting boatmen who moved precariously along the gunwhales as they pushed their long poles against the riverbed. On

3

the far bank one could see the long roof of the British Residency and the European Club with its wooden terrace built up on stilts above the water. Behind these rose the thousand-foot reddish-brown rocky hill called the Takht-i-Suleiman, with a prison fort on its lower slopes and a Hindu temple on the summit. In the distance, towering ten thousand feet above the valley floor, were the snowy crests of the Himalayas, which bounded our world to the north, as the Pir Panjal Range did to the south. During the three summer months, when the valley became uncomfortably hot, we left the houseboats for a wooden chalet at Gulmarg, "the meadow of flowers" hidden in a green hollow at nine thousand feet on the slopes of the Pir Panjal.

On our side of the river behind our moorings were only fields and footpaths, so most of our outings began by boat, summoned by shouting to the opposite bank. There the owners of small, puntsize *shikaras*, each furnished with a pair of facing cushioned seats under a central awning, clustered around the steps of the club looking for custom. Somewhere on the other bank my father kept a motor car, a long open Dodge tourer with a rumble seat, which he used mainly for shooting or fishing expeditions in the mountains or up the side valleys. We occasionally made longer excursions in the car, but our everyday transport was by a combination of shikaras and one-horse buggies known as *tongas*. My parents kept riding horses and probably used them on most days. In Gulmarg there were neither boats nor wheeled vehicles. At first I was carried up the four-thousand-foot escarpment in a little sedan-chair, but at the earliest possible age (four or five) I also rode.

I think that the first datable event that I can remember was my third birthday party, celebrated on March 30, 1926, with a picnic in an almond orchard in full blossom on a hillside near Srinagar. It was an occasion attended not, as one might have supposed, by parents but only by nannies and their charges, and I remember it chiefly because for some reason our transport arrangements broke down, and we had to walk most of the way home. It seemed a very long way, but it was also exhilarating. It was the first time I had conceived of walking as a means of travel, as distinct from an unwelcome form of exercise designed to give nannies their daily outings (they used to lead us to strange and unattractive places such as the European cemetery in the town).

As with many people of my generation and class, Nanny loomed much larger than parents. The first one whom I can remember was Mrs. Watson. She must have attended me for three years, and I became very fond of her. I was much intrigued that she was *Missus* and not *Miss*, and soon I began to pump her about Mister Watson. He was, she informed me, a "private soldier" who had not treated her well. A "private soldier" sounded to me very grand indeed, like a kind of freelance who fought just for the hell of

4

My Australian great-grandfather Owen Friend

My grandmother Bessie (Friend) Donaldson (1875–1965)

it. I was sorry that he had treated her ill, but I suspected that he must be all right at heart. It was probably during my discussions of military affairs with Mrs. Watson that I gained my first insights into world politics. Why, I asked, were we who lived in houseboats so different from those who served us and from those who poled their dungas past our windows?

6

My grandfather William Cattenach Donaldson (1869–1914)

Because, she replied, *we* were British, whereas *they* were Indians. And why was it that the British were apparently so few and the Indians so many? Because, she said, the British were in India only as rulers. Their homeland was a small island far away across the sea. I remember that this was a puzzling piece of information. How would the inhabitants of a small island come to rule over a great country like India? Mrs. Watson assured me that it was because the British were stronger. It was the way of things that strong countries ruled over weak ones, and Britain ruled over more weak countries than anyone else. So we were the most important people in the world.

All this was in one way rather uplifting. It made me walk taller. At the same time it had some practical inconveniences. For example, it was impressed on me that members of the ruling race were not expected to show their emotions and in particular not to cry in the presence of their subjects. I like to think that there were not too many tears. But I remember one occasion on which Mrs. Watson behaved in a quite uncharacteristic and unaccountable manner, which it took me all of twelve hours to decide to overlook. It was springtime in Srinagar, and we went for a walk with another nanny and her charge, who was younger than I and fortunate enough to be provided with a push-chair. I was on foot, and although the Himalayan sun was hot, I was dressed like my opposite numbers in Kensington Gardens—in a tweed overcoat buttoned to the neck and leggings of the same material. Naturally enough, I lagged.

The two nannies, deep in their discussion of the nursery world, did not notice anything amiss until I was far behind them. They thought it was my fault. I thought it was theirs. I was told there would be a display of physical violence when we reached home, but such threats had been made too often for me to take them seriously. In due course the push-chair party took their leave of us, and Mrs. Watson and I continued on our way, chatting peaceably enough. We ferried over the river, and I mounted the gangplank of the nursery boat with every confidence that any unpleasantness had been forgotten. My outer garments were removed, and I assumed that afternoon tea was about to be served. Suddenly this two-faced woman approached me from behind, turned me upside down, and began to whack me with the back of a hairbrush. Having contemplated this episode with puzzlement for more than a half-century, I can only conclude that the other nanny had put her up to it and that Mrs. Watson dared not face her again until she could claim that she had done it.

In general my relations with Mrs. Watson prospered over the years, to such an extent that when in 1928 I was offered the choice of accompanying my parents on a visit to England or remaining in her care in Kashmir, I unhesitatingly chose the latter. I had no objection to foreign travel, but what, I asked, would happen to Mrs. Watson if I abandoned her? My parents were quite definite that if I came with them to England, Mrs. Watson's employment would terminate. That settled it. In loyalty I elected to stay. In the event, my decision proved a considerable disappointment. In my simple way I had imagined that Mrs. Watson and I would be left in charge of the household but not so. On my parents' departure the houseboats in the valley and the mountain chalet were both shut up, the servants disappeared to their homes, and my guardian and I were consigned to Needu's Hotel in Srinagar and to a seedy boarding-house in Gulmarg. In those places the quality of life was by no means that to which I had been accustomed. We had no facilities for entertaining other nannies and their charges, and probably they felt that we were no longer nice to know. Moreover, that summer, exceptionally, the monsoon reached right into the Himalayas, forcing us to sit all day in our boarding-house bedroom while the rain poured down. Ultimately, I found that all my heroism had won Mrs. Watson only a short reprieve, for when my parents returned they soon decided that the time had come for a governess.

I was now five and a half, and in retrospect I sense that the remaining two and a half years of our stay in India must have been one of the most stimulating and enjoyable periods of my childhood. Certainly, it must bear favourable comparison with the corresponding period most European children spend at primary schools of one kind and another. I still lived in the nursery boat with the new governess, Norah Hottinger, but I was of an age now to be of some interest to my parents, at least to my mother, and the hourlong visit I spent with her in the late afternoons was a pleasurable part of the day. In the mornings I was learning to read, write, and count but only until eleven o'clock, at which time the Kashmiri groom would appear with two horses. He and I would ride together until lunchtime. This was not only a tremendous access to freedom but it brought me into regular touch with another world. The groom spoke no English. We had to converse in Urdu, a language that had been spoken all round me since birth but that I had now to employ actively if I did not wish to ride in silence. In fact, if I remember correctly, we talked incessantly as we rode through the incomparable scenery around the Dal Lake, and at least once he took me to his home in the old town of Srinagar. There we climbed upstairs to a vast room on the fifth floor of an old wooden apartment building where I squatted in a circle with his many relatives and was regaled with delicious freshly baked chapatties (a bread similar to pita).

In Gulmarg even more than in Srinagar, the horse provided me with an avenue to greater freedom and a wider society, for here I found not merely the small circle of European residents in Kashmir but a host of British visitors from the plains of India. Children of riding age used horses rather as their contemporaries in England used bicycles, for house-to-house visiting, for all-day picnics still higher up the mountain, and for the children's service at the local church. There was even a pack of mounted Wolf Cubs, fully equipped with lances and banners, that met for gymkhanalike exercises in a green meadow.

We spent the early months of 1929, when I was nearly six, in the plains of India. I can remember still the tortuous drive some two hundred miles

My mother Lorimer (Donaldson) Oliver (1899–1989)

My father Douglas Giffard Oliver (1880–1936)

down the Jhelum gorge to Rawalpindi, with an overnight stop in a rest house perched hundreds of feet above the rushing river. Next day we drove down the last hill into Rawalpindi only to see the train that had been due to take us to Lahore steaming majestically out of the station on its southward journey. It was my first train, and I can still see the green engine and the string of bright red carriages disappearing into the brown landscape. My parents set off to chase it by car, leaving Norah Hottinger and me to follow by the night mail train. I forget where we stayed in Lahore, but I remember the delirious excitement of two successive polo weeks, when the teams of the Indian cavalry regiments competed against each other with high panache. They interspersed their matches with exhibitions of tent pegging, in which thunderous charges of trained horsemen swept past us with lances lowered to pierce and carry away the rows of little white targets a few inches above the turf. For me the trip ended with a monthlong visit to the Hottinger parents at Sialkhot, where her father was a doctor in the Indian Medical Service. He spent a large part of most days driving round the villages of the northern Punjab inspecting clinics and other medical posts. I accompanied him everywhere and thought it a marvellous life.

The summer of 1929 was to be our last in India, and during it my mother and I were both seriously ill, she with dysentery and I with typhoid fever. Maybe these two events hastened our departure, and I suppose the problem of my continued education was another factor. But I think my parents had also come to realise that Kashmir presented special difficulties for their marriage. There, at least, they had no interests in common. My father was a man's man who lived for his shooting and fishing, drank his evening whiskeys with other men at the club, and found his home recreation in a well-equipped carpenter's shop located at one end of the nursery boat. My mother's most serious interest was in turning Kashmiri girls, destined for lives in purdah, into Girl Guides. To this end she cultivated the missionaries who ran the leading schools in the old town. And for the rest, her friends were of a different generation from my father's. They seldom went out together. They hoped that in Europe a better pattern of life might perhaps emerge. But in one matter at least they agreed to follow separate paths. As a young man my father had been a champion bob-sleigher, and now in 1929 the proprietors of the Cresta Run at St. Moritz were looking for a new secretary. The post involved three months' residence a year in Switzerland with free accommodation at the best hotel. My father applied for it and was appointed. My mother was sure that St. Moritz was not for her. Thus they would live apart for three months a year.

In November 1929, therefore, my father departed for his first season of duty in Switzerland. Rather than winter alone in northern Europe for the first time in many years, my mother and I were to spend those

Child of the Raj, 1924

months in Meerut, the garrison town some forty miles to the east of Delhi where the Indian Mutiny had broken out in 1856 and where the current commanding officer was an old friend. Sadly, then, we packed up the houseboats, dismissed all but one servant, and set off by car across the Banni Hal pass to Jammu, Lahore, Delhi, and Meerut. Our host proved to be an eccentric who believed himself to be a reincarnation of Napoleon and who made it a practice to keep his right hand tucked into his jacket whenever it was not otherwise employed, but our stay with his family was pleasant. I suppose that I did lessons with his children. We rode twice a day in the unbroken winter sunshine, watching the soldiers at their

13

exercises and enjoying privileged seats at their great occasions, when our host, who was distinctly portly, would mount his horse from a kitchen chair to take the salute. There was a hilarious event when the commander in chief, Edmund Ironside, came to lunch. Our host, posing carefully in front of a portrait of Napoleon that hung in the hall, asked Ironside if he did not see the resemblance.

At last, in March 1930, our life in India came to an end. With the one remaining Kashmiri servant called Aliyah, who had been with us since my birth, we drove to Delhi and caught the train to Bombay. We spent the night in the Taj Mahal Hotel and walked with Aliyah by the sea of which he and I had heard so much. Next day we boarded the Lloyd Triestino liner *Cricovia* that was to carry us to Venice. Aliyah saw us to our cabin, helped us to unpack, and took a long sorrowful farewell. I have thought of Aliyah often and especially of the secret early morning sessions before my parents and governess were awake, when I squatted round the brazier with him and his colleagues as they awaited the first summons of the day. I still think of him as I say the lines of Housman:

> The faithful valet to fetch and carry,
> The true, sick-hearted slave,
> Expect him not in the just city
> And free land of the grave.[1]

2

Unwillingly to School

(1930-36)

I have vivid memories of the journey to Europe—the radiant brilliance of the Indian Ocean; the schools of flying fish that skimmed the water beside us; the harbour at Aden with the fins of sharks gliding above the surface; a box of Turkish delight that made me horribly sick in the Red Sea; a solitary daylong stance astride the anchor chain in the bow of the ship as it nosed its way through the Suez Canal; the little ceremony in the eastern Mediterranean when those passengers not expecting to return to the East gathered by the stern rail and hurled their solar topees (pith helmets) into the ship's wake; a hotel in Venice where I allowed my bath to overflow and flood the rooms below; the Orient Express winding through the corkscrew tunnels of the Alpine passes; the undreamed-of verdure of the Kentish countryside in early spring; the florid features of my grandmother's chauffeur, Robinson, who met us at Victoria Station and drove us to her house in Eaton Place, Belgravia.

It was the first time that I had met any member of my family other than my parents, but my grandmother stepped at once into the very centre of my consciousness. Born in 1875 in Sydney, she was the second of twelve children of a prosperous banker and sheep farmer who had sent her and a younger sister, under sail, to school at Cheltenham Ladies College during the joint reign of Miss Beale and Miss Buss. As a special concession the two little girls from Australia were allowed the services of a lady's maid, and during the school holidays tutors took them travelling in Europe. They did not return to Australia until they were grown up, and on the steamship that carried them home my grandmother met and became engaged to William Donaldson, a young member of the family that owned the ship. Soon she was back in Europe to live for the next twenty years in a series of large country houses in Ayrshire and Stirlingshire and to bring up five daughters, of whom my mother was the third. Child-rearing

15

in those days was not a bar to travel, and my grandparents, in the interests of their family business, were constantly on the move—not rushing about in aeroplanes but in the staterooms of ships and drawing-room cars of railways the world over, meeting people of their own sort, with plenty of time to talk and to forge enduring friendships. Soon after my grandfather's premature death in 1914 at the age of forty-five, my grandmother moved to London to oversee the debut of her daughters and stayed there to provide a family centre and a hospice to relieve their subsequent catastrophes.

In 1930, when my mother and I arrived from India, the youngest daughter was still living at home unmarried. The second youngest, already tragically widowed, lived there also with a son of my own age and two older stepchildren coming and going from boarding school. Also in residence were the two daughters of the eldest, who had left them behind in a long course of marital adventures. So, for all its six floors and generous proportions, the house in Eaton Place was full to the brim, and where the eight servants slept I can hardly imagine. Our stay on this occasion was only a short one, but it brought the freedom of my grandmother's bedroom from six until eight o'clock each morning. There she would already have been sitting up since four in her high four-poster, typing long bulletins to her vast and scattered family. When I entered, she would put all this aside and tell me endless marvellous stories of her childhood in Australia, her first voyage to Europe in the windjammer, the San Francisco earthquake, the sinking of the *Titanic*, and the lives of countless acquaintances, particularly of those who, according to one of her favourite phrases, had "died in screaming agony"—a kind of termination I accepted with all the philosophic calm of childhood in the face of the ultimate.

During most of the 1930s my grandmother's household was the one fixed point in a constantly changing world. My parents had to decide whereabouts in England to settle and then to find a suitable house. Meantime, they made temporary bases in France and Belgium. In France it was Dinard, across the bay from St. Malo. We had a villa in the Boulevard Féart, which led up from the harbour to the cathedral and afforded a spectacular viewing point for the processional activities of the Catholic church. Almost every day a funeral cortège would pass our front windows, with nodding black-plumed horses pulling a huge high hearse, followed by mourners arrayed in every kind of crêpe drapery. On feast days half the town turned out to walk behind the clergy bearing the Blessed Sacrament under a golden palanquin (awning), sourrounded by images of the Virgin and the saints. By day I attended the English-language school of a Mr. Hogan, about which I remember nothing; the most important part of my education there was the company of our Swiss maid Louise, who taught me to speak French with an accent that was provincial but nonetheless convincing. In Dinard it was summer. The sea sparkled in the bay, and I learned to swim. It was a good billet for six months or so.

From Dinard we moved to Le Zoute, on the Belgian coast, where we at first rented a villa in the Avenue Lippens. In retrospect I see this as a really bad time in my life. Neither of my parents had faced the problems of providing a home life for an only child in a foreign country, now that nannies and governesses were done with. There was some kind of English-language day school, where I learned a little Latin and also the marvellous words of the General Thanksgiving from the Book of Common Prayer, which we said before we started work. For the rest, I breakfasted alone. I returned after school to a house empty except for foreign servants. I played golf by myself and fell prey to unwholesome fantasies. I suppose this was the classic problem of lonely single children. By the following summer things had begun to improve. We had moved into a part of the town where some other English people were living with children my age. I learned to play tennis and made some friends that way, but it was still an uphill struggle.

That winter passed somehow, and then in the spring of 1932 came the time for boarding school in England. It was a huge shock. The place was in Gloucestershire at one corner of Minchinhampton Common. It was called Beaudesert Park, and it was selected because my mother and one of her sisters had once been at school with the headmaster's daughter. The institution was a good one of its kind—very much a family business, staffed by the proprietor and his wife, two of their unmarried sons, a daughter, her husband, and just two or three hired hands. A bony blue-nosed matron supervised our dressings and our undressings, our hot baths and our cold baths; we stood in line before her each morning to have our heads yanked from side to side as she peered into our ears and down our necks. A retired sergeant major drilled us remorselessly each midmorning and, for the rest, ensured that we spent every moment of outdoor leisure running in pursuit of some kind of ball. On weekday afternoons we ran across Minchinhampton Common to a playing field where we played football (soccer) or cricket according to the season. On Sundays we wrote supervised and half-dictated letters home before marching in crocodile (two by two) to the local church. We wore blue serge suits with Eton collars and sported bowlers in winter and straw boaters in summer.

Indoors the scene was much dominated by the headmaster, known as Big Sir to distinguish him from all the lesser sirs. He was rather apt to address one as "you ghastly little hound" and, if irritated, would stretch out a hand, seize one's cheek between his two middle fingers, and shake it in a way that modern educators would not approve but that was humiliating rather than actually painful. His teaching of Latin and Greek was sometimes interspersed with his forebodings about what the

17

Unwillingly to school, 1932

world would come to if people like Stafford Cripps (the left-wing British statesman) ever got control of it. Nevertheless, he was an exceptional teacher, and his frequent simulated rages nearly always ended with an injunction to look him straight in the eye. For these contests he would remove his pince-nez, holding it in his left hand while his intimidating gaze gradually melted into a twinkle of fundamental kindness.

In retrospect I have often wondered whether the only thing I enjoyed about my preparatory school was the lessons. I certainly did not enjoy football, still less kicking balls aimlessly around playgrounds. I preferred cricket, even though we practised it three or four times each weekday and in our Eton collars on Sunday afternoons and evenings. On really searching my memory, however, I am surprised to find how many pleasant and companionable pastimes could still be fitted into our busy schedule. There was of course no television, and although Big Sir had a radio in his private quarters, I can remember only one occasion, in January 1936, when he invited a few of the older boys to come in and listen to the bulletins announcing King George V's approaching death. And so there were many long winter evenings, when some of us attended to our stamp collections, while others made dreadful fretwork knick-knacks— pipe racks and the like—to offer to admiring parents. And then there were the crazes that swept through the school with the speed of epidemics. One term it was yo-yos. Five boys returned from the holidays equipped with them, and within a week everyone had sent begging letters home. There followed ten more weeks for the highly competitive acquisition of ever-more-demanding operational skills. Another term it was tanks, which we fabricated on the premises out of a cotton reel (spool) with a rubberband threaded through the hole and held in place by a pencil on one side and half a matchstick on the other. With the rubberband thoroughly twisted we could set the contraption down on any flat surface, and it would advance in pursuit of other tanks or even confront them head-on. One hobby acquired on this Cotswold hillside has brought me pleasure throughout my life. Thanks to the enthusiasm of Big Sir's eldest son "Mr. Austin" many of us learned to love butterflies and moths. We caught them in nets and moth traps, killed them in stink bottles, and pinned them out in collecting cabinets. But we also studied them. We bought books and identified them. We made pill-boxes and mated the lepidopterans, keeping the eggs carefully until they turned into caterpillars and then into chrysalises. There was even a firm somewhere in Kent that supplied us through the post with the caterpillars of some of the rarer species we could not capture for ourselves. Of course, I soon stopped collecting, but the brief experience of doing so taught me to recognize all the English butterflies and some of the moths, and it gave me the eye to observe things in the countryside that many people never notice.

Still, when all exceptions have been made, the preparatory school years were not a happy time for me. Home life was better for a year or two, for my parents had at last settled in England in a pretty Jacobean farmhouse in the village of Thurston near Bury St. Edmunds. The neighbourhood was friendly, and my parents had good contacts there to start them on their way. There were children of my age within bicycling distance, and soon invitations to children's tennis parties, cricket matches, and Christmas dances poured in from all over the county. There was much to be done about the house and garden, and my father was an admirable handyman. Together with Jack the gardener, we felled trees, cut them up for firewood, laid out paths, and built a brick-and-rubble wall to enclose a new rose garden. In one of the outbuildings was a dynamo machine with which we made our own electricity. In another my father had a carpenter's shop with splendid tools, including electric saws and lathes. A hard tennis court was put down in a corner of the paddock, and neighbouring children were happy to come and play.

It should have been a formula for domestic bliss, but it was not to be. My father was absent every winter in St. Moritz, and my mother and I never joined him there, even for a week or two. He returned every spring, drinking more whiskey and getting up later in the morning. My mother did not restrain her criticisms, and we soon ate our meals in silence or with only the most perfunctory exchanges to keep up appearances before the parlourmaid. My father spent more and more time in his workshop. My mother dutifully drove me around to social engagements during the school holidays but otherwise retreated into women's bridge and the higher levels of Girl Guide administration. In due course I began to realise that she was planning to leave him and that meanwhile she was seeking to wean me from him. She said it would be "either or." That rather rankled.

During my last Easter holidays in Suffolk a pony I was riding fell at a jump and in the succeeding mêlée my left elbow was crushed into several pieces. As a result, I missed a part of my last summer term at Beaudesert and had to spend the rest of it carrying around a five-pound kitchen weight in a forlorn attempt to restore full movement to the joint. I am sure that I carried around with me too the consciousness of crisis at home. One weekend my father came to take me out. It was his first visit to the school and he came alone. He drove me to see his old school at Marlborough, and as we went he told me that my mother was about to leave him and not through any wish of his. He said she was an angel and he was not good enough for her. It was all very upsetting. I looked around at the other boys in my dormitory and felt inadequate, inferior, and uninteresting. It was in these circumstances that I had to go and sit for a scholarship at Stowe. I certainly did not expect to win one, and when the news of my success came through, I could hardly believe it.

I saw my father only once more, when at the end of the summer term of 1936 he took me to watch tennis at Wimbledon. During the holidays that followed my mother took me to Le Zoute, while my father travelled in eastern Europe. In September he returned to live alone in the Suffolk house. In November he died at the age of fifty-six after falling down a back staircase in the middle of the night.

3

Stowe and King's
(1936–42)

In September 1936, aged thirteen and a half, I entered public school at Stowe and stayed there until December 1940. Despite the wreck of my family life, or perhaps because of it, I remember feeling much at home there almost from the first day. My "house," which bore the secondary ducal name of Chandos, occupied the eastern half of the east wing of the great country mansion of the former dukes of Buckingham; several of the most famous architects of the eighteenth century had played some part in building it. The "house room," where the younger boys did their preparation and spent their leisure hours, had been the easternmost of the long sequence of state rooms on the south front of the building designed by Robert Adam, and its windows commanded the splendid vista that "Capability" Brown had created at the beginning of his career as a landscape gardener to the aristocracy. It descended between beech groves to the Octagon Lake and rose beyond it to the Corinthian Arch, which led to the double avenue of oak trees lining the road to Buckingham and the south. My first dormitory was high up in the same wing in what I suppose once was a servants' room, its windows looking west across the rooftops to the pediment of Vanburgh's portico, where a huge clock rang out the quarters in tones of uncompromising solemnity. The three names on the door, in alphabetical order, were Monaco, Oliver, and Phillips.

Monaco was indeed Prince Rainier, who has proved to be such a model of princely virtue that I hesitate to comment on his brief career as an English schoolboy, which lasted for only a term. Hilary Phillips was the son of an international bridge player, Hubert Phillips, who made an unusual livelihood devising crossword puzzles. Hilary, like me, was a scholar (scholarship student), so we spent our days as well as our nights in company in the two prestigious forms in which the more clever boys prepared for the school certificate before going on to specialise in the upper

22

school. We thus had the privilege of splendid teaching, because the most gifted and ambitious sixth-form masters came scouting for talent among us, hoping to attract us later on into joining their teams of competitors for university awards. English, history, French, German, and Latin were all superbly done. So, I believe, was mathematics, though I had no head for it. The science master was the only laughingstock among them. But the great treat of every week was the class taught by the headmaster, J. F. Roxburgh, who somehow managed to teach every boy in the school once a week and to know each of us unerringly by both Christian and surname. "J. F.," as we called him, was a magnificent vital figure, immaculately tailored in Savile Row, with one gorgeous handkerchief in his breast pocket and another in his cuff, not a hair out of place, a spring in his step, and an unmistakable whiff of some very discreet, very exotic scent as he swept past us into chapel or paced untiringly around a classroom. He drove, at reckless speeds, a maroon Daimler coupé, accompanied when occasion demanded it, by a chauffeur in breeches and leather gaiters. As the obituaries say, "he never married," but neither did he ever put a foot wrong. "Hilton Young," he would say musingly, as he strode into the classroom, "What is the French for a hairbrush?" When someone gratingly pushed back a chair, he would wince and exclaim, "Oh, my dear man, *please* don't throw the furniture about."

In this scene we were reared. In the afternoons we ran up the Grecian Valley to the playing fields beyond. If we played musical instruments, we did so in the Queen's Temple. If we played tennis, the path to the courts led us past the monument to the British Worthies—a semicircle of thirty busts, including Shakespeare, with his "power to astonish and delight mankind," and Newton, "whom the God of Nature made to comprehend his works." Members of the Officers Training Corps paraded at the Gothic Temple, which looked down on the Palladian Bridge. Those who swam or sailed or skated did so upon the Eleven Acre Lake, with the Temple of Friendship on its southern shore. Those who played golf enjoyed a green beside the Rotunda Temple, perhaps the most exquisite of them all. Before each meal the entire school assembled without any crowding in the Marble Saloon, which formed the centrepiece of the *piano nobile*. Outside it, whenever the sun shone during a leisure moment, the Adam portico on the South Front and the steps descending from it would have a sprinkling of grey-suited "Stoics" (as pupils of Stowe are known) gazing out over the enchanting landscape. Just to live at Stowe, even in the lower ranks of a community of 550 boys, was a pleasure that impressed me every day.

To live in beautiful surroundings is a wonderful privilege. It does not, however, insulate one from the troubles of life. My first term at Stowe was marred by my father's sudden death. It found my mother living temporarily with my grandmother, no longer in Eaton Place but in an

23

ample flat in Ennismore Gardens with a splendid open view over the churchyard of Holy Trinity Church to the Brompton Oratory behind it. It was from there that we went to bury my father at Kensal Green one cold and rainy November morning. It was there too that I spent my first Christmas holidays from Stowe. My eldest aunt, Gwen, at that time newly embarked upon her fifth marriage, was also a guest, and I thought her wildly attractive. She had chosen her successive spouses each a little further down the social scale. Number five was a dental mechanic in Capetown, South Africa, and he succeeded in holding her affection for many years. My grandmother, when asked to whom Gwen was married "just now," would set her jaw defiantly and reply, "Some kind of engineer, I believe."

My mother had sold the Suffolk house and was soon to rent a flat three doors from my grandmother at 37 Ennismore Gardens. It had a fine sitting-room looking straight up the east side of the gardens to Hyde Park and two bedrooms facing into Brompton Square at the back. This was to be our home until the outbreak of war in 1939. My father had not left much money, and it soon became clear that my mother would need to augment her income. She did so in an enterprising way, by buying a large house in Courtfield Gardens, South Kensington, that had just been converted to accommodate 20 one-room furnished flats. She put in a Belgian manager who employed the domestic staff and took his reward from the profits of catering in the common dining-room. My mother took the rents of the flatlets, which gave her a handsome return on her capital. For the rest, though still only in her thirties, she settled down to a middle-aged pattern of life, spending most of her afternoons at a bridge club. Her friends were those with whom she played cards, mostly women and mostly older than she. They did not often come to the flat, and during my holidays from Stowe I met few people outside the family circle, and they too were mostly women. It was pleasant enough, but it did not help me to grow up.

During my second year at Stowe my future began to be greatly shaped by the attraction of a truly outstanding schoolmaster, William McElwee, who was head of the history department. A former student of Christ Church, Oxford, who had researched the Austro-Prussian War of 1866 and written an elegant monograph on the foreign policy of Emperor Charles V, McElwee had tried university teaching at Liverpool but had soon found his real vocation among sixth formers, whom he treated in almost every way like Oxbridge undergraduates. In appearance he was a total contrast to Roxburgh—short, sallow, dark-haired, his brown eyes full of laughter with wrinkles fanning out from their corners right across his cheeks. He dressed like a well-bred tramp, in old suits, wore his cloth cap at a rakish angle, and drove a huge old open Lagonda, in which he would set forth every Easter holiday on extensive "culture tours" of the Mediterranean lands, accompanied by five or six of his senior pupils. During the term he lived with his wife Patience and a great many cats in a dilapidated and dirty house called Vancouver Lodge, just down the hill from Stowe in the village of Dadford. Here he kept open house for tea every day of the week, and those who were free from other engagements could come early and stay late. He had arranged his working day so as to teach throughout a long unbroken morning, much of it devoted to individual tutorials, when essays were read aloud and criticized and reading programmes were discussed in detail. His afternoons were spent sociably at the house or in its large unkempt garden.

Bill McElwee did his scouting for talent in the second-year scholars' form called The Twenty. The school certificate examination lay at the end of the course, but he paid it scant attention. Ceaselessly pacing the room, hands in pockets, shoulders hunched, he would present the personalities of kings, popes, ministers, and royal mistresses rather in the style of the seventeenth-century essayist John Aubrey, farts and all, yet without avoiding subjects of high seriousness where they existed. This opened new worlds to most of us. We knew his reputation as the most dashing and successful of the heads of departments. We knew that he was among us to fish and that at the end of the year he would cast his net at those whom he judged the most promising for his purposes. I soon knew that I wanted very much to be one of them, but I did not imagine that he would notice me. Yet he did, and so, during my third and fourth years at Stowe, I became one of the privileged history specialists who had access to his individual tutorials and to his home and the right, rare in those days, to call him and his wife by their first names.

There was nothing cosy about the tutorials. One sat beside him on a broken-down sofa, while he rolled and puffed at endless cigarettes as he waited to pounce upon clichés and illogicalities and strove to instill a sense of form in argument. He expected one to read a great deal, some of it in French and German. I remember his telling me that it was time I learned to read French as fluently as English; he handed me three volumes of the despatches written by Caulaincourt when he was Napoleon's ambassador in St. Petersburg, to be read within three weeks without using a dictionary. In general, however, he was adept at teaching one to use books quickly, and he would have shared Samuel Johnson's scorn for those who were "accustomed to read a book from cover to cover." Although individual tuition was at the heart of his system, for the rest he demanded of his historians that they work and play together as equals, dispensing entirely with the pecking order of seniors and juniors that divides most school societies rather strictly into age groups. From the age of fifteen and a half, therefore, one worked in class with boys one, two, or even three years older, and during the afternoons spent at Vancouver Lodge one met the same people socially on a completely equal footing. There was banter and camaraderie but also a total respect for the developing personalities of his circle of chosen pupils. In politics he was conservative, but he did not spurn the idealism of the left. In religion he was probably a sceptic, but he took the subject seriously enough to insist on teaching the compulsory period of divinity in the curriculum himself and to prescribe as a textbook not a scriptural text but the recently published report of the Archbishops' Commission on Doctrine in the Church of England.

I find it exceedingly difficult in retrospect to estimate how far I have been touched by religion at different periods of my life. But I do of course remember that in my first term at Stowe, I asked to be prepared for confirmation. It was an unusual request, because most boys waited to be herded through the rite during their third or fourth years. The impulse therefore did not come from any school influence, and I think it must have come, although subconsciously, from home, where it was my mother's practice to attend early services of Holy Communion on Sundays, to which I had already accompanied her for several years. I suppose that basically I just wanted to be able to do the adult thing. My housemaster, Major Haworth, an officer and a gentleman of the old school, though dubious about the idea, did not actually object, and he even tolerated the view I held at the time—that to be a Christian one should also be a pacifist and that one should make this position public by abstaining from membership in the Officers Training Corps (OTC). I suppose that in his wisdom he guessed that I would grow out of it more easily on my own than by any intervention of his. What is perhaps more extraordinary is that I do not remember suffering any persecution or even ridicule from my contemporaries on this account. Certainly, Bill McElwee, a keen territorial officer prominent in the OTC, always left the subject well alone; in fact, as the international situation moved on through 1938 and 1939, I gradually shifted my position. In the circumstances of 1940 to be in any doubt about pacificism was to be swept inevitably into the majority viewpoint.

War came when I was sixteen and a half. My mother and I heard the news of Hitler's invasion of Poland as we finished a game of family golf at Roehampton, and next morning we listened to the prime minister's radio announcement that the ultimatum had expired and that we were therefore at war with Germany. Within a matter of minutes we heard the howling of air-raid sirens, and we duly retired to the basement with our gas masks. The Belgian manager of the flatlet house in Courtfield Gardens had decamped without notice a few days earlier, and my mother had moved into a vacant ground-floor unit to take charge. She had twenty rooms to be kept clean somehow, and twenty hungry tenants to be provided with breakfast and dinner with all the problems of food rationing. She got what help she could find, but much of it was transient and she had frequent intervals when she had to cope almost alone. It was to be her "war work."

I, meanwhile, returned to Stowe for my fourth year and part of a fifth. There Roxburgh greeted us with a sombre address in which he warned us that the war would probably be a long one and that those of us who survived it would be unlikely to get the chance of a university education afterwards. We should therefore snatch at whatever shortened period of university education we could get before we were called up at the age of nineteen and meanwhile arm ourselves with the qualification of the higher school certificate in case we could get no further.

For the time being, school life went on much as normal. Some younger masters disappeared quite soon, but their places were taken by retired men who returned to help out. Fortunately for me, Bill McElwee, who was later to fight a gallant war, was not called up until late in 1940, so my work for the Cambridge scholarship examinations could go forward without interruption. During the Christmas and Easter holidays I returned to whatever accommodation could be found for me at Courtfield Gardens. In the summer of 1940 I went to work on a farm near Buckingham, where I must have been among the last young Englishmen to be initiated into the skills of horse-drawn harvesting machinery. The following autumn term was my last, and I spent it working early and late for the examination in late November that brought me the offer of a scholarship at King's. Eight Stoics won awards at Oxford and Cambridge that year, and five were McElwee's historians. In normal circumstances I would have remained at school until the following June and gone up to Cambridge in September, but in view of Roxburgh's advice it was arranged that I should leave at once and proceed to King's in January in order to get five terms at Cambridge before being called up for military service in June 1942.

If Stowe had been good, King's, even in wartime, was in every way much better. The sheer independence of undergraduate life there was absolutely miraculous. For the first time in my life I had two rooms of my own, on the sunny top floor of a modern hostel building overlooking the Arts Theatre in St. Edward's Passage. Although my scholarship was in history, most of the history staff of the college was away on war service, and the authorities agreed that a sensible plan would be for me to read the first part of the tripos (bachelor's degree) in English literature. I had George "Dadie" Rylands for a supervisor and he was first rate. He recommended that I attend about three lectures a week, and for the rest I read under his guidance Shakespeare and Milton; the metaphysical poets; Bunyan, Jeremy Taylor, Thomas Browne, Defoe, Pope, Wordsworth, Shelley, and Keats; and a broad swathe of the classical English novelists from Samuel Richardson and Henry Fielding to Henry James and Virginia Woolf.

Most of the books I needed were available in Everyman's Library at two shillings a volume, and with my scholarship stipend of £60 and a generous allowance of £200 a year from my grandmother, I could easily afford them. I read for many hours each day in my bright sitting-room, and once a week I took an essay to Dadie Rylands in his elegant rooms overlooking the provost's garden. There I would read to him aloud while he lay, eyes shut, on a sofa. The reading over, he would spring to life, darting about the room, pouring sherry, encouraging, criticizing, poking fun, helping me to grow up and planning my next week of pure pleasure. Dadie accepted my incomprehension of much literary criticism, although he warned me that it would present difficulties at the examinations. And so the name of F. R. Leavis was hardly mentioned between us, and the pages of the quarterly *Scrutiny* remained unread. My prime interest lay in placing English literature against its historical background—the approach exemplified by Basil Willey, whose lectures I specially enjoyed. "Roland," Dadie would say of me in gently mocking tones, "is interested in *thought*."

As with Bill McElwee, the astonishing thing about these King's dons was that they not only taught us but also played with us. There was, for example, the Ten Club, where week after week some of us would meet, after due preparation, to read Elizabethan, Jacobean, or Restoration drama in the company of people like Donald Bevis, the rich and jovial senior tutor of the college who lectured in French literature and collected antique glass; Philip Radcliffe, the gentle musician; Charles McBurney, the archaeologist and later excavator of the great Haua Fteah cave in northern Libya; Archie Graham-Campbell, the dean of chapel, a masculine aristocrat who was usually allotted elderly female parts; A. F. Scholfield, the university librarian, a Mephistophelian figure usually cloaked if not daggered and so practised a mimic that some claimed they had never heard him speak in his own voice; Dadie Rylands, of course; and several others. Though it never struck me at the time, all of them, like all of us, were male and unmarried. It was a very different climate from that which was to prevail in Cambridge after the war, when most dons were married and had families that demanded their presence in the evenings. But, equally, I do not recognize in my own experience any of the preoccupation with homosexuality painted by Noel Annan in connection with the Cambridge of a few years earlier.[1] In fact, I think the subject was hardly ever mentioned. Most of my friends were men, because there were still comparatively few women around. Girton was a long way out, but I visited friends at Newnham (then the only women's colleges), just as I did those in other colleges. During my first year, at least, most of my close friends were those who had come on with me from Stowe— Wayland Young, later a hereditary legislator; Peregrine Worsthorne of journalistic fame; John Rolleston, who later made a distinguished career

Cambridge undergraduate, 1941

in the Ministry of Defence; Francis Broughton, who somehow became metamorphosed as Charles Legh of Adlington Hall in Cheshire; John Tate of the sugar family, who became a director of the firm; James Sutherland, later a well-known architect and consulting engineer; and Roger Ellison, a musician and composer who was to be my neighbour and later my best

29

man. These were some of the people in whose company I experienced the thrill and happiness of being just grown up and with whom I felt able to share my glimpses of the profundities of life.

So far as I was concerned, these glimpses soon began to set in a Christian direction. It did not happen at once, because on first arriving in Cambridge I needed to celebrate my new-found independence by breaking with all the compulsions of school. I played no organised games. I dressed in a corduroy suit like any other aesthete. I smoked. I ignored the invitations of the Student Christian Movement and other religious societies. I avoided chapel services. But one day I received a note from the dean saying that it was customary for scholars of the college to take turns in reading the lessons at weekday matins: would I therefore kindly be present at 7:30 A.M. on three consecutive days in early March. It seemed a reasonable request, so I went to explore the premises and took some advice on procedure from a kindly verger (attendant).

Having duly acquired a white surplice, I entered the vast building shortly before dawn on the appointed Monday morning, made my way through the organ screen, and took up my position in the choir stalls where three or four candles cast a flickering light. No one else was in sight, and my eye travelled eastwards to where in the dim distance two more candles indicated the place of the high altar. Suddenly, from an unseen opening in the north wall there emerged a little procession of two white-clad acolytes followed by a portly priest in full eucharistic vestments who paused and bowed to the high altar and then disappeared through an equally invisible opening in the south wall. I wondered if I had seen some vision from pre-Reformation times, but my attention was soon called to the entry of the dean, Eric Milner-White, dressed now in cassock and surplice, by the same route that I had taken. With the help of only the verger, we said matins and went our several ways. The same sequence of events repeated itself on each of the two following days. On further investigation I discovered that down either side of the main choir ran an interconnecting series of side chapels by which it was possible to reach the east end of the building without passing through the doors of the organ screen. I likewise discovered that daily matins was preceded by a service of Holy Communion during full term.

There was no reason why this trivial experience should have had the effect upon me that in fact it did. It would have been more logical to have taxed "the royal saint with vain expense" and to have carried away some impression of the futility of providing unattended services. But my reaction was quite different. I felt that I had seen a glimpse of the Christian church at its faithful work throughout the centuries. It happened that soon afterwards I received a visit from a stranger in clerical dress who proved to be a Benedictine monk from Downside Abbey. He was called Hilary

30

Steuart. Like me, he was reading English, and he had heard of me from a mutual friend in London. I took to him at once, and we went for many country walks together during the spring afternoons. As he told me about his daily life at Downside, I felt I understood what he was saying. No word of conversion ever passed between us, but I began again to attend Anglican services and to look out for those among my contemporaries who were practising Christians. I never got to know Eric Milner-White, who left us in the summer of 1941 to become dean of York, but I made friends with the college chaplain, John McMullen, with whose help I began reading some ecclesiastical history, both that of the early church and that of seventeenth- and eighteenth-century France.

Having to put six terms' work into five, I stayed in Cambridge for much of the long vacation of 1941. My friend Wayland Young did the same, and we spent many happy afternoons together, walking and swimming by the banks of the Cam in what must have been an unusually sunny English summer. Towards the end of it he invited me to his family's country home at Fritton Hythe by a little lake in the Norfolk Broads. His father, the first Lord Kennet, was the most formidably educated man I have ever met, the owner of a splendid and much-used library filled with the classic works of poetry, philosophy, history, and economics. He had been a successful politician and a minister. He had fought in the navy during the First World War and had lost an arm at the battle of Zeebrugge. He had married, late, the sculptress Kathleen Scott, the widow of the Antarctic explorer and the mother of Peter Scott. Wayland was their only child. These were exciting people to stay with. They knew, or had known, the great in nearly every walk of life. Kathleen Kennet had been the intimate confidante of Herbert Henry Asquith, and her correspondence with him stood, bound, upon the library shelves. So did the diary of Captain Robert Falcon Scott, of which I have never forgotten the final sentence, scribbled in the tent just before he died: "How much better this has all been than lounging in too great comfort at home."

During my second year at Cambridge I enjoyed a really marvellous set of rooms in Wyatt's Court at the top of the staircase nearest to the river. The sitting-room had a long window looking out over the bridges of King's and Clare and across the great back lawn to the southern façade of Clare, which has always seemed to me the most pleasing example of seventeenth-century domestic architecture to be found anywhere. The room had a long window seat where I sat reading for many hours each day and a comfortable circle of chairs round the fireplace, which was laid for me each morning by Mrs. Perry, a Cambridge "bedmaker" of the old school who took an interest in her "young gentlemen" and liked to make them comfortable. Several close friends had rooms nearby. Stephen Toulmin, the future philosopher of science, was just across the staircase. Oliver

Lodge, later a queen's counsel at the chancery bar and chairman of many tribunals, and Oliver Scott, who was to become a leading figure in cancer research, were on neighbouring staircases. So were Adrian Carey, who became an Anglican clergyman, and his brother Hugh, who was to be second master at Stowe. I still took my essays to Dadie Rylands, but my closest friend among the fellows of the college was Alwyn Scholfield, the university librarian whose outlook on life was very different. An Etonian and a classicist, he had been keeper of the state records in India and then librarian of Trinity College before returning to King's on his appointment to the university library. A lifelong though regretful bachelor, he made a point of advising his younger friends to set their sights on matrimony. One needed an introduction to join his circle, but to those in it his door would be open between dinner and midnight on any day of the week, and one could be sure of crisp satirical conversation in the vein of Max Beerbohm's *Christmas Garland*, which was his favourite recreational reading. Wayland enjoyed him too, and on April 1, 1942, we sent him what I still think was quite a funny letter. It purported to be from one Montgomery Fitzroy, who described himself as public monuments conversion officer and, informed him that it had been decided to take over the tower of the university library for the purposes of Armed Forces Special Training, Group 6 (Dissent by Parachute). Special girders were to be erected at the four corners of the tower (Mark 4, Soldiers for the precipitation of), and it would also be necessary to camouflage the whole exterior surface of the structure in scarlet and gold. When we called upon him that evening, his hand was on the telephone and he was seeking to be connected with the vice chancellor. We were just in time to save the situation from escalation to undesirable lengths. It was the only time I ever saw him blush.

In preparation for the military service that would follow, I had on my arrival in Cambridge joined the University Training Corps and had had a successful interview with the colonel of the Welsh Guards for training for a commission in that regiment. I still had only limited movement in my left elbow, following the compound fracture I had sustained at the age of twelve. Although it had prevented me from playing some games and handicapped me in others, it had not been more than a minor embarrassment in the training corps, and it had never occurred to me that it would prove a barrier to military service. But at my official medical examination in the early summer of 1942 the doctors thought differently, and I was classified C-3. This meant that my normal military destiny would be the Pioneer Corps, a branch of the army that supplied unskilled manual services in support of the fighting troops. In these circumstances, when Donald Beves, the senior tutor of the college, one day suggested that he should submit my name for an interview for an unspecified type of intelligence work that he thought would interest me, I quickly assented.

The interview took place at St. John's College in the rooms of Martin Charlesworth, a clergyman who was a lecturer in ancient history. There I met a genial soldier, Brigadier John Tiltman, who began by asking me whether I played bridge. "Family bridge," I replied. "Ever do crossword puzzles?" he asked. I answered no. I forget what followed, but in the end he asked whether I would be prepared to "do a course." "A course in what?" I asked. "I am afraid I cannot tell you," he replied. I asked whether the work at the end of the course would be at home or abroad. He said, "It might be either." I asked whether it would be in uniform. He said, "It might be, or on the other hand it might not." A quick decision was required, and then and there I agreed.

4

Most Secret War

(1942–45)

In July 1942 I received two sets of call-up papers. The first required me to report in two weeks' time to the training centre of the Pioneer Corps at Maryhill Barracks in Glasgow. The second referred me in less peremptory language to a nondescript address in Bedford, which proved to be that of a perfectly ordinary small-town villa in one of the little streets leading down to the River Ouse. It turned out to be a school of cryptography where, along with some thirty others, I was indoctrinated over five or six months in the simple codes and ciphers employed during the First World War and still used to provide a few hours' secrecy in exposed situations where code books and ciphering machinery would be in danger of capture by the enemy. We learned about various systems of substitution and transposition and how to set about solving them. We were not taught anything about machine ciphers or given any information about the extent to which enemy ciphers were being read. Some of our time was spent in language study, in German and Italian, with a particular emphasis on the conventional phrasing used in official telegraphese.

It was interesting and stimulating work, and we did it in good company. The instructors were army officers of the kind who would lean over one's shoulder, place a finger on one's scribbling, and inquire gently whether one was not making too many "empirical assumptions." My classmates were of varied ages and experience, some of whom had made their way there through one or other of the armed services and so continued to wear their uniforms, but most were civilians like me. One whose company I greatly enjoyed and who was to become a long-term friend was Angus Wilson, not as yet a novelist but formidably well read in several languages. He already was a master of characterisation and mimicry, and his repertoire extended right across the social spectrum. He had been recruited directly from the staff of the British Museum Reading

34

Room. Another with whom I became friendly was Edward Boyle, later a Conservative member of Parliament and a minister of education in Edward Heath's government; he had come to Bedford straight from school at Eton.

At last, during the icy weather of January 1943 my cohort was transferred from Bedford to the Government Code and Cipher School at Bletchley Park. This was the central intelligence agency, serving all the armed services and the Foreign Office, to which intercepts of enemy wireless messages were teleprinted from a worldwide network of listening posts, and where they were, so far as possible, decrypted and turned into useful intelligence. For usefulness speed was of the essence. But even more important was secrecy—not so much the secrecy of any particular piece of information as secrecy about the source from which it came. It was the perpetual dilemma of those at the centre of power—how to get field commanders to trust the intelligence that came from decrypts without dangerously widening the circle of those who knew that enemy codes and ciphers were being read. So far as we at Bletchley were concerned, the most important element of security was that none of us should know more than we needed to in order to make our own particular contribution. We did not visit the offices of other sections unless we had business there, and we did not talk shop with any but our most immediate colleagues. We worked for eight or nine hours a day, six days a week, and most of us worked shifts—9 A.M. till 6 P.M., 4 P.M. till midnight, and midnight till 9 A.M.—changing every four days. We were billeted at Bletchley and in the surrounding countryside at distances of up to fifteen miles. If out of walking distance, we were taken to our billets in buses or utility trucks that departed fifteen minutes after the end of each shift. Although our company comprised a huge array of talent, social mixing was not made easy, except during brief mealtimes on the premises. In the words of a Christmas review, which applied to a wider circle than the clerical staff,

> The innocent ladies,
> Whatever their grade is,
> Are billeted miles away,
> And, just to be funny,
> There's Transport Money
> Deducted from their pay.

On arrival at Bletchley Park I was assigned to the Naval Section, headed by Frank Birch, a veteran cryptographer of the First World War and between the wars a history fellow of my college in Cambridge. On occasion he doubled as the Widow Twanky in the annual pantomime at the Lyceum Theatre in London. Within the section I was at first placed in the "Z Watch," a group of perhaps forty people divided into three shifts whose duty it was to receive the decrypted signals from all German naval networks and to turn them first into correct German and then into an accurate English translation. Some twelve to fifteen people sat round a long table at any one time, presided over during the day shift by Walter Ettinghausen, an Oxford professor of German who in 1948 was to become the permanent secretary of the newly founded Israeli Foreign Office. Ettinghausen or his deputy doled out the decrypts as they came in, and each of us probably dealt with seven to ten signals an hour. For us the essential problem was that the operators at the intercept stations, working in poor acoustic conditions, were often able to capture correctly only 60 or 70 percent of each encoded text. Every decrypt was therefore to this extent corrupt, and it was a fairly skilled operation, rather like doing a crossword puzzle in another language, to restore it to its original form. The work of translation that followed was by no means straightforward. The ambiguities of telegraphese had to be resolved but so did the technical jargon. We had another whole section, known as "the library," that kept tabs on every unusual expression that occurred in enemy signals, to which we found we needed to refer many times on each shift. Within the Z Watch the group with which I was especially concerned was one set up to handle signals from a newly decrypted network covering the region of the Black Sea. No doubt, anyone privileged to read the whole of our combined output would have found plenty of interesting and significant material, but we, working on the random items given out to us, drew little satisfaction from the content of what we handled—only the mild pleasure of doing a technical task quickly and efficiently. Later, in 1947, I was to find myself living for a few weeks in Hamburg among a group of professional interpreters engaged in the trials of war criminals, and I learned from overhearing their conversation that they had no interest in the human content of their court cases but only in the technical achievements and shortcomings of their colleagues. That was the case with the Z Watch also, and with my lack of experience and far-from-perfect command of German I did not really feel in the race.

Fortunately, within a matter of weeks another opportunity presented itself. Only a few doors away from the Z room was the headquarters of a small section that dealt with German naval hand ciphers. It was headed by C. T. Carr, later professor of German at St. Andrews University. Even in this egalitarian establishment no one ever called him anything but Doctor Carr, and he worked in a small room he shared with a no less uncommunicative teacher of German from the University of Edinburgh. What they did there I was never quite sure, but in the adjoining and somewhat larger room there worked, in three shifts round the clock, a close-knit team of six or seven cryptographers who regularly broke and decrypted traffic transmitted in a hand cipher called *Werftschlüssel*. It was, as its name implied, a humble "dockyard" cipher used to communicate with tugs, icebreakers, and other small vessels operating around the harbours of the North Sea and the Baltic, right up the Norwegian coast as far as the North Cape, and for a time in the Adriatic and Aegean. The users of "Werft" seldom had anything to say that would have been of any intrinsic interest to the naval intelligence officers at the British admiralty. They sent each other little messages about the weather and the ice and the layout of the minefields protecting their bases. Their significance to us at Bletchley was that they often said these things in identical language to that employed in the complex machine ciphers used in communications with the big ships and especially the submarine fleet, which also needed to be informed about the weather, the ice, and the position of minefields. Werft signals, especially the most routine ones, could thus be used as cribs by our colleagues working on the machine ciphers.

Basically, Werft was a system of bigrammatic substitution, in which every pair of letters was represented by a different pair, using a set of thirty substitution tables that were used in parallel and changed every month. Thanks to the successful capture of one of the little ships that used the system, we knew how to tell which of the thirty substitution tables had been used to encipher any particular message. By the second week in each month we were usually able to provide accurate and nearly instantaneous decrypts of some routine traffic. The settings of the important machine ciphers changed daily and could be broken only with the aid of embryonic computing machines, called *bombes*, that were capable of trying out a large number of possibilities within a short space of time. A crib successfully identified on the basis of the length of the signal and the time and place of its origin could reduce the number of possibilities to be tried from some quite impracticable trillions to some perfectly feasible hundreds or thousands.

This, then, was the operation I joined, very much as the young apprentice, in the early spring of 1943 and in which I continued for about a year. My colleagues, many of whom became my close friends, were an interesting and varied lot. There was an Oxford Egyptologist called Paul Smither, who was greatly liked by all but who was shortly to slip away and die of leukemia. There was John Barns, at that time a Greek papyrologist, who was later to become professor of Egyptology at Oxford. His was a retiring disposition that did not take easily to such modern innovations as the telephone. Whenever it rang, he approached it with stealth and held the receiver well away from his ear while he whispered into the mouthpiece. Convinced that Oxford would sooner or later be oblitered by a Baedeker raid, he had spent most of his days off during the first two years of the war illicitly transporting the more valuable papyri of the Ashmolean

Museum into hiding places in the rafters of a Naval Section hut. The hut was replaced by a brick building without rafters, so when I first knew him, he was engaged in transporting them all back again, two suitcases at a time. There was Christopher Morris, a history don from King's, whose specialty was the political thought of sixteenth-century England and who was to be my director of studies when I returned to Cambridge after the war. There was Ruth Briggs, the clever daughter of a canon of Worcester; she had recently graduated in modern languages at Cambridge and was probably the best of us at the work we had to do. As time went on we were joined by James Hogarth, a senior principal in the Scottish Office who was dressed for some reason as a sergeant major; Bentley Bridgewater, the secretary of the British Museum and a close friend of Angus Wilson's; and eventually Caroline Linehan, who was to be my wife for thirty-six years. Caroline was a well-known figure at Bletchley Park. She had been a member of the small prewar nucleus of the organisation and had become a much-respected authority on "wireless intelligence," which consisted of the analysis and interpretation of daily changes in the volume of traffic emanating from the different enemy sources. She was also active socially, a tennis player of county standard, a regular participant in amateur dramatics, and secretary of the Social Club. She joined the Werft party only after a long and debilitating illness had necessitated her replacement in her former position.

We tried to arrange things so that two of us would be in the room at any one time and also so that we changed partners every four days with the change of shift. Within this framework our efforts revolved around the monthiy change in the substitution tables of our cipher. The first two or three days in the cycle were a nightmare in which we looked at the growing pile of unreadable signals with anxiety, frustration, and despair. We indexed every bigram as it appeared, and from the resultant frequency table we began to get an idea of which were the most common. After that, using our knowledge of the traffic in previous months, we simply had to guess, and to go on and on guessing, at what might be the opening phrases of particular signals until at last someone got a set of tentative equivalences that also looked promising in other signals. By the third day we had usually achieved the initial breakthrough, with a half-dozen signals partly decrypted and perhaps two dozen firmly established equivalences scattered around the 676 squares of each of the new substitution tables. From here on things built up rapidly, and the work became progressively more enjoyable. By the fourth day we were usually able to take a recently received and fully decrypted weather report to our colleagues working at the daily changes of key in the various machine cipher networks. These changes occurred at midnight, and therefore our main aim was to supply a crib that had originated as soon after midnight as possible. These nocturnal visits were when we came nearest to a sense of achievement, because we could feel that perhaps we were making it possible for the machine-enciphered traffic of that day to reach its unintended destination on the desks of the British admiralty, the Joint Intelligence Committee, and even in some tiny, highly selected measure, the chiefs of staff and the prime minister himself. The supplying of cribs apart, our daily work for the rest of each month consisted of filling up the remaining blank spaces in the thirty new substitution tables until, usually by sometime in the third week, signals on any subject could be decrypted as they were received. We took a professional pride in trying to fill every square in the bigram substitution tables, but by the fourth week we usually found ourselves with plenty of time for idle conversation.

One advantage of doing secret work was that we could not take it home and therefore, in contrast to most of our later professional lives, we had some hours of daily leisure. The problem was where and how to spend them. A few were well enough off to acquire houses in the neighbourhood, and a few more managed to find comfortable lodgings in the homes of well-to-do local families. One party of mutually congenial academics were billeted in a country pub, where they trained the landlord to play the part of the master of the college and to preside over a high table dinner. As a latecomer of lowly status my first billet was in a drab council house in the brick-making suburb of Bletchley called Newton Longueville, where I shared two small rooms with a young mathematician called Donald Michie (later a professor of mechanical thought at the University of Edinburgh), who had just been recruited from school at Rugby. Our landlady gave us breakfast and high tea but made it plain enough that she and her husband would rather have their house to themselves. After a few months I was able to move to more spacious accommodation in a small manor house in the village of Broughton, where the daughter of the house was a colleague at the office. My private life, however, only began to hum towards the end of 1943, when I met Caroline Linehan, who invited me to several meals at the cottage in Woughton-on-the-Green that she shared with another colleague, Margaret Sawyer. The cottage was part of a picturesque black-and-white sixteenth-century farmhouse that had been allowed to fall derelict when a new red-brick farm had been built alongside it sometime in the nineteenth century. It had long been condemned for human habitation by the local planning authorities, but the sentence had been temporarily rescinded for the duration of the war. Margaret Sawyer had rented one end of it from the farmer for four shillings a week and had managed to make four or five rooms just habitable. A Bletchley Park driver was living temporarily in two rooms at the other end of the building, but the two middle rooms were quite empty, and the lower one was used only as a passage from the farm to the farmyard. Chickens, and occasionally even cows, wandered through it, leaving their droppings to add to the deposit on the crumbling brick floor. But a steep open stairway led to an upper room seldom visited and laden with the dust of ages. Here, it was suggested, and perhaps in the first instance jokingly, that I might make a bed–sitting-room. I could wash and have my meals with the women next door.

Joke or not, I jumped at the offer, and it proved to be one of the most momentous decisions of my life. Harry King, the farmer, agreed to a rent of two shillings a week, and within a few days I had acquired a second-hand bed and was able to move in. Conditions at first must have been spartan indeed. I forget exactly how and when electricity was introduced, but certainly there was a minimum of heat and light. Even next door I fancy that washing arrangements were confined to the kitchen sink, and the loo, such as it was, adjoined Harry King's pigsty, the occupant of which, known to us as Henry, was both communicative and malodorous. But we had the community of interests and the total independence that could not often exist in the relations between billetor and billetee. We could have nearby friends to visit and more distant ones to stay. And Woughton, which today has been totally engulfed by the new town of Milton Keynes, was then a lovely village. At one end of it the church and the pub faced each other across the main road from Bletchley to Newport Pagnell, and John Rose, the publican, played the organ in the church as well as providing recreation and good company on his premises. From the pub a side road led down past our cottage to a spacious village green of perhaps five or six acres with houses sparsely dotted around it. On the far side it was bounded by the Grand Union Canal, and we could see the tops of the passing longboats and hear the gentle thud of their submerged engines, a sound rather reminiscent of the knock of bat on ball. A pretty hump-backed bridge crossed the canal, and beyond it a dirt lane climbed the hill to the village of Loughton some three miles away. All this was our walking country, and we became so familiar with all the paths and gates and stiles that we could use them by night as well as by day. And we had a pair of tabby cats, called Romulus and Remus, which also enjoyed long country walks, when they would scamper ahead of us for a hundred yards or more and then call to us to catch up.

The base at Woughton made it much more possible to renew contact with my old friends from Stowe and Cambridge. Those of my age group who had joined the army had missed the desert war culminating in the battle of El Alamein and the advance to Tunisia but were in time for the invasion of Italy. Many of them were to perish on the beaches of Anzio. But those in the navy were mostly operating out of British bases, and Wayland Young and James Sutherland were among my earliest houseguests. Wayland in particular made light of our primitive lifestyle in comparison with his own conditions as an able seaman in a motor torpedo-boat flotilla on the east coast. There thirty-two people shared a commandeered seaside boarding-house, sleeping six to a room and with two enamel basins for the entire party to wash in—and this in the intervals between twenty-hour patrols in the North Sea "with the cold, the wet, the noise, the dark and the bumping," not to mention the danger. He pronounced my set-up to be magnificent.

Sometime in the autumn of 1943 Wayland must have introduced me to Elizabeth Jane Howard, who was at that time married to his half-brother, the artist and naturalist Peter Scott. Their house was in Clifton Hill in St. John's Wood. Peter, as a Royal Navy reserve commander of torpedo boats all round the southern coasts, was seldom at home, and Jane presided over a household of agreeable and intelligent women— Anne Richmond, who was already engaged to Peter Piper, the future director of the National Portrait Gallery and the Ashmolean Museum; Dosha Cropper, who was being courted by a charming painter, Barry Craig; and Audrey Tuck, who was to marry John Rideout, a Japanese linguist at the School of Oriental and African Studies. All these, together with a constantly changing company of friends and relations, came and went at Clifton Hill, and no one understood how, with the rationing system, they were fed. At all events, Jane soon gave me the freedom of the house, and for a year or more I went there almost whenever I had a day off. She was busily training herself to her calling as a writer of fiction. I read much of her early work and, under her influence, started some of my own. She was witty, kind, versatile, strong-minded, and upright. It would be difficult to exaggerate what I owed to her at a formative time of my life.

By the time of the Allied invasion of Normandy in June 1944, the naval war in the Atlantic and the North Sea was virtually over, and it was clearly no longer necessary to maintain a team working round the clock on an intrinsically unimportant cipher like Werft. During the remaining year of the war I therefore found myself moved around in a whole variety of short-term cryptographic jobs. I spent some weeks in a room with Alan Ross, the philologist who later achieved fame by his publications on "U" and "Non-U" in English daily usage. Together we studied intercepts in a German Mediterranean cipher called Henno, which had never been broken. Our efforts to do so were quite unavailing, and I remember only Ross's peering at me through his usual clouds of tobacco smoke and saying, "You know, Oliver, I've just been doing some sums, and I reckon that if we had a hundred girls, each working for sixteen hours a day for thirty years, we could solve this problem." Fortunately, we were not required to do so. After the Henno episode I was transferred to the Air Section, where I spent a happy three months or so reconstructing an Argentinian code book in which the five-figure equivalences proved to be conveniently arranged in

Pencil drawing by Peter Scott, 1944

alphabetical order. All the assistance I needed was to be found in a Spanish dictionary. Later still, I worked in the Military Section, under the same John Tiltman who had originally interviewed me in Cambridge. This was big stuff, but I was far too small a cog to really understand the total operation in which we were engaged.

The last small job that I did at Bletchley has, I find, been totally submerged in the mists of amnesia. I can remember the hut and the room in which I did it. I remember that I had the services of a nice young military clerk called Corporal Eccleston, who saw to it that I started each day with fresh blotting paper and beautifully sharpened pencils. And I remember that I subsequently recommended him to Peter Scott for a job in the newly founded Severn Wildfowl Trust to which he gave sterling service for many years. But what we did in that hut at Bletchley has completely escaped me. It cannot have been very important, and I suspect that by this time, the summer of 1945, and with the German war at an end, my thoughts, like those of many others, must have been concentrating on how to secure my release from the organisation in time to return to Cambridge for the next academic year. These were the circumstances in which young men took to practical joking, and I remember one episode in which the most senior officials in the place were invited in a circular letter to attend a lecture on dental hygiene in the Far East. It was said that most obediently did so. At all events, this was when the characterisation of ourselves in an earlier Christmas review came nearest to the truth:

> A backroom boy am I,
> We're here in countless numbers,
> We pass our days in slumbers
> And dreamy lullaby.

By September 1945 the diaspora from Bletchley was well under way. I undertook with Maurice Wiles (later Regius Professor of Divinity at Oxford) a successful mission to Cambridge to ask the help of the vice chancellor in securing the release of former students who wished to return to the university in time for the new academic year. And from our household at Woughton Margaret Sawyer departed to Edinburgh, soon to marry a young minister in the Church of Scotland. Caroline continued for the time being in employment at Bletchley Park, and it therefore suited her to keep her tenancy at the cottage. I likewise kept my room there as a retreat for weekends and vacations. We were still in our own eyes dear friends and nothing more, but it must have been clear to those who knew us well that, despite the difference of nearly thirteen years in our ages, our paths were destined to converge.

43

5

Two Towards Africa

(1945–48)

In October 1945, war service completed, I packed my few possessions into an ancient Morris motor car that I had bought from Margaret Sawyer on her departure from our community at Woughton-on-the-Green and drove the fifty-odd miles to Cambridge to resume my career as an undergraduate at King's. In many ways it was like a joyful homecoming. There was the place itself, which I knew and loved so well. There were the people who had stayed there through the war years and kept things going, including most of those who had taught me and played with me and generally treated me like a grown-up and an equal when I was still only a raw schoolboy. And there were a good many of the friends of my own age who, like me, had been away and were now returning to finish their studies. As I drove over the hill from St. Neots and recognised the pinnacles of Henry VI's great chapel sparkling in the afternoon sunlight, I felt all the same excitement and expectation as Wordsworth riding in by the same route a century and a half before. And in most respects I was not disappointed.

On the other hand, I was now twenty-two years old, and I still had little idea of the direction my life would take. The academic friends I had made at Bletchley had sown the seeds of hope that I might follow in their footsteps, but I knew that they belonged to a small and highly competitive elite to which the approach would be lengthy and full of risk. My starting base was not a strong one. I held a scholarship in history and that was where my developing academic interests were leading me, but I had read the first half of my degree in English literature. As I surveyed my new rooms in Webb's Court, looking out upon the college library, I realised that I now had just nine months in which to reestablish myself as a historian qualified to begin in the research that might lead to a fellowship. I had to work fast and well and also to explore alternative means of

44

livelihood. I went for an interview with Gladwyn Jebb, who was then in charge of British recruitment for the new United Nations organisation, and I entered my name for the civil service examination to be held the following summer.

Meanwhile, the first step was to exercise my options about the kinds of history that I would study. I knew that, if I was ever to become a professional, the field in which I would wish to begin would be some kind of ecclesiastical history. I had already during my spare time at Bletchley taught myself something about the first four centuries of Christian history and something about the post-Reformation period in Western Europe. About the medieval period, however, I was still almost ignorant, and it seemed that an outline course on medieval Europe would be one obvious choice. A further option pointed in the same direction. This was due to the arrival in Cambridge as professor of medieval history of the Benedictine scholar David Knowles, previously a monk at Downside Abbey and the author of a revered work on the monastic order in England. Knowles was now offering as a "special subject" a course on the sources for the life of St. Francis. My friend Wayland Young, who had just returned to Cambridge from the navy, was also interested, and we went together to call on Knowles and to ask him whether our little Latin and less Italian might be sufficient. We encountered a character of singular gentleness and retiring charm who, without ever suggesting that it would be easy, agreed to accept us as disciples if that was what we really wished. It was a choice I think we both found to be formative, engaging our hearts as well as our minds in the search for historical truth in a field from which mystery could not, even in the most rigorous analysis, be altogether excluded. I have long forgotten the technical historiographical problems that so absorbed me at the time, but the "little, poor man of Assisi" with his wry smile has in a sense been a companion through life, often out of mind but never far away.

I made one other other choice, not seemingly as significant as the first but in the event rather more so. It was to read, as my modern subject, the newly developed version of colonial history called the "expansion of Europe." This was not recommended by my advisors. I remember Christopher Morris's telling me that it was the kind of choice that might be made by someone who was going to get a third-class degree. It was true that it was not at that time a well-designed course, nor was it taught by any of the more exciting teachers in the university, and the college had a real problem in finding someone competent to supervise my work. Nevertheless, with my Indian background and as a contrast from my long incarceration in England during the war, it appealed to me, and in the performance it led me to the idea that my wish to work in ecclesiastical history might well be carried out in relation to the expansion of Christianity in colonial lands.

That idea, however, still needed to incubate over several months, and meantime it was Franciscan scholarship that held me in thrall and to the extent that I actually discovered, by close textual comparison, something of value about the sources used by Thomas of Celano in his two lives of the saint. Knowles was sufficiently impressed by it to introduce me to John Moorman, later bishop of Ripon and principal Anglican representative in ecumenical discussions with the Church of Rome, who at that time was the leading English scholar on Franciscan origins. Moorman kindly came and spent an afternoon with me in my rooms at King's and was alleged to have remarked, no doubt light-heartedly, to a friend at dinner that he had just met a young man who seemed to know more about St. Francis than he did. In the event, however, it was Moorman who strongly counselled me not to try to undertake a doctoral dissertation in Franciscan studies from any base in an English university. He painted for me an entirely convincing picture of the massed weight of Franciscan scholarship that existed within the Order of St. Francis in Rome and other centres throughout the world, which would make it a slow business for any outsider to gain recognition.

Of course, it was impossible to live in Cambridge during that first postwar year without enjoying a great deal of happy friendship, good talk, and stimulating recreation. The Ten Club still met regularly to read plays. Chapel services apart, the college was full of marvellous music. Despite the continuance of food rationing and other shortages, the dons somehow managed to be endlessly hospitable. The social circle of contemporaries was large and varied. For all that, it seemed to me a very different and more serious place from the carefree Cambridge of 1941 and 1942. Most of us had been out in the real world and had returned for a definite purpose before going out into it again. Even for those few of us whose aim was to remain in Cambridge, being an undergraduate again was a more consciously transitory experience than it had been before. I think that I worked extremely hard, probably too hard, at my books and that when I took a day off, it was usually to drive over to Woughton to spend a Saturday or a Sunday with Caroline, who was still working at Bletchley Park.

I still have most of the correspondence that Caroline and I exchanged during that academic year and the next one, and I am interested to see that it still reads more like that of two old and intimate friends rather than that of lovers in any ordinary sense. On Caroline's side the letters tell of the escapades of our two cats, Romulus and Remus; the cow that slipped its leading rein and blundered through the garden into my downstairs room where, finding a little haven of privacy, it proceeded to have diarrhoea before it could be extricated. Angus Wilson and Bentley Bridgewater had been to call. Our close friends Harry Hinsley and Hilary Brett-Smith, who rather like ourselves had been left as the joint tenants of a cottage in the next-door village of Simpson, had become engaged to be married.

46

Sometime around Christmas 1945 the third unit of our cottage fell vacant, and the landlord let it be known that he would be glad to sell the whole building. The question therefore arose whether Caroline and I should jointly buy it, initially in order to preserve our respective occupancies and in the longer term as an investment that we might improve by reconverting the three units into a single house and selling it. Much of our correspondence during the early months of 1946 was concerned with problems of planning permission and with the feasibility and cost of making the essential improvements. I think we finally closed with the owner for what nowadays seems the absurdly small sum of £400 in June of that year, and during the following eighteen months we carried out, piecemeal and mostly with the help only of the village odd-job man, a radical rehabilitation of the whole premises, which were to be our home until 1954.

Meanwhile, my undergraduate career had ended, if not in disgrace at least without the glory of a first-class degree, which I so badly needed in view of my future plans. During the month or two before the final examination I had been showing signs of strain, but on the occasion all went reasonably well until the final paper, which consisted of a "general essay" to be written in three hours. I seem to remember that the subject specified was *walls*. I looked at the sheet in desperation, and my mind went almost blank. The clock ticked remorselessly round the first hour and then the second and then the third, and all I had written in my answer book was my name on the cover. Instead of handing it in, I threw it into the wastepaper basket and left the room. In so doing I had, all unwittingly, broken the rule that stated that candidates for a degree must answer all the papers. Fortunately for me, an alert proctor noticed that my answer book was missing and organised a search of the wastepaper baskets. I was still in trouble, but through the charity of the examiners I emerged, after an agonising wait of three weeks or so, with a result in the upper second class. Also, what seemed to me even more extraordinary, some three weeks later again the college authorities elected me to a research studentship. My show was still on the road, and I spent a happy month building a walled rose garden at the back of the cottage and driving with Caroline for a brief holiday in Skye and the Outer Hebrides.

I cannot now remember the process of thought by which a general desire to work on some aspect of the nineteenth-century expansion of Christianity was translated into a precise project of research. I described it as "The Missionary Factor in East Africa," which became successively the title of my fellowship dissertation, my doctoral thesis, and my first book. Certainly, the decision owed nothing to any professional advice given me in the college or elsewhere in the university. I remember that Christopher Morris, when talking to me about the award of my studentship, told me that henceforward my time would be very much my own and that if, after a year or so, I felt it necessary to come and discuss my progress with him or any of his colleagues, that would be quite in order. He added that if I did so more frequently than that, they would not think me very good at the job.

I think it was suggested to me several months later that perhaps I ought to give some consideration to the question of whether I should register for the doctoral degree—a qualification not really necessary for those destined to make their careers in Cambridge but nevertheless one that was increasingly insisted upon by lesser universities where I might one day need to earn my living. The regulations decreed that all doctoral candidates should have supervisors appointed by the university, and in view of the subject I had chosen this would probably mean looking outside the college to some such person as the professor of imperial and naval history, Eric Walker, the author of the best-known history of South Africa. I countered with the suggestion that it might be the recently appointed professor of ecclesiastical history, Norman Sykes, who, though lacking any African experience, might be expected to have an interest in the expansion of Christianity. In due course I did become Sykes's pupil, and he did then invite me to come and see him about once a month during the term. But that was long after I had defined the scope and character of my research

Apple Tree Cottage, Woughton-on-the-Green, built in the 1560s, restored by us in 1947

without any expert help or advice. Sykes was conscientious in reading what I wrote and in telling me whether there was anything he could not readily understand. But because his own field of interest came no closer to mine than the history of the Anglican Church in England in the eighteenth century, he could be of only limited help to me. There was certainly no such thing as a research seminar, either in ecclesiastical or imperial history, where one could meet and discuss professional problems with one's peers. In fact, John Fage, with whom I was to collaborate on many different projects throughout my later career, was also my contemporary as a research student in Cambridge, but we made only glancing contact at the time. So also were Ronald Robinson and Jack Gallagher, who were later to collaborate in the writing of a famous book called *Africa and the Victorians* (1961); I knew Robinson a little but Gallagher not at all. I feel that in any properly organised place of learning we should have been meeting round a table with some of our mentors about once a fortnight and helping to educate each other. Although I know from long experience that research of any kind is necessarily a lonely business, I do not think that any research student in any of the universities in which I have subsequently taught was ever subjected to quite the tests of self-reliance cultivated in postwar Cambridge.

The consideration that caused me, as an ecclesiastical historian, to specialise in Africa rather than any other continent was the much greater impact of Christian missionary work in Africa south of the Sahara, as compared with the Asian countries where the earlier establishment of other world faiths had presented much greater obstacles. Latin America might have been even more interesting, but I was much less aware of it. What took me to the eastern side of Africa was the shorter and therefore more managable span of the Christian missionary effort there. The missionary penetration of the East African interior had begun only about 1875, but it had been remarkably widespread, and in most places pioneer missionaries lived under some kind of indigenous African rule for about fifteen or twenty years without the protection of a colonial system. Unlike the exploring travellers who had only narrowly preceded them, the missionary pioneers had been long-term residents, concerned to learn the vernacular languages and study the law and custom of African societies. Their early records should thus have a value that had been little appreciated. I was aware of one determining condition from the first. It was that any study of the kind I had in mind had to be undertaken in a completely ecumenical spirit, if only for the reason that in Africa missions of different denominations and of different national origins had everywhere worked side by side, if not always in full Christian amity. However tempting it might be to confine the search to a single set of archives in a single sending country, it would be pusillanimous to avoid the opportunities for comparative study of one Christian tradition against another and unsound to neglect their differing perceptions of the African peoples among whom they lived.

At the same time this last decision posed large problems of practicability that had to be solved by compromise. Among Roman Catholics alone I would be dealing with six missionary orders, with motherhouses in London, Paris, Algiers, Verona, Turin, and Reichenbach in Bavaria. The German Lutheran missions, so important in what is now Tanzania, were based in Berlin, Leipzig, and Bethel-bei-Bielefeld. Only the English-speaking societies were easily accessible in London and Edinburgh, and these comprised Anglicans of both high- and low-church persuasions, Presbyterians likewise divided between Established and Free Kirk missions, the Wesleyan Methodist Missionary Society, the London Missionary Society, and the Africa Inland Mission. Clearly, it would not be possible for me to do archival work in all these places, and in any case it soon transpired that few had archives open for research. The Roman Catholic congregations mostly did not even reply to my letters. Of the German societies, two were in the Russian zone of occupation. Of the English societies, the Church Missionary Society and the London Missionary Society were the only ones that offered me a ready access to their papers. In general, therefore, it would be a matter of working from published sources.

There was, of course, a considerable literature of specialised printed books in English, French, and German, consisting of the general histories of missionary societies and the biographies and autobiographies of their leading members, which were mostly obtainable in the Cambridge University library or that of the British Museum. There was also, as I soon discovered, a wealth of primary evidence to be recovered from the printed periodicals of the various missionary organisations. The key fact here was that missionary societies of every denomination had to raise their operational funds from supporters in the sending countries; to do so successfully during the late nineteenth and early twentieth centuries they had to feed these increasingly literate supporters with regular bulletins of current information from the main fields of action. Every missionary society or congregation had its published journal, and to my considerable surprise these journals included a mass of first-hand material written by missionaries in the form of reports to their parent societies in the course of their daily work. Of course, what was printed was only a selection, but, so far as it went, there was no doubt of its authenticity.

From these materials I found that I could reconstruct a hitherto completely unsuspected picture of missionary operations during the precolonial period. It showed that, with rare though significant exceptions, the pioneer missionaries did not really work within African societies but rather in between them, by setting up communities of their own from the outcasts of African societies, such as ransomed slaves and political refugees. In such communities all aspects of daily life, the economic and political no less than the spiritual, were directed by the missionary settlers in the region. From these people were made most of the early converts to Christianity. Only here and there, as in the royal court of Buganda (now part of Uganda), was the Christian message preached at the heart of a free society in which individuals could make specifically religious choices, even if they did so at the peril of their lives. It was no wonder that Buganda produced both the first martyrs and the first mass movement or that the communities of Christian outcasts formed elsewhere seldom grew into the schools of future evangelists that their founders intended. It was plain that in most of East Africa the Christian message found willing audiences only after British and German colonialism had forced African societies to change politically and economically on a scale that needed the interpretation offered by missionary education.

Altogether I found the act of historical research of completely absorbing interest. Reporting to Caroline on my final interview with the civil service commissioners, in which I had had some unsympathetic exchanges with the novelist C. P. Snow, who was on the panel, I said, "It remains to be seen how much weight he carries, but as to the result, my feeling at the moment is that I simply don't care. I become increasingly convinced that this work here is what I should be doing, even though I don't at the moment know where it is going to lead. I have never felt more strongly the certain value of anything I have been doing." And I know that to several of my closest friends it became apparent that I had found a new assurance of outlook and a new authority about my work.

So great was my enthusiasm for the things of academe during this autumn and winter of 1946–47 that I gravely neglected even Caroline and our joint effort to rebuild the cottage at Woughton. Our correspondence continued in its usual affectionate style, but with contrition I now see in it the signs of her unhappiness and frustration at being left with so much of the daily responsibility when she too had left her employment at Bletchley and was seeking to rethink her professional future. In retrospect I suppose that these were the last few months during which each of us was trying to face up to the prospect of life without the other one, but whereas I had established a clear career ambition that had to take priority over other considerations, she was still searching. I have no record of where I spent Christmas that year. Possibly, it was with my mother, who had sold her flatlets in Courtfield Gardens and bought a charming little house in Victoria Grove, just off the Gloucester Road, which was to be her home until 1980. During the first three months of 1947 England lay mostly snowbound, and travel between Cambridge and Woughton was unthinkable in my ancient motor car. I remember that Wayland and I at last made the journey together at the end of March and that we had to drive far out of our way to avoid the floods in the Ouse Valley caused by melting snow.

In May 1947 Caroline took a demanding job in the visitors department of the British Council that involved arranging the travels, accommodation, professional contacts, and entertainment for distinguished visitors from foreign countries. These people were always missing their trains, getting lost in the north of Scotland, or requiring urgent medical attention in the middle of the night, leaving Caroline and her colleagues with plenty of amusement but hardly any leisure. Therefore, we saw little of each other that summer, and in the latter part of it I was away on a research trip in Germany. While there I experienced the sense of detachment necessary to review the whole nature of our relationship and to conclude that it had in truth gone far beyond the dimensions of ordinary friendship.

The purpose of my visit to Germany was to find and study the printed sources for the German missionary enterprise in East Africa. I had foreseen correctly that the best collection would probably be in the library of the former German Colonial Institute in Hamburg. The only difficulties of the expedition were those of operating in a country still in tatters after losing the war and still subject to military government by the victorious Allies. Non-Germans were not permitted to stay in German houses or German hotels, and therefore the only way to obtain food and lodging was to be formally attached to the Control Commission and billeted in a so-called officers' mess. Long-distance travel was likewise possible only on military trains, and it was in this fashion that I entered the country after travelling on the military ferry from Harwich to the hook of Holland. We crossed the German frontier at Bentheim, where a voice on the loudspeaker announced, "You are now in the British zone of Germany. Passengers are reminded that it is illegal to give food to German civilians. Anyone throwing food out of the windows of the train is liable to prosecution." As we drew out of the station, I suddenly noticed that people lined both sides of the track. The men and women just stared. The children waved—for food. It went on right down the line to Osnabrück. Every few hundred yards children ran beside the embankment waving frantically, while their mothers held out baskets or bent down to teach their children how to beg. In Osnabrück, as later in Bremen and Hamburg, and above all in the Russian sector of Berlin, I saw huge areas of rubble still uncleared after the wartime bombing raids. People in the streets carried baskets that they used for scavenging among the ruins.

In Hamburg I was directed first to the luxurious Atlantic Hotel, which had been taken over by the Control Commission as a transit camp, and thence after a few days to a pleasant villa on the northern side of Alster Lake, which was described as the Mechanical Engineers Officers' Mess but which was in fact inhabited by a half-dozen fairly elderly male interpreters and a similar number of young female clerks who giggled dutifully at their seniors' wisecracks. From here I got in touch with the education control officer and was introduced to the extremely helpful and friendly librarian of the university, who found me the volumes I needed from a series of dusty packing cases stacked in an attic above the lecture room of the Oriental seminar. Because no reading room was functioning, I was allowed to remove what I wanted, a carload at a time, to the mess, where during six weeks of torrid weather I did most of my work on a covered balcony overlooking a delightful garden.

It was, as I remarked at the time, a typically colonial situation. I was living in a German city, surrounded by German people, working in their language on an aspect of their history, but I could have no contact with them beyond an official interview. I could not eat or drink with them because of the sharply different rations, which required separate systems of supply. Non-Germans bought nearly all their requirements at Control Commission stores and paid for them in a special form of paper currency called BAFs. The unscrupulous, of whom there were many, then traded the surplus through their German employees into the black market. Cigarettes, of which the non-German ration was ninety a week, became the common currency for small transactions between the two systems. Theoretically, a person producing a British passport could board a German bus or tram, but these were so overcrowded with people clinging to the running boards and even sitting on the roofs that one would have been ashamed to do so. Instead, one hailed a Control Commission taxi and tipped the driver a cigarette. The economic apartheid had been made almost total by the inflation of the German currency by roughly 1,000 percent during the two years since the war and by the maintenance of the official exchange rate of forty marks to the pound at a time when the market rate should have been about four hundred. Obviously, one avoided marks and used the BAF currency as much as possible. As I wrote in a letter to Caroline,

One sees only too clearly how all these colonial race problems grow up. How can one expect to have satisfactory relations with people when one's standard of living is their wholetime envy? And yet where would one find the officials who would serve abroad on the same level as the natives? There is an old friend of mine here who is running some kind of Christian welfare school for Germans. He lives with them, pools his rations with them, and because of his work the government allows him to do so. But he is the only Englishman I've met who really knows any Germans.

It was on that balcony in Hamburg in June and early July 1947 that I became progressively convinced that I must rethink my relationship with Caroline in the context of love rather than friendship. It was not just that I was lonely, though I was. It was much more that I was encountering a whole new world of experience, and I knew only one person in the world with whom I wished to share it. I still have the draft of a letter written on July 11 in which I said,

Being out here has made me see things more clearly, and the conclusion I am forced to is that you and I must act decisively, and that soon. . . . This business of each having our own lives is not going to work. As long as we are in contact at all, I, at any rate, am going to want you so much more than anything else that having our own lives will just be a misery. And, if we must part, then every week we delay it is going to make it more impossibly difficult.

I did not post this letter from Germany but brought it home with me, and soon afterwards we discussed it. A day or two later a pencilled note from the British Council offices in Brook Street brought me her reply:

When you told me (or when I first really realised) the serious proportions our relationship had reached for you, I was . . . suddenly aware of the very tremendous thing we have achieved. . . . The discovery alone gave me great happiness. [Until then] my feelings for you amounted to this: very deep, warm-hearted, emotional affection, combined with a great enjoyment . . . in your company. . . . But I have never remotely associated myself with your future, beyond a hope that (other relationships we might respectively acquire permitting) there was a normal friendship in it which might last for our lives. . . . Roland, if we both really want this thing . . . it can, in spite of thirteen years, be made a roaring success.

And so it proved to be.

Having taken our decision, we moved quickly, announcing our engagement in early October 1947 and planning our marriage for two months later. Not all the preliminaries went smoothly. Our friends were support-ive, but we had to face quite hurtful disapproval from some members of both our families, the brunt of which had to be borne by Caroline, who was still working for the British Council in London and therefore more accessible than I was in Cambridge. I for my part was working as hard as I have ever done, writing the first three chapters of my book, which were due to be submitted as a fellowship dissertation early in the new year. The most serious problem of our marriage was that of our future means of support, and it was nothing short of providential that, sometime in late October, my archaeologist friend Charles McBurney dropped in to see me bearing an advertisement that he had noticed in the *Times* for a lectureship in the

Marriage to Caroline, 1947

tribal history of East Africa at the School of Oriental and African Studies at the University of London. At first sight it did not seem to me in the least promising. I objected that I was an ecclesiastical historian and that if there was such a subject as tribal history, I was certainly not qualified to lecture about it. He said he felt sure there must be such a subject and that I probably knew more about it than anyone else. I consulted Norman Sykes, who happened to have a friend on the staff of the school through whom he could make inquiries. The result was most encouraging, both as to the standing of the school's department of history and the drive and enterprise of its young head, Professor C. H. Philips, who held the chair of Oriental history at the university. It was explained that the lectureship would initially be a research post and that the incumbent would be given every opportunity to learn the subject before being required to teach it. It was to be the history department's first venture into the African field, and it was intended that, if successful, further posts would follow. The somewhat exotic title of the lectureship was likewise experimental and was intended merely to emphasize that regional rather than colonial history was the main objective. I realised that it would involve a major change of my chosen course, but in the end I decided to apply, and at the time of our marriage in December an interview was in prospect for the following month.

Our wedding took place on December 10 at my mother's local church in Victoria Road, South Kensington, and the dean of King's, Archie Graham-Campbell, soon to be nominated as bishop of Colombo, came up from Cambridge to officiate. We spent our honeymoon at Cara Lake in Kerry and afterwards returned together to my rooms in St. Edward's Passage, Cambridge, where we lived rather merrily as the only married couple in a household of single research students. I went on with my writing and added a little to our scanty income by teaching a handful of Colonial Service cadets destined for posts in Africa. Among those who brought me essays was the young *kabaka* (king) of Buganda, Frederick Mutesa, who was completing his education in this rather surprising company. We were to meet again in very different circumstances. Meanwhile, it became clear within a few weeks that my stay in Cambridge would be a short one. On January 20, 1948, I was interviewed at the School of Oriental and African Studies, and the next day I received the offer of the post, to start on April 29 at a salary of £525 a year. My income would thus be almost doubled, which indeed it needed to be. It remained only to try to finish my dissertation before we moved back to the cottage at Woughton to begin my new career.

6

The First Exposure
(1948–49)

The School of Oriental and African Studies, as I first knew it, was a place of extraordinary privilege and exciting promise. It was founded in 1917 "to give instruction in the Languages of Eastern and African peoples, Ancient and Modern, and in the Literature, History, Religion and Customs of those peoples, especially with a view to the needs of persons about to proceed to the East or to Africa for the pursuit of study or research, commerce or a profession." Its promoters and its pioneer teachers had mostly belonged to the small minority of British officials and educators who had concerned themselves deeply with the languages and cultures of the Indian empire. The First World War, with the breakup of the Ottoman empire, had seen an expansion of British interests in the Middle East and had underlined the need for Orientalist skills concerning that region also. The case for an academic centre of Oriental studies had thus been made, but the constituency of active supporters was small, and the founders had had to struggle through the 1920s and 1930s on a shoestring budget to build up a staff of about thirty teachers, many of them employed on a part-time basis. The Second World War, however, spreading across so much of Southeast Asia and the Far East and employing troops drawn from almost every part of Africa, brought to the cause a wholly new appreciation of the scale and urgency of what was required. It was beginning to be understood that the postwar world would demand a fairly speedy end to formal empires and that future relations between Europe and the Third World would need to be conducted on the basis of much more knowledge and respect for Asian and African civilisations and cultures.

In 1946 the Interdepartmental Commission of Inquiry under the chairmanship of Lord Scarbrough recommended that the government finance a ten-year programme of expansion that would carry the staff of the school to a teaching strength of 256 posts by 1957. With rare enlightenment the commission's report recognised that the recruitment and training of these teachers would have to run far ahead of the anticipated demand for their services. A cadre of specialists on the various regions would have to be created by recruiting young graduates in the traditional academic disciplines and giving them the opportunity to retrain themselves by study and by regular travel to the regions of their concern. Collectively, they would get to know the different regions of Asia and Africa and the intellectual leaders of the newly emerging states and nations. In the ripeness of time a new generation of Western students would flock to learn from them. Most astonishing, at least in retrospect, the government accepted the report, and the Treasury funded the first five years of the programme with scarcely a murmur of protest.[1]

Such, then, was the community I joined in April 1948. It was one that numbered comparatively few elders, not many more in midcareer, and what was soon to become a large majority of young novices and postulants, most of whom had acquired their initial orientation in the course of some kind of war service in Africa or the East. The older hands included some who had quite busy teaching schedules, notably those who taught Japanese, Chinese, and Arabic, which were the only Oriental languages already in heavy demand. Most of us, however, enjoyed several years unburdened by teaching of any kind. Our only duty was to develop our subjects by research and writing, and to a large extent we were left by our seniors to judge the priorities for ourselves. In my own case, Cyril Philips made clear that he expected me to devote my first term to the preliminary study of an East African language. Thereafter I could take a year reading the ethnographic literature concerning eastern Africa in preparation for a further year of extensive travel, in the course of which I would try to examine the local sources, both written and oral, for the precolonial history of the region. I should also take every opportunity to complete my doctoral thesis and publish it as a book. The rest was up to me.

Therefore during the summer term of 1948 I travelled daily to London, spending an hour or two each morning with Laurence Hollingsworth, who, following many years in the Colonial Education Service in Zanzibar, was now the school's principal teacher of Swahili. In the afternoons I explored the African holdings of the school's splendid, though already gravely overcrowded, library. I got to know some of those who were to be my colleagues through many years. In my department these already included Bernard Lewis, who taught and wrote with equal grace, wit, and learning over an enormous range of Middle Eastern history; A. L. Basham, Kenneth Ballhatchet, and John Harrison, who worked directly under Cyril Philips in Indian history; Bill Beasley, who was to become the leading British historian of Japan; and Denis Twitchett, soon to leave us for the chair of Chinese at Cambridge and who initiated our work in Chinese history. Outside the history department my closest contacts were among the African linguists; after Hollingsworth I soon became acquainted with Malcolm Guthrie, the austere former Baptist missionary in the Belgian Congo who was already deeply engaged in a twenty-five-year project on the classification of the Bantu languages, and also with his much more approachable colleague Archie Tucker, who studied and classified the Sudanic family of languages. Both helped me greatly to understand the place that language study should occupy in my future work. They taught me how many African languages there were and how few were spoken by more than a hundred thousand people. During a journey of familiarisation such as I was about to undertake, I would be passing through the arenas of many hundreds of languages. I could not hope in the time available to learn any one of them sufficiently to obtain primary historical data in the vernacular. I would have to use interpreters. What mattered for me was to know the African language families and, within each, how closely or distantly the member languages were related to one another. Swahili was a special case. It was the indigenous language only of the harbour towns of the Indian Ocean coast, whence it had spread inland with the trading caravans of precolonial times. Outside its area of origin it was a lingua franca, comparable with English or French, useful for asking the way but not for interviewing old men about traditional history.

Another member of the Africa department who played a considerable part in my initiation was Diccon Huntingford, officially a lecturer in Nandi, a language spoken in the western highlands of Kenya for which there was unlikely at any time to be any student demand. In practice, however, Diccon was an amateur ethnographer of the old diffusionist school. He had started his adult life as a farmer in Kenya, learning the language spoken by his African neighbours and employees and taking a deep interest in their oral history and customs. During the war he had been much in demand as an army education officer who gave courses for British servicemen on the social background of the African soldiers with whom they were working. He had travelled widely over East Africa and had taken part in the reconquest of Ethiopia from the Italians. He had in fact competed for the post to which I was appointed, and certainly at that time he knew much more about the tribal history of East Africa than I did. We soon became good friends, and I feel sure that it was he more than anyone else who helped me to see that if there was such a thing as an *inter*tribal history of East Africa in precolonial times, the most likely place to find it would be in the so-called interlacustrine region, comprising southern Uganda, northwestern Tanganyika, and Rwanda-Urundi. Here there had been strong kingdoms, organised along similar lines and with

59

dynastic traditions apparently extending over four or five centuries. These I could probably check against each other to produce at least the outline of a common history. I planned to direct most of my journey to this region.

Meanwhile, at home Caroline during that summer of 1948 became pregnant with our first and, as it was to prove, our only child. It was of course the most important event of our married life, and had we been differently circumstanced, it might easily have delayed, curtailed, or changed the character of our coming travels. As it happened, however, my brother-in-law Dermot Linehan and his wife Barbara had a young family growing up in Melrose with a sweet and affectionate Scottish nanny to help them. Long before our daughter was born, they most kindly offered a place in their nursery during our absence. We were living at a time when air travel was still little developed and when family separations were generally accepted as the price of working in the tropics. After some heart searchings we decided to accept the offer and go ahead with our plans. Sarah was born at our home at Woughton-on-the-Green on April 2, 1949, the first day of that memorable summer when, except for a few thunderstorms, the sun shone out of a blue sky for six and a half months. Day after glorious day her cot sat under the apple tree in the front garden, the watching shared first with a monthly nurse and then with a succession of nice young women from Switzerland and Italy who came to learn our language in exchange for their help in our home.

Against this idyllic background our preparations for travel went ahead. We pored over maps. We studied a cheerful little guide published by the Automobile Association called *African Throughways*, which contained entries like the following: "The route is believed to lie some sixty miles west of the Nile. It was last attempted by a party of four Frenchmen, who never returned." We corresponded with all manner of people who might be able to help us with local contacts or specialised advice. We made our wills. We laid in the drugs recommended by the London School of Hygiene and Tropical Medicine. We visited a missionary outfitter in the Faringdon Road recommended to us by Malcolm Guthrie and bought camp equipment, mosquito boots, and the rest. We practised photographing documents in the open air with a splendid Leica loaned to us by the university, and we experimented with a Wirek recording machine manufactured by the musical supply company Boosey and Hawkes. No pocketsize tape recorders were available in those days. This clumsy instrument, weighing about thirty pounds, had, in the absence of a regular electricity supply, to be powered from a motor car battery, which in turn needed to be simultaneously recharged by a dynamo machine, which looked and sounded rather like a motorcycle engine. When in use, the dynamo had the nasty habit of backing away from the vehicle it was servicing and pulling out the connecting plug. In those postwar years motor cars were still in short supply, particularly cars suited to African conditions. For our local transport we arranged to take over a 1937 Canadian Ford stationwagon that Malcolm Guthrie had been using for a field trip in what was then the Belgian Congo and French Equatorial Africa. This determined our starting date and our point of departure. On returning to Leopoldville (Kinshasa), Guthrie would ship the car and the recording gear by river steamer one thousand miles up the Congo to Stanleyville (Kisangani). We would fly to Stanleyville and begin our land journey from there by driving about five hundred miles through and around the Ituri forest to Uganda.

And so we came, at the end of September 1949, to the traumatic parting with our baby daughter. Early in October we departed initally to Brussels and thence to the heart of Africa. I remember how we stood with about thirty other passengers on the tarmac at Melsbroek airfield in the cold half-light of dawn, while a Sabena air hostess called the roll. Most of us duly answered in French *présent*, but it was comforting when one, described as "Monsieur Major," replied *here* in a very English accent. We were to see much of Mr. Major during the next few days. He proved to be a wholesale buyer for the great firm of Unilever, which, in addition to its palm oil plantations, owned shops and trading stations throughout the Belgian Congo. Mr. Major spent most of his life in distant travels. He could walk into a village market anywhere in tropical Africa and see at once how the fashions in cotton prints were changing and which cooking pots and razor blades were in favour. He taught us that our programme of travel need not alarm us. He probably told us there was nothing to it.

The little plane in which we flew was a DC4. It took six hours to get to Athens and another four hours from there to Cairo, where we spent twenty-four hours comfortably lodged at the Heliopolis Palace Hotel. After a day of sightseeing we took off late in the evening for Juba in southern Sudan, where we waited in a grass-roofed shelter for the plane to be refuelled. A spectacular red dawn broke over the brown plain, promising a day of burning heat. A couple of hours later we were flying over the Congo forest on the last lap of our journey. It was a vital part of our experience to see, as was only possible from above, the sparseness of human settlement in this immense green landscape. During the nineteenth century the explorers and the early missionaries who ascended the waterways had had a very different picture of river banks crowded with villages and rivers busy with canoe traffic. The colonials had carved a few motor roads through the forest, like the one we were to follow to Uganda, but these, no less than the rivers, created an utterly false demographic impression. The great spaces of the Congo forest remain hidden from the land-based traveller. As I was to learn later, this was very different from the West African forest region, where dense vegetation appears to press upon the roadsides but is often little more than a screen concealing large clearings and dense agricultural settlement.

Stanleyville in 1949 was the prosperous capital of the Belgian Congo's eastern province. Built beside the river at the foot of the series of small rapids known as the Stanley Falls, it was the eastern terminus of a thousand miles of uninterrupted waterway connecting it with the Stanley Pool and the colonial capital of Leopoldville (Kinshasa). During the late nineteenth century it had been the meeting point of trading systems from the eastern and the western coasts of equatorial Africa. The first foreign settlement there had been planted by Tippu Tip, the richest and most powerful of all the Zanzibari caravan traders operating in the East African interior. The descendants of his followers were still easily identifiable as the inhabitants of a suburban village beside the falls, speaking the Swahili language and following the Islamic faith of their founders. King Leopold had blocked the traders' westward advance with his river steamers, and gradually the Belgians had replaced the old trade paths to the east by building a railway round the cataracts to Ponthierville (Ubundi). From there another navigable stretch of the river led upstream to Kindu, the port for Albertville and Lake Tanganyika. During the 1920s two main motor roads had been cut through the Ituri forest to the east and the north. Stanleyville was thus the communications hub for the whole eastern half of the colony. The gold, cotton, and coffee of the far interior all passed through its docks, as did all the imports from the outside world. Stanleyville was thought to be a place with a great future. At the time of our visit a large brewery had just been completed, and several important factories were under construction. On our way to the Hotel Stanley we drove along tree-lined boulevards filled with new and outsized American motor cars. Behind the long waterfront of the Congo River, here nearly a mile wide and flowing strongly, we passed the double-storeyed cream-coloured offices of the great monopoly companies responsible for most of the economic development of the colony and, beyond them, the tidy villas of their European staff, each set in flowering shrubbery of hibiscus and bougainvillea. To us, coming from the drabness of postwar England with its annual foreign travel allowance of £25, the standard of life enjoyed by the Belgian colonial elite seemed quite astonishing.

At the Hotel Stanley we soon ran into the only British resident of the town, Paul Burton Roberts, the local representative of the British-American Tobacco Company, a man of great intelligence, broad experience, and wide reading who helped us greatly in our acclimatisation to a new scene. On our first evening we dined with him at a chic restaurant by the banks of the river called the Pourquoi pas?—the kind of place to which sole and lobster from the North Sea were flown out daily by Sabena Airlines but where our choice was the Nile perch known throughout the

Congo as capitaine, the fish of the steamer captains, on whose skill and sobriety so much else depended. With the distant roar of the falls in the background and the lights from the far shore twinkling across the broad water, Paul explained to us many of the real workings of the "model colony." Peasant farmers were compelled to live beside the roads and each to cultivate a quota of primary produce for sale to monopsony companies on pain of up to six months' imprisonment with a beating every Friday. During the coming months we were to receive much confirmation of these conditions from Congolese refugees in Uganda. No doubt these practices were greatly responsible for the explosions of destructive hatred that characterised the aftermath of Belgian colonialism in the 1960s.

Over the weekend of October 26–27, 1949, we rested, making short expeditions with Paul to the Swahili village by the falls and to a colourful market on the Tshopo tributary of the Congo, where we found our travelling companion Mr. Major already at his business in company with the staff of the local Unilever subsidiary. On Monday morning we went in search of our motor car. The Leopoldville steamer, the *Colonel Chaltin*, was tied up at the dock, but no car had been unloaded from it. We asked if we could go on board and make inquiries but were told on no account to attempt it, as monsieur le capitaine was *en train de boire* (the captain was having a drinking bout) and had already dealt roughly with a post office employee who had gone on board to search for some missing mailbags. Soon, to our great consternation, the whistle sounded, the *Colonel Chaltin* backed off from the dock, and sailed away downstream. The steamer would not return for some three weeks. Our frantic inquiries to the shipping company eventually established that an old car had indeed been landed on the opposite bank of the river and been placed among the goods destined for Ponthierville. We crossed by the ferry and found it standing alone in a railway siding. It did indeed look old and tired. Its brown box-body leaned to one side, its hinges creaked, its paint was badly scratched, and it resolutely refused to start. Moreover, we found no sign at all of the four cases of recording gear, spare parts, and camp equipment that should have accompanied it. We were told that the nearest mechanical help was across the river in Stanleyville, but we did not know how to get to it. We need not have worried, however, for in no time a crowd had collected, and we found ourselves being propelled in the vehicle, first to the ferry and then through the streets of Stanleyville to the garage to rhythmical cries of "*H-r-r-r Nya-nya, H-r-r-r Nya-nya*." We had no idea of how such a crowd would expect to be rewarded, so we picked a ringleader and paid him what we thought we could afford. As a system it seemed to work, and the crowd dispersed quite amiably.

However, we still faced the problem of the missing cases, without which we could hardly set out on our overland journey. Paul Burton

63

Roberts came to the rescue. Together we called on the general manager of the shipping company, and Paul gravely asked whether he realised that this was no mere tourist matter but the Oliver Scientific Mission, no less, supported by the British government and with an important rendez-vous with the governor general of Uganda in just a few days' time. He was sure that the general manager was fully capable of solving the problem unaided, but if by any chance a telegram to the British consul general in Leopoldville would assist matters, he would be glad to send one. The general manager looked suitably dismayed and asked us to leave things to him until the following morning. True to his word, he telephoned at breakfast time to say that the cases had been identified on board an upcoming steamer, the *Reine Astride*, which was due in two days. We never did hear whether there had been a loading error at Leopoldville or whether the formidable captain of the *Chaltin* had been persuaded to effect a transfer of baggage to the *Reine Astride* in midstream. At all events, the Oliver Scientific Mission, its transport now in working order, and its leader having paid a courtesy call on the provincial governor, M. Bock, was now ready to depart.

We were of course more than a little scared of what lay ahead of us. We had been exactly a week in Africa, and all of that still in a world of paved streets and running water, telephones, and electric light. Now we had to cross the largest tract of primeval forest on the continent—in the wet season with rivers running high and earth roads deeply rutted in liquid mud. Most of all we were frightened by our lack of mechanical knowledge. We had still to learn that a breakdown in Africa, though it might be inconvenient, was seldom disastrous. Sooner or later help would arrive. We therefore decided, almost at the last minute, that we would spend more money than we could easily afford to hire a driver from the garage to accompany us on this first leg of about 450 miles to Beni. In the event, he did not have to do anything for us. Because we had no common language, his companionship was a perfectly silent one, but his presence on the backseat relieved us of the worst of our anxiety. Indeed, it enabled us to positively enjoy the forest drive and gave us, at the end of it, the confidence to carry on alone.

The first day out of Stanleyville was an easy one that took us to a little roadside inn at Kilometre 229. The sun shone straight down, lighting up the red murram road between its high green verges, and there was enough human company to forestall any sense of isolation. The colonial government had deliberately concentrated the population beside the road, and every few miles a village street took off to left or right, each within a semicircle of cleared fields surrounded by a belt of oil palms. At a village called Mganga we turned aside to visit a Baptist mission, to which we had been recommended by the Baptists in Stanleyville. The man of the house was away, but his wife, a Mrs. Carrigan, gave us cooling drinks and talked to us about their work. Though trained as a nurse, her main field of activity had been linguistic. For many years she had been translating the Bible into the two local languages, Bali and Kumu. Now, with the work nearly done, the mission was having to restrict the sale of Bibles, as so much of their content was disturbing to the local people. The war years had seen a spread of Watch Tower doctrines, here known as *Kitawala*. The Jehovah's Witness initiates attempted to put into practice the saying of Jesus that the first should be last and the last first by working themselves into a state of hypnotic trance. In trance they went through the motions of driving motor cars, riding bicycles, and engaging in other enviable pastimes of the white man. At the height of the troubles a few Europeans living in isolated places had been kidnapped, and the authorities suspected that the movement had gained a foothold among the African police of the district. This had led to drastic repression and had been one of the main motives for the government's policy of villagisation. Mrs. Carrigan left us in no doubt that the mission fully approved of the government's action.

A stray question from Caroline about whether the villagers practised any metal working elicited from Mrs. Carrigan the response that until recently the great specialty of the local smiths had been the manufacture of the iron "leopard's claws" used by members of secret societies to attack their victims. She evidently had no doubt that the attackers consumed the remains of the victims, and she had witnessed the public hanging of two men convicted of this crime. She said that her Bali neighbours in the village refused even to talk of such happenings but that the Kumu who lived nearby in the valley of the Tshopo River, and among whom she had recently spent some weeks in camp, had no such inhibitions. In retrospect I find it strange that this, our first field interview, should have been concerned with matters quite so lurid, the like of which we never encountered in any of our later travels. I do not disbelieve the broad outline of Mrs. Carrigan's evidence. I can only say that there cannot have been many African peoples who lived as far from any beaten track as the Kumu and that it seems to be in small isolated communities that people appear to live in the greatest fear of their neighbours.

Beyond Kilometre 229 we entered hillier country, which made the trees seem even taller. And twice or more each day we ran through violent thunderstorms that transformed our pleasant road into a series of ski slopes. We climbed each hill with skidding wheels and slithered crabwise down the other side to a bridge consisting of two narrow planks at the bottom. And so we came on the evening of the second day to Mambasa, where, as at Stanleyville, a section of the town was inhabited by the descendants of the Swahili traders of the nineteenth century and by those of their local followers. There, in the Hotel des Pygmées,

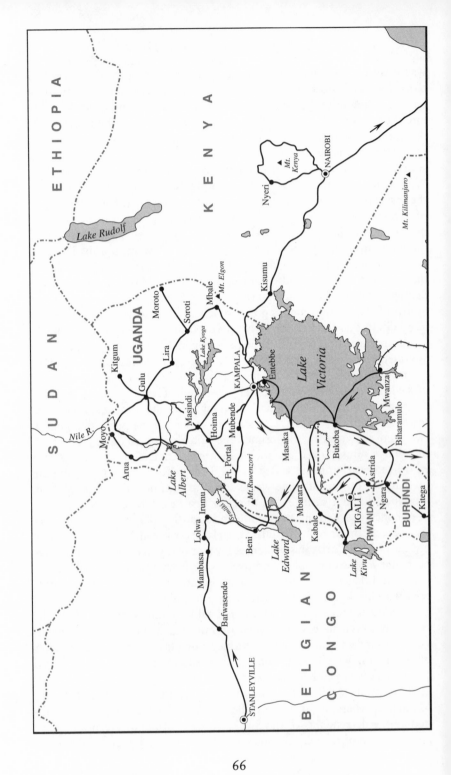

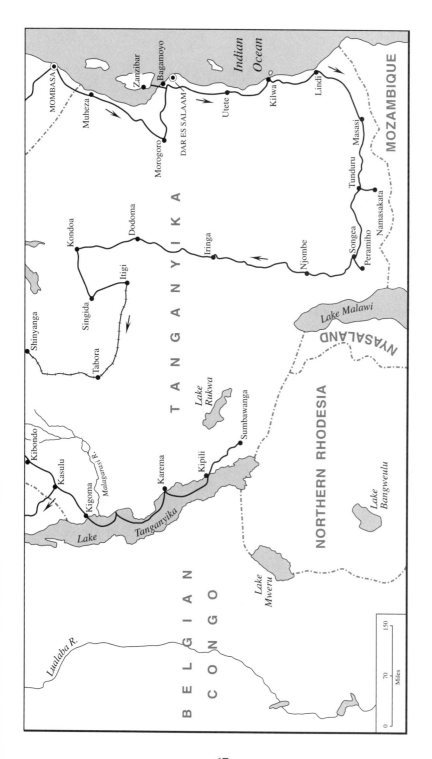

we met a Dr. Woodham, an American of private means who had lived in the neighbourhood for more than twenty years, running his private medical mission to the local Pygmies. We gratefully accepted his invitation to lunch on the following day, and there found a happy American family at home in the Ituri forest. His wife had cooked a delicious meal, complete with ice cream, and we ate with two teenage children recently returned from schools in the Midwest. The attractive daughter of fifteen was a little apprehensive that she might find the forest dull after Chicago, but the son of twelve seemed keenly alive to the adventure of it. Outside on the veranda was another boy, a hopeless invalid from birth who would probably never leave the forest and with whom one of his parents had always to stay. As we talked, Dr. Woodham came in from his morning clinic, worried and sad because a Pygmy woman with a terribly wounded head had been unable to stand the confinement of his hospital and had fled into the forest during the night. Understandably, he did not invite us to meet the rest of his elusive patients. Just how understandably came home to us that afternoon, when our progress was halted by a huge tree that had fallen across the road. A Belgian official, travelling in the opposite direction, had returned to the nearest village for help, and soon a team of thirty stalwarts arrived with their axes and ropes. While they worked, a troop of ten or twelve Pygmies walked down the roadside in single file, their bows and arrows slung on their shoulders, looking straight ahead and entirely oblivious to the activity around them. When they reached the tree, they climbed straight over it and continued on their way without pause or spoken comment. We realised that here was a far wider cultural gap than that between European rulers and African peasant subjects. The hunter-gatherers inhabited a totally different world.

When the obstruction was finally cleared from the road, it was almost sunset, and many forest miles still lay between us and the next hotel at Irumu. Greatly daring, we turned in uninvited to a mission settlement in the nearby village of Lolwa, where we were soon greeted by a young missionary wife. She was walking down the garden path with a child on either hand and saying, "I hear folk talking English, and I hope they're spending the night." This was just what we were hoping too, and soon we were seated in her lamplit sitting-room with a bowl of fresh-cut roses on the table and the distant sound of children's voices practising "Silent Night" in preparation for Christmas in a forest clearing. Our hosts proved to be Plymouth Brethren, and their Lolwa mission consisted of three generations of a single family. The grandparents had come from Stornoway in the Outer Hebrides and had been posted to the Ituri forest after earlier assignments in California and Panama. At Lolwa they had brought up a large family, consisting of several sons and one daughter, all but one of whom had stayed to work at the mission. The daughter, our

The main road to Uganda, Ituri forest, 1947

hostess, having trained as a nurse, had married an American colleague in the mission, Bill Spees, who was now the head of the station and soon came in from his work to join us for the evening meal. Besides his evangelistic duties, he was the headmaster of a school with four hundred pupils, the supervisor of a leper colony serving the whole of the eastern Ituri, the manager of a large dispensary, and the master builder and odd-job man of the entire establishment. If pig or elephant were trampling the gardens of the villagers, it was he who drove the creatures off with his gun. If food was short, it was he who led the hunting parties. Next morning early he took us on a tour of inspection, and when we had seen the church, school, dispensary, workshop, and brick kiln, he asked whether we would like to see the lepers. It would have been unthinkable to have refused, and we accompanied him for perhaps a mile down a forest track from which a little village street climbed up the side of a hill. At the sound of our approach the inmates, most of them horribly maimed and disfigured, emerged one by one from their houses and gathered round us, talking, laughing, and asking who we were and where we came from. We were told that each leper had at least one undiseased relative living with him, even though at some peril, to care for him and grow his food. Even some young children were living with diseased parents, and, providing that they slept in separate rooms, they were thought to have a good chance of remaining

69

immune. Bill Spees told us that the lepers were carefully trained never to touch other people; nevertheless, when he and his wife had returned from their last overseas leave, they found the entire population of Lolwa lined up to shake them by the hand and, at the end of the line, a hundred lepers, each with a hand outstretched. "There was nothing for it," he said. "We shook hands with the whole lot."

We left Lolwa and drove on eastwards through dense forest, until suddenly we came upon a sight so surprising that we stopped dead to take it in. Before us the road dipped down again to one of the innumerable river valleys that we had crossed throughout our journey. But this one was different. On the far side of it we could see in the distance, over the tops of the trees, a grassy mountain. Since leaving Mambasa our road had been following, more or less, the route taken by H. M. Stanley in his expedition to rescue Emin Pasha in 1887. On the previous day we had stopped, alas in a thunderstorm, to visit the site of his Fort Bodo, where he had waited in conditions of mounting privation for the rear column that never came. Now we were gazing upon the scene he described in his book *In Darkest Africa* (1890) in the following words:

This then was the long promised view and the long expected exit out of gloom. Therefore I called the tall peak terminating the forested ridge, of which the spur whereon we stood was a part, and that rose two miles East of us to a height of 4600 feet above the sea, Pisgah—Mount Pisgah—because after 156 days of twilight in the primeval forest, we had first viewed the desired pasture lands of Equatoria.

Stanley went on to tell of the reactions of his Zanzibari porters, who, "feverish with exultation," turned and cursed the forest for its cruelty:

They compared it with hell, they accused it of the murder of one hundred of their comrades, they called it the wilderness of fungi and wood-beans; but the great forest which lay vast as a continent before them, and drowsy like a beast, with monstrous fur veiled by vaporous exhalations, answered not a word, but rested in its infinite sullenness, remorseless and implacable as ever.[2]

After a mere four days of fairly comfortable motoring, we had no cause to castigate the forest in this way, but the sudden change of scenery as we reached Mount Pisgah was curiously moving. We emerged from the forest, as from a tunnel, into a landscape practically bare of trees and soon afterwards turned south, keeping the sharply defined forest margin well in sight on our right-hand side as we moved towards our next stopping place at Mutwanga in the western foothills of the Ruwenzori Range. At the little town of Beni we parted from our driver, who would return to Stanleyville by bus. Alone for the first time we drove down the escarpment of the

70

western Rift Valley to the Semliki River, which flows round the western side of the Ruwenzori from Lake Edward to Lake Albert. We crossed it by ferry and climbed up some four thousand feet on the other side to the little mountain resort of Mutwanga, where we were to enjoy the warm hospitality of Mr. and Mrs. Kline of the Africa Inland Mission (AIM).

Despite their loose affiliation to the AIM, the Klines and one other family with which they shared their station represented the missionary outreach of a single nondenominational congregation in Philadelphia. They told us that their remuneration depended entirely on their individual success in presenting the significance of their work to their home congregation. They had just returned from a fund-raising furlough, and it had enabled them to bring back a new car, a refrigerator, and other luxuries. Their colleagues on the station had had no such luck. They had borrowed money for their last home trip and had failed to repay it, so it was now doubtful when or whether they would get home again. Perhaps because of these background uncertainties Mr. Kline, when saying grace before meals, managed to inject a good deal of pleased surprise into the phrase "Lord, we have some food." And before we departed the following morning, our own twelve-year-old vehicle was made the subject of our breakfast-time prayers—alas, to small avail. The engine had sputtered ominously as we climbed up the escarpment to Mutwanga, and it sputtered again as we now worked our way round to the southern shoulder of the mountain, where the road crossed the frontier into Uganda. At the crest of the ridge we saw the Belgian flag flying, and on giving our name to the official at the tiny frontier post, we were greeted with "*Ah, la mission scientifique Oliver!*" Our credentials, presented at the Belgian embassy in London six months previously, were lying on the table, and we were proud to think that the "mission Oliver" had succeeded in arriving on the precise date specified. "*Vous avez ni ivoire, ni peaux de léopards, monsieur? Bon, passez, je vous en prie. Bon voyage*" (You are carrying neither ivory nor leopard skins? Very well, sir, please pass. Have a good journey.).

It was a marvellous route by which to enter Uganda. The car purred its way down the eastern side of the ridge towards the blue waters of Lake Edward sparkling in the sun. We quickly noticed that, unlike their opposite numbers in the Congo, all the Africans whom we passed on the road were riding bicycles. Their wives were dressed in long bright cotton dresses and seated with perfect balance on the pillion brackets. Bales of cotton or bundles of green bananas balanced on the handlebars. We soon passed the little lakeside trading centre of Katwe and then left all signs of population behind us as we entered the Lake George Game Reserve, now a part of the Queen Elizabeth National Park.

The road to Mbarara, which still had to cross the Kazinga Channel by ferry, went off to the right, while we took the northerly route towards Fort

Portal. A road sign indicated that we were crossing the equator, and soon afterwards our car engine gave two small gasps and expired. As we were to discover later, a vapour lock had developed in the petrol pipes, because of the rapid changes in our height above sea level. The standard remedy was to sit and wait for several hours until the engine had completely cooled. Meanwhile, in our inexperience the situation seemed quite alarming. We were in a game reserve. We had encountered no other traffic since leaving Katwe. The midday sun shone down relentlessly, and there was no shade anywhere within sight. A troop of large baboons soon gathered to observe us. It seemed clear that we should not leave the vehicle. In the event, we only had an hour or two to wait, but it seemed like an age.

At last we heard the sound of an approaching car, and there drew up beside us one of the small community of white coffee farmers settled around Fort Portal. His name was Gunn, his nickname was Bunduki, which is the Swahili for *gun*, and his car was full of guns. He shared our ignorance of internal combustion engines but volunteered that a friend of his called Lemon—Squash Lemon—was visiting friends nearby and would probably be able to help. We all set off and duly found Squash Lemon, sitting outside a caravan and drinking brandy. Indeed, he had drunk so much brandy that he was convinced that we were Belgians from

Customs post at the Belgian Congo-Uganda frontier, 1949

the Congo, and he didn't know our "lingo." Nevertheless, he came and after a brief diagnosis told his African servant to put his mouth to the petrol intake and "bloody well blow." Now, he said, "It bloody well *must* go." And it did.

Fort Portal, the district headquarters for the Toro kingdom, was a place to which we would return later in our travels. On this occasion we stayed there just long enough to have the car attended to and then made straight for Kampala, down two hundred miles of dusty serpentine road, passing here and there through patches of forest but mostly weaving in and out of the swampy valleys between the flat-topped hills characteristic of central Buganda. We found that the eye learned only slowly to recognise the pattern of human settlement in such a landscape, with the houses scattered unevenly across the slopes and concealed within the groves of banana trees that supplied the staple food. There were no compact villages along the route—only the halfway township at Mubende, the administrative centre for western Buganda, and the two trading centres of Kyanjojo and Mityana. It was therefore with some surprise and excitement that we suddenly saw the dome and twin towers of two cathedrals standing out boldly on the eastern horizon and lit by the evening sun. This was the very heart of Christian Buganda, which had been the centrepiece of my missionary studies. And this, we both felt, was the end of the introduction to our travels. We had reached the starting point of our serious initiation.

7

Three Kingdoms
(1949)

In Kampala we needed entrée to three areas before we could properly get on with our work. The first was obviously that of the protectorate government, radiating outwards from the administrative capital of Entebbe twenty miles to the southwest—a real bureaucrats' paradise, built in a semicircle around an immaculately mown golf course that dropped down to the blue waters of Lake Victoria with a view of Kome Island in the distance. The government offices stood at one end of the semicircle on a little peninsula running out into the lake, and my dominant memory of our first visit is of how small and intimate it all seemed. I had a letter of introduction to the administrative secretary, Barry Cartland, who was the third most senior officer of the government. He sat in one of about six rooms, all opening onto a grassy quadrangle that, together with the offices of the attendant Goanese clerks, constituted the secretariat. The office of the governor was in a two-storeyed building just next door; the lower storey housed the archives. Perhaps a half-dozen other similarly modest establishments accommodated the directorates of the main government services—public works, agriculture, medical services, lands and survey, and some others. Education was, with rare exceptions, still a missionary preserve, though subsidised and inspected by a government director who had his office in Kampala.

The secretariat lay at the centre of a web of authority that spread out through the four provincial headquarters to the sixteen main districts into which the country was divided for administrative purposes. At the headquarters of each district would be a district commissioner and one or two assistants who were responsible for supervising the judicial and police work and the collection of taxes carried out by African "native authorities" operating at the district, county, and subcounty levels. Some technical departments would be represented at the district level, and

74

therefore a district headquarters might have six to eight European officers and their families living in moderately comfortable bungalows, built typically around a rough golf course with a clubhouse, a tennis court, and some kind of rest house for visiting European staff. My plan was to visit every district in the protectorate for one to two weeks, to inspect the archives and photograph the materials most relevant to my interests, interview the leading authorities on the precolonial history of each area, and seek out vernacular books and manuscripts dealing with the subject. Therefore what I needed from the system was to be introduced by the district commissioners to the relevant native authorities and to be given access to their archives and rest houses. Somehow, in a matter of about half an hour it was all satisfactorily arranged.

A second area to which we needed access was the local missionary world, in which I had both a direct interest because of my book and an indirect one as a source of contacts for my work on traditional history. Fortunately, only two main Christian denominations were represented in Uganda. The Roman Catholic Church had three dioceses in the southern half of the country, all served by the White Fathers; one diocese was in the north, served by the Verona Fathers, and another was in the east, served by the Mill Hill Fathers. The Anglican Communion was organised in two dioceses, Uganda and the Upper Nile, both served by the Church Missionary Society (CMS). The missionary door was enchantingly and unforgettably opened for us by the Anglican bishop of Uganda, Simon Stuart, and his gifted wife Mary, who came within a few days of our arrival and scooped us out of an uncomfortable lodging to stay with them in their simple but superbly sited "palace" at the top of Namirembe Hill, from which one looked out across the whole width of Kampala and its suburbs, with glimpses of Lake Victoria in the distance. A few hundred yards away at the opposite end of the hill stood the red brick cathedral with its copper dome. Every Sunday morning a vast and colourful crowd of worshippers wound its slow way up the spiral approach road for a two-hour sung Eucharist in the Luganda language. Beyond and below the cathedral a broad tree-lined avenue led down to the old royal capital of Mengo, where my sometime pupil, Kabaka Mutesa II, held court in a silver-domed palace (*lubiri*) surrounded by the straight-woven reed fence that was a symbol of royal authority. At his gate was the *Lukiko* hall, the meeting-place of his traditional council, and all around it were the European-style houses of the Ganda royals, aristocracy, and upper bourgeoisie.[1]

As guests of the Stuarts we made many of our earliest African contacts within this favoured circle, and it was good for us to learn so soon that there were Africans who shared our education and values and with whom we could talk and laugh as equals. We were asked to lunch by the kabaka's parents-in-law, Christopher and Pomola Kisosonkole—he a graduate of

Fort Hare, the leading secondary school in South Africa, and she a Zulu with a keen appreciation of the difference between conditions in a British protectorate and those of a colony of white settlement. When we had eaten, Christopher carried the plates to the kitchen door and handed them to the maid, saying, "We are becoming very anglicized, you see." Mary Stuart had gathered a number of such people into a kind of salon to discuss public affairs rather than politics, and there we made many long-lasting friends like the newspaper proprietor Eridadi Mulira and his wife Rebecca, and Thomas Makumbi and his wife Eseta, who had acted in a well-known film called *Men of Two Worlds*; she had lived for a year in the English film world and had now returned with relief to her own society. We visited the elite boarding schools—Budo for boys and Gayaza for girls—where such people had gained their secondary education and where such a large proportion of the CMS missionary force was concentrated. We saw and met more people when we attended the celebrations for the kabaka's birthday, beginning with a full-dress service in the packed cathedral and continuing with a garden party at the lubiri and an impressively decorous football match between Buganda and Busoga for "the Kabaka's Cup."

Back at the bishop's house the days were full of interesting visitors, and during the intervals between them I was often able to sit with him in his office and pose my professional questions about how an African diocese was organised and financed. The visitors included many of the African clergy; I quickly realised that none of them—not even the assistant bishop, Abere Balwa—spoke English and that all were middle-aged or older. These men were clearly not products of the elite schools but people who had enjoyed just a few years of primary education and who had achieved success as rural evangelists and teachers in bush schools before being recruited for a little further training for the ordained ministry. I felt bound to ask whether such a system, however appropriate for the management of the first mass movements to Christianity during the early twentieth century, could possibly be adequate to a situation in which the leaders in African society were increasingly being drawn from those who had received formal education for six, nine, or even twelve years. Simon agreed that it was the most crucial question for the future, but he feared that the ethos of a rural ministry, paid at a level of bare subsistence, had become so entrenched that it was almost hopeless to expect better-educated volunteers to come forward. The Roman Catholic Church had from the beginning pursued a very different policy of steering likely ordinands at a young age into junior and senior seminaries from which most dropped out along the way but from which the few survivors emerged with an education comparable to that of their opposite numbers on other continents. The numbers of African clergy in the Catholic Church were still small. One Catholic diocese had recently been set up in southern

Buganda with an African bishop and clergy, but in the rest of the country all clerical functions were still performed by foreign missionaries.

In 1949 Simon Stuart's diocese included the whole of southern Uganda, Rwanda-Urundi, and a slice of the Belgian Congo to the west of Ruwenzori. In the course of visiting its many deaneries and parishes he and Mary would drive about forty thousand miles a year, all along dirt roads and many along byways maintained only by the local populace, using *pangas* (reaping knives), hoes, and tin basins. One of our earliest experiences as their guests was to accompany them on a typical two-day sortie to a rural deanery in northern Buganda. After an early start from Kampala, and after picking up the African rural dean at the boundary of his deanery, we reached our first stopping place about midmorning at a little mud-walled village church that, though founded early in the century, had never had a visit from a bishop. The confirmation service was followed by speeches of welcome and then by a feast served under a canopy of thatched banana fronds. There were big bowls of soup and mountainous helpings of boiled and mashed bananas topped with guinea-fowl and green vegetables. The village chief waited on us in person, and while we ate, two sheep, a pig, some hens, and baskets of fruit and vegetables were brought in and presented before being despatched to Namirembe to await our return. We departed in the heat of early afternoon to keep two similar engagements with thirty or forty dusty miles between each. At the first some kind of religious revival had resulted in ninety candidates for confirmation, which put us badly behind schedule. At the second we participated in a really big feast, six courses provided by the rich chief of the entire county, and then a group photograph, which involved at least an hour's discussion of who should stand where. Once more we drove on, to arrive long after dark at a girls' boarding school run by English missionary ladies. Eight white-frocked little girls had been waiting many hours for their confirmation, which finally took place by lamplight before we retired, exhausted, to our beds. We had witnessed a day in the life of a colonial bishop, and it was in every way a good preparation for the work that lay ahead of us. We had sampled the bush and had found it full of apparently happy and friendly people. We would have liked to have been able to speak to them directly in their language rather than in interpreted English or halting Swahili, but we had seen that some personal communication was nevertheless quite possible.

Even while we were staying at Namirembe, another opportunity was opening for us on the neighbouring hill of Makerere, where a former government college of arts and technology was being transformed into the University College of East Africa, serving Kenya, Tanganyika, and Zanzibar as well as Uganda. Like the other university colleges founded at about the same time at Achimota on the Gold Coast, Ibadan in Nigeria, and

Khartoum in the Sudan, Makerere was being developed in a "special relationship" with my university in London. This meant that London degrees
would be awarded on the basis of teaching syllabuses and examinations
approved by the sponsoring university. Recruitment to the academic staff
would be assisted by the so-called Inter-Universities Council for Higher
Education in the Colonies, operating through a small but immensely influential secretariat directed by Walter Adams, later the founding principal
of the University College of Rhodesia and Nyasaland and director of the
London School of Economics. At the time of our visit Makerere was still
very much in a state of transition. The professor of education, Bernard de
Bunsen, was the acting principal, not yet confirmed in his new post. Behind
a shy, apparently bumbling, exterior he was developing an admirable
vision of what a university in tropical Africa should aim to become, and
he had the personality and background to move as an equal among the
high officials of the four East African territories. At Makerere he was
clearly visible by all during the hour or two before sunset, when he would
be walking round and round the hill, always in earnest conversation with
one or another member of his staff.[2]

We did not at first seem to have any obvious point of contact with
Makerere. As yet it had no department of history, and the subject was
being taught only part-time by the wife of a lecturer in English. But we had
a letter of introduction to the librarian, Julie Larter, who soon invited us to
use her spare room and share her housekeeping during our visits to Kampala. Through her we soon met many leading figures at Makerere—Hugh
Trowell, the well-known specialist on African diet and famine diseases,
and his wife Margaret, who was making an international reputation as
a teacher and patron of East African artists; Kenneth Baker, the devoted
founder of an outstanding department of geography; the anthropologist
Aidan Southall, soon to be joined by Audrey Richards, recruited from
the London School of Economics to set up the Institute of Economic
and Social Studies; the chaplain and church historian Fred Welbourn and
Hebe, his doctor wife; Leonard Beadle, the professor of physics; and Klaus
Wachsmann, the gentle musicologist who was the curator of the Uganda
Museum, where he had trained a team of African musicians to accompany
visitors from one exhibition hall to another, playing charmingly upon their
instruments the while. We quickly felt the attraction of such a society but
were nonetheless dumbfounded when, a bare three weeks after our arrival
in Uganda, Bernard de Bunsen asked to see us both in his office. He offered
me the job of building his history department with the starting rank of a
university reader (associate professor).

The proposition presented me with one of those comparatively rare
moments of fundamental choice that occur in a professional life. In
London I was, and would remain for a long time, a person of little

consequence in a large organisation. As head of a department at Makerere I would have an assured position and one that would bring me into daily contact with the African students whose education I was deeply concerned to promote. On the other hand, for that education to be properly relevant to African needs I would have to develop a whole new conception of African history that had to embrace the entire continent. I felt that was a task that would be better initiated from outside Africa than locked too closely into a single region within it. To have stayed in East Africa would have been personally agreeable to both of us, and we had already seen enough of the circumstances to be confident that a family life would be possible while based there. But we could also visualise the inevitable conflict between running a teaching department and practising research and writing. It was at bottom a choice between the students and the subject, and I am interested to find that in the letter in which I reported the offer to Cyril Philips in London, I said, "I am sure that for many years to come the best books on African history will be written not here but in England, and the same probably goes for most serious academic work by African students." It was in fact in the training of African research students based in London that I was to make my main contribution to African university education. Meantime, having decided to decline the offer, we were at last ready to begin the next stage of our travels.

In many ways it could have been tempting to start our inquiries in the kingdom of Buganda, where by 1949 precolonial history had already received far more serious study than anywhere else. It had been a passionate interest of several early literate Christians, including the great Apolo Kagwa, who had been prime minister of the kabaka's government from 1891 until 1927. Kagwa had been in a unique position to summon the living repositories of oral tradition, and he had worked in close contact with an unusually able missionary ethnologist, John Roscoe, who had no doubt helped him to order his materials according to the prevailing conventions of European historiography. Both men had published their main results during the first decade of the twentieth century. Both were in substantial agreement about the order and foremost events of the reigns of some thirty-three kabakas, representing some nineteen generations of rulers under whom the kingdom had grown from minuscule beginnings to include roughly one-quarter of the territory and also of the population of the modern Uganda protectorate. They had clearly mapped the successive stages of this expansion as well as the constitutional changes whereby the kabakaship had been transformed from a simple presidency over competing clan heads into a strongly centralised monarchy operating through appointed officials.[3]

All this we knew, but we had nevertheless determined to go first to Bunyoro, the traditional kingdom adjoining Buganda to the north and west and at one time the dominant power in the whole region. Unsuccessful nineteenth-century wars had reduced Bunyoro to a mere rump of its former size and importance. Accordingly, on November 23 we set off for Hoima, which was both the district headquarters of the protectorate government and the capital of the traditional ruler of the kingdom, the *omukama* (king) Tito Winyi Gafabusa IV. The rest house there was of the simplest noncatering kind, with three small bedrooms and a common dining-room that we had to share with other visitors. The narrow open veranda that ran down one side of the building became our workplace. Here we brought files from the district office for study and photographing, and I sat for long hours with a well-mannered and extremely assiduous mission schoolteacher called Joseph, who was seconded to us as an interpreter by the local White Fathers. I had of course already studied what had been published in English about the history of Bunyoro, including three articles that had appeared in the *Uganda Journal* under the initials *K. W.*, generally believed to stand for King Winyi, that is to say, for the omukama himself.[4] There was, however, a small book by a former minister in the omukama's government, John Nyakatura, that was available only in Lunyoro (the Nyoro language), and my first task was to master its contents with Joseph's help before getting involved in any interviews.[5] The district commissioner, John Bessell, made his office records available to me and took me to make an introductory call on the omukama. In the evening Bessell demanded our presence on the tennis court, where the fourth player was a White Father who was required by the rules of his order to perform in his cassock; all things considered, he did so very well. Afterwards, we dined with John Bessell and there met the Yale-educated prime minister in the omukama's government, Balamu Mukasa, who represented the old kingdom's modern face.

The omukama, Tito Winyi, belonged to an earlier generation than Kabaka Mutesa. He was in fact a late-born child of the omukama Kabarega, who in the late nineteenth century had made his kingdom the centre of the opposition to British occupation. He had fought the British from one place of retreat to another and had finally been caught and exiled by them to the Seychelles. Tito Winyi had been born and brought up in the islands, where history had understandably been the main topic of conversation of a court in exile. A much older brother ruled in Bunyoro, enduring all the indignities of early colonial rule, including the dismemberment of the country and the temporary imposition of Ganda chiefs. But Tito Winyi had been trained to embody the traditions of a more glorious past. I suppose that he understood that the interest of a British historian could not be harmful to the continuing plight of his country and that it might even be of some help. At all events, he quickly invited us to witness the "morning ceremony," which he had performed daily since his accession in 1924. This was basically an inspection of the ritual structures in the palace compound. Dressed in the bark-cloth robes used by his ancestors before the advent of imported textiles, he emerged from his throne room in the main dwelling built in the European style and walked along a narrow strip of bark-cloth carpet, which was unrolled before him as he moved and rolled up behind him when he had passed. His route took him through a succession of seven sacred huts, all built in the traditional round form, lined with reeds, and topped with conical thatched roofs. The first was the throne room of the "queen sister," who was next in precedence to the king and on all important occasions had to sit there enthroned to greet him as he passed. The second hut was that of the princes, the king's half-brothers who had business to perform at court. The third and fourth huts were traditionally reserved for the reception of ambassadors from neighbouring states, and in the courtyard leading to them a court official stood holding the omukama's sacred spear of office and the bow and quiver that were part of his regalia. The fifth and sixth huts were courtrooms where offending chiefs used to be tried. The seventh hut was the royal dairy, where the cows supplying the needs of the household were milked. En route to the dairy was the courtyard of the sacred fire, which had to be kept burning day and night while the king lived. Here the omukama paused under a canopy facing the fire and went through the symbolic motions of hearing lawsuits and delivering judgments.

The return journey to the residence was made by the same route. On reentering his throne room the omukama mounted his throne, which was covered with a great pile of leopard skins, and sat there in state while his courtiers knelt in a semicircle and told him the happenings of the previous night. Then, after disappearing briefly to change into European dress, he showed us in detail the regalia kept in the throne room and, above all, the collection of beaded crowns with long flowing false beards of colobus monkey fur that he had inherited from his predecessors. He drew our attention especially to three or four crowns in which the headpiece was surmounted by a tall thin cone of copper; these had belonged, he said, to a dynasty earlier than his. It was obvious that most of these items of regalia, made of impermanent materials in the first place, must have been frequently repaired or even completely renewed. Drums had been recovered, spears rehafted, and one of the supposedly older crowns had a glass butterdish of clearly recent European origin woven into its beaded headpiece. Nevertheless, a real and impressive attempt had been made to preserve the possessions of previous generations of rulers.

From the throne room we moved to the wide porch outside that had three vacant chairs set for the omukama and us. At right angles to these, two benches already were occupied by a dozen elderly gentlemen, all respectably dressed in the long white cassocklike robes called *kanzus*, which were worn under European jackets and were the standard uniform of African gentility throughout the protectorate. These were the crown wearers, so-called because on state occasions they wore the same beaded and bearded headgear as the king. Their functions were approximately those of a college of heralds. On our arrival they rose and then knelt to the omukama, who introduced us and invited us to put our questions. Taken somewhat by surprise, I asked them to tell us how they had acquired their special knowledge of their country's history. They told us that in the days before literacy young men and boys around the royal court were trained to remember the orders and messages sent by the king to his chiefs all over the country as well as the diplomatic communications between Bunyoro and other states. They described how they had been made to repeat their messages immediately after they were entrusted with them and how they were severely punished for any mistakes. Often, too, after starting on their missions, runners would be despatched to recall them so that they could be tested again. This, they said, was also the way in which historical knowledge was transmitted from one generation of experts to the next, and certainly their speeches flowed fluently enough to have been deliberately committed to memory and kept alive by frequent repetition. What they did not volunteer, and what I lacked the sophistication to elicit, was who decided what should be committed to the pool of memory in the first place, what should be eliminated, and what should be manipulated in the course of its onward transmission.

I was able to have two or three more sessions with the omukama and his crown wearers, in the course of which I saw all too clearly that a serious researcher could profitably spend two or three years in Bunyoro, learning the language and recording historical information in this peculiarly favourable environment. It was with some sadness that I reminded myself that my mission was one of wide-ranging reconnaissance—I must be prepared to glimpse and then move on. What seemed of greatest relevance in all the ground we covered was the fascination of my hosts for what they clearly saw as a historical period preceding that of the current dynasty. At that time Bunyoro and all the surrounding states were briefly included within a single great empire of Kitara, encompassing the whole of southern Uganda and northwestern Tanganyika and ruled by a conquering dynasty from outside the region that tradition remembered as the Chwezi. The Chwezi had not been a numerous people, although they had posessed large herds of cattle that had been widely dispersed across all the areas suitable for grazing. At first they had been welcomed by the local people, who respected them for their riches and their powers of organisation, but after a couple of generations they had lost their prestige. Their unitary kingdom had disintegrated into a series of smaller states ruled by the founders of new dynasties that mostly survived until colonial times. To me, still in my

Interview with king of Bunyoro and crown-wearers, 1949

first flush of naive diffusionism, it seemed that such a scenario would, if true, hold a double attraction for the modern historian. On the one hand, the conquest theory would explain the similarity of political and social structure among the peoples of this region. And on the other hand, if all the ruling dynasties of the area had taken their origins in a single historical event, it should be possible to study their traditions side by side within a single chronological framework of dynastic generations running back from the recent past to the time of the Chwezi conquest. Only slowly did I learn that it was a characteristic of traditional history to explain the relationships between neighbouring states in terms of descent from a common ancestor who had divided his possessions among his children, whereas the historical reality, in every state that I investigated in detail, showed the gradual growth of a few larger units from a multitude of smaller ones. Meanwhile, however, the search for the Chwezi provided a useful thread of continuity as we moved from one district of southern Uganda to another.

The period of history between the departure of the Chwezi and the defeat and exile of the last independent omukama by the British in 1899 seemed from the traditions to have lasted for some sixteen or seventeen dynastic generations, perhaps therefore for some four hundred to five hundred years. During this period, beginning somewhere around 1450 to 1500 A.D., a state ancestral to modern Bunyoro had been ruled by Tito Winyi's forebears, who belonged to the Bito clan. Bunyoro traditions were quite explicit about the origins of the Bito dynasty. They had come from the north, from the Acholi district of modern Uganda, and the first three rulers of the dynasty had been carried back to the north, to the neighbourhood of modern Gulu, for burial. As with many of the other larger states of precolonial Africa the Bito state was composed of a core area, ruled directly by the king, and tributary states that varied in number and size at different periods. The core area was relatively stable, and it was clear from the geographical references in the recorded traditions that its centre lay well to the south of modern Bunyoro. In fact, as Tito Winyi was careful to explain to us, the royal tombs of all the kings before his father, Kabarega, lay in two of the three large counties awarded by the British to Buganda in exchange for Ganda military help at the time of the 1895 conquest. The British administration, cognizant of the importance of the tombs, permitted the government of Bunyoro to keep one official, the *mugema*, or prime minister of the dead, in the area of the tombs; he was charged with their maintenance. We asked if we could visit this official and be shown some of the tombs, and so one day towards the end of our visit we picked up the assistant mugema, who lived at Hoima, and set off down the narrow country road leading towards Mubende that traversed Bunyoro's "valley of the kings."

We found the mugema at home but not well enough to accompany us, so we continued with his assistant to a point some twenty miles farther on. There we left the car and climbed a hill to the tomb of Tito Winyi's grandfather, Kamurasi, who had reigned through the middle years of the nineteenth century. It consisted of a group of round houses set in a dense grove of giant fig trees and surrounded by a royal fence of straight-woven reeds. The tomb occupied the largest house, with the grave site marked by nine iron hoe blades. If the ethnographic evidence collected by John Roscoe in the early 1920s is correct, the burial was filled in, not with earth but with layer upon layer of bark-cloth, and the corpse of the king rested in the arms of two of his widows, who were smothered to death by the grave cloths. Although we had arrived at the place without notice, it was guarded by a tiny wizened lady, a descendant of one of Kamurasi's widows, who seemed pleased to see us and shuffled round, pointing out the various personal possessions of the dead king that were preserved there— drums and spears, bows and arrows, and pieces of beaded jewellery. We gathered that other widows' representatives lived within the precincts and shared the guard duty. We spent the rest of the day visiting other tombs scattered along either side of the same long valley. All conformed to the same pattern, and all had their guardian widows. We came away impressed by the evidential value of the guarded tomb as a test for the orally transmitted genealogies of this and other royal dynasties of southern Uganda. It seemed to us beyond the bounds of probability that such places could have been established with the sole intent to deceive.

Before leaving Bunyoro, we said our farewells to the omukama and his queen, the *omugo*, at a private dinner served in their modest dining-room, which was furnished, apart from the table and chairs, with only a large refrigerator. The king had only halting English and the queen none, so we passed most of the time in an amiable silence as we ate our chicken and they their beef from the herd reserved for royalty. Outside a violent thunderstorm was raging, and we were a little concerned when, after dinner, the queen rose to her feet, seized Caroline by the arm, and propelled her out into the pouring rain. I think that they had one small umbrella between them, and thus they progressed arm in arm across several reed-fenced courtyards to a gateway labelled *Females*, only to

A royal tomb in Bunyoro, 1949

find it locked. The only key was evidently in the omukama's pocket, so back they had to come and apply for it with much happy laughter before setting out for the privy again. They returned in due course, triumphant if also somewhat bedraggled. It all helped to make a nice friendly evening.

From Hoima we paid a three-day visit to the headquarters of the western province at Masindi in order to sample the contents of the provincial archives. We found the place in a state of seige by the employees of Metro-Goldwyn-Mayer. They were engaged in shooting scenes for the film *King Solomon's Mines*, which had been located, most improbably, some forty miles away in the neighbourhood of the Murchison Falls. Deborah Kerr and Stewart Granger were rumoured to be installed in electrically lit tents equipped with long baths and running water. We worked hard at our archives for two days and on the third drove to Butiaba, the port at the northern end of Lake Albert, to try to get a closer view. There we found both lake steamers in full occupation by hordes of sunburned Americans, all hung round with dangerous-looking knives and fishing off every accessible part of the decks and jetties. These, however, proved to be merely the rag, tag, and bobtail of the MGM expedition. "Deb and Stew," they told us, had already completed their assignment and had departed for the greater comfort of the Lake Hotel at Entebbe. We withdrew, feeling that at least we had enjoyed an unusual view of Lake Albert.

Leaving Bunyoro with regret, we moved 120 miles on December 10 to the neighbouring kingdom of Toro, with its attractive administrative headquarters at Fort Portal, built at more than five thousand feet above sea level in the eastern foothills of the Ruwenzori. Approaching it towards evening from the eastern side, we were rewarded with an unforgettable view of the elusive mountain range with its whole line of snowy peaks turning into a crest of fire in the sunset. We put up for the first few days at the same Mountains of the Moon Hotel where we had stayed on our first arrival in Uganda from the Belgian Congo, and we now used it as the base for our work on the district archives. We rejoiced in the cool clear air, brilliant green foliage, and pale blue blossoms of the jacaranda trees that lined every avenue. The district staff was welcoming and hospitable and so too, in a sociable way, was omukama of Toro, George Rukidi III. His palace and the seat of his local government were perched dramatically on the top of the nearby Kabarole Hill. The style and outlook of George Rukidi was, however, very different from Tito Winyi's. When we called on Rukidi by appointment, he was playing ping-pong and he at once invited us to join him. His English was fluent, and when we paused to drink beer, he was happy to talk about the economic prospects of his kingdom, about the copper just beginning to be mined at Kilembe some forty miles to the south, and about the forthcoming 250-mile extension of the Uganda Railway from Kampala to Kilembe that would make large-scale exploitation possible. On historical matters, however, he was not quite so impressive and with some reason. In terms of precolonial history the nucleus of modern Toro had originated as a tributary of Bunyoro ruled by a cadet branch of the same Bito dynasty. The tributary status had been left behind in the early nineteenth century but had been firmly reimposed by Kabarega of Bunyoro in the 1880s. During the early 1890s a prince of Toro, Kasagama, living as a refugee in Buganda, managed to elicit the support of the British in his claim to the throne by aiding them in their war against Kabarega. Kasagama was rewarded by the transfer from Bunyoro of a large county on his eastern border. Therefore Toro was something of a parvenu among the kingdoms of southern Uganda. There were no crown wearers or other official repositories of tradition to whom he could refer us. We were free to look around, but we would be on our own.

We addressed ourselves next to the CMS mission, where Canon and Mrs. Dobson quickly put us in touch with an impressive young couple of Makerere graduates, the Kabuzis, both teaching at the well-known secondary boarding school for boys at Nyakasura, a few miles out of Fort Portal. He was a Ganda and she a Toro, and it was an interesting marker in social history that theirs was the first intertribal marriage to take place between Makerere students since its founding in 1922. Marjorie Kabuzi's father, Canon Kamuhigi, was a senior cleric in the Anglican Church who had the reputation of an amateur historian of Toro. He had some vernacular notes and manuscripts that he read to us with Marjorie interpreting. Most were not very enlightening, but I took notes on one that summarised his information concerning the Chwezi. He drew many comparisons between the Chwezi and the later British conquerors of his country. He told us that the Chwezi, like the British, could kill animals at a distance, they had the means of lighting their houses at night, and they often moved about at night carrying some kind of lanterns. Above all, he told us, they had been clever at using their superior knowledge to impose their rule on others. But in the end people had learned to see through their trickery and so their power evaporated. They just gathered themselves together in one place and then left. I had the strong impression that Canon Kamuhigi had been telling us a parable. Yet it was not one that he had deliberately invented in order to criticize colonial rule in covert terms but a parable that had emerged from his reflections on traditional history in light of his experience. It seemed to me to offer a marvellous lesson in how oral tradition could be subconsciously remoulded in the course of its transmission from one generation to another.

On our last Sunday in Fort Portal we drove over the northern shoulder of Ruwenzori and down an incredibly tortuous traverse road to the little county headquarters fifty miles away at Bundibugyo in the Semliki Valley. We took with us as a passenger a slim Munyoro woman of seventeen from the secondary school at Kabarole. Her father was working as an agricultural officer in this out of the way corner of Toro. Her name was Sarah Nyendwoha, and little did we suspect that she was destined to be the first East African woman to graduate at Oxford, later to become the wife of the first Tanzanian high commissioner in London. She also was to become a lifelong friend. Our own reason for visiting Bundibugyo was that this area was inhabited by two ethnic populations, both related linguistically more closely to peoples on the Congo side of Ruwenzori than to those of Uganda. These were, on the one hand, the Amba of the Semliki Valley, and on the other the Konjo, or Nande, who cultivated the mountain slopes between about four thousand and nine thousand feet above sea level. Historiographically, the strange thing was that Konjo traditions claimed a common origin with the Ganda, and many actually belonged to Ganda clans. We did not solve the problem during our brief visit, but a month or so later we did. While in the mountains of western Ankole we found ourselves among a community descended from Ganda refugees from a civil war fought in the late eighteenth century. These refugees had fled in several directions and had settled among many different ethnic groups, including the Nande to the west of Lake Edward and the Konjo of Ruwenzori. In the course of time the refugees had in most respects become assimilated with their hosts, but they had brought with them both a great migration story and a historical consciousness that their hosts had nothing to rival. In these circumstances the host societies had adopted the traditions of the refugees. As my experience of traditional history grew wider, I was to discover many other cases in which traditions presented as those of an entire people proved to be those of a minority within them. The phenomenon became known within my circle as Oliver's Law.[6]

On December 21 we left Fort Portal for a Christmas break of ten days in Kampala. With us in the backseat travelled a new member of our expedition, Benjamin Munya, a Toro from Kabarole. He was small and not very handsome, but as Caroline put it so well, "Nature had made him a gentleman, and a series of district commissioner masters had made him a gentleman's gentleman." He was to travel with us continuously for the next eight months without ever causing us a minute's irritation. He had no vices and many virtues, including honesty, modesty, cheerfulness, patience, and tact. He was always there when needed and never when he was not. Like us, he had left his family behind. Unlike us, he did not write to them, but he saved nearly all his pay to take to his family when he returned. Once only did he receive a communication from them. It was a telegram to say that his wife had had a baby. I asked him whether it was a boy or a girl, but he said the telegram had not mentioned the sex, and he took no steps whatever to find out.

One of Benjamin's first tasks was to polish us up like anything for a grand dinner party given by the Stuarts for the general secretary of the Church Missionary Society, Max Warren, who was visiting Uganda with his wife Mary. The only other guests were Kabaka Mutesa and Damale, his queen. It was already fairly widely known that all was not well between them and that Mutesa was really in love with Damale's sister Sarah. But they still did the public duties together convincingly enough, and on this evening they did them quite splendidly until, as we rose from the table, Simon Stuart led the way into his private chapel. There, in Mutesa's words, "We prayed for Christian marriage in general and for my marriage in particular. Strangely enough, though I was very surprised, I was not in the least angry." All the same, it put a premature end to an otherwise successful evening. After that we spent the interval between Christmas and the new year at Makerere and in a much more light-hearted way. On January 2, 1950, we were on our travels again.

8

Pastoral Pursuits
(1950)

On the second day of 1950 we set out on a formidable twenty-five-hundred-mile journey of rather more than two months that was to take us as far from our base as the southern tip of Lake Tanganyika, to the frontier of what was then Northern Rhodesia, the modern Zambia. Our first stopping point was at Mbarara, the capital of the Ankole kingdom in the grasslands of southern Uganda, midway between Lake Victoria and Lake Edward. As far as Masaka the scenery was that of Buganda with its typical alternation of flat-topped hills and papyrus-filled swamps, the foreground much obscured by elephant grass growing six to eight feet high; as we turned west, the countryside began to open out, with long views across gently rolling downlands. The rectangular houses set in their surrounding banana groves disappeared in favour of the round beehive shelters of the pastoralists. Soon we began to encounter dense herds of cattle moving from one grazing place to another, their massive lyre-shaped horns knocking against each other as the beasts swayed from side to side. The herders were slim sharp-featured men and boys, dressed in bright red-and-gold waist-cloths with a short upper cloth knotted over one shoulder, striding along holding their sticks behind their necks, both arms raised.

The rest house in Mbarara was a dream, set in a garden of roses on a gentle slope of mown grass above the district office with a grand view of the Rwampara Hills to the southwest. The district commissioner, Tony Malyn, had made admirable preparations for us, including appointments with the *omugabe*, George Gasiyonga II, and the apostolic vicar of Ruwenzori, Monseigneur La Coursière, who headed the White Fathers mission in southwestern Uganda. But best of all, he had found for us the perfect intermediary and interpreter, in the person of Kesi Nganwa, who happened by a fortunate chance to have a fortnight's leave while changing jobs. He had been organising teacher of the CMS schools in Ankole and was to become inspector of schools for the education department of the protectorate government. Looking back over a lifetime of friendships with Africans from almost every part of the continent, I can think of none who did more to stimulate in both of us a lasting love of their country. Already the father of eight children with all their varied calls on his time, Kesi gave us the whole of his brief holiday. The job he was just relinquishing had taken him all over Ankole, travelling mostly by bicycle. He knew the roads and the byways and he had contacts in every county. He could take us straight to the right people everywhere. But above all, it took him less than two hours of conversation with us to believe in the value of our mission and to be prepared to spread that belief by infectious advocacy wherever we went together.

The first visit we made in his company was also the most important. We drove out twenty miles from Mbarara to the country home of Lazaro Kamugungunu, a former *enganzi*, or prime minister, in the omugabe's government. Kamugungunu was now living in patriarchal style on his private estate of one square mile, which was but the nucleus of his pastoral operations, for he was thought to possess some eight thousand head of cattle dispersed around the country in the care of client herdsmen. He was out inspecting his cows when we arrived, but messengers were despatched in search of him, and soon he came striding in, a tall authoritative figure in his early seventies, dressed in a long white kanzu and a tweed jacket. The main purpose of our visit was to see a manuscript history of Ankole that he had put together from a collection of traditions built up by his father-in-law, Nuwa Mbaguta, who had been his predecessor as enganzi and had held that office for no less than forty-three years, from 1895 until 1938. Kamugungunu had known Kesi Nganwa since childhood as he was the son of the parson of the parish; nevertheless, it took all of Kesi's considerable eloquence to bring the old man to a favourable decision. At last he gave orders for the precious manuscript to be brought, and he solemnly entrusted it to us to study together, after which he would see us again and answer our questions.

The manuscript, which Kesi translated orally to me at all spare moments during the next few days, was basically the same as that published in 1955 in Runyankore under the names of L. Kamugungunu and A. G. Katate, and it was a great advance on anything previously in print.[1] Like Nyakatura's book on Bunyoro, it presented the beginnings of continuous history in terms of a brief episode of rule by the Chwezi, when Ankole had formed part of a larger kingdom that had its last capital at Bigo, a few miles beyond the frontier of modern Ankole to the northeast. When the Chwezi departed, they left behind their royal drum, *bagyendanwa*, which passed into the hands of Ruhinda, the eponymous ancestor of the Hinda clan. The Hinda clan henceforth supplied the ruling dynasty of the kingdom of Ankole and also that of Karagwe and other smaller states to the south of the Kagera River in northwestern Tanzania. The manuscript provided at least brief information about the reigns of nineteen kings of the Hinda dynasty who had ruled during the period between the departure of the Chwezi and the establishment of a British protectorate in 1894. The Hinda thus seemed to have been the contemporaries of the Bito dynasty of Bunyoro, emerging sometime in the late fifteenth or early sixteenth century A.D. and expanding gradually from a core area in the grasslands north and south of Mbarara to embrace large territories to the west and northwest that had previously belonged to the independent kingdoms of Buwheju and Mpororo. Twice in its history Ankole had suffered major invasions from Bunyoro, when the victors had seized the entire cattle population of the country, requiring the rebuilding of the pastoral economy from the foundations up. These episodes were clearly remembered in the traditions of both countries and thus provided a means of tying both traditions into a single chronological scheme.

It was in Ankole that our overelaborate recording equipment at last came into its own. While in Bunyoro I had attempted to record some of my interviews with the crown wearers, but it had caused unbearable stress both to them and to me. The dirty old car hunched against the palace steps, with its dynamo thudding away in the background and microphone cables littering the royal veranda, quite spoiled the essential dignity of the scene, and I found it almost impossible to combine the work of an interrogator with that of a disc jockey. In the privacy of the Kabuzis' home in Toro I had successfully recorded Canon Kamuhigi's dubious accounts of the Chwezi, but in a case like this simultaneous interpretation was quite sufficient. During my second visit to Kamugungunu with Kesi Nganwa, however, I raised with him the question of whether there were in Ankole any examples of historical recitations that were learned word for word by heart. He stepped to his front door and called a name, and a young man appeared with a herdsman's staff in his hand. In response to Kamugungunu's next instructions the young man assumed a threatening posture, raised his staff to shoulder level as if preparing to hurl a javelin, and leaped towards us while uttering a torrent of staccato recitation that lasted for several minutes. He paused, still glaring at us, while it was explained that this was an *ekyevugo*, a warrior's boasting speech, delivered to the omugabe or his representative when summoned to the colours by the beating of the big war drum. It recalled the deeds of prowess of the speaker and his close kin, sometimes covering the events of several generations. It could also be kept up to date in relation to colonial times by adding verses that detailed visits to Kampala on government business or trips to England under the auspices of the British Council. What was above all remarkable was that it was a form of oral literature that was still alive and practised sufficiently often to be at the forefront of the speaker's mind. The explanation offered was that the herdsmen's way of life involved much staying awake on watch, both for wild beasts and for cattle thieves, and that they avoided drowsiness by intellectual activities of this kind.

We persuaded Kamugungunu's young relative to repeat his performance so that I could record it, and when we played it back to him, his face lit up with a wonderful smile of amusement and pleasure. He congratulated the black box both on the excellence of its memory and on its skills as a mimic and then withdrew to tell his fellows of his experience. We soon found that he had provided us with an unfailing key to the goodwill of the pastoral communities that we were about to visit in different parts of the country. Kesi would send messages ahead to the county chiefs to announce our coming. When we arrived we would find quite large crowds of people who had walked in from the surrounding pastures to see the black box that could talk Runyankore, Luganda, Swahili, and even English. I would invite the chief to say a few words to open the proceedings, and the playback would invariably be greeted with warm applause and much laughter. I would then play the specimen ekyevugo and call for volunteers to compete. There was never a shortage, and before long groups and individuals would produce harps and lutes and offer songs. The most impressive choral performance was one sung by forty or fifty men sitting in a semicircle. At one moment they would go through the motions of milking, while their voices reproduced the hissing of milk dropping into the wooden pail. At another moment they would raise their hands in imitation of the cattle horns, and their clicking fingers would convey the gentle knocking of horn upon horn in a densely packed herd.

The culminating episode in these proceedings was an afternoon session at the omugabe's palace on Kamukuzi Hill on the outskirts of Mbarara. There the main residence had been made unsafe by a swarm of warrior bees, and we were directed to a more modest building, roofed with thatch, that housed the royal regalia, including the drum bagyendanwa, which was the main symbol of the historical link with the earlier kingdom of the Chwezi. In precolonial times bagyendanwa had been considered so important that it had its own capital, with its own palace set in its own royal enclosure surrounded by the dwellings of its own court officials, supported from its own herds of cattle. In fact, bagyendanwa consists of a pair of drums, male and female, and, as we saw it, the two lay on their sides on an altarlike table with the sacred fire of the kingship burning perpetually beside it. The faces of both were covered with white cowhide with black markings, and they stared at us out of the smoky gloom like a pair of enormous eyes. Meanwhile, outside the house a colourful crowd was assembling—musicians, spectators, and would-be performers, some brought in by lorry from outlying places. And soon, down the hill from the bee-ridden palace there came a procession of large ladies, made larger by their billowing draperies. They were the queen (the omugo) and her attendants. These were all Hima women of the old school, sedulously fattened by unnatural quantities of milk literally forced upon them from their teenage years onwards. Slowly, they subsided onto the ground beside us, their heads veiled in bright cloths, the ends of which were held across their mouths to muffle their conversation and hide their laughter. Last of all came the omugabe and his treasurer dressed in European suits. As usual, Kesi presented us and described our mission, and we played his speech back, to the delight of the assembled crowd, while the large ladies beside us quivered from inside their draperies like a row of jellies. Self-styled warriors rushed up to the omugabe and declaimed their ekwevugo recitations. And then lutes were brought, and the royal ladies were invited to sing some of their songs of courtly life, called *enanga*. They did so in tones that sounded gentle and appealing, but by no means could they be persuaded to remove their head cloths, and all attempts to record them proved futile. It made, nonetheless, a great afternoon.

Unfortunately, when we replayed our recordings at the rest house, we soon realised that they presented problems far beyond our capacity to solve. The speed of the diction was too rapid for even a native speaker to transcribe with accuracy in the time available. Moreover, even the partial texts that Kesi was able to recover proved too full of archaisms and hidden meanings for any useful standard of translation to be possible without deep linguistic research. Some years later a colleague at the School of Oriental and African Studies, Henry Morris, was to publish a learned work, *The Heroic Poetry of the Bahima of Ankole*, based upon long study of the ekyevugo genre.[2] Later still one of my research students, Samwiri Karugire, was to make extensive use of it as historical source material in his *History of the Kingdom of Nkore*.[3] Meanwhile, all that Kesi and I could do in the short time at our disposal was to open up the topic, but for us it at least provided a lively insight into the lives and culture of the specialised pastoralists of Ankole. Of course, it had left us completely perplexed—as we were to be again in Rwanda and elsewhere—about any historical explanation of the existence, side by side, of two apparently different races in the Hima pastoralists and the Iru cultivators. The almost inevitable diffusionist tendency was to conclude that one lot must have come from the outside and imposed itself on the other lot by a combination of cultural superiority and martial skills. On the other hand, we had seen enough of the pastoralists to realise that most were poor and not very skilled, except with cows. We knew that, among the better-off, some Iru were just as well educated and forward looking as any of the Hima aristocrats—Kesi Nganwa was a good example. We knew that there was some intermarriage and some possibility for individuals to move from one category to the other. What we failed to observe was the obvious economic fact that, given the right environment, it was much easier for a successful pastoralist to become rich and powerful than for any cultivator of the soil. A rich cattle owner could spread his herds widely over the country and in doing so attract clients and dependents on a scale that made him look like a member of a ruling race. But there were few such rich pastoralists.

Before leaving Ankole we took a three-day trip to the highland region of Bunyaruguru, which overlooks the eastern side of Lake Edward and formerly was part of the kingdom of Mpororo. We paused at the county headquarters at Bushenyi to make some recordings. Then we proceeded about forty miles to the headquarters of the northernmost subcounty, where most of the population consisted of refugees from Buganda whose ancestors had settled there around the middle of the eighteenth century. They were known locally as the Kunta, and they still spoke Luganda and maintained their membership of Ganda clans. The protectorate government had recognized their separate status by nominating a subcounty chief from their number so that local government could be carried on in their language. According to the tradition related to us by one Abudara Baraba, the name *Kunta* was originally that of a military formation recruited by a Ganda prince called Semakokiro to overthrow the reigning kabaka Junju. The coup was successful. Junju was killed and Semakokiro became kabaka, whereupon, instead of rewarding his followers, he accused them of regicide and ordered their massacre. Intelligence of his intentions leaked, and most Kunta managed to save their lives by flight. They fled in all directions, some eastwards to the Kavirondo Gulf of Lake Victoria and some westwards, where they settled in pockets all around Lake Edward, and even, as we saw in Chapter 7, among the Konjo of Ruwenzori. Only in Bunyaruguru had their settlement been dense enough for their language to survive. Baraba was a travelled man who had worked in Buganda and visited many of the Kunta settlements around Lake Edward and knew which Ganda clans were represented in each. I thought his testimony interesting enough to telegraph to my Seventh-day Adventist friends on Ruwenzori and ask them if they could assemble a representative gathering of Konjo people to meet me the following day. I wanted to determine whether they knew the story of Semakokiro and Junju, and I found that they did. It made a long drive, but at the end of it I felt richly rewarded.

Leaving Ankole with great regret, we moved about one hundred miles on January 18, 1950, to Kabale, the headquarters of the Kigezi district in the southwestern corner of the country. There a dense and rapidly burgeoning population of Kyiga people cultivated every square inch of soil in the high and healthy mountain valleys running down from the volcanic peaks of the Mufumbiro (Virunga) Mountains. Only a generation earlier the upper slopes of these valleys had been covered with natural forest. Now they were quite bare of trees. It was the only district of Uganda where overpopulation was already recognized as critical and where a dynamic agricultural officer, John Purseglove, having successfully promoted every possible measure for the prevention of soil erosion, was now busy organising a controlled migration of Kyiga cultivators into the patches of lower-lying agricultural land still available in western Ankole. As our travels progressed, it became increasingly clear that the areas of densest population in eastern Africa were to be found in the lands high enough to be free of malaria. As an historian I had to think deeply about the long-term role of population increase in mountain areas and of consequent continual migration from highland regions into the surrounding lowlands.

We were in Kigezi only for a week, and much of our time there was wasted by mechanical breakdowns that resulted from the inability of our carburettor to cope with the combination of steep hills and high altitudes. It was a great pity, because a helpful district commissioner invited us on our first day there to join him at a meeting of all the county chiefs of the district, who were sitting as a court of appeal in actions involving customary law. When the legal proceedings ended, we were asked to play a selection of our recordings from Ankole, and the assembled chiefs at once understood what we were after. Had we been able to get to them in their county headquarters as planned, we should doubtless have had a most fruitful time. As it was, we spent our days waiting for help by distant roadsides and our evenings giving encouragement to a superb Indian mechanic in Kabale. The mechanic really gave us his best and in the end sent us forth in a condition to tackle the many hundreds of mountain miles that lay ahead of us. For the rest, we did our usual work on the district records, held what interviews we could manage in Kabale town, and on January 25 set out on schedule for Rwanda by the unforgettable route up and over the eastern wall of the Rift Valley, using the so-called Kanaba Gap. At ten thousand feet above sea level the gap leads to what must surely be one of the most splendid views in the world, sweeping across the broad lake-strewn trough of the Rift to the three magnificent volcanic cones of Muhavura, Gahinga, and Sabinio astride the Rwanda frontier.

Our visit to Rwanda was prompted by the intimate links between its precolonial history and that of southern Uganda and northwestern Tanganyika. It was necessarily a brief one, if only because our Belgian colonial francs were limited to the surplus from our earlier journey through the eastern Congo. I was, however, eager to make contact with local historians, and especially with Abbé Alexis Kagame, who was beginning to be known in the outside world for his translations of traditional Rwanda poetry. He was a Catholic priest, of Tutsi pastoral ancestry, and closely enough connected with the king, the *mwami*, to have gained permission to sit with the local equivalent of the Nyoro crown wearers. Here these officials were known as the *abiru*, and Kagame had been permitted to record the secret recitations of dynastic history that they learned and transmitted in verbatim texts in the presence of the king and his immediate circle. Although he was a well-known person, none of our advance information had told us where, exactly, Kagame was to be found. It was suggested that we consult the White Fathers at their headquarters at Kabgayi, close to the royal residence at Nyanza in the centre of the country.

It took us two long days of tortuous but utterly enchanting travel (about three hundred miles) to reach Kabgayi. The first night we spent at Kisenyi on the northern shore of Lake Kivu. On the second day we pursued our way over three successive mountain ranges to the Belgian administrative capital at Kigali, pausing to pay a courtesy call on the resident, M. Sandrart, whom we found in a state of trauma following the departure of a visiting mission of the U.N. Trusteeship Council. We were told that one member had taken off from the Sandrarts' dinner table to interview the domestic staff and to inspect their sleeping quarters, while another member had disappeared during a tour of the botanical gardens. "*Oui, oui, perdu dans la brousse . . . avec une négresse, vous savez*" (Yes, yes—lost in the shrubbery with a black woman, you know). Ours was a different sort of mission, however, and they received us with all kindness and despatched us to Kabgayi with their blessing. We reached there after dark, and after several more hours of magnificent but no less contorted driving, we were amazed to find an ecclesiastical city set on a hill and, wonder of wonders, electrically lit. It comprised a cathedral, senior seminary, junior seminary, novitiate, hospital, printing works, museum, residences for European and African clergy and lay brothers, and, above all, dormitories and refectories for hundreds, if not thousands, of catechumens attending six-month courses for baptism or confirmation. It was indeed quite difficult, especially in the dark, to decide to whom we should present ourselves. We arrived more or less by chance at the senior seminary; in the courtyard one of a dozen slim Tutsi ordinands stepped forward courteously to offer assistance. He conducted us to another courtyard, with its own chapel in the centre, which was the novitiate. The father on duty, whom he called to talk to us, told us that regrettably the guest-house was occupied by a Belgian honeymoon couple, but he offered us a pair of adjacent narrow cells and the hospitality of the refectory table.

And so we dined that night in company with some ten Louvain-educated Belgian White Fathers and a smaller number of young Rwanda clergy and senior ordinands, and they talked to us with some enthusiasm of their daily work. We gathered that in Rwanda the White Fathers had, from their first implantation in the early years of the century, put far more of their effort into the training of a native clergy than had their colleagues in Uganda and Tanganyika. As a result, nearly two hundred African clergy were now working in teams of five or six, in twenty-six large parochial districts that were entirely in African hands. The first White Fathers bishop, Monseigneur Hirth, had established the strategy of using to the full the social prestige of the Tutsi pastoral class in positions of leadership in the church, and we had only to look around to see that the same strategy was still in force. The seminaries were populated almost exclusively by Tutsi students, whereas among the catechumens, who were sent from all over the diocese to Kabgayi for their prebaptismal training, the great majority were of Hutu farming stock. In due course we asked about Kagame and were told that, just at present, he was working in a rather remote country parish at Kigarama near the headquarters of the southern province at Astrida. It was hinted that there had perhaps been some disagreement between him and the diocesan authorities.

Next day, after attending the impressively crowded daily mass of the catechumens in the cathedral, we continued our pursuit, calling on the administration at Astrida and installing ourselves in a spectacular country rest house at Rusitira. Beside it Metro-Goldwyn-Mayer had recently reconstructed a mwami's palace of precolonial times in the traditional materials of reed and thatch, in which MGM had filmed some scenes for *King Solomon's Mines.* Outside it the studio had added a simple observation tower for the cameramen, from which it was possible to get a comprehensive view of the whole interior layout with its many different buildings enclosed within a maze of reed fences. Here, while we were settling in, a little boy came running up the drive holding a stick. In the split end of the stick was an envelope bearing the address Oliver c/o Resident, Ruanda. It contained a telegram from the British district commissioner in Bukoba, in northwestern Tanganyika, which was to be our next main port of call after leaving Rwanda. He just wanted to know the expected date of our arrival, but we felt that the mode of the communication was well suited to the theatrical setting in which it reached us.

It was from Rusitira that we at last ran our abbé to earth in his simple clergy house at Kigarama. He lived with six or seven other African priests, none of whom had ever been out of Rwanda, but all of whom were quite able to carry on a sophisticated conversation in French, as perhaps also in Latin. Books and newspapers were lying around in their common room and also a radio to which they were clearly devoted listeners. It was an experience to sit down to lunch with them and to take part, over the chicken fricassee and crème caramel, in a conversation that ranged

98

from the forthcoming general election in England and the personalities of Winston Churchill and Clement Attlee, to the Kravchenko trial then going on in the Soviet Union and the Chinese travels of the "red dean" of Canterbury.[4] All these men were Tutsi, and several of them showed, as did our host, the effects on the Tutsi physiognomy of the abandonment of one kind of pastoralism for another. Kagame was large in every sense of the word. He combined bounding energy with genial good nature and sweeping intelligence. He was to spend much of the 1950s at the Gregorian University in Rome, where he wrote a doctoral thesis the Bantu idea of 'being.' But for a conservative nationalism, which aligned him with the Tutsi struggle for political dominance, he would have been a splendid candidate to be the first African cardinal.

As an historian Kagame had followed the openings suggested to him by a sequence of missionary predecessors, all of whom had been to some extent influenced by imagined parallels between the political consolidation of Rwanda and that of medieval France. He had learned to see the history of his country through the eyes of the ruling dynasty, and while doing so he had come to realise the potential importance of the historical recitations circulating in the mwami's court, which only a native speaker with the right connections would be able to record and transcribe for study. Kagame had done much of this work, publishing some of it in French translation and producing his version of Rwanda history in two slim volumes in the Kinyarwanda language that corresponded very much to Nyakatura's work on Bunyoro and to Kamugungunu's on Ankole.[5] Kagame's history has since been superseded by that of Jan Vansina and other outside professionals, because Kagame kept so close to the traditions of the court, and to the interpretations of tradition offered by the ritual experts there, that he presented a picture of systematic military conquest of one province after another by a culturally superior Tutsi kingdom. In fact, it was a much more gradual and essentially economic process of infiltration by pastoralist groups from the low-lying arid grasslands of eastern Rwanda into the lusher foothills of the Nile-Congo divide where cultivating peoples predominated until every hilltop was grazed by pastoralists, with client cultivators in the surrounding valleys. As Vansina was to show, the institutions of the Rwanda state emerged from a series of compromises between pastoralists and cultivators, rather than from the imposition of one superior system upon the rest.[6]

Meantime, I gained enormously from three days of talks with Kagame, and it was with real regret that I turned to the second purpose of our visit to Rwanda, which concerned the Protestant side of my missionary studies. Before we left Kampala Simon Stuart had strongly advised me to make some first-hand contact with the part of his diocese that lay within Rwanda and was served not by the CMS but by a small Anglican society with fundamentalist leanings called the Bible Church Missionary Society. Around 1945 a revivalist movement of some considerable power had emerged from this area, and it had spread, and was continuing to spread, among Anglican Christians and also among members of other denominations across much of East Africa. Like other such movements, it was proving both revitalising and deeply divisive. On the one hand, its practice of public confession was said to have created a wholly new sense of unity between white missionaries and African church leaders. On the other hand, the revivalist movement had been intolerant and censorious of all who could not share in its special experiences. Simon had warned us that, when we encountered them, the revivalists would lose no time in asking whether we were saved. When I asked what reply we could truthfully make, he answered without any hesitation, "Saved but not safe."

While in Astrida, therefore, we called on a charming and saintly couple, Mr. and Mrs. Stanley Smith, who ran a hall of residence for the Protestant students of the government technical college, out of which the University of Rwanda was to develop in the early 1960s. They told us that it was unthinkable that we should leave the country without visiting the effective headquarters of the movement at Gahini in northeastern Rwanda, where Dr. Joe Church ran both an important hospital and a centre for revivalist preachers. There was no way to forewarn the Churches of our arrival, but we undertook to carry the mail, both to Gahini and to an intermediate station, which would be a sure passport to their hospitality. Our hundred-mile route took us right across the Bugessera Desert, once perhaps the homeland of the Tutsi pastoralists and the base from which they infiltrated the higher and better-watered lands of the Hutu cultivators, but in modern times virtually uninhabited and uninhabitable. It gave us in fact one of the most frightening days of all our travels, running on sandy tracks, hard to detect and quite without signposts, through harsh thorn bush with only the occasional impala for company. It was late when we arrived at Gahini, but we found the Churches at home and entertaining, as our fellow guest, a well-known Ganda evangelist, William Nagenda, who had been the cofounder with Church of the movement commonly known as the *Balokole*, or saved ones. They had in fact both just returned from a preaching mission in Europe, and in our tired and overwrought state we could only listen with growing desperation to their mutually admiring accounts of how successfully they had testified in aeroplanes and elsewhere. They were good people but impossible to converse with, and it was with some relief that we departed early the next morning for our journey into Tanganyika.

9

To Lake Tanganyika and Back

(1950)

In 1950 Bukoba was a pretty little harbour town situated half-way up the western shore of Lake Victoria. It was a regular port of call for the two steamers that circulated the lake, one in a clockwise and one in a counterclockwise direction, each taking about a week for the four-hundred-mile round trip. Bukoba was roughly equidistant by either route from the terminus of the Uganda Railway at Kisumu. Southwards, it was much closer to Mwanza, whence the Tanganyikan Central Railway led via Tabora to the coast at Dar es Salaam. To the north of the harbour the curve of the bay was marked by a fine sandy beach, from which it was then considered quite safe to swim, except between six and seven o'clock in the evening, when the hippopotamuses came ashore to crop the grass around the government offices and to spend the night calling to each other from a series of reed-filled pools that encircled the government rest house. The north end of the town housed the Swedish Church mission, which had an impressive array of schools and hospital buildings; at the southern end the French-Canadian White Fathers had built their cathedral on a rocky promontory that jutted into the lake just beyond the harbour. Much of the social life seemed to turn on the comings and goings of the lake steamers, when the white population, both lay and clerical, would gather to meet or see off friends and stay to drink in the ship's bar. For our accommodation we tried the government rest house but we found the hippopotamus nightlife rather overpowering, so we retreated to the greatly superior comfort of the Swedish mission, to which we had been given an introduction by the missionary scholar Bengt Sundkler, who was soon to return there as bishop.

In colonial terms Bukoba was the administrative headquarters of the Haya people, who lived by a combination of banana planting and small-scale cattle husbandry on the attractive green downlands stretching all the way down the western shores of the lake. They grew large quantities of robusta coffee, as an economic crop that they exported by the lake steamer to the international market in Mombasa. Politically, the Haya were organised in seven large chieftaincies, the dynasties of which all claimed descent from the same eponymous Ruhinda who had supposedly fathered the omugabes of Ankole, whereas an eighth dynasty, that of Kiziba, situated nearest to the Uganda border, belonged to the same Bito family as the rulers of Bunyoro. The eight hereditary *bakama*, as they were called, had been brought during the period of German colonial rule into a kind of federation, with an appointed secretary general who acted as their collective intermediary with the colonial administration.[1]

The first secretary general, Felix Lwamgira, had been a major figure, in every way comparable to Apolo Kagwa in Buganda and Nuwa Mbaguta in Ankole, and like them he had devoted his leisure hours to the recording of oral tradition. His main effort had been concentrated in Kiziba, where he had worked in collaboration with a Catholic missionary priest, Father E. Cézard.[2] But he had also written smaller histories of the other seven kingdoms in the Luhaya language, and it was with these that I most needed to begin my inquiries. Forewarned of my arrival by the district commissioner, the current secretary general had drawn up a schedule of appointments for me in each of the eight capitals and had found me a most efficient interpreter and travelling companion, Michael Lugasiya, a medical student at Makerere who happened to be at home on vacation. Together we spent the next ten days driving all over the district, and everywhere we went, we found assembled big gatherings of men who filled to overflowing the courthouses of the several bakama. My predominant memory of those days is of being pressed in upon, often in the semidarkness of the large round thatched houses still then used for ceremonial purposes, by crowds of people, many of them intoxicated and smelling strongly of banana wine. Faced by such scenes, which could all too easily have become unruly, the entertainment value of my recording equipment came repeatedly to the rescue. There was little possibility of serious historical questioning, but at least we came away with our collections enhanced and with good humour prevailing.

On February 11, 1950, we rested from our labours, and entertainment was provided instead by the governor of the colony, Edward Twining, who was touring the northwestern province accompanied by some lesser officials and a large brass band. On that Saturday morning he held a *baraza*, or public assembly, on the green lawns by the lakeside. Centre stage was occupied by the band, with chairs for officials on one side and for missionaries and civilian guests on the other. The eight bakama sat in a row with their secretary general, and the ordinary Haya people (Bahaya) stood around in their thousands, the men in white kanzus and the women in their brightest cotton prints. The band played the national anthem. The governor, a portly figure crowned with feathers, mounted the dais and began to read a speech so extraordinary that its key phrases, remain indelibly printed in my memory. "Bahaya," it began, "I am very pleased to be in your beautiful country." And then, with a note of gathering menace, it continued, "But, Bahaya, news has reached my ears that you, alone of all the tribes of Tanganyika, are not increasing your numbers. I hear that you are a lazy, drunken, disease ridden, idle, litigious, decadent, and utterly dissolute people." He paused for emphasis between each adjective, while the interpreter searched for the correct Luhaya equivalents and the crowd began to manifest symptoms of consternation. Then came the crescendo. "Your women, Bahaya, are famous throughout the length and breadth of East Africa." It was all too true that they were. "Mark my words, Bahaya, down this path damnation lies. My government will do all in its power to help you to overcome these grave defects." The crowd by now was grunting its displeasure, when it was told that this lecture would be enough for one morning but that there would be more, for those who cared to hear it, at the headquarters of the Maruku chieftaincy at four in the afternoon.

We did not go to Maruku, but we did go to a sundowner party given that evening at the European Club at which the governor took over the baton from his bandmaster for "Rule Britannia" and other popular numbers. Little did we suspect that political independence in Tanganyika was just eleven years away.

Our stay in Bukoba was rushed, but it was long enough to make us conscious of a type of political organisation, common in precolonial Africa, of a cluster of little states, sharing a common language, observing similar customs and social institutions, and claiming a common origin at least at the aetiological level. At the historical level it was lacking a thread of common experience that could explain the similarities. I suppose that at the time I was still obsessed with the notion of state building by conquest, and I was looking for an interpretation of the Ruhinda legend that could be applied to the formation of border baronies around the fringes of the central core of larger kingdoms represented by Rwanda and Burundi, Ankole, Buganda, and Bunyoro. In so doing I was missing the much simpler socioeconomic explanation, based upon the gradual integration of predominantly pastoral and predominantly agricultural communities in the areas surrounding the central grasslands of the interlacustrine region—an explanation equally valid for the formation of the larger states as for the smaller ones. Nevertheless, even if I was following a false trail, my quest for a historically meaningful definition of the interlacustrine region was a real and useful one. It supplied the guiding motive for the still more rapid and wide-ranging finale to this part of our journey, when we were working our way round the southern fringes of Burundi through the still smaller polities of the Ha, Vinza, and Jiji lying between Bukoba and the Lake Tanganyika port of Kigoma.

In part, however, our trip was also an escapade. If Tanganyika as a whole was the back alley of British colonial Africa, confiscated from the Germans in 1918 and never developed in case it had to be given back, the four-hundred-mile stretch of country we had now to cross was the back alley of Tanganyika. It had no cosy semisuburban district centres. At Biharamulo, Kibondo, and Kasulu district commissioners chosen for their qualities of self-sufficiency had their homes and their offices within the fortified *bomas* built by the Germans that also housed the police station, the post office, and other local services. One of these egregious gentlemen kept pythons as pets. They occupied his spare room. Another, using large inherited wealth, had imported a Rolls Royce in which to tour the exiguous road system of his remote district. We stopped at these places only long enough to inspect and photograph the relevant sections of the district books. Even the single main road connecting them was all but bereft of other traffic. Long stretches were tsetse ridden, and it was often difficult to maintain the speed of about thirty miles an hour needed to escape the attentions of the fast-flying and viciously biting insects that homed in on any moving object in sight. Three days of hard driving brought us at last to Kigoma and to the S. S. *Liemba*, which was preparing to sail for the south end of the lake the following evening. Meanwhile, we lodged Benjamin at a friendly mission house, established ourselves on board, and spent the day of our departure photographing the Kigoma district records on the deck of the steamer while the other passengers assembled.

Tradition describes Lake Tanganyika as "a vast expanse of water, almost completely surrounded by White Fathers," and a glance around the *Liemba*'s first-class accommodation afforded much support for this view. The upper deck was full of pacing priests, breviaries in hand, saying their offices. Fore and aft from here, however, one looked down into the open hold, where several hundred African passengers were trying to find what comfort was possible. Meals were being cooked on wood-burning stoves and eaten in family groups. Clothes were being washed and hung out to dry. Women and girls were dressing each other's hair into the small spiky ringlets favoured in this area. Most of these African passengers were the so-called migrant labourers returning to their homes around the lake after a year or more of employment on the sisal estates of the coastal regions. On our return journey we would be picking up their replacements. Twice a day we would stop for an hour or so off some tiny settlement, and canoes would come out to collect or deliver passengers and to sell food to those remaining on board. One day, however, at one such insignificant place, winched aboard, complete with gun cases and other expensive luggage, was a caricature of an English retired colonel who, after a brief inspection of the other passengers, sat down beside us and entered into conversation. His name was Athill, and his business was buying the mica collected from the surface of the soil on the hilltops all round the lake. Hundreds, if not thousands, of people participated in the collection, selling their produce piecemeal to middlemen, mostly small Arab merchants with whom Athill did his business. After telling me all this he screwed his monocle into position, turned to me, and said, "You know, Oliver, I can't quite *place* you. What *are* you?" I said, "A lecturer at the School of Oriental and African Studies," to which he replied, "So am I, so am I." It transpired that he had worked for many years in Ethiopia and that he had learned Amharic well enough to be placed on a panel of qualified teachers of the language who could be called upon for help in emergencies. In the event, he never had been called upon, and the panel had long been obsolete, but thus strangely did professional colleagues meet on the waters of Lake Tanganyika.

On February 18 we anchored off Karema, a place already embedded in my consciousness, for it was here in 1879 that King Leopold II of the Belgians, when scouting for his later African empire, had established the first of what was intended to become a chain of scientific stations stretching across equatorial Africa from coast to coast. King Leopold's grand design had fired Cardinal Charles Lavigerie to follow with his White Fathers in the king's footsteps. When in 1885 Leopold transferred his line of approach to the Congo River, the White Fathers inherited the fort at Karema and turned it into a mission station for ransomed slaves whom they settled in a village around its walls. This arrangement protected the people when necessary with an armed force commanded by retired papal *zouaves* (the Swiss Guard and others) specially recruited for this unusual type of missionary service. At the time of our visit the slave origins of the villagers were still well recognized, for their relations were not to be found among the local Bende people but among a whole scatter of ethnic groups living on the other side of the lake. Moreover, among those who greeted us as we landed on the beach was an old man dressed in black knee-breeches, yellow stockings, black shoes, a white coat, and a tall red tarboosh with a long black tassle. His name was Adrian Athman, and he had been born somewhere in the Sudanic belt of West Africa. While still a boy he had been captured as a slave and exported across the Sahara to North Africa, where he had eventually been ransomed by the local White Fathers and sent by them to Malta for medical training. Along with two others who had been freed in the same way he had volunteered to serve with the White Fathers' mission in East Africa, and he had walked up to the lake with the third missionary caravan in 1889. He had been there ever since, and he told us in his excellent French that he had cared for all the missionaries who had ever served there. By the church at the top of the hill Caroline met an old nun, Sister Geneviève, who had lived at Karema almost as long as Adrian Athman. She had arrived in 1893 and had never been away. She was walking up and down, saying her office, when she suddenly noticed Caroline, and perhaps overcome by the rare sight of a young white laywoman, the nun led Caroline to a bench, took both her hands, and began to sob. "*Voilà cinquante-sept ans que je suis ici,*" she said. "*Peut-être que j'ai pu faire quelque chose pour le bon Dieu—peut-être*" (Look, I have now been here fifty-seven years. Perhaps I have been able to do something for the good Lord, perhaps).

The following day brought us to Kipili near the southern end of the lake. We knew of it as the port for Sumbawanga, the least accessible of all sixty-four district headquarters in Tanganyika. And we knew of Sumbawanga as the administrative capital of the Fipa people who, like the societies to the north of the lake, were said to consist of a class of specialised pastoralists living among and dominating a much more numerous agricultural peasantry. The question I wanted to answer was whether the Fipa plateau should be regarded as an extension of the interlacustrine region or not. In principle, therefore, we wanted to get to Sumbawanga, but in practice we supposed that it would be impossible, for we had left our car at Kigoma, and no public transport was available over the hundred miles or so of mountain road that led there from Kipili. On the jetty, however, we met a young Mauritian farm manager who offered to drive us there in his car and to put us up in his employer's residence when we arrived. We would have to be back in Kipili four days later in order to catch the *Liemba* on its northward journey, and how we would do so was quite problematic. But we decided to risk it.

Our host, Roger Borain, was kindness indeed. He took us to call at the oldest White Fathers' mission on the plateau, at Chala Mountain where we met another old West African freed-slave doctor, a colleague and contemporary of Adrian Athman's. He even helped us track down the local Catholic bishop, Monseigneur Holmes-Siedle, who gave us coffee beside the tent in which he was camping and discussed with frankness the problems of running a diocese so remote from central church affairs. In Sumbawanga we called on the district commissioner and loaded up the car with a selection of his archives before driving up a final steep escarpment to the farm where we were to spend the next three nights at nearly eight thousand feet above sea level. The proprietor, Mrs. Damm, who was away from home at the time of our visit, was a second-generation

German settler who had trekked into the area, driving her own cattle, during the 1930s. She had built up a big business trading cattle to the Fipa people and in buying and exporting the wild honey they collected in the forests. She had the reputation of never having had to take two shots at a lion. On her veranda we worked at our papers, guarded by her pack of magnificent Rhodesian Ridgebacks. We were there quite long enough to satisfy ourselves that the historical connections of the Fipa were with the peoples to the south and west of Lake Tanganyika and that there was no trace of any migrational drift of pastoralists down the eastern side of the lake. As I wrote rather portentously—and revealingly—to my masters in London, "This means that we have to look for the origins of the pastoral and monarchical states in southern Africa to the comparatively narrow corridor of highland pastures between Lake Tanganyika and the Congo forest."

Meanwhile, as we worked, heavy rains had fallen, and Roger Borain became more pessimistic every day about the chances of getting us back to Kipili in time to catch the all-important steamer. Finally, we solved the problem by chartering a lorry from an Indian contractor in the little town. We agreed with him for a fairly large sum but on the understanding that we would deduct from it any fares that we might take by picking up passengers and goods along the route. In the event, the state of the escarpment road was not nearly as bad as predicted. We camped overnight in a mosquito-ridden mud rest house beside the jetty and were thankful to see the *Liemba* appearing over the horizon in the half-light of dawn.

Our return journey from Kigoma to Kampala was not without excitement, for we decided, with the connivance of the district commissioner at Kasulu, that we would make a diversion through southern Burundi. The area had no frontier post but only an unmarked track that led through the mountains from Manyovu to Makamba, crossing the upper Malagarasi River by a ford. Somewhere near Manyovu the car had one of its attacks of mountain sickness and stopped dead. We knew that it was most unlikely that any other vehicle would pass that way, but a mile or so farther back we had passed a small gang of workers patching up the road with their bare hands and to them we now repaired. They told us that there was a white man's house some way ahead, and one offered to act as runner. From ten in the morning until five in the afternoon we sat and admired the view, but at last a little old car chugged into sight, driven by an American Seventh-day Adventist missionary called Sparrow who tinkered without success and finally carried us to his home for the night. We returned to our car on the morrow, and it responded to the first touch of the starter. There remained the Malagarasi ford, which we negotiated successfully. But while climbing the hill on the far side, we slid gently but decisively into an erosion gully from which only lifting could rescue us. The situation did not look promising. Evening was coming on, and we were on a byway that had only the most occasional use. But we saw on the left of the road a banana plantation, which had to spell human habitation somewhere nearby, and soon it became apparent that the plantation was full of moving forms, some of which carried spears. We were in fact under observation. All we could do was to call out the Swahili greetings and hope that they would be understood as a declaration of our peaceful intentions. Soon indeed we were surrounded by a crowd of entirely amiable people who saw exactly what we needed and lifted the car bodily back onto the road. It was an incident that did much to give us confidence in all our subsequent African travels.

The day's experiences were not, however, at an end. We set off into the dusk, and it seemed an interminable journey to Makamba, which turned out to be just a square of traders' shops, quite unlit and all locked up for the night. We drove round it, looking for anything that might be a rest house and at last found one building with a bell. The door opened, and from a brightly lit interior a voice said in English, "I know you." It was another passenger on the flight from Brussels to Stanleyville the previous October who now turned out to be the English wife of a Greek merchant in this out-of-the-way corner of Belgian Africa. Soon we were recuperating in a long hot bath, enriched with fragrances by Elizabeth Arden, the prelude to a sumptuous meal.

Next day we resumed our route, by winding mountaintop roads amid spectacular scenery, to the administrative capital of Burundi at Kitega. It was March 3 and a Friday afternoon when we arrived, and all the government offices were shut for the weekend. There was no hotel, and to gain government shelter the only possible meeting-place with Belgian officialdom was the Cercle, the club, which was not quite a club in the British colonial sense, for it included all Europeans, right down to the *petits blancs* who typed the letters in the government offices and the African elite—the hereditary ruler, the *mwami* and his ministers. Here in fact the mwami could be seen playing darts and drinking beer with the petits blancs, a role quite unthinkable for the kabaka of Buganda or his fellow rulers in southern Uganda. The Belgian elite was present also, though not playing darts, and it so happened that our first encounter there was with the resident of Burundi, Robert Schmidt, who had been at school at Winchester and spoke perfect English. He asked us from where we had come and we told him. He then flagged down a M. François, the administrator for the southern district, and said to him, "François, that track that comes in across the Tanganyika frontier from Kasulu—it is quite impassable, isn't it?" "Absolutely, Monsieur le Résident," was the reply. "Interesting, François, because these people have just used it."

In retrospect I marvel at the time and trouble that these senior Belgian officials were prepared to devote at short notice to a young academic visitor, still very much feeling his way into a new subject. There was not even a rest house at Kitega, but we were quickly provided with an empty government quarter. The following day Schmidt invited me to spend most of the morning at his residence in an extended historical discussion with the mwami and one of his ministers. Schmidt was above all interested in my work on the Hinda dynasties in Ankole and Buhaya, for it was from this direction, rather than from Rwanda, that the mwamis of Burundi traced their origins. The pastoralists of Burundi were in fact sharply divided in their clan affiliations between the Tutsi, who claimed an origin in Rwanda and belonged to the same clans as the Tutsi of Rwanda, and the Hima, who claimed to have come into Burundi from the east and whose clan names were those familiar all the way from Ankole through Buhaya and on southwards to Buha. Though referring to themselves in public merely as *baganwa* (princes), the Burundi royals clearly belonged in the Hima rather than the Tutsi category. In origin they were pastoralists who had spread southwards through the grasslands of Karagwe and Buha and who then began to interpenetrate with the agricultural Rundi living to their west in the foothills of the Nile-Congo watershed. As with the Tutsi penetration of Rwanda, but some two centuries later, the nucleus of a militarised state emerged in central Burundi. During the eighteenth and nineteenth centuries this state successfully incorporated its weaker neighbours.

I did not keep notes of that meeting, and I cannot be sure how far my recollections of it have been coloured by my reading of subsequent work by Jan Vansina and others. But I have no doubt that enough was said to pull together my tentative explorations from Ankole southwards and to enable me to see the dispersion of Hinda dynasties in a more meaningful way.

From Kitega we made our way back to Tanganyika by the official route, passing through the little district of Bugufi, where a former pupil from the course for Colonial Service cadets in Cambridge, George Gordon, was the district officer. He was a man who liked to observe the formalities, and he was much concerned about how to deal with our passports. The Belgians in Kitega had written a small essay on one of the visa pages, recording our arrival in Burundi, but Gordon's problem was how to admit us to Tanganyika because we had never officially left it. I forget how he finally salved his conscience, but at least he made no difficulties about surrendering his district book for our inspection. Bugufi was a miniature Burundi, a little state ruled by a pastoralist dynasty that, for at least a part of the nineteenth century, had been tributary to that of Burundi. However, when Rwanda-Urundi had been separated from the rest of German East Africa after the First World War, Bugufi had been placed on the Tanganyika side of the frontier. In Kitega we had been told how our friend Robert Schmidt had attempted to retrieve Bugufi for Burundi and how the matter had been referred by the Trusteeship Council of the United Nations for adjudication by two retired proconsuls, Pierre Ryckmans and Alan Burns. They had duly visited the district and recommended that things be left as they were. Gordon now told us how the news of the award had been received over the wireless by Governor Twining during a recent visit. Schmidt had crossed the border to meet him as a gesture of courtesy and heard the result only during Twining's baraza speech. We were relieved to hear that "Rule Britannia" had on this occasion been omitted from the musical programme and that Schmidt and Twining had ended the evening by joining hands and singing "Auld Lang Syne" on Gordon's lawn.

After leaving the district headquarters of Bugufi at Ngara, we spent one more night in the company of the hippopotamuses at Bukoba before returning to Kampala on March 8, 1950. It had all along been our plan to spend the rainy season at our base at Makerere, and in the event we had to drive the last twenty miles of our long journey through a massive thunderstorm that more than once brought us to a complete halt. It gave us a foretaste of how travelling conditions would be affected during the next two months or so on the soft murram roads of the Uganda countryside. This therefore would be the time to work more intensively at the secretariat archives in Entebbe and to fill out the experience we had gained in our travels by further study in the university library. Besides, though still in excellent health, we were in need of rest.

10

The Martial Races
(1950)

For all but two months after returning from Lake Tanganyika we remained in Kampala, staying with Julie Larter in her long wooden bungalow at the back of Makerere Hill, which looked across a little valley filled with elephant grass to the great thatched cone of the mausoleum of Kabaka Mutesa's three most recent ancestors. As I see from our surviving letters, it was an immensely busy period. The negatives of all the documents we had photographed had to be developed in the stifling conditions of the darkroom lent us by the department of physics. We had the spools of recorded recitations in six different languages and hoped to find competent transcribers and translators among the students of the university. I knew by this time that these were likely to be of no more than marginal value as historical sources, but I understood that my linguistic colleagues in London would be interested in securing examples of oral literature, and this they most surely were. My search for the right helpers in this task brought us into contact with a number of highly intelligent African students, some of whom came and worked regularly with me in the house and stayed to talk freely about their aims and aspirations. The Uganda Society, which published a useful journal, invited me to take part in its programme of public lectures. And above all we now addressed ourselves in earnest to the secretariat archives in Entebbe.

There was as yet no trained archivist and therefore no catalogue or guide to the materials, most of which had simply accumulated in the order in which the secretariat clerks had deposited them whenever they needed more space for current files in their offices. We simply had to work our way along the shelves, making our own inventory as we went. So far as we could discover, nothing at all had survived from the first ten years of British rule. But for the early years of the twentieth century the records seemed to be both complete and readily accessible, and from them

111

I learned much that was to be relevant to my future career as a director of research. In particular I learned how little of the information that flowed into a colonial secretariat from its representatives in the provinces and districts was passed on to the metropolitan government in London. Thus I also learned how defective was so much of the research carried out by doctoral students in colonial history, most of whom relied entirely on metropolitan archives, which were more concerned with policy than with actual effect or response. I realised that valid work on the history of the African peoples during the colonial period would require taking full account of local sources. I resolved that when my turn came to set the fashions in research, I would do my best to ensure that historians of modern Africa had the opportunity to visit the countries they were studying.

Meanwhile, at Makerere Bernard de Bunsen was still trying to involve me in his new department of history, for which he had recruited the first lecturer in the person of Kenneth Ingham—a contemporary of mine with a gallant war record and an Oxford doctorate on the missionary history of India. Kenneth had arrived to take up his post at the end of March, and I naturally thought that that had settled it. But Bernard still talked of wanting me to head the department and of being prepared to wait up to three years for me, which would give him time to establish a chair in the subject. Meantime, he asked me to prepare a paper for the academic board setting out my suggestions for the development of the department. I still have a copy of that paper. I argued that, although for some years to come the demand for formal education in history might be mainly for English and European history, African history was bound to become a major subject of history teaching at Makerere. I said that the future emergence of textbooks worthy of university studies would depend greatly upon the speedy collection and preservation of the wealth of historical evidence that was still in an oral state and that was nowadays being passed on only sporadically from the older to the younger generation. I stressed that Africans outside higher education had already started both to read history and to write it and that a university department of history should keep pace with and try to guide this vibrant concern in the community at large. I therefore suggested that a department of history at Makerere should aim to recruit as soon as possible one or two African members of staff with the linguistic skills to devote their research effort to such work. I pointed out that any development of this kind in the history department would also be of relevance to the emergence of a department of African languages and literature, for which no plans apparently existed but nonetheless was an imperative for any African university. The bottleneck I foresaw would be in the supply of candidates equipped with an honours degree in history, for Makerere's ceiling at that time was a general degree taken in three subjects. It would therefore be necessary, with the help of the East African governments, to send likely candidates overseas for more specialised training than they could obtain at home. I had already sounded out the director of education in Uganda, who had promised his support in the award of scholarships, and de Bunsen had commissioned me to open the question with the directors of education in Kenya and Tanganyika when I passed through those countries in July.

I remember the meeting of the academic board on April 23, 1950, at which my paper was discussed, and I remember the doubts expressed by its all-white membership. Looking round the room, I realised that many of these people, though they were clearly devoted to their work and rightly proud of it, were primarily concerned with implanting European culture in Africa. For the scientists and mathematicians among them this was natural enough: physics and chemistry required no adaptation to the local scene. But some teachers in the humanities evidently felt nearly as strongly that languages, politics, history, and education should be taught in Africa as nearly as possible as they were taught in Europe. Above all, there must be no compromising of academic standards, even in the interests of preserving what otherwise would disappear. Nevertheless, thanks to de Bunsen's strong support, my paper was accepted "for action as soon as possible." I remember thinking with some relief that henceforward it would be Kenneth Ingham's task to fight these battles and that my contribution would be to train his auxiliaries in the more cosmopolitan atmosphere of London.

At last, then, in early May 1950 we were ready to set out on the next phase of our travels, a five-weeks tour of twelve hundred miles that would take us through the northern and eastern provinces of Uganda. This, we knew, would be an environment quite different from any that we had yet experienced, and we had little idea of what we might find there. We knew that most of the region was populated by people who spoke Nilotic languages resembling those spoken in the southern Sudan and quite unrelated to the Bantu speech we had encountered so far. We knew that these people grew grain rather than bananas for their staple food and that, the climate being somewhat hotter and drier than that of southern Uganda, they wore few or no clothes. To the Bantu speakers of the south they were the *bakidi*—the naked people. We also knew that within the ranks of the colonial administration the north had its enthusiasts who admired the northerners for their manliness and candour and for their apparent indifference to outside influences. We knew that it was from among the northerners that most soldiers and police were recruited. They were the "martial races"—brave, loyal, and uncomplaining.

We drove on May 9 about 250 miles to Gulu, headquarters for both the northern province and the Acholi district. It was an easy enough journey, except for the ferry that crossed the Somerset Nile at Atura, midway along its course from Lake Kioga to Lake Albert. This was also the boundary between southern and northern Uganda, and it was symbolic of the disjunction between the two halves of the country that the main road connecting them was dependent on an engineless boat propelled by two paddlers and two punters. Once on the far side we quickly realised that we were in another world. The vegetation changed from elephant grass to the orchard bush composed of deciduous trees twenty to thirty feet high and growing as far apart from each other as those in a typical apple orchard. The orchard bush extends right across Africa in these latitudes. Beneath the woodland the whole landscape seemed flat and featureless, save where the occasional inselberg (mountain) thrust a few hundred feet of bare rock towards the sky. Human habitation was sparse and showed none of the signs of economic progress already visible in the south. Houses were uniformly round and windowless, and their roofs were all of thatch. Women dressed in leather skirts, and men were mostly naked. All this betokened not merely an ethnic difference but one of geographical remoteness from the centrifugal forces of colonially inspired change. In Uganda both colonial administration and missionary education had made their appearance a full generation later in the north than in the south. Even in 1950 the entire northern region still lacked a single school of full secondary standard.

Looking back to precolonial times, it was obvious that the key question affecting the whole of the northern region was how one group of Nilotic languages, the western group, had come to impose themselves upon so wide an area, stretching almost to Khartoum in the north and to the Kavirondo Gulf of Lake Victoria in the south. Working from the most elementary evidence of linguistic classification, it was clear that the ancient centre of these languages had been in the marshy areas of the southern Sudan, where two of its three subdivisions—the languages of the Nuer and the Dinka—had been stably located within a comparatively small area at the heart of this region. The third subdivision, usually known as Lwo, was the one that had achieved wide dispersion and within such a brief period that its component languages were still mutually intelligible. Therefore it seemed that one had to envisage a fairly rapid movement of Lwo-speaking peoples, who had swarmed all round the nuclear area and had in particular given rise to a major migration towards the south and southeast, embracing large parts of northern and eastern Uganda and a fertile and populous part of western Kenya. It was, again, at the southern end of the Lwo sphere that the precolonial history of northern and southern Uganda had met and interacted. The traditional historians of Bunyoro clearly stated that their ruling Bito dynasty had had its origins in the north and that the first three kings of the dynasty had been buried there (see Chapter 7). The migration of Lwo peoples had therefore to be seen in a wider context than that of their linguistic expansion. In some areas the migrants had succeeded in imposing their language upon those among whom they had settled. In other areas the migrants had lost their Lwo language but had nevertheless imposed themselves politically upon large communities of Bantu-speaking people. The mystery was how the Lwo people, who in modern times were very much the poor relations of the northern Bantu, had in the past been able to exercise so wide an influence upon them.

With these thoughts we arrived in Gulu to see what we could learn in a short time about the central group of the Lwo-speaking peoples of northern Uganda—the Acholi. The district commissioner, Dick Stone, was out on tour, but his able young assistant Bob Menzies gave us free use of the papers in the district office. We took them away to the rather grand catering rest house for study and photographing. They helped to flesh out our picture of an Acholiland, comprising in all some 250,000 people who were organised politically in some thirty chiefdoms of varying size under chiefs called *rwots*. Each rwot was in theory the head of a ruling clan of Lwo-speaking origin that had established its authority by conquering an earlier population of non-Lwo origin at some time in the not-too-distant past. One or two of the rwotships, notably that of Patiko, claimed dynastic genealogies extending backwards through sixteen or seventeen generations and therefore to some time in the sixteenth century. The great majority, however, claimed only about twelve generations or less, thus placing their arrival in the seventeenth or even the eighteenth century. One part of Acholiland had totally escaped conquest and settlement by the Lwo, and this, significantly, was the low-lying valley of the White Nile, flowing northwards from Lake Albert to the Sudan. Whatever use the Lwo migrants may have made of the river as a means of access, their preferred places of settlement were in the higher country to the east and west, where cattle could be kept without danger from the tsetse fly that infested the valley itself. The language spoken by the riverain people was Madi, which belonged to the Central Sudanic language family. It was reasonable to suppose that Madi had been the ancient language of most of the rest of Acholiland before the Lwo conquest.

We asked about the current survival of oral tradition, but Bob Menzies explained to us that the little rwots of Acholiland had been far less successful than the larger dynasties of the Bantu south in resisting the pressures of colonial administration. Many rwots had been dismissed for incompetence or malpractice, and even normal succession situations had been manipulated; thus modern rwots tended to be retired police or interpreters who were no longer surrounded by the traditionalist elements of the royal courts of the past. He did nevertheless help us to arrange day visits to two of the more important rwots—those at Patiko and Padibe—where we were greeted with song and dance but not of a kind that appeared to merit recording. The last two days of our stay we spent at Kitgum, the former district headquarters of northern Acholiland, a remote station nestling under the Imatong Range, which divides Uganda from the Sudan. The station had been abandoned by the white members of the colonial administration when the improvement of the road system enabled them to work out of Gulu. Its circle of pleasant bungalows was therefore occupied by the Asian and African staff of the technical departments, and, as we noted prophetically, it looked as much of Africa would look when the white man had left. On our return journey to Gulu we paused beside a brick building, which we presumed to be a local courthouse, where a European man in typical bush clothing was descending the steps. It proved to be Lucian Usher-Wilson, the Anglican bishop on the Upper Nile, who pressed us warmly to stay with him at his headquarters on the slopes of Mount Elgon at the end of our tour, which, to our great pleasure and profit, we did. As Bob Menzies recalled to us that evening, the similarity of architecture employed for churches and courthouses had once got him into serious trouble, when he had entered what he presumed to be a courthouse and walked up the aisle to what he presumed to be the bench, only to meet Lucian processing towards him in full ceremonial dress at the close of a confirmation service. Both processions came to a halt. Menzies held out his hand and said, "Doctor Livingstone, I presume," but the quip was not appreciated.

Thursday, May 18, 1950, was Ascension Day, and we attended mass at the splendid Italianate basilica that the Verona Fathers had built as their cathedral in Gulu. One father explained to us that the order was fortunate enough to have two lay brothers, one an architect and the other a painter, who had put their best efforts into the work over many years. Its construction required 1.1 million bricks, of which 600,000 had been contributed by the African parishioners of the diocese who had come in, village by village with much singing and laughter, to help with the unskilled work. Several fathers had also spoken to us about their colleague, J. P. Crazzolara, who had been researching for a quarter of a century on the history and ethnography of the Lwo peoples. He was now stationed at Arua, the headquarters of the West Nile district, whither we were bound later that day. Like Acholiland, West Nile was an area in which an ancient population, speaking Central Sudanic languages, had been partially incorporated into Lwo chiefdoms, here using the generic name of Alur. As in Acholiland, unincorporated Madi were still living in the valley of the Nile, while on the plateau to the west of it, astride the Congo frontier, were other Central Sudanic peoples like the Lugbara and the Lendu, some of whom were ruled by Lwo chiefs, and still others lived outside their sphere of influence. As Aidan Southall was soon to show in his excellent book on the Alur, the process of assimilation by the Lwo was quite recent at the fringes of their territory and still going on.[1]

Leaving Gulu, then, we crossed the White Nile by ferry at Pakwach, passing through country emptied of its human population by sleeping sickness, and therefore alive with game and especially with elephant, and then climbed up the western escarpment of the valley to Arua. There our first European contact was with that most civilised of social anthropologists, John Middleton, then a research student at Oxford and working on the religion of the Lugbara. He had only recently arrived and was living in camp a few miles out of Arua and deliberately allowing himself and every detail of his daily life to be studied by his Lugbara neighbours before he began to worry them with his questions about their beliefs. One of his initial problems was that he had been provided by the Colonial Social Science Research Council with a bright red van, closed in at the back, and the rumour had gone round among the Lugbara gossips that he used it to go out and steal babies to eat before touching up the paintwork with their blood. He had had to get a mechanic in Arua to install rear windows so that all and sundry could more easily inspect his possessions. Although he was in the course of developing a deep respect for the Lugbara way of life, he did acknowledge that it was sometimes a bore not to be able even to clean his teeth without submitting to the curious gaze of a circle of spectators. It was John Middleton who told us of the many Lugbara refugees from Belgian colonial rule who had crossed the nearby frontier to escape compulsory cotton cultivation under the threat of draconian penalties. He also told us that the Lugbara firmly believed that the Verona Fathers were married to the Verona Sisters. Although they lived in separate establishments, there was the undeniable fact that the Verona Sisters all wore wedding rings.

From Arua we made a memorable excursion in the company of Aidan Southall to the high hills overlooking Lake Albert to the south, where he was making some final inquiries for his study of the Alur. It was a perfectly clear day, and, as we picnicked at lunchtime, we could see right across Acholiland to the Imatong Mountains on the Sudan frontier, more than a hundred miles away. We learned much from Aidan about the redistributive functions of Lwo chiefs that made their rule not only acceptable but positively desirable to their Alur subjects and actually caused chiefless communities at the periphery of their little states to apply for Alur citizenship. The greater part of our visit to Arua was, however, rightly spent with Father Crazzolara, who received me with infinite courtesy and gave me an advance sight of the first part of his monograph on the Lwo that was to be published later that year. He had thought it best to try to write it in English, and he asked me to give him a little help with his use of the language. Needless to say, I was glad to do so, and I spent several long days with him in his room at the mission. As its readers will know, this first part of his work presented an overall view of all the migrations of all the Lwo peoples. He finished by posing the gigantic and wholly relevant question of whether the credit for state formation among the Bantu peoples of the interlacustrine region and beyond, hitherto usually assigned to some quite putative contact with the Hamitic peoples of Ethiopia, should not rather be given to the Nilotic Lwo. He suggested that not only the Bito dynasty of Bunyoro but also the antecedent kingdom of the Chwezi and its southerly Hinda derivatives had their origin as a result of successive waves of Lwo conquest.[2]

Looking back on it with the advantage of more than forty years of further research by historians and archaeologists, it must be said that Crazzolara's Nilotic hypothesis has stood the test of time much better than the earlier Hamitic hypothesis put forward by C. G. Seligman and others. Where Crazzolara fell short was in presenting it as the culmination of a single cataclysmic migration of Lwo peoples that had spiralled around the whole periphery of the southern Sudan and northern Uganda, depositing a dozen different Lwo groups along the road before breaking on the northern edge of the Bantu world. To this extent he took his sources too literally, ignoring the tendency of oral tradition to telescope its accounts of the more remote past. A slow drift of pastoral peoples always in search of new grazing lands, and perhaps accelerating from time to time in response to natural disasters like drought or disease, was not something that oral tradition was capable of describing. Likewise, oral accounts of the actual process of migration and conquest, of the assimilation of war captives and the submission of conquered peoples, were apt to be generalisations from a few comparaively recent examples. Again, working from the genealogies of the surviving small dynasties of northern Uganda, Crazzolara placed his single great migration during the seventeenth and eighteenth centuries and spurned the longer genealogies of the Bantu-speaking dynasties of the south as inflated. But never mind. He had forged an indestructible link between the precolonial history of northern and southern Uganda, which greatly increased the general understanding of the subject. I left Arua feeling that I owed him a great debt.

We returned to Gulu on May 29 by the northern route, pausing briefly at Moyo to have lunch with the hospitable district officer, Sandy Weekes, who administered this northernmost outpost of the Uganda protectorate with its miscellaneous population of Madi, Kakwa, and other ethnic fragments. As we sat on the veranda of his pretty crescent-shaped house looking north to the border hills, we little imagined that inside twenty years the whole of Uganda would be subjected to the tyranny of a rough tough soldier from this remote corner of the country called Idi Amin,

Cathedral built by Verona Fathers, Gulu, Uganda

who must at this time have been already working his way up through the noncommissioned ranks of the King's African Rifles.

We stayed only a night in Gulu before travelling on eastwards through the endless orchard bush to Lira, the headquarters of the Lango district, the homeland of Milton Obote, who was to be first the predecessor and later the successor of Idi Amin as president of an independent Uganda. Needless to say, at the time of our visit the possibility of any such developments was well below the political horizon, and the district office was occupied by a half-dozen able young Englishmen, all of whom expected to complete their careers in the Colonial Service.

The most baffling problem of precolonial Lango history seemed to be that here were 300,000 people, speaking a Lwo language almost indistinguishable from Acholi and yet bearing no signs of ever having experienced even a minority Lwo presence. The Lango political system turned not on rwots but on a multitude of clans and subclans akin to those of the pastoral peoples on their eastern frontier, like the Didinga and the Jie. In linguistic terms these peoples were eastern Nilotes related, though only remotely, to the western Nilotes who had given birth to the Lwo. Of the Lango, therefore, one could only say that they seemed to be people of eastern Nilotic origin who had voluntarily abandoned their language in favour of the western Nilotic Lwo speech of their Acholi neighbours. I met and had long talks with a charming and vivacious, Verona Father. Angelo Tarantino, who was considered to be the best

119

Interior of the cathedral

authority on the ethnography of the Lango, but we had to conclude that there existed no evidence by which the problem could be solved. There were Lango traditions extending over three or four generations of clan leadership to a period of sustained migration of Lango clans from the northeast to the southwest of the region during the first three-quarters of the nineteenth century but with no surviving consciousness of an earlier Lwo presence to account for a change of language. My inconclusive talks with Tarantino were not, however, without result. Fifteen years or so later I was in a position to direct two excellent research students, John Tosh and John Lamphear, towards this region, and between them they were able to resolve this and many other problems.[3] Historical research in any new field must have its scouts.

From Lira we moved eastwards on June 3, 1950, to Soroti, where Jerry Lawrance, a district commissioner of outstanding ability and great charm, presided over the affairs of the Teso people in what had become by far the most densely populated district of northern Uganda. The Teso spoke an eastern Nilotic language, and their traditions were nearly unanimous in claiming an origin to the northeast in the dry plains of neighbouring Karamoja. Taken at its face value such a tradition would have implied that people who could only have lived in Karamoja by practising a rather specialised system of pastoralism had moved into a very different, rather moist, environment in which they had become sedentary cultivators of grain crops in a land so empty of earlier inhabitants that they had had to begin by clearing the forests. All this had supposedly happened since the time of the grandfathers of the older generation of living people, but, significantly, the traditions of migration and resettlement were strongest among the northeastern Teso, who were presumably the last to arrive. Probably, the true scenario was much more extended in time, and as in so many other places the traditions of migrant newcomers, being so much more memorable, had come to dominate those of longer-settled families. At all events, it seemed to me clear that in Teso there would be scope for an inquiry into the history of agricultural settlement very different in character from those centring upon political evolution that had preoccupied me hitherto.

Soroti, as I remember it, was not a beautiful place, but Caroline and I both seem to have greatly enjoyed our brief stay there. We spent two days interviewing elderly informants in their villages about the history of settlement and recorded some interesting musical performances in which the instrumentalists played a kind of horn called *usukusuk*, made of large gourds with stems about ten feet long, while the dancers jumped rhythmically into the air and somehow brought their bare feet down together to produce a steady background thud in place of the usual drumming. We paid a visit to the Agricultural Research Station at Serere that had been so important to the development of cotton cultivation in Uganda as a whole. We played evening tennis with the district team, and with the local Catholic missionaries, who belonged to the Society of St. Joseph at Mill Hill, London, but who seemed in practice to be Dutchmen from well-heeled families. They turned up in new cars and well-pressed white shorts and no nonsense about having to play in their cassocks. We even played bridge after dinner with Jerry Lawrance and the district magistrate, who brilliantly described the murder trial that he had been conducting in Karamoja, where the courtroom had been filled with men wearing nothing more than a blue ostrich feather stuck into their carefully dressed hair. Two layers of interpretation had been necessary to translate the evidence from Karamojong into English. Nevertheless, the proceedings had still to begin in Norman French, with the clerk crying "*Oyez . . . Oyez,*" while the blue plumes nodded sagely in the background.

Clearly, after such an introduction we had to get to Karamoja, although it was a "closed district" in which people still went about armed and where the safety of travellers could not be guaranteed. But Jerry Lawrance was happy enough to write us a permit to study the archives at the district headquarters at Moroto, and we drove there on June 8. It was not in fact at all frightening. It was true that every male Karamojong carried a spear, but government regulations required that spear blades had to be protected with a little leather glove. This was held in position with a lace that had to be tied with a neat bow. The idea was that murder by spearing occurred mostly during rapid fits of temper, following an initial exchange of insults. If both sides had to pause, even for the few seconds necessary to undo the laces, tempers had time to cool. It struck us as a model of intelligent legislation. Our first personal encounter with a Karamojong occurred when we reached the banks of the Aswa River, where the road took a sharp dip and disappeared beneath its turbulent waters. A cheerful-looking old gentleman waved us forward vigourously with his spear, and, when we still hesitated, he strode forward into the water to demonstrate that it did not come above his knees. At Moroto the rest-house attendant arrived for work each morning with both his spear and his bow and arrows, planting the first firmly in the flowerbed by the front door and hanging up the latter on two hooks in the kitchen, after which he performed his domestic duties with complete suavity. Only when we went for an evening drive was there a slight hitch. We were flagged down by a martial figure standing right across the road. He wanted a lift, so we took him on board, spear and all, and it seemed to be going well enough when Caroline told me rather emphatically that she wished to go home. I turned the car round and did my best to explain to our passenger that we were going no farther. We parted on the best of terms, but when we were alone, Caroline explained that she had been resting her arm along the back of my seat and that this had evidently been too much for our friend's curiosity. For fifteen minutes or so he had been running his fingers gently up and down her skin, no doubt in order to discover in what measure it resembled skin with which he was familiar.

Moroto was nothing but a village street but built on the lower slopes of a rather splendid mountain nearly nine thousand feet high that bestrode the border between Uganda and the Turkana district of Kenya. It looked out westwards, southwards, and northwards over the immense plain covered with dry thorn scrub over which the young men of the Karamojong, Jie, and Dodoth circulated with their cattle. The old men, women, and children grew a few vegetables and herded a few goats around the stockaded villages known as *manyattas*, the only places of fixed habitation. The colonial administration of such an area had been restricted virtually to the maintenance of law and order, and above all to the prevention of the intergroup violence caused by competition for the best pastures and watering places. The Land Rover had not yet made its appearance in East Africa, and district officers still did most of their travelling on foot, setting out for two or three weeks at a time accompanied by a few armed police, thirty or forty porters, and a herd of goats to supply the evening meal for the caravan. The goats were written down in the record of official expenses, but after their consumption their skins had a value, of which the lords of the local treasury, by long convention, took no account. Hence "the goat bag" had come to mean the small fund that could be spent on improving the local amenities without reference to higher authority. In Karamoja in 1950 the goat bag was still of some significance.

During our first two days in Moroto we did our accustomed paperwork in the district records and on the third, which was a Sunday, attended the local church, where the service was conducted by a white missionary who had come in specially from his station in the bush at a place called Lotomi. It was the only Anglican mission station in Karamoja, and he invited us to spend a night there, which we were glad to do. The following morning he took us parish visiting to the local manyatta, where we crawled on hands and knees through many low doorways leading from one family unit to another, the inhabitants greeting us cordially enough as they went about their daily business but not really pausing to talk. The experience gave us a valuable glimpse of the early days of mission work, which had been so long and so completely superseded elsewhere.

From Lotomi on June 13 we drove to the opposite end of the ecclesiastical spectrum, the charming little hilltop settlement of Buwalasi, where Lucian and Muriel Usher-Wilson presided over the headquarters community of the Upper Nile diocese. Their house was set in a glorious rose-filled garden and looked across a deep green valley to the rotund pale blue dome of Mount Elgon that filled the eastern skyline. We were now back in the Bantu-speaking world, here represented by the Gisu people whose dwellings, each set in its little banana grove, rose tier upon tier up every ridge and side valley of the great mountain to a height of perhaps seventy-five hundred feet, where first the bamboo forest and then the high heathlands led up towards the summit. The Gisu had first been colonised not by the British but by a Ganda warlord, Semei Kakungulu. With the connivance of a still small and hard-pressed protectorate administration he had set out with one to two thousand followers to establish a new kingdom among the unsophisticated peoples of the eastern region where he hoped to be recognised as the kabaka. The British had allowed him to buy firearms that he had paid for by hunting ivory and that he had also used to impose his authority and to take tribute from those in whose midst he had settled. It was at Kakungulu's invitation that the first Anglican and Catholic missionaries had settled close to his capital at Mbale, and they had brought with them hundreds of Ganda evangelists, the fruits of the mass movements of conversion in their homeland around the turn of the century. Lucian's diocese had thus been built upon the strange conjunction of buccaneering Ganda soldier-settlers and young literate Ganda Christians with Bibles in their baggage packs, eager to build village schools and establish Christian congregations. Within ten years or so an increasingly prosperous and confident protectorate government had elbowed Kakungulu out of his political authority, but the Ganda evangelists had remained and had pushed out new tendrils of Christian influence across the whole of the northern region—hence the location of the episcopal seat in the southeastern corner of a diocese that now stretched right across to West Nile and into the Belgian Congo to the west of Lake Albert.

Lucian Usher-Wilson, like Simon Stuart, was often away visiting his scattered flock, but when at home he was a meticulous administrator whose files were in apple-pie order. I found him a perfect informant, always able to put his hand on the facts and figures that I needed about the numbers and skills of those in church and mission employment and the different ways in which they were all supported. He also was willing to talk frankly about the relations of church and government, past, present, and future. His theological college was on the doorstep, and he made a point of getting to know the ordinands personally. They were invited regularly to meals in the house and made to play carpet bowls (an indoor game played with miniature bowls) with his other guests. I feel sure that the experience was of benefit to all concerned. Lucian also sent me out on my own to visit the African archdeacon of Mbale. He knew that there would be linguistic difficulties in our communication, but he judged that I would learn more that way than with the formality always imposed by the presence of an interpreter. One detail of that visit I have always remembered was how our servant Benjamin was automatically included in the welcome given us by that African family. He was as much a stranger as we were, but he was waved into the already crowded family parlour, where he seated himself in a corner but took part without any embarrassment in the general conversation. Ever since then I have observed with admiration the elasticity of African social customs as compared with those of Europe. An African friend once told me that he thought of London as a place where, if your brother knocked at your front door when you were giving a dinner party, you would send him away hungry and tell him that he should have made an appointment before coming. On the whole, I think that his characterisation was fair.

Caroline and I had both been hoping that there might be an opportunity to get closer to Mount Elgon, if only to climb up through the forest into the high grassland, with its giant lobelias and tree-heaths (heaths of tree height), about which we had heard so much. But alas it was not to be. We set off one morning up the side valley that had the highest-reaching road, intending to camp at the uppermost village, but long before we got there our old car gave up the struggle, and we were left in a place from which rescue was difficult to arrange. We walked a long way under a pitiless sun before we were able to send a message and waited many hours before a mechanic arrived from Mbale. When we finally got back to the Usher-Wilsons, Caroline was obviously unwell. Although a day in bed restored her, it was thought to be an attack of suppressed malaria, and we decided that it was high time to return to our base in Kampala and get our affairs into order for our next big journey. We felt just a little guilty as we drove without pausing through the important Busoga district, but with this one exception we had completed our plan to visit every district in Uganda. And as our friends in the government assured us, we had seen far more of the country than any of them were likely to see in the course of an entire career. Above all, we had seen and learned enough to be confident that there could be a meaningful study of the country's history beginning several centuries before the period of European exploration and the imposition of colonial rule. We had accomplished the primary purpose of my first study leave.

11

The East African Horizon
(1950)

We now had little more than two months left of our study leave, and I was determined to spend most of the time trying to widen our horizon, even if in a comparatively superficial way, to include something of Kenya, Tanganyika, and Zanzibar. Having devoted most of my time in Uganda to questions of precolonial history, I was content now to leave these aside, except for the most accessible materials such as the tribal history sections of the Tanganyika district books. From now on I decided to concentrate first on the further experience and information I needed to complete my missionary book as soon as possible after our return to England and, second, to introduce myself and the relevant objectives of the university I represented to the education departments of these countries, as I had already tried to do in Uganda. On July 2, therefore, we drove eastward to Kisumu, the harbour town at the northeastern corner of Lake Victoria and the headquarters of Kenya's western province. From there on the following day we climbed through the immaculate tea plantations at Kericho to the Mau summit at nine thousand feet above sea level, with hardly a gasp of protest from the car, and then dropped down again into the Rift Valley with its tarred roads, trim European farms, and three lakes circled with the pink sheen of a million flamingoes feeding round their shores. On the eastern wall of the Rift there was in those days only the one steeply hairpinned road past the little chapel built by the Italian prisoners who had been employed on it during the war. A few miles beyond the crest a sideroad led off to the Church of Scotland mission station at Kikuyu, where we stayed for a week as the guests of George Calderwood, the head of the mission. It was almost on the outskirts of Nairobi, and we drove there daily to do our business with the Kenya government and work in the archives of the Christian Council of Kenya. The mornings and the evenings we devoted to the affairs of the Church of Scotland mission and of the so-called Protestant Missionary Alliance, of which it had been the linchpin. Our daily pabulum came from the contents of a tin trunk that George Calderwood kept in his house and that contained the correspondence of the successive heads of the mission from 1900 onwards.

I had long realized that the missionary history of Kenya had a very different flavour from that of Uganda, where Christianity had been represented by only two main denominations and where missions and colonial government, whatever their mutual criticisms, had always felt themselves to be engaged in the same basic task. In Kenya many more denominations were competing for converts, and the Christian population was more mobile, both between country and town and between peasant holdings in the reserves and agricultural employment on European farms. From early in the twentieth century strong reasons had existed, for Protestant missions at least, to try to cooperate with one another in pastoral work and church discipline, including attitudes towards African customs. Also, and increasingly from about 1905 onwards, missionaries had realised that the presence of European settlers posed a threat to the interests of their African clientele—a threat in relation to which the colonial government was bound to favour the cause of the settlers, who had been encouraged by the metropolitan government to make their homes there. In Kenya, therefore, missionaries felt themselves to be the natural protectors of African interests, and this again was an objective they had to pursue as far as possible in common.

Because of its central geographical position, near Nairobi but not in it, the Church of Scotland headquarters at Kikuyu made the perfect venue for ecumenical activities. The first head of the mission, Henry Scott, and his successor J. W. Arthur began to meet regularly with J. J. Willis, the Anglican archdeacon of Kavirondo, in 1907. The Anglican bishop of Mombasa soon started to join them and also the head of the nondenominational Africa Inland Mission, the headquarters of which was only twenty miles away at Kijabe. In 1913 the Kikuyu meetings made ecumenical history by holding a common service of Holy Communion, at which the bishop of Mombasa, J. W. Peel, presided and offered the Sacrament to all those present. It led to terrible trouble when Frank Weston, the high-church bishop of Zanzibar, denounced two of his brother bishops to the archbishop of Canterbury for "promoting heresy and committing schism," but the Kikuyu meetings went on and led in 1918 to the formation of the Protestant Missionary Alliance, which in due course sponsored the Alliance High School, the best-known secondary school in East Africa, and the United Theological College at Limuru.

The Alliance was likewise the natural channel for missionary protests to the colonial government about the implications for the African population of its postwar policy of intensifying white settlement by encouraging the migration of British war veterans to establish farms in Kenya. Already by 1919 administrative officers had been instructed to put heavy pressure on the African peasantry to go out and work as migrant labourers on the European farms instead of developing their own commercial agriculture, and to the missionaries it seemed that this was but the spearhead of a more general intention to restrict African development by importing skilled workers from outside the country instead of training those already there. The missionary protests issuing from Kikuyu were heard in London as well as Nairobi and were represented to the highest levels by J. H. Oldham, the outstandingly able secretary of the International Missionary Council. In his hands the protests developed into a positive counterpolicy of stepping up the quality of mission education in all the British African colonies by instituting a system of government inspection and government grants for the qualified teachers in mission employment. This was accepted by the British government and implemented at a special meeting of the governors of all the African colonies convened in June 1924. The effect on missionary strategy all over the continent was revolutionary. On the one hand, as I had been discovering in Uganda, government subsidies for educational work soon came to figure more highly in ecclesiastical budgets than the combined revenue from the home constituencies of the missions and the contributions of the local church communities. On the other hand, a large proportion of both missionaries and the most skilled African church workers was diverted into educational rather than evangelistic effort.

All these developments, so important for the closing chapters of my book, had in a sense had their origin at Kikuyu, and certainly no one with whom to discuss them was better qualified than George Calderwood, who as Dr. Arthur's successor had spent most of his missionary career dealing with them. It was at his house that we met the great missionary headmaster Carey Francis, who had left a Cambridge fellowship in order to found the Alliance High School and had stayed there long enough to educate a whole generation of Kenya's future leaders. One subject that frequently came up for discussion during that week was the decisive attitude taken by the Church of Scotland mission since the 1930s towards the custom of female circumcision as practised by the Kikuyu people of central Kenya. They had in fact gone so far as to forbid it to all their adherents and to excommunicate those families that disobeyed the rule. As a result, they had lost a large portion of their members, and some of those who had left the church had set up the Kikuyu Independent Schools Association, which employed ex-mission teachers to found a network of independent schools throughout Kikuyuland, for the support of which they succeeded in claiming the government subsidies previously paid to the mission. Rightly or wrongly, I decided that I could not deal with this issue in my book. It was highly technical, it concerned only one of the

128

many peoples of East Africa, and chronologically it was at the very limit of the period I was trying to portray. The decision did, however, have one consequence about which I subsequently had many regrets. George Calderwood told me that, just at the bottom of the hill at Dagoreti, there lived the president of the most prestigious of the independent schools, a certain Jomo Kenyatta, who had fairly recently returned to Kenya after a long absence in England and whom I might like to meet. Alas, I never did so.

I suppose that, had we trolled the district offices of Kenya in the same way that we had done those of Uganda, we might have gathered some hint that all was not well in the body politic of the colony. Nowadays we know that, already during the first six months of 1950, more than one hundred Kikuyu had been prosecuted and imprisoned for taking part in oathing ceremonies of a kind thought to be obscene or blasphemous rather than seditious. Such talk as we heard was mostly of movements of religious rather than political dissent. And in fact another two years were to pass before the declaration of the state of emergency that goes by the name of Mau Mau. Meantime, in Nairobi the Norfolk Hotel and the New Stanley, not yet swamped by international tourists, were still patronised by English gentry in town for a few days' break from their farms. The assumption was that everyone knew everyone else and that, if they didn't, they ought to. It was all extraordinarily friendly and completely confident. With the Royal Technical College, soon to be the University of Nairobi, springing up beside the Norfolk, and with the residence halls for students already climbing the hillside opposite, leading up towards Government House, there could be no real doubt about who was ultimately destined to rule in Kenya, but the transition from European dominance still seemed a long way off.

When our work in Nairobi was finished, we took three days off to drive around the base of Mount Kenya, passing through the most densely populated parts of the Kikuyu Reserve, visiting the largest of the Presbyterian mission stations at Tumu Tumu, and spending a luxurious night at the White Rhino in Nyeri, where our old motor car, full of cooking pots and camp beds, looked distinctly out of place. Then, on July 18, we made for the coast, down the terrible three hundred miles of potholed dusty gravel road to Mombasa. The road was said to be deliberately left in that condition to keep the state-owned railway in business. We had been entertaining high hopes for our visit to the Kenya coast, but they were not to be realised, because as we drove down Chamgamwe Hill, the last escarpment leading down to the causeway to Mombasa Island, we were struck from behind by the largest kind of army truck, which had been despatched by some irresponsible officer at the British base at Mackinnon Road to have its brakes mended in Mombasa. Fortunately for us the driver of the vehicle bravely drove it off the road to avoid hitting us a second time, but the episode lost us a week, which we spent marooned in a hotel at Port Reitz while the bodywork was being repaired. There was nothing for it but to cancel our Kenyan plans and keep to the programme I had arranged for Tanganyika.

Caroline, probably wisely, decided to withdraw from this stage of the expedition and to return to Kampala. Never good at early morning starts, I think she was apprehensive about the pace of travel necessary to cover the ground during the time at our disposal. She was also attracted by the idea of spending the last month of her freedom from motherhood cares reading in the Africana section of the library at Makerere and perhaps trying out her skills as a writer. So with great sadness I put her on the train at Mombasa on July 23 and, as soon as the car was ready, set off southwards with Benjamin to Tanga. It was in those days a beautiful road, bright with sun and sand, which passed through village after picturesque village set among coconut palms and inhabited by the Digo people, who lived by farming and fishing on the coastal plain. At Tanga the solidity of the government buildings round the harbour reminded us that we were once again in former German territory, and here we turned inland, through great sisal estates, towards our first stopping place, the station of the Universities Mission to Central Africa (UMCA) at Magila, where the Anglican bishop of Zanzibar, Bill Baker, had his mainland headquarters.

The UMCA had been founded as the response of the British Tractarians, a high-church movement, to David Livingstone's appeal for the evangelisation of tropical Africa, following his coast-to-coast journey of 1856–58. The mission had started work in Nyasaland (now Malawi) but soon retreated to found a settlement on Zanzibar for slaves freed at sea by the British navy. It was hoped that, after education and training, some recaptives would return as missionaries to their homes on the mainland, and Magila, founded in 1869, had been the first, not very successful, attempt to promote this. Situated near the Pangani Valley trade route into the interior with the Usambara Mountains to the north of it, the mission had built up its clientele among the Bondei and Zigua peoples living on the southern peripheries of the Shambaa kingdom, where the slave trade was fed by intermittent warfare and where people had been glad to associate with a body of influential outsiders who had the ear of the Zanzibar sultanate. During the period of German rule Lutheran missions from Germany had settled in the mountain regions to the north and south. Magila, with its later offshoots, had kept its operations close to the German-built railway running inland from Tanga to Korogwe.

I had long been fascinated by the quite special missionary ethos cultivated by the UMCA, which deliberately emulated the material poverty of those it served. Its missionaries were probably the best educated of any

130

working in the East African field, but they were paid ten shillings a week and their keep, and they took pride in having in their houses no furniture or equipment that an African successor, supported by the local community, would not be able to take over from them. The entire system rested upon the observance of celibacy, required of all missionaries for as long as they remained with the mission, but this did not apply to the African clergy trained by them, nearly all of whom were married men. Now here I was in their midst. My host, Bill Baker, had been an undergraduate at King's College, Cambridge, where he had been known by irreverent but affectionate contemporaries as "the lamb of God." His father and grandfather had both been clergymen who had served the same parish in Bedfordshire for sixty-eight years. Now as bishop he lived in a house built of mud-and-wattle with a roof of corrugated iron that had three rooms, one of which was a private chapel. There was no mission motor car. His comings and goings from Zanzibar, and from Dar es Salaam and its hinterland, were all by public transport, starting with a four-mile walk to the little station at Muheza. His visitations of the local parishes were all conducted by train and on foot. At Magila he ate with the archdeacon and the parish priest in the old stone clergy house built in the nineteenth century. Some fifteen English nuns of the Community of the Sacred Passion lived in a stone convent higher up the hill beyond the massive parish church built in the style of Gothic Revival at its most forbidding. The unworldliness of it all was deeply impressive, but it was perhaps more like a rural deanery than a diocese. Bill Baker's entire flock was estimated at thirty thousand. In Uganda Simon Stuart was the spiritual leader of a half-million.

It took me two long days of driving to get the two hundred miles from Magila to Dar es Salaam, where I stayed for a busy three days with the UMCA parish priest, Cedric Frank, who with the help of one African colleague served the spiritual needs of the European community of the colonial capital and those of the increasingly urbanised migrant workers from the mission's rural bases in the northeastern and southern provinces of the territory. Most of these people were living in separation from their families and away from the social restraints of their rural communities. They were strangers in a predominantly Muslim town in which even the other up-country migrants spoke different vernaculars and observed different customs. To such as these the community life of an urban parish fulfilled a vital need. My visit to Cedric Frank thus gave me my first real glimpse of missionary work in an urban setting. During my brief stay I was also able to see the director of education about scholarships for a few Tanganyikans so they could break through the bottleneck of the honours degree by studying in Britain and see the secretary for African affairs, John Lamb, about archival problems. With his help I tracked down the surviving German archives in the lands office and went over their contents with the kindly German curator who still looked after them. It was likewise in Dar es Salaam that I had a chance encounter with W. M. Macmillan, who, as King George V Professor of Imperial History at the University of Cape Town, had done some outstanding work on the political influence of Christian missionaries in colonial South Africa. He had also, in the 1920s, played an active part in J. H. Oldham's campaign to persuade the missionary societies of the Western world to extend and formalise their educational work in tropical Africa. We therefore had much to discuss as we strolled around the harbour area of the town. He took the most kindly interest in all my doings but astounded me, as we parted, by assuring me that it would be my main duty in life to teach the Africans that they had absolutely no history of their own.

On July 31 I flew the thirty-odd miles to Zanzibar in a minuscule biplane that carried only one other passenger and installed myself by Bill Baker's invitation in his rooms adjoining the massive cathedral built by Bishop Edward Steere on the site of the town's main slave market during the decade following the British-induced abolition of the sultanate's export slave trade in 1873. The cathedral had, I suppose, always been more of a triumphalist declaration of faith than a response to local needs, for Zanzibar was a Muslim island on which the only African Christians were members of the temporary community of freed slaves awaiting the opportunity to return to their homes on the mainland. At the time of my visit its ministrations were performed by a single rather elderly missionary called Archdeacon Clarabutt, who made no bones about the fact that his congregation consisted of the handful of active Anglicans to be found among the colonial administration. Sometimes, he said, a few Africans came to the services, but he really didn't know why.

The main purpose of my visit to Zanzibar, however, was to meet the chief justice of the protectorate, John Gray, who could accurately be described as the doyen of the amateur historians of Africa. The son of Arthur Gray, master of Jesus College, Cambridge, and author of the world-famous textbook on anatomy, John Gray had read history at King's during the years before the First World War and in 1920 had joined the Colonial Service as an administrator in Uganda. There he employed some of his spare time reading for the bar and so became first a district magistrate and then a judge. From then on his apparently ample leisure was devoted to the history of the African countries in which he served. While in Uganda he read the works of the European explorers and missionaries, comparing them with the oral traditions collected by Kagwa and others, and wrote a series of highly original articles in which the late nineteenth-century rulers of Buganda were treated not as savage despots but as intelligent statesmen who tried their best to assess and control the new forces from the outside world that were breaking in upon their country. While in Gambia, where he spent ten years as judge in the Supreme Court from 1933 until 1943, he wrote what is still the standard work on the history of successive colonial administrations of the area. In Zanzibar, where he spent the last ten years of his service as chief justice, he once again devoted his evenings and his weekends to the ample history of the island and its relations with the adjacent mainland. His large work on the subject was completed during his retirement.[1]

I had been warned by my old Swahili teacher Laurence Hollingsworth that in Zanzibar Gray was known by the nickname of *sahani moja*, meaning literally 'one plate' and metaphorically 'the one who dines alone'. It was no doubt true that he had never been one to spend his evenings drinking in a colonial club, but the Gray I encountered was welcoming, hospitable, and positively jovial. On my first evening we met and talked for three hours, and he invited me to meet him in his chambers early the following morning. I do not know what happened to the business of the high court that day, but on my arrival he informed a deferential but evidently puzzled Goanese clerk that he would be "*in nubibus*" (in the clouds) for the rest of the day, whereupon we sallied forth into the town on foot and rapidly acquired a large following of urchins to whom Gray dispensed sweets from his pockets. We called first on the resident, Vincent Glenday, and next upon the sultan, whom we found impressively seated with his entourage on a wide balcony of his palace looking out over the harbour. There we had coffee and then retired for the rest of the morning into the museum, which in 1950 housed the archives of the British and German consulates of precolonial times. In the afternoon we drove across the island, looking at ancient mosques and modern clove plantations, and in the evening sat down to a sumptuous dinner in his lodgings. His anecdotes were superbly told, and I particularly treasured one in which he related how, when acting as governor in Gambia in September 1939, he had received a telegram asking him to declare war on Germany. "And I said, 'Surely the Colonial Office must know that we *don't* do things like this on a Saturday morning in Gambia. It must wait till Monday.' " On a more serious note we talked about our respective ambitions in research and publication, and I see from a letter I wrote to Caroline next day that I even toyed with the idea that the University of London might be persuaded to enlist him as its first professor of African history. In retrospect it strikes me as an idea that I am glad to have had.

I returned from Zanzibar to Dar es Salaam on August 2 and two days later set out along the single terrible road connecting the capital of the territory with that of its southern province at Lindi. The distance was only three hundred miles, but the road was submerged for six months of every year, and during the other six it was passable only by driving at ten miles an hour. The first day took me to Utete, a district headquarters in the Rufiji Delta with no building more modern than the splendid 1910 German fort in which the district commissioner lived, worked, and entertained travellers between tours of inspection that had to be carried out mostly by boat. The second equally arduous day brought me to Kilwa, the seat of the richest and most powerful sultanate on the eastern coast of Africa during medieval times. The medieval town had been built on an island a half-mile offshore, which gave it protection from the people of the mainland and also a safe roadstead for the long-distance shipping that rode the monsoon winds from the Persian Gulf and southern Arabia. The island town had been squeezed out of business by the Portuguese, who occupied it briefly at the beginning of the sixteenth century and diverted its trade into their own channels. It had been replaced in the eighteenth century by a new town, built on the mainland opposite, by a new dynasty from southern Arabia that had developed the inland trade in the slaves and ivory of the region around Lake Malawi. In the mid-nineteenth century this dynasty became tributary to that of Zanzibar, and it was beside this mainland Kilwa that first the Germans and then the British had established their administrative headquarters in the area. At the time of my visit there was talk of a new future for Kilwa, as a deepwater port for circum-Africa shipping, with better supplies of freshwater than Zanzibar's. In anticipation of a growth of tourism a charming young English couple had built a pleasant hotel called The Travellers' Rest overlooking a small nearly circular bay and close to the district office; I was happy to spend three nights of luxury at the hotel in the course of an otherwise spartan tour.

The district commissioner at Kilwa, Pat Allsebrook, had been a classmate at Stowe, and he obligingly lent me his official motor launch to visit the island ruins in the company of his assistant Jimmy Hildesley. He and I spent an agreeable day there, but it was definitely a case of the blind leading the blind. I knew the history of the place in the bare outline presented by the literary sources, but nothing in my education had as yet given me the slightest awareness of historical archaeology as an independent source of evidence. Together Hildesley and I poked about in the ruins of the Great Mosque and those of the adjacent palace at a time when nothing whatever had been done to clear or restore them. Rubble filled the bottom half of every structure we entered. The glazed pottery bowls decorating the multidomed ceiling of the Great Mosque were close above our heads, but neither of us had the knowledge to guess at their date or provenance. The ruins of the splendid Husuni Kubwa palace at the northern tip of the island were as yet undiscovered. I think it was only later that summer that my future friend and collaborator Gervase Mathew, the brilliant Dominican scholar from Blackfriars in Oxford, paid

134

his first fleeting visit to Kilwa in the course of a holiday spent with his brother, Archbishop David Mathew, who was the apostolic delegate in British tropical Africa and had his headquarters in Mombasa.

Meanwhile, the more immediately tangible result of my brief stay in Kilwa was that Jimmy Hildesley conceived an unaccountable admiration for my motor car and made an offer for it that I knew would be acceptable to my employers. The agreement we made was that I should complete my trip round the southern province and then freight it from some point along the central railway to Dar es Salaam, while I would return in the opposite direction to Uganda by train and lake steamer. That would give me, I reckoned, just about two weeks in which to reach the railway, and I was determined to make the most of them in terms of missions visited and district books consulted.

On August 7, therefore, I drove with Benjamin the last ten hours of that inexorable coast road to Lindi and put up at a squalid hotel, whose other guests were all connected with the British government's ill-conceived attempt to establish highly mechanized ground-nut (peanut) plantations some fifty miles inland at Nachingwea. Next day we drove westwards to Masasi, the scene of the UMCA's attempt during the 1870s to settle recaptive slaves from Zanzibar in free communities on the mainland. It was now the seat of the Anglican diocese, where I was kindly received by two archdeacons and a lady doctor; my appearance gave them the rare opportunity for an after-dinner game of bridge before they retired to say Compline in Swahili. At their suggestion I spent the following night at the diocesan theological college at Namasakata that consisted of a church and twelve thatched rondavels built in a clearing in the forest near the Mozambique frontier, many miles from the main road and inaccessible from it for six months of every year on account of the Rovuma River floods. Here a tiny band of senior catechists were being prepared for the priesthood by a single celibate white missionary, and even in those slow-moving and apparently secure colonial times one wondered whether this could be the way to build a church capable of standing on its own in the modern world.

The Roman Catholic Church in southern Tanganyika was in the care of the monks and nuns of the Benedictine congregation of St. Ottilien, with its home base in Austria and southern Germany. I visited its two great powerhouses—the abbey of Ndanda between Lindi and Masasi and that of Peramiho to the west of Songea. At Peramiho my Benedictine guide led me round all the monastic buildings, the abbey church, schools, seminary, barns, and workshops of a huge agricultural estate and brought me finally to the graveyard of the monks, where he paused and said, "You see, we have completed three rows—*successfully* completed, we trust." As far as I could see, there was no essential difference between

135

the monastic pattern of missionary work and that of the missionary congregations like the White Feathers at Kabgayi in Rwanda, for example, except for the sad fact that, after nearly seventy years in the field, the Benedictines could not point to a single African priest trained by them to take their place in the future. The monastic ideal, which had attracted many East African women, had apparently not made any comparable impact upon East African men, while the monks had probably found it more difficult than other missionaries to adapt their patterns of life for a secular African clergy.

From Peramiho and Songea my route ran northwards through the splendid highland country of the Livingstone Mountians, where the last of the great northward migrations of Nguni people from the militarized Zululand of Shaka during the early nineteenth century had finally come to rest. There they established two "Ngoni" kingdoms, each with its ruling class of former warrior migrants. I would happily have stayed there longer, but my time was now so constrained that I had to limit myself to brief stops at the various district headquarters through which I passed. I stayed at Njombe, Iringa, Dodoma, Kondoa, and Singida and learned at least what the colonial administrators knew, or thought they knew, about the Bena, Hehe, Gogo, Sandawe, and Iramba peoples. It was much better than nothing, and I came away with a real picture of the arid sparsely populated centre of the huge territory, which constituted the essential problem for its economic development.

At last, on August 20 I came with Benjamin to the little wayside railway station of Itigi, midway between Dodoma and Tabora. There we packed up our camping gear in a series of sad little bundles, cleaned up the old motor car as well as we were able, and entrusted it to the stationmaster for transmission down the line to Dar es Salaam, while we caught the evening train that dawdled its way westwards, depositing us at Tabora in the middle of the night to await the branchline service to Mwanza, the southernmost port on Lake Victoria. From the steamer's deck we had a last view of Bukoba. Next day we were at Port Bell, six miles from Kampala. Julie Larter was waiting on the pier at Port Bell to meet us with the news that Caroline was ill with suspected tertian malaria. There remained just ten days before our flight back to England.

12

Taking Stock
(1950–53)

Our homecoming from East Africa in the early September of 1950 was
not an easy one. The three days of comfortable roomy travel by flying
boat from Port Bell to Southampton, with leisurely overnight stops at
Alexandria and Augusta in Sicily, should have made a delightful transition
from one lifestyle to another. But Caroline had to do it with a temperature
of 102, and on arrival she had to go straight to the Hospital for Tropical
Diseases, where she stayed for nearly a month. Our much longed-for
reunion with our daughter Sarah had to be postponed until the middle of
October. Never had the English climate seemed more depressing than in
that rain-sodden autumn and winter of 1950–51. And for the first time in
our married life we felt desperately poor. The Labour government, now
in its sixth year of office, had still not succeeded in liberating the economy
from wartime controls. Prices had risen during our absence. Our income
had stood still. Caroline was a long time in recovering her health and
strength, and she needed more domestic help than we could afford. I
think it was at this time more than any other in our thirty-six years of
marriage that the difference in our ages asserted itself. I was twenty-eight
and still at the bottom of the professional ladder. She was forty-one and
beginning to need some of the comforts of life. I do not doubt that all this
contributed to her strong feeling that our family should not be enlarged.

Nevertheless, our life at Woughton-on-the-Green slowly reestablished
itself. We opened up the cottage, and Sarah, now one and a half, at last
arrived with the faithful Nanny Bisset, who had written to us every single
Sunday of our absence and always reassuringly. She had evidently put
much thought and sound imagination into preparing Sarah for our return,
and I can still see the look of lively and expectant curiosity on her face
when we met them at the station. Nanny stayed with us for ten days.
After that we were on our own, except for our next-door neighbour,

Mrs. Christine O'Reilly, who had cleaned the house for us since 1943 and now opened her home and family circle to Sarah whenever Caroline and I needed to be out together. In fact, during the next four years of our life there we were a great deal at home. I had already discovered that time spent at the university when not actually teaching was apt to be time wasted, and I learned to do nearly all my work at Woughton. The cottage was roomy, and I had a study inaccessible enough to be insulated from most domestic activities. There I was able to work long days broken only by interludes for meals, conversation, and exercise, and I therefore had the opportunity to complete writing *The Missionary Factor in East Africa*, present it for examination as a doctoral thesis in Cambridge, and prepare it for publication by Longman, all within the academic year of 1950–51. It finally appeared in 1952, was kindly received by reviewers, and remained in modest but steady demand for the next thirty years with only one revised edition along the way. Its principal conclusion, which I think has gained acceptance from both scholars and church officials, was that the main reason for the phenomenal success of Christianity in modern Africa was because, when the disparity of knowledge between Africa and Europe was greatest, Christian evangelism offered a means of education that enabled colonial Africans to participate in modernisation instead of being overwhelmed by it.

Meanwhile, at the university I had to address the much wider question of how African history could be developed into a regular subject of study, not only in London but also in the emerging university colleges in tropical Africa that were preparing their students for London University degrees under the system of special relationship described in Chapter 7. During my absence Cyril Philips had been successful in establishing a second post in the subject and had already appointed to fill it Robert Hamilton, a history graduate of Oxford with a postgraduate qualification in social anthropology who was proposing to make his debut with a detailed study of the oral traditions of the Chewa people of central Malawi. There was also the promise of a third post, the incumbent of which would specialise in some part of West Africa. There was therefore the clear prospect of an African history section within the history department that would stand alongside the existing sections concerned with the Middle East, South Asia, Southeast Asia, and the Far East. Thus far it was all very encouraging, but one could not but be aware of the yawning gap in scholarly achievement and literary output that still separated the study of African history from that of the Orient, where no one doubted the existence of high civilisations expressed in ancient literary languages that must obviously be worthy of scholarly study. Would-be historians of Africa had by contrast to face the open incredulity of nearly everyone they met about whether their whole endeavour could possibly be worthwhile.

What had Africa ever contributed to the world but servile labour? Was it not true that Africans had never invented even the wheel? What, in the memorable words of Hugh Trevor-Roper, could be the purpose of investigating "the meaningless gyrations of barbarous tribes in remote and irrelevant parts of the globe"?[1] By 1963, when the last phrase was uttered, the opinions it conveyed were beginning to be old hat, but in 1950 they were common currency among all but our closest colleagues.

Clearly, we had to begin by winning the trust of other historians and of these the nearest to us were those specialising in imperial and colonial history. It was therefore a piece of great good fortune that my return from Africa coincided with the move from Oxford to London of Keith Hancock as director of the newly founded Institute of Commonwealth Studies, situated just round the corner from SOAS in Russell Square. Hancock was by any standard a professional heavyweight—a fellow of All Souls who had held chairs in Adelaide, Birmingham, and Oxford and was soon to be knighted for his general editorship of the official series of civilian war histories, and he was at this time starting to work on his great biography of Jan Smuts. On my first day back at the school I had a message from him asking me to call, and there and then he invited me to become a regular member of the seminar he was inaugurating on the history of the tropical dependencies. From then on we met weekly on a professional basis, and later, when Caroline and I moved from Woughton to London, we were to become his neighbours in Newton Road, Bayswater, where Caroline became an intimate friend of his gifted and artistic wife Theaden. It was from Keith Hancock that I learned how to organise a seminar and how to work with postgraduate research students of many different nationalities. It was in his company that I began to be interested and involved in the politics of decolonisation in Africa. He read, and took an active interest in, all my early writings—something that cannot often be said of relations between older and younger colleagues. After his return to his native Australia in 1957 we corresponded regularly until his death in 1987. Whenever he visited England, he stayed a few nights with us, and then we would talk with scarcely a pause for eighteen hours a day.

Hancock's seminar in its early days included among its staff members Jack Fisher, the brilliant economic historian from the London School of Economics, and Fisher's economist colleague, R. A. Knox, who later went to the International Monetary Fund; John Barnes, an anthropologist with historical interests, recently returned from field studies among the Angoni of Malawi, who was later to hold chairs in Sydney and Cambridge; Kenneth Kirkwood, then a visiting fellow from the University of Natal and soon to be appointed the first Rhodes Professor of Race Relations at Oxford; and Alison Smith, the research officer of the institute who, although she never held a teaching post, was to become a major contributor to many African publications, including especially the *Oxford History of East Africa*. Among the research students who attended were the first two African scholars to become professional historians of their continent, Kenneth Dike and Saburi Biobaku. Both were Nigerians and students of Gerald Graham, the Rhodes Professor of Imperial History at King's College. Dike, I think, was on the point of finishing his thesis, *Trade and Politics in the Niger Delta*, and made only occasional appearances before returning to take up a post at the University College of Ibadan, where he was eventually to become the first professor of history and later the first African vice chancellor. Biobaku, however, was around for longer, working at a thesis, *The Egba and Their Neighbours*, which was to lead him to the directorship of the Yoruba Historical Research Project and eventually to the vice chancellorship of Lagos University.

Besides these, there were two or three research students from the Caribbean, but it was essentially an Africanist group, and together we examined some of the problems involved in setting up colonial adminis-trations in tropical Africa during the late nineteenth and early twentieth centuries. We looked at the initial lack of local revenues and the rapid rise and slow fall of imperial grants-in-aid, which were finally eliminated only about 1914. We marvelled at the tiny cadres of colonial officials, which were all that could be afforded until they could be supported out of local revenues. We studied the introduction of economic crops and the slow development of roads, railways, harbours, and inland waterways, without which there could be no access to international markets and no significant increase of taxable wealth. We measured the costs of military activity, which ate up so much of the initial grants-in-aid, but we did not perhaps spend as much time as we should have on the actual nature of military operations, which contemporaries described as "pacification," whereas later generations saw them only as "warfare" and "conquest." We cer-tainly did not give enough attention to the ways in which early colonial administrations obtained their supplies of local labour—by conscription, tribute labour, and winking at the continuance of local systems of slavery so long as part of it contributed to serving colonial needs. But at least we taught ourselves enough to realise that a real, if still somewhat fuzzy, distinction could be drawn between the traditional interests of colonial history and the history of the African peoples during the colonial period. I found my experience with the local archives in East Africa was much in demand, and I gained greatly from the opportunity to compare notes with those who knew parts of western and southern Africa at first hand.

At SOAS Robert Hamilton and I tried to build a corresponding group of those with marginal interests in precolonial history. Diccon Hunt-ingford, who had been transferred to our newly created department of cultural anthropology, was now devoting his time increasingly to Ethiopia

140

and produced a series of papers on the Oromo and Sidama states to the southwest of the Christian empire, where he sought to locate the origins of the state systems of eastern and southern Africa. Anthony Arkell, who had recently retired from his post as commissioner for archaeology in the Sudan and was now curator of the Flinders Petrie Collection at University College, was an early and enthusiastic member. He too was interested in the diffusion of kingship systems, in this case running westwards from the pre-Christian kingdom of Meroe through Darfur to the interior of West Africa. Then there was the singular and engaging Father A. M. Jones, an ex-missionary linguist and musicologist who had discovered that many peoples of both eastern and western tropical Africa shared with many peoples of Southeast Asia the practice of singing in thirds. The same peoples on both sides of the Indian Ocean also made and used xylophones, while those who lived near the seacoast often built seagoing canoes equipped with outriggers. Because it was indisputable that the indigenous languages of Madagascar belonged to the Malayo-Polynesian family, Father Jones was led to postulate a long line of seaborne diffusion that started in Borneo and led first to the eastern coast of Africa and then proceeded round the Cape of Good Hope to the Bight of Benin. Soon, the banana, Asian yam, and the disease commonly known as elephantiasis were added to the list of common traits linking the two sides of the Indian Ocean, and we were faced, as some of our more light-hearted members put it, with the picture of Sea Dayaks from Borneo sailing across the Indian Ocean in their outrigger canoes, munching their yams and bananas at mealtimes, and in the intervals playing their xylophones and singing in thirds, while dangling their elephantiasis-ridden legs in the water to assuage the pain.

Such highlights apart, we settled down to the long slog of reading, digesting, and summarising, region by region, the ethnographic literature of Africa for what it might have to teach us. Here we might have expected to get some help from the social anthropologists who enjoyed a near monopoly in African studies at the time, but in fact we got little. I wrote to Daryll Forde, the director of the International African Institute, to ask whether either he or any of his colleagues at University College would join in our efforts and received a reply in which he expressed sympathy for the predicament of those who were employed to teach a subject in which they had no competence. Only much later did we become good friends. Again, I was invited to give a lecture at the Royal Anthropological Institute on the traditional history of Bunyoro, Buganda, and Ankole, after which Raymond Firth of the London School of Economics made a statement from the chair to the effect that I had given yet another example of the naïveté of historians in giving credence to the traditions of neighbouring peoples on the ground that they appeared to corroborate each other. Social anthropologists, he said, knew well that king lists and dynastic genealogies claimed in oral tradition were merely expressions of the social organisation of the peoples concerned. After that experience I treated social anthropologists with circumspection.

In a way, the most significant event of my first year back in England was the renewal of my hitherto slight acquaintance with John Fage. We were put in touch again by a director of Longman, C. S. S. Higham, who had been handling my missionary book and who was already on the lookout for a pair of authors to write a general textbook on the history of Africa. Fage was at this time teaching history at the recently founded University College of the Gold Coast, and during the long vacation of 1951 he came to stay with us at Woughton so that we could discuss the matter at leisure. I still have the draft synopsis we sent to Higham in September and about which we corresponded actively for more than a year, and in retrospect I can feel nothing but relief that it was overtaken by more pressing commitments on both sides. Although I had by this time reached a stage at which I could have planned a history of Uganda that was not too Eurocentric in conception, our attempt to see things on a continental scale was still helplessly dependent on external influences and frames of reference. In the event, it was nearly ten years later, when we were working together at SOAS, that the project reemerged in a much more satisfactory form as the Penguin *Short History of Africa*.

Meanwhile, however, my meetings with John Fage in 1951–52 had one important by-product—we conceived of convening a conference on African history and archaeology at which the teachers of history in the African university colleges could meet, while on summer leave from their posts, with those in Europe who had some close interest in the subject. The organisation of it naturally fell to me, and in September 1952 I wrote to sound out the departments at Achimota, Fourah Bay, Ibadan, Khartoum, and Makerere. That brought us our first fifteen acceptances. Then, in the absence of any comparable institutions in French tropical Africa, I wrote to Théodore Monod, who directed the scientific research organisation called the Institut Français d'Afrique Noire (IFAN) in Dakar. Monod accepted for himself and for the head of his archaeological section, Raymond Mauny, who was then just completing his great monograph on the historical geography of West Africa. Mauny was learned, enthusiastic, and bilingual, and he was to be a great ally in the years ahead. A search for further archaeologists brought me to A. W. Lawrence, who had a chair at Achimota and researched on the trade castles of West Africa; Keith Murray, the director of antiquities in Nigeria; Bill Fagg of the British Museum; the veteran scholar Gertrude Caton-Thompson, who had excavated the Desert Fayum in the 1920s and Great Zimbabwe in the 1930s; O. G. S. Crawford, the editor of *Antiquity* who had worked much in the Sudan; Gervase Mathew, the Dominican polymath from Blackfriars, Oxford. Through Mathew I came to know Mortimer Wheeler, the former director general of antiquities in India, at this time secretary of the British Academy and already well known at every British fireside for the genius he displayed almost weekly in an early television parlour game called *Animal, Vegetable, Mineral.* As the list lengthened, the historians began to look like the babes in this wood. Most were still in their twenties with their reputations still to make. But they included four of the eight volume editors of the future *Cambridge History of Africa,* ten future incumbents of history chairs at British and African universities, and— wonder of wonders—three African members, all of whom rose to be vice chancellors of universities in their countries.

The preparatory work for the conference was in large measure done in my seminar, which had by this time been strengthened by the recruitment of a third member of staff in the person of Douglas Jones, who came to us from the University of Liverpool in the autumn of 1952 to be our specialist in West African history. Our seminar produced succinct regional surveys, first of the extent to which the oral traditions of African peoples had been recorded by literate observers during the period of European contact, and next of the known sites of archaeological interest that might be used to extend and complement the oral evidence. All this material was circulated to conference members in advance, and our hope was that they would add to it in discussion but, even more, that those engaged in teaching history in Africa would be made aware of the resources that existed. I find that even after the passage of some forty-five years it reads pretty well. In our commentaries we made many of the essential points. First and foremost, that oral traditions were almost never to be seen as the traditions of entire peoples but rather of ruling groups and others interested in the preservation of special rights and privileges. Second, that traditions of migration were seldom to be interpreted as mass movements of entire peoples over long distances but more often as the local interchange of minority groups, either as conquerors or a refugees, in which those who moved usually lost their original language and learned that of those among whom they settled. Third, that even in the most favourable circumstances traditions could not be much older than the ruling groups that propagated them, and that by and large a period of about twenty generations was about the limit of the historical depth that could be reached by this means. In most areas the period of remembered history was much shorter, but even in the least favourable conditions the approach through oral tradition could make possible a more Afrocentric perspective than that which began with the records of exploration by outsiders.

Our archaeological summaries were, surprisingly enough, far more tentative than their historical counterparts, and one has to remember that in 1953 carbon dating was still so much in its infancy that the only reference to it came from Gertrude Caton-Thompson, who reported an obviously erroneous date of 600 A.D. for a wooden beam from the Elliptical Temple at Great Zimbabwe. We had, as a matter of policy, deliberately excluded the Stone Age from our purview, and what would today be called the Early Iron Age was then little known, if only for the lack of any valid dating method applicable to simple single-level occupation sites. Conference communications therefore concentrated on the later Iron Age sites that were presumed to belong to present-millennium—sites such as Koumbi Saleh in southern Mauritania, the supposed site of the capital of the medieval kingdom of Ghana, that had been excavated by Mauny and his colleagues over three seasons between 1949 and 1951; Ife and Benin, neither of which had as yet been extensively excavated but were known to have produced sculptures, some of them in bronze, which implied the existence of a high culture in the area; the Sudan, where Arkell drew attention to the need for much more excavation at Meroe and the sites of Christian Nubia; the stone harbour towns of the Indian Ocean coast, where it was hoped that the existence of datable imports, such as Islamic and Chinese pottery and glass beads from western India, would one day provide the means of dating interior sites also, as indeed they were beginning to do at Zimbabwe and elsewhere in Southern Rhodesia. Perhaps our aim was best of all expressed in a note by Gervase Mathew on the group of earthwork sites in western Uganda, headed by Bigo and Ntusi, which were associated in traditional history with the Chwezi dynasty; here was a clear example of where archaeology could be used as a control on the evidence from tradition—a control that in the course of the next forty years was to carry the later Iron Age history of that area back to the tenth century A.D.[2]

As preparations for the conference went on, I came to know Gervase Mathew really well and to look to him for many different kinds of help. Gervase travelled through the world in a rumpled black suit, with an egg-stained shirtfront and an ancient haversack on his back. "That man a priest!," said Mrs. O'Reilly incredulously when he dropped in to lunch with us one day at Woughton. She was indeed so overcome that she bicycled into Fenny Stratford to consult her spiritual advisor, only to be told that, regrettable though it might be, members of the mendicant orders enjoyed a certain licence in sartorial matters. But the Mathew clan was large and well connected, and Gervase seemed to have entrée to every Government House in the empire and to be on a first-name basis with their incumbents. Whatever the problem, he always seemed to know someone who could help. One really fruitful idea, the realisation of which I was to be concerned with through the rest of my professional life, was that of the need for a research institute on the lines of the British

With Caroline and Sarah, 1953

Academy's "schools" in Rome, Athens, Ankara, and Jerusalem that could act as a centre of initiative and a place of training for a new generation of scholars concerned with the borderline between precolonial history and archaeology. It was an idea that Mortimer Wheeler, as secretary of the academy, was peculiarly well placed to further, and the three of us agreed that at the final session of the conference Wheeler would propose it as a formal resolution. In the event, it took five years to bring the British School of History and Archeology in East Africa (later the British Institute in Eastern Africa) into existence, but the place of its conception was certainly Gervase's fertile mind.

Again, it was Gervase who introduced me to Oliver Woods, the long-standing and highly respected colonial correspondent of the London *Times*. Oliver, like Gervase, patrolled the Government Houses of Africa, whose occupants well understood that his despatches would be read with attention in Westminster and Whitehall and took trouble to see that he had access to the best information about their territories. He proved a ready and accurate listener to our story, and on the final day of the 1953 conference he treated us to an editorial titled "Africa's Past," in which he noted that archaeologists and historians from many parts of Africa south of the Sahara, including the French territories, had been meeting at the School of Oriental and African Studies in London to pool their knowledge. "Their discussions," he wrote, "raise the question whether the sombre picture of darkness and ignorance pervading the African continent before the coming of the white man is not largely due to our own failure to unearth the past."[3] With rare understanding he commented that it was not the more publicised examples of relics, such as the stone buildings at Zimbabwe or the plastic art of Nigeria, that seemed the most significant but rather "the impression that these finds were largely fortuitous and that the surface of Africa is still barely scratched in the attempt to reconstruct its history." He referred to the young historians from the university colleges in Africa who would be returning with added interest in the local histories of the territories in which they worked. "The immediate need," he concluded, "is to prevent destruction of existing sources and to speed up research."[4] For me, to read all this in such a public place was indeed to feel that my subject was at last on the map.

13

The Political Kingdom
(1953–55)

It was one of the happiest privileges of my career as a university teacher that during my first ten years I had only graduate students, and all were working for research degrees. In those days research students in most branches of history were rather rare creatures, and their supervision tended to be the jealously guarded monopoly of the senior professors. My first research student came to me when I was twenty-eight, in the person of Richard Gray, who arrived from Cambridge in 1951. Later, after working for some years in Central Africa and the Sudan, he was to be my colleague for a quarter of a century and eventually my successor as professor of African history at the University of London. He was joined the following year by John Flint, Ruth Slade, and Marie de Kiewiet. In 1953 I took on my first African research student, Ade Aderibigbe, a Nigerian who had courageously obtained his first degree at Birkbeck College while working night shifts in the post office. He was to teach African history for many years at the universities of Ibadan and Lagos, where he also became deputy vice chancellor.

This was already an interesting circle, and it was much enlarged and enriched when, that autumn, Gerald Graham went as visiting professor to the Gold Coast, leaving me the care of his imperial history seminar at King's. This brought me into touch immediately with the brilliant Nigerian Jacob Ajayi and in succeeding years with several more of his countrymen, like Emanuel Ayandele, Christopher Ifemesia, Ibaro Ikime, and Takuna Tamuno, all students of Graham's at King's but who came to me regularly for advice. It meant that I was able to reorganise the work of my seminar, so that, instead of being a discussion group for colleagues with a marginal interest in African history, it became a place of training for future teachers of the subject in most of the emerging universities of English-speaking tropical Africa. From 1956, with the arrival of Adu Boahen, directed to

147

us by John Fage from Achimota, there began to be a regular flow of students who had taken their first degrees at one or other of the African university colleges in West and East Africa.

The first and most serious duty of supervisors is to help their clients find the right topics for their research. Supervisors have to think not only in terms of what will make good training but also of what most needs to be done to fill the gaps in existing knowledge. They also have to carry the consent of their colleagues and especially of their senior colleagues. At London University, when I started out as a research supervisor, there was a board of studies in history and within it a higher degrees subcommittee, composed of the heads of history departments in all the different colleges and a few other senior people. Most were specialists in the history of England or some part of Western Europe. A few represented ancient history or American or colonial history. Cyril Philips spoke for the whole of Asia and Africa. The chair was Lillian Penson, who was also the vice chancellor of the university, probably the most formidable personality with whom it has ever been my lot to deal. She was a diplomatic historian who had once revised the celebrated textbook by A. J. Grant and Harold Temperley, *Europe in the Nineteenth and Twentieth Centuries* (1927, 1940). She was also on the governing councils of several African university colleges. So she reckoned to know about Africa, and it was to her committee that I had to bring detailed information about the qualifications of the research students I had accepted and my proposals for their thesis topics.

It would not have been politic for a newly recognised teacher to bring avant-garde proposals to Lillian Penson's committee, but as a matter of fact I was in no hurry to do so. Our early research students were feeling their way into the subject, much as I had done. We had no funds with which to send them to Africa, and their three-year grants did not allow them enough time to learn and use an African language. They were looking for topics that could be opened up from sources in Europe. It was obvious to them, as it was to me, that the main mines to be worked, but always with a view to the African history that could be extracted from them, were the archives of those missionary societies that had been operating in Africa in precolonial times and the official diplomatic archives arising from the consulates scattered around the coasts of Africa during the period of transition from the slave trade to legitimate commerce. Richard Gray, in his 1961 *History of the Southern Sudan 1830–1880*, which quickly became a standard work, was an admirable pioneer in demonstrating how much truly African history could be distilled from the correspondence of the consuls in Cairo and Khartoum, and that of the Verona Fathers, who settled on the upper Nile from the 1840s on. Ruth Slade worked on the records of the Baptist Missionary Society, whose agents had been on the Cameroon coast since 1852 and on the Congo since 1877.[1] Flint was interested in the origins of the Royal Niger Company and therefore in the local operations of the older West African trading companies from which it had been pieced together by George Goldie. This situation was best studied in the correspondence of the Oil Rivers consulate at Old Calabar.[2] Ajayi and Aderibigbe worked on the archives of the Church Missionary Society and those of the colonial administration in Lagos but very much with an eye to what they had to tell about trade, diplomacy, and warfare among the southern Yoruba during the nineteenth century. Adu Boahen addressed the archives of the British consulates in Tripoli and Tunis and in 1964 produced an outstanding book, *Britain, the Sahara, and the Western Sudan, 1788–1869*, centring upon the caravan trade of the central Sahara in the early nineteenth century.

Such was the institutional background to my decision in the summer of 1953 to take as the subject of my second book the life of the explorer, painter, naturalist, linguist, consul, and pioneer colonial administrator Harry Johnston, who had lived and worked in so many different parts of tropical Africa during the 1880s and 1890s and had regarded them all with the eyes of an artist and a scientist as well as of a man of action. He had been in Tunis during the preparations for the French occupation. He had travelled widely in Angola and the Congo just as Stanley was laying the foundations of King Leopold's private colony. He had lived as a naturalist in the still independent Chagga kingdoms of Kilimanjaro and travelled as a vice consul among the stateless people of the Cross River in southeastern Nigeria. He had brought Cecil Rhodes into touch with Lord Salisbury and had carried out the treaty making on which British claims to Northern Rhodesia (Zambia) and Nyasaland (Malawi) were based. He had established the protectorate government of Nyasaland and reorganized that of Uganda, and during a long retirement he had continued with his scholarly work, culminating in his 1919–1922 *Comparative Study of the Bantu and Semi-Bantu Languages* in which he presented and analysed vocabularies drawn from some three hundred languages, many of which he collected.

Sir Harry Johnston and the Scramble for Africa (1957) was not a magnum opus. It was completed in little more than two years during the intervals of my other work. Its great merit for me was that it took me to the same archives and private collections as my research students and enabled me to help them more effectively while spotting openings for their successors. It taught me a great deal about the inner workings of the Foreign Office during the later nineteenth century, and it brought me close to the mind of Lord Salisbury during his great period as prime minister and foreign secretary. It did not bring me much closer to African history, unless perhaps in teaching me about the problems of power in early colonial situations, when 150 trained soldiers were deemed sufficient to control populations of two or three million among whom the use of firearms was already widespread. It made me realise how much of early colonial government was a matter of nods, winks, deals, and alliances and therefore how much continuity there was between precolonial and early colonial times. The extensive use of force by colonial governments in general came much later on, when colonial power had built up and when demands for taxes and labour had presented Africans with something more concrete to resist.

With Johnston himself I managed to maintain a decently respectful relationship. When I told Margery Perham, who was then engaged in her fifteen-year task with the biography of Frederick Lugard, what I was doing, she said, "What, *that* little man—I can't think how you could!" But two years later, when she had read what I had written, her comment was, "At least, *your* little man, unlike *my* little man, was never a bore." There was some truth in both judgments. There was a sense in which Johnston was not quite trustworthy. I checked his book on the Kilimanjaro expedition carefully against his private diary for that period, and it was obvious that events reported in the diary as trivial had been greatly embroidered for the purposes of publication. His much younger brother, Alex Johnston, who worked as his private secretary from 1898 until 1909 and wrote the first biography of him after his death, once said to me, "If Harry saw a blue flower somewhere, it was likely to appear in published form as 'a lake of blue.'" And it was not just a matter of hyperbole. There was a preparedness to deceive, which showed itself, for example, in his kidnapping of a Niger Delta ruler, Jaja of Opobo, to whom it would appear he had actually offered safe conduct, an action that in Salisbury's judgment "could not be defended according to European standards of honour." It may be too that in Johnston's eagerness to make Central Africa British, he may have made promises to Cecil Rhodes and grants of land to the British South Africa Company that went further than he was prepared to confess to the imperial government. If so, his defence would surely have been "Better Rhodes than the Portuguese," and it would have been an honest statement of his motives. There is not a shred of evidence that Johnston was financially corrupted by Rhodes, and once freed from Rhodes as a paymaster Johnston developed a concept of protectorate government that reflected a very different outlook on the future of the African peoples. With his naturalist's eye he was better able to foresee the economic development of the African peasantry that would become possible with the advent of mechanical transport, and there was a place in his thinking for the educated Africans that they were denied in Lugard's alternative system. Altogether I thoroughly enjoyed the two years I spent in his company.

It stands out clearly from my records that 1953, when I began to work on Johnston, was also the year in which Caroline and I began to be seriously involved in current African affairs. Up until this point, while keeping our eyes open, we had taken the political environment in which I had to do my academic work rather for granted. While I was still a postgraduate student, we had watched the transfer of power in British India without any conscious realisation that it would carry nearly immediate implications for Africa. From 1948 onwards we had watched South Africa starting to turn the clock back but had read it as nothing more than the final victory of Afrikaners over South Africans of British descent. We knew that on the Gold Coast comparatively minor disturbances had led to the granting of representative institutions, with the promise of eventual self-government to follow after a period of tutelage of undecided duration. We knew that what happened on the Gold Coast would have to happen in Nigeria also as soon as the interregional tensions there could be brought under constitutional control. But West Africa was a long way from East Africa, both geographically and in terms of economic and educational progress, and the East Africa we had seen during a year of intensive travel had not seemed either ready or even eager to rule itself. As educators we tended to measure things by our own standards. We knew that in West Africa there were already thousands of graduates, whereas in East Africa there were fewer than one hundred. In Uganda, the most advanced of the East African territories educationally, there were still only eight full secondary schools. It never occurred to us that independence movements could be launched and countries ruled by leaders with little more than primary education. Therefore we did not worry about how soon independence would come to Africa, so long as the course remained firmly set in that direction, and in East Africa, as in West Africa, we were confident that it was.

Into this comfortable scenario there burst, in the autumn of 1952, the news of a revolution in Kenya grave enough to require the declaration of a state of emergency and the despatch of British troops to reinforce the local garrison. Here, so it seemed at the time, was a situation comparable with that in Malaya, with guerrilla bands operating out of impenetrable forest bases tacitly supported by some civilian populations and terrorising the remainder into a reluctant acquiescence. The Malayan emergency had already lasted four years, tying down some forty thousand Commonwealth troops and a sizable proportion of the British strategic reserve forces. One had to wonder how many more such situations it would take to put an end to imperial power the world over. One had also to wonder what a successful military suppression would do to colonial policy, not just in Kenya but right down the eastern side of Africa.

Significantly, it was at this moment that the British government announced that it intended to proceed with a long-discussed plan to federate the two protectorates of Nyasaland and Northern Rhodesia, governed

151

hitherto through the Colonial Office, with Southern Rhodesia, where a small but rapidly growing white minority had enjoyed practical self-government since 1923. It was clear from missionary sources, no less than from the statements of the politically conscious local elites, that African opinion in the two northern territories was totally opposed to the scheme, but few people in England at the time seemed to think that Africans were capable of having a valid opinion on such a matter. There was much talk of trustees having to do what was best for their wards, alongside much more talk of creating bastions of British strength in Central Africa. I am interested to see from my surviving papers that this was the first issue on which I tried to exert some tiny speck of political influence, by writing to my old friend from Bedford and Bletchley, Edward Boyle, now a young and highly esteemed Conservative member of Parliament. I told him my conclusion that the proposed safeguards for African interests, though they might prevent actual regress, could do nothing to guarantee "the very rapid progress in the status and opportunities of Africans which . . . seems to offer the only hope of avoiding a cataclysm in both East and Central Africa in the near future." It is obvious that I was much influenced by the situation in Kenya, for I concluded that one did not need to be an expert to imagine what sort of a bastion Kenya would be if we removed the Lancashire Fusiliers. One result of the correspondence was that Caroline and I sat right through the parliamentary debates on the federation in March and April 1953. In the House of Commons we were much struck by the rows of empty benches from which the trustees were exercising their powers of decision in the best interests of their wards. The House of Lords debate, which lasted through two full days, was a much better-attended and more impressive affair. My principal memories of these debates are of how the archbishop of Canterbury, Geoffrey Fisher, visibly influenced the doubters with a brilliant presentation of his early hesitations about the scheme and how they had been overcome, while Lord Hailey, the great official expert on colonial government in Africa, was singularly ineffective in trying to explain his waverings in the opposite direction.

It was, however, in late November of 1953 that we were thrust into deep involvement with a political situation in Uganda, when we read in our morning newspaper that the kabaka of Buganda had been summarily arrested at Government House, Entebbe, following an interview with the governor, Andrew Cohen, and that the kabaka had been driven straight to the airport and put on the next plane to London without even the opportunity to go home and pack. We did not at that time know Cohen personally, but we had friends in common, and everything we knew about him thus far had predisposed us in his favour. In his previous position as head of the African department of the Colonial Office he had been associated with the first moves towards decolonisation in West Africa, and when appointed to Uganda in 1952 he had made it clear that he also intended to take that country a big step in the same direction. He had been active in promoting economic development and in trying to ensure that there would be enough educated Ugandans to fill most managerial posts. He was above all concerned to see Africans participating in the central government of the country, and the great problem here was to secure an equitable representation of the different regions, which had been so unequally developed in the past. The natural opponents of such a levelling policy were the Ganda, who, as both the largest ethnic group and the most centrally placed, had enjoyed the first bite of every kind of modernisation introduced during the colonial period and therefore had the most to lose. Relying on the treaty signed with Buganda by Harry Johnston in 1900, Cohen had required the kabaka to support his policy. The kabaka, facing the certain wrath of his people, had refused his assistance and so had incurred the deportation. It was clearly a tragic situation but, at least as we first saw it, no more than that of any other public official who must obey orders or face dismissal.

Very quickly, however, we learned that this was not how the event was seen in Buganda. We had some contacts among Ganda students in England, and before long they were writing to us to express their feelings of personal insecurity as members of a society that had lost its king. In a matter of two or three weeks a delegation from the Lukiko, the parliament of Buganda, had arrived in London and went at once to seek the advice of Simon Stuart, now retired from his Uganda diocese and living as a canon and assistant bishop in Worcester. Simon took the delegates to the archbishop who, having earlier that year presided at the coronation of Queen Elizabeth II, was quicker than most to see that

> Not all the water in the rough, rude sea
> Can wash the balm off from an anointed king.[3]

He promised his help on condition that, if Mutesa's return could be secured, the Lukiko would respond by cooperating with the governor's policy for the country as a whole. Unfortunately, such a simple solution was made impossible because of the number of times on which both Cohen in Uganda, and the colonial secretary, Oliver Lyttelton, in London had publicly announced that their decision to withdraw recognition from Mutesa was final and irrevocable. News was filtering through that Cohen's preferred solution was to secure the election of a new and more amenable kabaka, but the effect of this news was to unite the Ganda against him and to bring about the first serious talk of violent resistance.

Meanwhile, the delegation from the Lukiko remained in England and tried to take its message to a wider audience. Sometime in January 1954

Caroline and I attended a meeting arranged by the Fabian Colonial Bureau in a committee room at the House of Lords, to which the delegation would present its case. A large and distinguished gathering assembled and ten minutes after the appointed time for the meeting was showing signs of restiveness. Suddenly, the delegates entered at a run, removing hats and mackintoshes as they came panting to the rostrum.

Ladies and gentlemen, we are so very sorry to keep you waiting, but we have been listening to the wireless, and we have heard the most terrible news that the governor of Uganda, Sir Andrew Cohen, has been kidnapped, and that he is now a prisoner, and that he is thought to be in a canoe, in which he is being conveyed to the Sese Islands, in the middle of Lake Victoria. Ladies and gentlemen, we are so very sorry to be the bearers of such grave tidings.

It was beautifully done, by our friend from Namirembe days (see Chapter 7), Tom Makumbi. The distinguished audience was visibly shaken. Members of Parliament were rushing to the doors to get the news to their colleagues around the building. Journalists were scribbling their reports, while they waited for more details. At last there came, in the dry voice of Lucy Mair, a professor of social anthropology at the London School of Economics, "*What* wireless?," at which Tom Makumbi let down the pressure, saying, "Well, ladies and gentlemen, we have tried to give you a practical demonstration of how the people of Buganda felt when they heard that you had deported our kabaka."

On a more sombre level Max Warren, general secretary of the Church Missionary Society, was consulting me about letters received from John Taylor, the principal of Mukono Theological College who was reckoned to have closer contacts with the Ganda than any other member of the mission. Taylor's message was that, although British administrators might think that monarchy was an institution that they understood, the Buganda model in fact bore a closer resemblance to that of King David than that of Queen Elizabeth. He wrote,

I think it true, that the Kabaka is still the great husband-figure to nearly all the women here, and one might almost say that from him all husbandhood derives. . . . So also every man feels that emotionally his authority in his home, and to a lesser degree in other spheres, derives from the person of the Kabaka. . . . In Buganda I doubt if there are a score of Africans who have really lost hope that the Kabaka will be restored to them. That is the gist of their prayers in the Churches.

It seemed increasingly clear that, whatever one's general sympathy for Cohen in his desire to build a united country, any constructive settlement of the crisis would have somehow to include a restoration of Kabaka Mutesa.

154

Just at this time all roads seemed to lead me back to the affairs of Uganda. I have a note that on February 23 I went to see Keith Hancock, who told me that Andrew Cohen, who was in England for consultations, had invited him officially, through Oliver Lyttelton, to spend three months in Uganda as a special commissioner to examine the constitutional relations between the protectorate government and that of Buganda and to make recommendations for a revision of the agreement of 1900. He said that the restoration of Mutesa was to be specifically excluded from his negotiations and that all those whom he had consulted so far had advised him that this need be no bar to the success of his mission. What did I think? I replied that I thought it would be impossible to separate the constitutional questions from that of Mutesa. I said that the concession needed was not great, that it was probably only necessary that a door should be left open for Mutesa's return after the end of Cohen's term of office, but that without this measure of concession it was difficult to see how any Ganda negotiators would be able to hold their constituency to the terms of a revised agreement. Keith then said that before giving Lyttelton his decision, he would like to meet the members of the Lukiko delegation—could I somehow arrange for this without disclosing the precise reason for the meeting? As I knew two of the delegates personally, I agreed to try.

As a result, I spent an interesting morning at the Strand Palace Hotel, where the delegates were staying. They knew nothing of Hancock, but they agreed to meet him, and I then asked them how they assessed the chances for their mission to London. They spoke of the possibility that a violent situation could develop but were confident that it could be avoided, providing only that a way existed for the kabaka's ultimate return. They were quite prepared to think that this might be postponed until after Cohen's retirement and that it might be to a scene that had been radically transformed in the direction of a constitutional monarchy. I then returned to Hancock and told him that, were I in his position, I would accept only if the government would give an assurance, however privately and confidentially, that it did not regard Mutesa's future as absolutely settled. Next day he told me that he had seen Cohen and extracted a promise that, as a last resort, at the conclusion of his negotiations and not before, he would be free to make a recommendation one way or the other respecting the kabaka's return. I felt that in a small way I had helped to make history.

Keith Hancock's departure for Uganda was scheduled for late June, and during the intervening months some of us who were close to him used to join in the briefing meetings he held with officials from the African department of the Colonial office. These were always based around a constantly lengthening document called "The Buganda Querist" in which he formulated questions concerning the constitutions of the Buganda kingdom and of the protectorate government that he would need to discuss with the representatives of each during his stay there. I seem to remember that in its final state the list had 243 entries. What we all came to realise, as the briefing went on, was that the only way to allay the fears of the Ganda about the fuller incorporation of their government into that of the country as a whole was by offering them a more assured representation in the larger body and one measured not just in votes but in official positions within the hierarchy. We were in fact talking about a situation in which self-government lay just around the corner. This was a surprise to all of us, the Colonial Office men included, and it led to some quite rough exchanges. "But Professor Hancock," one of them would say, "There just aren't any Ugandans as yet who are ready to be ministers." And Hancock would look at him over the top of his spectacles and reply, "Well, I don't know about that. I spent this morning talking to a young man whom I thought would make an admirable minister unless, of course, you gentlemen were to put him in prison, in which case he would probably be *prime* minister." In the event as we would all learn, the real problem would not be the shortage of suitable ministers but the almost total lack of junior officers, both civil and military, who were trained and ready to become senior officers and, even more, in the private sector of junior executives ready to become senior executives.

As the time for his departure drew nearer Keith Hancock became increasingly concerned about the problems of maintaining a publicly neutral stance between the Lukiko and the colonial government. I think it was I who suggested that Namirembe Hill might be the best location for the discussions, and the new bishop, Leslie Brown, went further by offering full accommodation for the Hancocks and their staff in a separate building in his compound. Again, sometime in May Keith asked me if I could write something for the British press that would stress his role as mediator between two governments rather than the temporary employee of one of them. In journalistic terms it would have to be a send-off article, published on or near the date of his departure, and one that explained to a wide audience the broad reasons for his mission, which had hitherto received little publicity, mainly because of Andrew Cohen's excellent relations with the British press. In what I wrote I dwelt first upon the constitutional changes necessary to protect traditional rulers in African countries from the impact of democracy in local government, which was bound to mean that they were exposed to conflicting pressures from below and above. I went on to say that with foresight, such changes should be capable of peaceful resolution but that in the case of Buganda they were having to be tackled against the background of a crisis of confidence of quite unforeseen proportions arising from the deposition of the kabaka. I tried to express the sanctity of the kabakaship in the eyes of the Ganda and suggested that the deposition was the first event in their history that had brought home to them the fact that they were a conquered people. In the belief of most Ganda the agreement of 1900 had established them as the allies of the British in ruling the rest of the protectorate. Now they had been subjected to a cruel national humiliation, just as though the colonel had arrested the adjutant on the paradeground in front of all the troops. Hence the need for a mediator to help set right the damage and to clear minds sufficiently to prevent a recurrence in other parts of East and Central Africa.

I sent my article to the *Observer*, which was then edited by David Astor, who returned it to me with the remarkably disinterested advice that, because it was clearly politics rather than journalism, it would carry more weight in the London *Times* than in his paper. I therefore went with it to Oliver Woods, who had been so helpful with my conference, and on June 18 it appeared as an opinion piece on the editorial pages and was followed next day by an editorial written in sufficiently forthright terms to warn the governor that he could no longer count on the unquestioning support of the British press. The article brought me an interesting batch of mail, the most surprising component of which was a letter of five closely typed pages from Andrew Cohen, who had sent a copy to Oliver Woods. Though not actually hostile in tone, it was highly defensive and based on an extraordinary misreading of what I had written. It gave me the opportunity for an equally full reply in which I was able to show plenty of sympathy for his predicament but also to conclude that perhaps by deporting Mutesa he had unwittingly applied the one shock powerful enough to winkle the Ganda out of their comfortable tribalism and also had given himself a lever, by agreeing to let bygones be bygones, to induce them to cross the bridge from the medieval to the modern world. I said I felt sure that, if he would only use it, the weight of public opinion in England would only applaud his magnanimity. While not addressing this particular sentence, he wrote again in markedly more friendly style, looking forward to a meeting when opportunity offered.

My Buganda file goes on through the rest of 1954. It gives interesting glimpses of the Hancock mission at work on Namirembe Hill, conducting what was in effect an extended seminar on the constitutional law and practice of plural societies, in which the pupils were twelve Ganda notables elected by the Lukiko and four senior officials of the protectorate government. Relations with Cohen were at first difficult but improved dramatically after he and Hancock took to meeting secretly for Sunday lunch at the country home of Hugh and Margaret Trowell, half-way between Kampala and Entebbe. By the third month of the mission Cohen had been won round enough to be prepared to see the constitutional proposals linked with the kabaka's return. There then remained the problem of persuading a new secretary of state, Alan Lennox Boyd, to reverse his predecessor's supposedly final decision. Lennox Boyd started from the position that, while a terrible mistake had been made in deposing the kabaka, what was done was done, and it took heavy pressure from the archbishop of Canterbury, and several highly charged meetings with Hancock after his return to England, to convince him that the constitutional reforms would create "a new situation" in which the kabaka could function as a traditional ruler without entering directly into relationships with the protectorate government. Thus the way was at last cleared for Mutesa to return to his kingdom in 1955 and so to emerge in 1964 as the first and, as it happened, the last constitutional president of an independent Uganda so far.

In June 1954 our friend Mary Stuart had reminded me of the don's prayer, "Lord, use me, if only in an advisory capacity," and in retrospect I think the cap fits. I did not enter into the affairs of Uganda out of a desire to meddle but only in response to the requests of people who consulted me. Mutesa, for example, could perfectly well have been one of them, but in fact he was not, and I took no steps to seek him out in his exile or to join the coterie of overt supporters that was flown out to celebrate his return. But I certainly enjoyed responding, both to Hancock and to my ecclesiastical contacts, like Max Warren and Leslie Brown, in whom I saw such a real and disinterested effort to see the truth and to work for it, and through whom I got ceaselessly fascinating glimpses of relationships at the level of governors, archbishops, and secretaries of state. For a working historian it made a priceless addition of relevant experience.

14

A Chair Declined
(1955–57)

During the spring of 1954 Caroline and I decided with infinite regret that we ought to dispose of the pretty cottage at Woughton-on-the-Green that we had rescued from ruin and had been our happy home for ten years. Sarah had reached school age. Caroline looked forward to pursuing her interests in a less sequestered environment. And I had a profession that was ramifying into a whole range of extracurricular activities and increasingly demanded a London base. Caroline did the hunting and came up with a solution we thought we could just afford, in Newton Road, W.2., a street of rather elegant small, very early Victorian houses in an otherwise insalubrious part of Bayswater, off Westbourne Grove. Our neighbours there were nearly all people of our own kind. The Hancocks we already knew. Daphne and Desmond Crawley, with their two children, came and went in between diplomatic postings to various Commonwealth capitals. John Scott, then the literary editor of the *Spectator*, lived there with his wife Helen and two boys of Sarah's age. Ronald Searle, the artist and children's author, lived and worked there with Kay, who ran the children's department of Penguin Books. Eldred Hitchcock, the sisal king of Tanganyika, owned two adjacent houses occupied by his wife and children, although during his almost fortnightly visits to London he was generally to be found in a suite at the Ritz. There was a village life for the adults and for the children a street gang that met after school hours on most days to play cricket against the lamp posts or to be drilled by Oliver Scott in preparation for raids planned against the children of Kildare Gardens, which fortunately were never executed.

Our house, Number 38, stood behind three lime trees, which gave us welcome privacy, though dropping copious libations of sticky resin on any motor car that ventured to park beneath them. Indoors it had a pair of rather handsome intercommunicating rooms on the main floor, with a

159

kitchen and playroom beneath and two and a half bedrooms above. As in so many other London houses of the same period a tiny bathroom had been built out over the backdoor when piped water became available, and gas fires had been installed in the bedrooms, but there were no radiators, and the main sitting-room was heated only by coal. By the time we had repaired the roof and the chimneystack and redecorated the interior, we were much too broke to undertake any further modernisation, so that our circumstances were at first almost as spartan, and certainly much more cramped, than they had been at Woughton. But the economy in travelling time was a great improvement, and in many ways London was much more habitable then than now. One could drive to the university, or the Public Record Office, or to a Pall Mall club and keep almost all of one's professional and social engagements quickly and comfortably without recourse to public transport. One could do many more things in the day. But the greatest of all the advantages of a base in central London was the ability to welcome our many friends from Africa and the professional colleagues from all over the world who were passing through England on visits too short to allow a trip to the country or even a trek to the suburbs. Caroline was the most informal of hostesses. She hated to send out written invitations or to pin people down in advance. But no one was ever readier to put away what she was doing to entertain a surprise visitor, whether known or unknown. It was how we made many of our best friends.

We moved to Newton Road in September 1954. At the university it was about the time when my work as a research supervisor was beginning to build up. Although I had now two colleagues, neither was as yet trained and ready to help. Robert Hamilton was between two yearlong spells of fieldwork among the Chewa, the ultimate outcome of which was to be his decision to seek another type of work as warden of a hall of residence at Makerere. Douglas Jones, who was to remain with us until his premature death in 1979 and who was to do distinguished work as a teacher of West African history, was still undergoing initiation with a year's secondment to John Fage's department at Achimota, followed by six months' fieldwork in northern Ghana.

At home I was spending every spare moment completing my life of Johnston, which was ready for the press early in 1956. I was also responding to a variety of calls that came my way, mostly without my seeking them. The close partnership I had built up with Max Warren over Buganda carried over into other problems. From Uganda the main focus of our mutual concern switched to Kenya, where the reports reaching him from missionaries in the field suggested that with violence among the Kikuyu increasingly under control, a heavy-handed colonial bureaucracy encouraged by the white settler lobby was misusing the army and the police to intimidate and brainwash large number of Kikuyu detainees held

160

in camps around the country. This was occurring at a time when policies of economic and political reconstruction should have been encouraging hope for the future rather than fear and hatred of the foreign rulers.

More generally, from his vantagepoint at the heart of a great missionary society, Max Warren saw more clearly than most people how rapidly decolonisation would come to Africa and how ill prepared the emerging African leadership of the churches would be to meet it. As early as 1953 he had involved me in a working party set up by the Christian Frontier Council under the chairmanship of Alec Vidler, the formidable editor of *Theology*, to study the problems of promoting a sense of political responsibility among Christians in Africa. Under the guise of seeking advice we tried to alert bishops and other missionary leaders in the field to the need for action in this area, and in 1955 an inner group sat down to plan the outlines of a short easily affordable paperback book. The author chosen was John Taylor, who had just returned from Uganda to become the Africa secretary of the CMS. It was published as a volume in the Pelican African series under the title *Christianity and Politics in Africa* (1957), and it presumably reached a wide audience.

I knew that Warren was regularly briefing the archbishop, who appears cryptically in our correspondence as "the South Bank."[1] On occasion he despatched me to the south bank—for the first time, when my friend Kesi Nganwa from Ankole, Uganda (see Chapter 8), recently elected first minister of his country, paid a visit to England and wished to impress upon the archbishop that his people were not yet ready to do without missionary help for their schools and churches. We drove into Lambeth Palace together and were shown into a drawing-room, where Geoffrey Fisher, who was inordinately proud of being the father of six sons, started by asking Kesi how many children he had. The reply was twelve. Fisher was visibly crestfallen and launched into a gale of flowery talk that allowed Kesi no possibility of making his point, and after an hour or so we withdrew with the promise that his chaplain would send a signed photograph. Altogether it seemed a sad encounter to have witnessed between an outstanding African Christian and the head of the Anglican communion.

The Suez crisis of 1956 was of course a landmark in the lives of nearly all the politically conscious people of my generation, but it had a special poignancy for those of us who were engaged in any kind of Asian or African studies. I must have discussed it almost daily among friends and colleagues at the school, but the best surviving record of my views at the time occurs in a long letter to Max Warren on December 8. He had, I knew, been up to the eyes in exercises of damage limitation among Christians in Egypt and Israel. I wrote to say that I thought we would all need to reassess our attitudes to the entire African situation in light of the public

161

humiliation inflicted on the two main colonial powers on the continent by one small newly independent African state. I suggested that the effect on emerging nationalism in Africa might well prove comparable to the effects on nationalism in Asia of the Japanese victory over Russia in 1905:

What we face, in fact, is a strengthening of nationalist sentiment, accompanied by a radical change in the calculation which every nationalist leader is always, consciously or sub-consciously, revising in his own mind, about the consequences of challenging established authority. To calculators all over Africa the facts of power will be seen quite differently as a result of the events of the last month. At least, so I think.

I went on to speculate on the likely course of events, stressing that we must think not in terms of what might happen in individual British territories but also on what might happen in French and Belgian possessions and the repercussions of that on the situation as a whole:

My own guess, for example, would be that the first big blow-up may be the extension of the nationalist struggle from French North Africa into French West and Equatorial Africa, both of which are predominantly Muslim and look constantly in the direction of Egypt. I also think it likely that we shall find the Belgian Congo figuring more prominently in the nationalist picture than it has done to date. And that would radically affect the situation in both East and Central Africa.

Turning specifically to East Africa, I said it was likely that Britain would now have to try to do in five years what it had hoped to do in fifteen and that even if the British government failed to see it that way, it was to be hoped that the churches would do so and make the necessary preparations.

I do not know whether my views ever penetrated to the "South Bank." I do know that they were sent *in extenso* to the Anglican bishops in Uganda and Kenya as well as to the CMS regional secretary. But I am not in the business of claiming influence, and my only reason for quoting the letter at such length is that the writing of it reflected one of those rare occasions of trying to look at a whole continent at a particular moment in time.

Among our most intimate visitors at Newton Road at this time was Michael Scott, the saintly founder of the Africa Bureau who at one time probably touched both of us more closely than anyone else we ever met during our married life. Although he later acquired a tiny flat somewhere in Hampstead, I do not think that at this period he even had a room he could call his own. He would turn up unannounced at ten or eleven in the evening, and when we had talked for a couple of hours, Caroline would ask him where he was spending the night. He would reply, "Oh, 'er, I hadn't really thought," and he would gracefully accept the offer of an uncomfortable divan in Sarah's playroom. When we came downstairs for breakfast, he would invariably have already left. Though utterly banal as a platform speaker, he was a spellbinding raconteur, and we would listen entranced at his accounts of his experiences as chaplain to the bishop of Bombay, where it had been his special task to visit the prisons. He would report his findings to the bishop as they took their evening exercise together on the Malabar Hills, and the bishop would say, "Well, Scott, we have to remember that it *may* be acceptable for a few thousand people to suffer atrocities in our prisons, if the result is to give good government to hundreds of millions." For Michael it was not acceptable. He would have wanted to be one of the prisoners and to have shared the atrocities. Later, when he was a missionary priest in South Africa, the city authorities in Durban decided to move some Indian families from a mainly white suburb, and the Indians attempted nonviolent resistance and were arrested on the street in front of their homes. Michael, who had travelled down from Johannesburg to stand with them, was arrested and imprisoned also. "You know, it's actually quite *difficult* to practice nonviolence," he would say with a rueful smile. "These fellows don't just arrest you. They have rifles, and they take good care to bring the butts down right on your feet while they are doing it." Some years after Michael's death, Archbishop Desmond Tutu, who had never met him in the flesh, travelled six thousand miles from Cape Town to dedicate a stained glass window in a Sussex church to his memory and said in his address that it had been Michael's example that had first taught him it was possible to be both white and good.

Quite early in our friendship Michael dropped in one evening to tell us about a thoroughly characteristic escapade he had made to Nyasaland (Malawi), where the colonial government had been putting pressure on the chiefs to express support for the Central African Federation. Gomani, paramount chief of the southern Angoni living in the hill country close to the frontiers with Northern Rhodesia (Zambia) and Mozambique, had refused to do so. His action was in a way similar to that of Kabaka Mutesa in Buganda. The government issued Gomani an ultimatum: either he obeyed orders, or he would be arrested. Michael decided to be arrested with him, bought an air ticket to Blantyre, and made his way to Gomani's village capital. It was dark when he arrived, and the headlights of the police cars were visible all along the mountain roads. Gomani's capital was full of people who had left their homes in the surrounding villages to support the chief in his hour of trial. Gomani decided that his best course was to flee on foot to Portuguese territory, starting under cover of darkness and before the police cordon tightened. Michael offered to accompany him, and they set off with a handful of followers on the two-day walk. Arriving exhausted at the nearest Portuguese administrative post, they were promptly arrested and returned to Nyasaland under police escort.

There they were separated, and Michael was taken off to breakfast by the district commissioner. "Such a nice chap," he said. "He told me over eggs and bacon that I was under arrest and would be deported back to England on the next plane."

Earlier in the day on which he told us this story Michael had told it to the colonial secretary, Oliver Lyttelton, who closed the interview with the proverb "He who raises the dust, reaps the whirlwind." But I still think that the episode was more than a futile gesture. It was a signal to the people of Malawi that the outside world was not entirely against them, and it was not quite without significance that Lyttelton bothered to hear him. A prophet has sometimes to express himself in symbolic actions. It was this quality in Michael that made me eager to give him the help he asked. His Africa Bureau was an overtly political organization, set up to assist the budding politicians of African colonies to lobby the British government, and I did not think it consistent with my own academic calling to appear publicly on its council. But some of its activities could accurately be described as providing education and information and could be hived off from the main body as registered charities, and to two of these I gave much time over many years. One was the Africa Educational Trust, set up to help African students seeking to enter British universities and technical colleges without the aid of government scholarships. The other, which has a place later in this story (Chapter 24), was the Minority Rights Group.

During much of 1955 my own and Caroline's forward thinking was dominated by the establishment of a chair of history at the new University College of Rhodesia and Nyasaland, which had been founded two years earlier as a symbol of the multiracial intentions of the Central African Federation. The college was bound by its charter to accept qualified students regardless of race, and it was to start its life, like the other university colleges in tropical Africa, in special relationship with the University of London, which would ensure that staff recruitment and teaching programmes would conform to internationally acceptable standards. The first principal of the college was the greatly respected former secretary of the Inter-Universities Council for Higher Education in the Colonies, Walter Adams, whose work had brought him into contact with all the recently founded universities in Commonwealth countries. No one could doubt that here was a leader who could be trusted to see that the new institution lived up to its proclaimed ideals. To head a history department there seemed to me, at the age of thirty-three, to be an attainable and wholly worthwhile ambition. Caroline too saw much to attract us to a life in Africa with interesting work in a sunlit highland climate, with excellent schools available for our daughter. I did not have much hesitation in entering my name for the competition, and in the autumn of 1955 I was offered the appointment.

Difficulties began to arise when the contract arrived and we studied the small print, which made it clear that Salisbury, Rhodesia, was going to be a much more difficult place to get away from than Makerere and the other colleges in tropical Africa. The conditions were set to attract migrants happy to make a large investment in local housing and to forgo paid fares for home leave. Reluctantly, we decided that this was not for us, and we backed out. The college found a superb replacement in Eric Stokes, a historian of India who had begun his career at the university college in Singapore and was to end it as Smuts Professor of Commonwealth History at Cambridge. His principal assistant in Salisbury was Terence Ranger, who, following his deportation for political reasons in 1963, was to build a renowned school of history at the University of Dar es Salaam before passing on to professorial chairs in Los Angeles, Manchester, and Oxford.

At first Caroline and I had many regrets about our decision, but we gradually learned to put them behind us. In London I had to wait three more years for promotion to a readership and another five for the creation of a chair of African history, but there was much satisfaction in being able to carry to fruition the enterprise I had taken through its earliest stage. The arrival as doctoral students of some of the first history graduates of the West African university colleges gave promise of an industry that might one day serve the whole continent. Meanwhile, the first priority was to consolidate the achievement of the 1953 Conference on African History and Archaeology by organising a second and larger one to be held in the summer of 1957.

Whereas the first conference had been essentially a clarion call by a handful of historians and archaeologists about what African history might in the future become, the second was much more a demonstration of what it was actually in the process of becoming, as professional scholars began to take over the initiative from the earlier miscellaneous amateurs. During nine months of intensive preparation, which began in the autumn of 1956, I tried to locate and contact every relevant historian, archaeologist, archivist, and museum curator in every territory of tropical Africa as well as in the four metropolitan countries of Britain, France, Belgium, and Portugal. My inquiries brought me into touch with some two hundred individuals, more than one hundred of whom managed to find the time and money to attend. The university colleges of Anglophone Africa were there in force, with nine staff members from Ibadan, five each from Achimota and Makerere, and two from Fourah Bay. Although most were still British expatriates, Ibadan was already under African leadership, with Kenneth Dike and Saburi Biobaku both present. The University of London accounted for another twenty-one members, nine from SOAS. Other British universities supplied thirteen, including seven from Oxford. Among the British archaeologists not in university employment, Desmond Clark, already a scholar of wide-ranging competence, came from the Rhodes-Livingstone Museum in Zambia, William Fagg from the British Museum, Frank Willett from the Manchester Museum, along with Kenneth Murray, the surveyor of antiquities in Nigeria, and Peter Shinnie, the newly appointed director of antiquities in Uganda. Basil Davidson, then still very much a professional journalist, joined us at his own request. I little imagined that he was destined to become the most popular of all the general exponents of the subject.

The French were still only just in the course of planning their first university in Francophone Africa, which was to open at Dakar in 1958. But there was still the indefatigable Raymond Mauny from the Institut Français d'Afrique Noire, and a half-dozen members of research organisations in metropolitan France, like the archaeologists Jean-Paul and Annie Lebeuf; the Egyptologist Jean Leclant; the historian of Madagascar, Governor Hubert Deschamps; the historian of Togo and Dahomey, Robert Cornevin; and the keeper of the colonial archives, M. Laroche. The Belgians had narrowly outdistanced the French, having founded two universities in the Congo, at Lovanium near Leopoldville in 1954 and at Elizabethville in Katanga in 1956. The latter was soon to have as its rector the distinguished physical anthropologist and Iron Age archeologist Jean Hiernaux. Meanwhile, African history was represented by Jan Vansina, who was at that time employed by the Congo research organisation widely known as IRSAC. The Museum of the Belgian Congo at Tervuren sent four members of its staff. Louis Jadin, the historian of the sixteenth- and seventeenth-century kingdom of Kongo, came from the University of Louvain, and Jean Stengers, the great expert on King Leopold's Congo, from Brussels. With Stengers I had already formed a fast friendship, based on our mutual research interests. Through him I had been invited to give lectures in Brussels in May 1957, and I was to return there as a visiting professor in 1961.

What is most striking in retrospect about the composition of the 1957 conference is that it included only five Americans, three of whom were still graduate students. This was was not the result of my negligence; rather it reflected the still tentative nature of African studies in the United States at the time. I had early on approached Melville Herskovits of Northwestern University, the acknowledged doyen of American Africanists, and he had been able to suggest only one name, that of an anthropologist with some historical interests. John Fage, who was visiting at Wisconsin during the spring of 1957, wrote to tell me that I should invite Dan McCall of the newly founded African Research and Studies Program at Boston University and also his own host at Wisconsin, Philip Curtin, whom he described as "known so far only for his work in Jamaican history, but positively interested in African history and bringing something of it into the teaching here." Within a very few years Curtin would recruit Jan Vansina from Belgium and would turn Madison into the foremost postgraduate school of African history in the United States. By the mid-1960s, and not without the help of SOAS, the situation in both the United States and Canada would be completely transformed.

We had asked all members of the conference, and also a few others who were unable to attend, to send us, if possible on one sheet of paper, a statement of their research activities since 1953, and we had undertaken the considerable task of circulating these papers in advance of the meeting, where they would be taken as already read and where regional discussions of the research outlook in history and archaeology would take place in a series of plenary sessions. There was indeed much of common interest to discuss. In eastern Africa Gervase Mathew, who had been paying annual visits there, was already able to suggest that the ancient harbour towns of the Indian Ocean coast should be seen not as the remains of Persian and Arab colonies but as the urban centres of African societies that had been gradually Islamised through the presence of Persian and Arab traders. His travels had likewise taken him to the earthwork sites of western Uganda associated in tradition with the Chwezi (Chapters 7 and 8), which he correctly prophesied would prove much older than the twenty generations allowed by the dynastic traditions. "What we have in Uganda," he said, "is a palimpsest of cultures, of which only the last is remembered."

In western Africa the borderland between history and archaeology was being most consciously addressed in Nigeria where, to supplement the work of an already active antiquities service, Kenneth Dike and Saburi Biobaku had each succeeded in attracting financial support for large research projects, concerned in one case with the history of Benin and in the other with that of Yorubaland. The core of each project was intended to be the collection and recording of oral traditions, which were believed to extend over some seven centuries in this region. But documentary historians were also being employed to make fresh searches of Portuguese and Dutch archives of the sixteenth, seventeenth, and eighteenth centuries, while anthropologists were studying the social organisation and ritual practices relevant to the interpretation of the rich sculptural traditions revealed by archaeology. Although neither scheme had as yet advanced much beyond the prospectus stage, their very existence seemed to illustrate exactly the lines along which the subject as a whole should be developing.

There was an exceptionally lively session on the teaching of African history, in which everyone, but especially the teachers from the African university colleges, insisted that, whether one was dealing with the evidence from archaeology or oral tradition or written documents, African history must from now on be Africa centred. Doctoral students must be steered away from topics concerned mainly with European activities or the policies of the colonial powers. Everything that had been done by colonial historians must be rethought in light of the new criteria. Everything still to be done must be relevant to the African consumer. Documentary research must be directed to local as well as metropolitan archives. Literary evidence, so largely generated by outsiders, must be tested from eyewitnesses or oral tradition. Most new research must be undertaken at least partly in African countries, and historians must, as their numbers grew, pay as much attention to evidence in African languages as anthropologists and sociologists had long been in the habit of doing.[2]

All of this did, as we shall see, have a real effect upon the character of future research and in due course worked its way into the published literature. Meanwhile, teachers still bemoaned the lack of textbooks suitable for students of African history, and here we were able to announce, as a pointer to what might be expected elsewhere, a grant of £16,000 by the Colonial Social Science Research Council to enable the Clarendon Press in Oxford to undertake a collaborative history of East Africa in three volumes, the first of which would be devoted exclusively to the precolonial period and would be edited by Gervase Mathew and me. The early chapters in this volume would be contributed by archaeologists, the middle ones by specialists in oral tradition, and the concluding ones by documentary historians with interests in the precolonial period.

So far as I was concerned, this was the culmination of a long story of negotiation that had begun in 1951, when Philip Mitchell, then governor of Kenya, had persuaded his fellow East African governors that they ought, while there was still time, to commission an official history of the British connection with the region. Mitchell had visited SOAS to interview me as a potential author, and I remembered how on that occasion he had delivered himself of the opinion, especially remarkable in the head of a government that employed the services of Louis Leakey, that until about five hundred years ago East Africa had probably been uninhabited. Negotiations had dragged on for more than five years, first with the East African High Commission and later with the Colonial Social Science Research Council in London. Now all was at last settled. The contributors had been chosen and briefed, and the volume was to be my main literary commitment from 1958 until 1960. Gervase was to prove an admirable collaborator, even though his side of our correspondence was mainly conducted on rather grubby postcards in an all but illegible hand.

At the 1957 conference many references were made to the need for a journal of African history, particularly as a means of keeping historians and archaeologists up to date with each others' findings, and this was in the event rather quickly achieved. During the autumn of that year John Fage and I began to negotiate with Robert July of the Rockefeller

Foundation for a grant of £5000 to the Cambridge University Press to assist with the launching expenses. July was at first highly sceptical. He told us that the foundation had given up making grants to journals because the grantees had invariably come back for more money. But he finally agreed to recommend it. The journal began publication under our joint editorship in 1960 and succeeded in making itself financially viable without further subsidy. That it did so was undoubtedly the result of one factor we could not have predicted when we made the application. This was the sudden surge in African studies that took place in the United States and Canada during the early 1960s. I think that from its earliest days the journal found about half its circulation in North America. North American contributions to its contents grew more slowly, but certainly the existence of the North American market enabled us to do something that would have been quite impossible for our opposite numbers in France and French-speaking Africa.

Meanwhile, the school had approved my application to spend the academic year of 1957–58 in making a second long journey in Africa. Six years had now passed since my earlier visit to East Africa, and the growing interests of my department made it desirable that, besides renewing my contacts there, I should also add some first-hand experience of western and southern Africa. I had always been a strong believer in the continuity offered by surface travel by car. It also had the practical advantage that Caroline and Sarah (now aged eight) could accompany me with little additional expense. At John Fage's initiative the University of Ghana had invited me to spend a term there teaching in his department, and my plan was to drive right across the continent from there, spending some weeks in Nigeria on the way. In Uganda I would do some field research, concentrating on the borderline between history and archaeology by trying to identify on the ground the royal tombs and capital sites mentioned in the dynastic traditions of the grassland kingdoms. There, as also in Tanganyika and Zanzibar, I would do business with the local contributors to the *Oxford History*, and we would then make our way southwards through Central Africa to Johannesburg and Cape Town.

For all of this the choice of the right vehicle was crucial. I needed a new car this time, and a strong one, and it seemed at first that many arguments favoured the Land Rover. We went to the showroom in Piccadilly and asked for a demonstration drive. When we got to Richmond Park, we were already aching in every limb, and I asked the salesman if he had ever driven one of these vehicles a long distance. "Oh yes, sir," he said. "I once drove one to a place called Nairobi. I'm not sure where it was, but it was a very long way." Incredulous, I asked whether, on the way to Nairobi, he had crossed a big desert. "Yes, sir," he replied, "There was a very big desert; it took us about two weeks to cross it." "And how did

169

it perform in the desert?" I asked. "Between ourselves, sir," he said, "It was absolutely dreadful. It boiled the whole way." We then asked him to demonstrate the system whereby the seats were supposed to fold into beds when required. "Sir," he said, "I wouldn't advise you to try that. You'll bark your knuckles every time. Besides, when you have driven this thing all day, you'll want to get as far away from it as you possibly can at night." Greatly admiring his honesty, if not his salesmanship, we thanked him for his help and directed our search towards a large comfortable estate car, called in those days an Austin Countryman. We had it delivered to us in England, so that we could break it in and get to know its ways, before shipping it from Liverpool to Takoradi, Ghana, where we would meet it in October. It was to do us proud.

Having many other preparations to make before our departure, we spent the summer vacation of 1957 with close friends Kit and Iseult Ward in the Berkshire village of Frilsham on a wooded hillside overlooking the valley of the little river Pang, which rises in the open downland five or six miles to the north and flows in a wide curve to join the Thames at Pang-bourne. Noble woods of beech, birch, oak, and holly crown the hilltops on either side, sheltering the rich farmlands with their wheat fields that run down to the water meadows by the riverside. A chaplet of unspoiled villages follows the valley from Hampstead Norreys, past Frilsham church and manor, to Bucklebury, Stanford, Dingley, and Bradfield and the whole area is criss-crossed with quiet footpaths for the walker. It is still, for me, the most enchanted place on earth. From there we made arrangements to let our house in Newton Road. From there we remade our wills and went for our various inoculations. From there we replenished our tropical camping gear. Then, on September 21 we flew to Accra.

15

Introduction to West Africa
(1957)

Ghana, when we landed there in September 1957, had been an independent country for just six months, and there were as yet few visible signs of its change of status. Kwame Nkrumah still ruled as prime minister, not yet as president, and the continuing Commonwealth connection was symbolised by a British governor general, Lord Listowel, who occupied the residence of the former Danish and British governors at Christiansborg Castle. Despite great efforts during the transitional period to train and promote Ghanaians to fill the leading positions in government service, a great many former British colonial officials were still employed on a contract basis. Both the army and the police force still had British commanding officers, and in fact the main fears of the ruling nationalist politicians were concentrated less on expatriate influences than on their ability to command the loyalty of the small indigenous elite of businessmen, lawyers, administrators, and senior teachers, all of whom were much better educated than they were. In these circumstances it did not seem too strange that an embryo university with 550 students in all subjects should be staffed by 120 teachers, 110 of whom were expatriates and held all the senior positions.

John Fage was at the airport to meet us, and with him we drove through the eastern suburbs of Accra to the old campus of the university college at Achimota, where we were to live for the next three and a half months in a shabby but rather attractive prefabricated bungalow on the perimeter of the site, overlooking the African bush. The building was almost completely shrouded in bougainvillea, which harboured some unwanted wildlife but gave us much-needed shade, especially on the wide porch where we ate our meals and spent our leisure time. The garden, save for grasscutting, had been long untended, but pineapples still grew there between the inevitable pawpaw and frangipani trees, and just beyond it

171

the wild elephant grass stood eight to ten feet high. The main railway line to Kumasi and the interior ran up the valley beneath us; we could not see it because of all the vegetation, but we could hear the mournful hooting of the daily train. From our domestic viewpoint it was much more rural than Makerere—more like a bush mission station at the back of beyond.

Not so the new campus three miles away at Legon that was still partially under construction. There on a fine conical hill dominating the surrounding plain was growing up a small town of dazzling white-walled buildings with red-tiled roofs turning upwards at the eves like those of China and Japan. It was divided down the middle by a dual carriageway, which approached from a main entrance gate more than a half-mile away and spiralled up to the summit, which was crowned by a great assembly hall and by the central university offices. Student residence halls clustered around the main road and up the slopes of the hill, with attractive houses for married staff well spaced along curving sideroads so as to give the greatest privacy. The student residences were designed on the lines of Oxbridge colleges, in quadrangles surrounded by chapels, dining halls, common rooms, and sets of individual students' rooms, each with a private balcony. There were lily ponds stocked with goldfish to eat the mosquito spawn and paved walkways on which the lizards basked and scuttered.

All this was to embody the idea of a tropical university resolutely propagated by the founding principal, David Balme, who had reigned there from 1948 until 1957. As he saw it, a university in Africa, no less than in England, should be not merely a place of instruction and research but a home fit for scholars to live in and bear each other company—a school of manners that should bind its junior and senior members by strong ties of sentimental attachment and send its alumni out into the world with an enduring vision of the elegant life. Even more than on the lecture hall and the laboratory the emphasis was to be upon the dining-room, the common room, and the individual tutorial given in the lecturer's room or private house. The professors with their departments were not to dominate the scene but to find strong rivals in the masters, tutors, deans, and councils of the collegiate halls who would never forget that the primary purpose of the place was to provide civilised leaders in church and state. In defiance of the climate the teaching staff was expected to lecture in academic gowns and to wear them for the formal "high table" dinners, held about once a week, when staff and students ate together, though at separate tables, in each hall of residence.

Balme had left Ghana shortly before we arrived, and I did not meet him until several years later, when he had been transformed into a modest and retiring professor of classics at Queen Mary College, London. But at Legon folklore had it that he had once circulated among his colleagues a note that said he had looked out of his window at one o'clock in the morning and had seen only one other house lit up, so how could they possibly be burning the candle at both ends as they were expected to do? I suppose that his guiding vision must have been that of Plato's Guardians; the flaw in that vision has always been that, while Guardians may make admirable civil servants, they do not get elected to Parliament in sufficient numbers to ensure the perpetuation of their kind. True, the Gold Coast had been by far the most prosperous of the British African colonies, but even so no popularly elected government of an independent Ghana was likely to go on allocating the resources needed to support such a luxurious and elitist institution in the style to which it had been accustomed.

Such then was the wider context of John Fage's department of history, of which he had been the effective founder, although not quite the earliest member. After nearly ten years on the job he had assembled an impressive band of colleagues, only one of whom had managed to avoid any contact with the history of Africa. Jack Lander was an English medievalist, the author of a distinguished book on the reign of Edward IV. He was unmarried and, as tutor of Commonwealth Hall, occupied a spectacularly elegant apartment overlooking most of the Legon site, where, besides working immensely hard, he smoked cigarettes through the longest of holders and was well supplied with the palest and driest of sherries. He was popular with his colleagues and greatly admired by his African students. He spent his summers in London, where he shared a beautiful eighteenth-century house in Islington with the literary critic Raymond Mortimer. Lander was to end his career at the University of Western Ontario. Another old-timer was Edgar Metcalfe, a colonial historian who, outside his teaching, was occupied with the biography of George Maclean, the brilliant mid-nineteenth-century governor of Cape Coast and creator of the Gold Coast protectorate. Metcalfe was soon to move on to the University of Hull. A new arrival on the staff was Graham Irwin, a handsome Australian who had already been teaching for some years at the university in Singapore and was a specialist on the Portuguese and Dutch in the East Indies; it was hoped that he would transfer these skills to the corresponding period of West African history. Graham was to be John Fage's successor as head of the department from 1959 until 1965, when he was appointed to a chair at Columbia University in New York. There was Margaret Priestley, who worked on the African merchants who organised the long-distance trade of the European forts on the Gold Coast during the eighteenth and nineteenth centuries. The youngest member of the staff, who was to marry a Ghanaian woman and outstay all his early colleagues, was Robert Sprigge. As a young bachelor he had already adopted the "old Coasters'" style of life by building up a household of half-adopted African children who lived with him, took his surname, and attended the local schools at his expense. He was our near neighbour on the Achimota site, and we loved to hear the tinkle of young voices emanating from his house and garden.

Such was the team of expatriate historians that initiated the teaching of the subject at university level in Ghana. In less than a decade these historians had developed the department to the extent of specialisation required for a London honours degree, and two of their first graduates were already in England, training to join them and before long to take their places. My brief contribution to the work was to pioneer the teaching of East African history to West African undergraduates. It was also my initiation in undergraduate teaching, and like all beginners I found it desperately hard work to provide "an ordered exposition of the subject" at the rate of two or three lectures a week. The supreme problem in presenting the history of precolonial Africa lay in the sheer numbers of small ethnic societies that had to be identified by name and placed on the map before any useful generalisations could be attempted, and I quickly learned that to West African students the peoples of East Africa seemed as distant and as different as those of China or Peru. Pan-Africanism was a political concept and, even so, one that was more easily intelligible to those who had lived outside the continent. As a goal for historians to practise in their studies, pan-Africanism evoked little response.

Outside the formal lectures the students would come in ones and twos to the house to discuss their essays and plan their reading, and there they would mostly seem as able, and also as open and friendly, as one could wish. Once, when I was sitting with a student on the porch of our house, we heard a rustling sound and saw a long green snake make its way along the foundation wall and disappear into a pile of gravel surrounding the kitchen drain. The student identified it as a green mamba and highly venomous, and when I asked him what we should do about it, he sensibly suggested that I might perhaps ring up the department of zoology. Sure enough, within about ten minutes there appeared a little wizened man on a bicycle, with a forked stick under one arm. When we showed him the place, he put his bare hand into the gravel, felt around, and soon withdrew it, holding the snake firmly by the neck. He carefully wound its writhing body around his arm, climbed onto his bicycle, and rode away. "And now, sir," said my companion, "do you still refuse to believe in juju?"

Despite the somewhat cloistered atmosphere of Legon we did not feel at all cut off from the big world in the Ghana of that time. Because of its pioneering leap into independent nationhood the foreign correspondents of the world press descended there. Oliver Woods of the *Times* of London was an early visitor, and Colin Legum of the *Observer* was travelling the country from end to end during almost all the time we were there. Whenever he was in Accra we used to meet, either on the lively terrace of

174

Asafo society at Grossfriedrichsburg, Ghana, 1957

the Ambassador Hotel, or else on the beach at Labadi, where swimming was strictly superintended by a character called Big Man, who doubled as chief of the village and head lifeguard. There we would lie and watch the local Ga fishermen bring in their boats through the surf, while their relatives on shore hauled, twenty or more at a time, at the lines that held the nets. Barbara Ward, the greatly respected freelance economist, came regularly to Ghana to stay with her husband, Sir Robert Jackson, who was still the government's advisor on development, and that autumn of 1957 she lectured at Legon on urbanisation in the Third World. In December the World Council of Churches held its triennial conference in Accra, which brought a host of old friends, like Max Warren and Bengt Sundkler. And in January 1958 Nkrumah hosted an important pan-African meeting, from which nationalist leaders from the Belgian Congo and the British territories in East and Central Africa carried away the impulse to step up their demands for an end to colonial rule throughout the continent.

Our difficulty was not that of keeping touch with the outside world but rather that of how to find time to be away from the campus long enough to make some contact with the traditional side of West African life. Quite soon after our arrival some kind friends took us to witness the annual *odwire*, or yam custom, of the little Akan state of Akwapim that was held in the capital town of Akropong, some forty miles inland from Accra. Here we witnessed the culmination of a weeklong ceremony

175

that had its roots far back in the history of West African kingship, when rulers sacrally controlled the agricultural cycle, initiating the seasons for sowing and planting by publicly casting the first seeds or turning the first sod. With the enlargement of political structures these ceremonies had in many areas become occasions when representatives from every family in the state would congregate in the capital and when subordinate chiefs would demonstrate their loyalty to the paramount by doing homage and presenting gifts. They were also occasions for the public display of wealth and power, intended to keep the populace in a proper state of awe and admiration. Now, as the guests of Nana Boafo Asante II, *kro ntihene* (paramount chief) of Akwapim, we were given seats on a decidedly rickety covered balcony on the first floor of the palace, from which we had a splendid view of the processions. The various local chiefs, in ascending order of importance in the processions, all dressed in silk *kente* cloths of scarlet and gold and wearing an astonishing array of golden jewellery, were carried in their litters, shaded by huge coloured umbrellas and followed by their drums of state, which throbbed insistently in their wake. Last of all came the paramount himself, preceded by his gold-embossed stool of office, his drums louder, his umbrellas more splendid, bobbing up and down and twirled by their carriers, while troops of young women danced beside his litter, waving fans and fly whisks all around him. To relieve the heat of the day the sweltering guests on our balcony were served successively with tumblers of beer, whiskey, and champagne, and the written record alleges that our eight-year-old Sarah landed one of each. If so, it would have been in line with the spirit of happy rowdy exuberance and ostentation, which we could not associate with any of our memories of demure royal occasions on the other side of Africa. It was beautifully reproduced at a children's nativity play that we witnessed soon afterwards at a mission school in Togoland; the three kings arrived at the Bethlehem stable with drums beating, umbrellas twirling, and their stools carried ceremonially before them.

My search for a wider experience of the country soon brought me into touch with the university's outstanding department of extra-mural studies. The founder, David Kimble, had come there from the Extra-Mural Delegacy at Oxford, and had attracted colleagues of real quality, whom he trained at headquarters and then scattered round the country in the guise of resident tutors whose business it was both to teach themselves and to recruit, each of them, a team of part-time voluntary assistants capable of conducting a weekly class for the literate community in their neighbourhoods. The prime targets were the clerks in local government offices, the teachers in full primary or junior secondary schools, the district nurses and dispensers providing medical services at the grassroots, agricultural demonstrators, forestry officials, and the like. All these people could read and write English, but, posted around the countryside in rural backwaters, their literacy tended to become thinner and less fluent. A club for self-improving literates was what they needed and what Kimble's department aimed to provide. Several of his resident tutors performed real feats of mobility, driving a thousand miles a week along dirt roads on their regular rounds of teaching, inspection, and encouragement. What was even more remarkable was how many managed to keep their scholarly standards in good enough order to produce real contributions in research.

At the time of our 1957 visit Kimble was keeping very much out of sight, while working on his *Political History of Ghana, 1850–1928* (1963), but his assistant, Dennis Austin, who was to write his own first-rate book, *Politics in Ghana, 1945–1960* (1964), took me with him on some of his shorter trips into the countryside and helped me to arrange my tour to the northern province during the Christmas vacation. In December I duly set off with a student companion, a Fante from southern Ghana who bore the ethnically misleading name of John Sykes, and we drove northwards through the great forest to Kumasi, the capital of the Asante kingdom, which, at the height of its power during the late eighteenth and early nineteenth centuries, had ruled a territory more or less the size of modern Ghana. There we stayed with the resident tutor, Bill Tordoff, who in addition to his teaching duties was already collecting material for an important monograph on Asante during colonial times. He took us to see the sights of the town, and next day we resumed our northward journey to Tamale, the provincial capital of the north. We were now beyond the main traffic routes, and soon the tarmac road was replaced by gravel, and children playing by the roadside rushed for cover with screams of *oboroni*—'white man.' Gradually, the forest thinned into low bush as we entered the so-called Middle Belt, an unpromising lightly populated region bridging the forest and the open savanna. The frontier of the northern territories was at the ferry crossing of the White Volta at Yeji, and here my companion tactfully changed his Western dress for a northern smock in deference to the sartorial preferences of what would be from here onwards a predominantly Muslim population.

And so we came to Tamale and to the imposing figure of Ivor Wilks, whom I remember as bronzed, mustachioed, Welsh, and altogether strongly reminiscent of portraits of the young Stanley. He was married in those days to a Ghanaian woman who came from the royal house of Ada state near the mouth of the Volta River. Their young son Sebastian was one day to be a student of mine in London. Meantime, Ivor was the resident tutor for the whole of the northern province, and during the next few days I was to accompany him on one of his weekly teaching visits to the most northerly part of his domain. We set off early in the morning and drove to Gambaga in the northeastern corner of the country

Our second African journey, Ghana to Uganda, 1957–58

and from there worked our way slowly westwards to Navrongo and on to Sandema, keeping close to the frontier between Ghana and the French colony of Upper Volta, known nowadays as Burkina Faso. All this was flat country with scarcely a tree in sight, and it was occupied by a seemingly dense agricultural population, living not in villages but in family groups of twenty and thirty in mud-walled compounds evenly scattered across the landscape at intervals of a few hundred yards. In terms of precolonial history these were small-scale stateless societies that survived in the no-man's-land between the Mossi and Dagomba kingdoms to the north, with their armies of horse-borne slave raiders, and the forest-based musketmen of Asante to the south. During the colonial period these peoples, though no longer raided for slaves, became the main source of paid labourers in the gold mines and cocoa plantations of the south and also for the rank-and-file of the army and police force.

The country folk living around our main destination at Sandema were the Kanjaga, and they numbered about twenty thousand, but it is unlikely that any of them formed part of Ivor Wilks's audience that evening, for Sandema was essentially an administrative centre, and its literate population, though mostly of northern origin, had been posted there from more accessible parts of the province. There were in fact only about thirty of them. Half were schoolteachers, and the rest were local government officials—accounting clerks, postmasters, storekeepers, and the like. Outside their professional lives they were the local leaders of political party organisations, Christian church activities, and social welfare groups. Collectively, they were the spearhead of the new Westernised lifestyle against the traditional pattern of life in the family compounds of the surrounding countryside. To this significant minority, holding on in difficult circumstances to their hard-earned literacy and education, Ivor's weekly lecture was the pivot of their cultural life. Nearly all attended. Nearly all attempted some serious reading arising from it. Nearly all joined vigorously in the subsequent discussion. The most aspiring contributed essays and papers.

It was about five o'clock in the afternoon when we edged our way down the main street of the little town, hooting loudly to announce our arrival and coming to rest on a patch of grass beside the mud-built council hall. We were now 540 miles from Accra and 140 from Ivor's headquarters at Tamale. The government offices were already closed, but a table and blackboard had been set ready in the open air, facing a thinly occupied circle of chairs and benches. We rested briefly, while the chairman of the class bustled off to round up latecomers from the pub and the marketplace. By the time all were assembled, dusk was falling, and a pressure lamp was brought out and placed on a packing case beside the blackboard. "Gentlemen," said the chairman rising,

"Tonight we shall be continuing our course on the history of Ghana." With quiet assurance Wilks launched into a formal lecture that could have been given with credit in the auditorium of any university. On previous Tuesdays he had been tracing the medieval history of the states that had grown up around the great bend of the Niger some five hundred miles to the north of us and dwelt upon the kinds of influence these states might have projected southwards into modern Ghana. This afternoon he turned his attention southwards towards the Atlantic coast and spoke with authority on the rise of the Akwamu empire, which from the mid-seventeenth until the mid-eighteenth century was the main supplier of slaves to the Danes, the British, and the Dutch based in the trade castles along the eastern sector of the Ghana coast. It was detailed and difficult stuff, far beyond the reach of any textbook then existing, much of which he had quarried from the Dutch and Danish manuscript sources. He moved through it with ease, using a wealth of contemporary analogies that his audience could readily understand. Question time was lively. The one or two southerners present, who came from the region he had been describing, tried hard to catch him out but were no match for him. The audience ended up with a picture of the internal aspect of the African slave trade that taught them much about the whole process of state formation in this part of Africa. Next time they would follow the same process among the Asante, and piece by piece the origins of their newly independent county would build up before their eyes.

It was late in the evening before we were able to retire to the privacy of a very basic rest house. Next day we stopped more briefly in Bolgatanga before returning to Ivor's hospitable home in Tamale. A day or two later I left with John Sykes for Accra. Ivor left Ghana in 1966, and after hesitating for some years between openings in Britain and the United States he settled in 1971 for Northwestern University in Evanston, Illinois. When his great book *Asante in the Nineteenth Century* was published in 1975, I felt proud to have witnessed, however briefly, the circumstance of its gestation.

We spent Christmas 1957 in Accra, but over the new year we took a week visiting a selection of the forty or so trade castles built by the Portuguese and Dutch, British, Danes, and Brandenburgers along the three hundred miles of coastline between Accra and Axim. For a base we were fortunate to be given access to a curator's flat high up in Fort St. Jago at Elmina. This was the subsidiary fort added by the Dutch to improve the landward defences of the great trade castle built by the Portuguese in 1482 that was captured by the Dutch in 1637. The flat had a private terrace on the ramparts, commanding the best view of the African town, with the main castle standing on a rocky promontory beyond it, and thither we repaired when, very early on January 1, 1958, we were awakened by a tumultuous shouting from the town below us, accompanied by the boom of cannon and the sharp crack of gunfire. The entire population seemed to be on the streets and brandishing some kind of ancient firearm. Soon it was explained to us that Elmina was celebrating "the Dutch New Year," meaning the Dutch capture of the Portuguese castle, an enterprise that was mounted from the earlier Dutch trading forts at Mori to the east of Elmina and Kommenda to the west, with the all-important aid of their African hosts and neighbours in those places.

Nothing could have better opened our eyes to the true nature of this "castle colonialism" that lasted for three and a half centuries on this coast. Seen from the angle of imperial history, the Dutch capture of Elmina fulfilled the grand strategic aim of assuring a regular supply of slaves for the newly conquered Dutch colony in Brazil. Seen from the angle of African folk memory, what was annually reenacted was the conquest of the African townsfolk of Elmina by their African neighbours and competitors. Though it might be referred to as the Dutch New Year, no one dressed up for the occasion as a Portuguese or a Dutchman. What was celebrated was an African war that changed the organisation of the inland trading networks and of the African middlemen who managed it. We encountered a similar surprise when we visited the most beautifully sited of all the castles, that of Grossfriedrichsburg, dominating a lovely palm-fringed bay to the east of Axim. We wandered enchanted through its ruins, and on our way out were met by a picturesquely dressed party of the local *asafo* society, meeting to practice traditional songs and dances. The leader praised us for our visit and said, yes, it was a sad thing about those Brandenburgers who had come to live with them for a short time during the seventeenth and eighteenth century. When they left, they had promised solemnly to return, but they never had. This was clearly not the folk memory of a people who felt themselves to have been oppressed and exploited by foreigners from across the sea but rather that of a society that had seen gain for itself from the foreigners' presence.

By this time we were getting within a few days of our departure from Ghana, and while we were still at Fort St. Jago, I drove into Accra to meet the fourth member of our expedition who was to accompany us on the journey across the continent to Uganda. Thinking back to the motoring problems of our last long trip in Africa, Caroline and I had decided before leaving England that another pair of strong young hands would be very desirable, and our old friend Mary Stuart had come up with the name of her nineteen-year-old nephew, Christopher MacRae, who would be completing his national service in the navy in December and was hoping to do some adventurous travelling before going up to Oxford the following October. Both of his parents were doctors and had been medical missionaries for many years in Ghana. His cousin, Andrew Stuart, was in the Colonial Service in Uganda and would give him hospitality from the time of our arrival there. It looked like an admirable arrangement, and so it happily turned out. In a sense, therefore, our transcontinental journey may be said to have started from our first evening together on the battlements of Fort St. Jago. After that we spent only two more nights at our bungalow at Achimota. Then on January 10, 1958, we were off.

16

West to East

(1958)

We had allowed ourselves, in terms of engagements at the other end, two months for the four-thousand-mile journey from Ghana to Uganda, but we were always clear that half this period should be spent in Nigeria, where my professional links with the university college at Ibadan were close, and likely to get closer, and where so much more was going on in the overlapping fields of archaeology and oral tradition than in any other African country. The implied consequence, that we would have to rather rush through the French and Belgian territories along our route, was sad, but it had to be accepted. From Accra we followed the coast road nearly all the way to Lagos, crossing the Volta by ferry at Tefle into the eastern part of ex-German Togo, which had been a French mandate since 1918 and was to become an independent country in 1958. Our stay there was confined to a single night in a charming rest house in a grove of palm trees beside the sea at Denu and to the acquisition of some CFA francs at a slightly reduced rate of exchange from one of the many Hausa traders, armed with briefcases, who flagged us down on the approaches to the capital city of Lomé.[1] Next day we crossed into Dahomey, known today as Bénin, and there we made a diversion northwards of something less than one hundred miles to visit the capital of the precolonial kingdom of Dahomey at Abomey. After their occupation the French had made their colonial capital on the coast at Cotonou, and soon afterwards they had abolished the traditional kingdom, converting Abomey into a provincial headquarters and recognising the head of the royal line only under the ambiguous title of *le représentant du roi* (king's representative), the current holder of which lived in a modest house on the outskirts of town. The palace area, occupied and added to by nine successive rulers of the eighteenth and nineteenth centuries, had become a museum that also housed the local offices of the Institut Français d'Afrique Noire (IFAN).

After paying our respects to the French officialdom we installed ourselves at the government rest house, where the superintendant, a huge and imposing figure, introduced himself as Prince Innocent Soglu. He certainly did no menial work and occupied the table next to ours in the dining-room, while numbers of very small black waiters scurried round him. Next day we went to the palace, where I had hoped to meet Pierre Verger, the historian of Afro-Brazilian relations who was the local director of IFAN. Unfortunately, he was away in Brazil, but his deputy guided us round the museum, which housed the shrines of the kings, each with their stools of office and other items of regalia arranged behind them. There were also hundreds, if not thousands, of wrought iron objects, looking like the stems of standard lamps, each surmounted by a bowl-shaped top of open filigree work; these were described to us as the shrines (*autels*) of lesser royalty and palace officials. The atmosphere of the place was extraordinarily sinister and gloomy, and here alone during the whole of our long journey Sarah, now eight, was suddenly overcome by floods of tears.

It was a relief after this to walk in the bright sunshine through the palace site, in which one vast mud-walled courtyard led into another, as each successive monarch had built right up against the premises of his predecessor. We tried to imagine these courtyards filled with the teeming population of a royal household, and especially the bodyguard of female soldiers, the famous Amazons of Dahomey, employed in this most militarised of African kingdoms. Inevitably, we found ourselves thinking also of the barbaric scenes that had been enacted here at the annual "customs," when hundreds of war captives, gagged and impaled, had been sacrificially slaughtered under the eyes of the king and his courtiers in ceremonies described by a long succession of European eyewitnesses invited as official guests from their trading factories on the coast at Whydah (Ouidah). Such ritual killings, though by no means unknown in other West African kingdoms, seem to have reached a uniqueness of scale in mid-nineteenth-century Dahomey.

That afternoon Prince Innocent Soglu had arranged for us to be received by the représentant du roi in his colonial bungalow, which nevertheless boasted a kind of throne room into which he made a formal entry, supported on each side by two of his fifteen wives. Chairs had been placed for us against the wall on his left, and we addressed each other in stilted courtesies through the official linguist who sat facing him. Nothing of any interest transpired, and we eventually moved out into the garden, where we were told that photography was permitted. The royal party grouped itself appropriately, with the junior wife holding a miniature state umbrella over her master's head, while he produced from

184

his pocket an interesting piece of insignia, the like of which I have never seen. It looked like a pair of silver tea strainers joined by a hinge, which he placed over his nostrils and was held in place by two side pieces that hooked over his ears—*pour ne pas sentir ses ennemis* (so as not to smell his enemies, as the linguist kindly put it). Caroline duly obliged with the Leica, and we said our farewells. The linguist followed us to the car to make sure that we did not omit to leave a tip.

Next day we drove across the Nigerian frontier to Lagos along a freshly reconstructed tarmac road through beautiful, gently undulating, forested country. There we stayed at the Church Missionary Society's guest-house on the Marina, where mealtime talk was all about the Commission on Minorities headed by Henry Willink that was travelling round the country collecting evidence on whether Nigerian independence, already scheduled for 1960, should be based upon the existing federal structure of the colonial government. The British government, in appointing it, had supposed that the issue was the comparatively simple one of how far the three dominant ethnic groups—Hausa in the north, Yoruba in the southwest, and Ibo in the southeast—would be willing to work together once the lid of colonial overrule had been removed from the pot. But no

The king of Dahomey, 1958

sooner had the commission arrived than it was submerged in petitions from much smaller units, which had little to fear from a remote central government but much more from the constitutional entrenchment of a locally dominant group. It was a problem that was to lead to a tragic civil war only seven years after independence and was to be solved only by greatly increasing the number of the constituent states of the federation. Meanwhile, some of its expressions could be irresistibly comic. Philip Mason, a commissioner, told me of one instance in the far southeast of the country, where a villagesize community had hired an expensive lawyer to argue that it would be impossible for it to share a state government with a neighbouring community of similar size. When asked why not, the people said, "Well, you've only got to look at the disgusting way in which they stack their yams."

From Lagos we soon moved on to Ibadan, where the university college had kindly placed an empty house at our disposal and had even arranged for Sarah to attend the local primary school, as she had done throughout our stay in Ghana. Though architecturally less striking than Legon, Ibadan in 1958 certainly gave one the impression that it was heading to become a university of international standard, and history in particular was represented by a team of professionals who were destined to make a mark in universities all round the world. The principal of the place was the well-known historian of the Spanish colonies John Parry, who went on to be vice chancellor of the University of Wales and ended his career as professor of oceanic history at Harvard. The head of the department was Kenneth Dike, destined to be Ibadan's first vice chancellor as an independent university. His next most senior colleague was Charles Smith, an Englishman who married a Fulani woman, became a Muslim, and took Nigerian citizenship; he was later to create a remarkable school of northern Nigerian historians at the University of Zaria. There was John Omer-Cooper, a South African émigré who later wrote the standard history of the nineteenth-century Zulu diaspora and took the study of African history to New Zealand. There were Roger Anstey, who wrote about Britain and the slave trade and became the first professor of modern history at the University of Kent at Canterbury, and Colin Newbury, who moved on to a long career in Oxford. Living on the campus, even so briefly, we got to know them all more easily and informally than is usually possible for a passing visitor.

On a site adjoining that of the University College of Ibadan, which was funded by the central government, was the Ibadan campus of the nascent University of Ife, which was supported by the government of the Western Region and was intended to serve the needs of the Yoruba-speaking community. Here my old friend Saburi Biobaku, in the intervals of his main job as secretary to the cabinet of the Western Region, presided over the Yoruba Historical Research Scheme, which was the Yoruba counterpart of Dike's corresponding project on the history of Benin. On our first Saturday in Ibadan Saburi drove us the fifty miles over to Ife, where we visited what must be one of the most extraordinary local museum collections in the world. I believe that the building has long been replaced, but in those days (1958) it consisted of a rather dark barnlike structure, not at all well protected, that housed nearly all the known examples of the justly world-famous tradition of naturalistic sculpture in terra cotta and cast bronze unearthed in this city since the German anthropologist and collector Leo Frobenius stumbled upon the treasures of the Olukun grove in 1907. Fortunately, the then-district commissioner heard of Frobenius's activities in time to prevent him from exporting his booty, and the finds from all the more recent excavations have, with few exceptions, been kept there. The result is that visitors are confronted by the originals of a score or more sculptures with which they are already familiar through published illustrations.

Our tour of the collection finished, we went to call on the *oni* of Ife, the traditional ruler of the city-state, from whose dynasty nearly all the other kings of Yorubaland claim some kind of legitimation or descent. His palace adjoined the museum. He told us how two months earlier a local building contractor had brought him a bronze figurine of a king and queen, dressed in royal regalia and with their arms and legs intertwined, that had been unearthed by his workmen in the course of digging the foundations for a cooperative warehouse in the suburb of Ita Yemoo. As luck would have it, on that very day Bernard Fagg, then the commissioner for archaeology in Nigeria, happened to pay a rare visit to the oni, who was thus able to greet him with the throwaway remark that a fellow had just called with something that might interest him. Some frantic telephoning followed, construction was halted, and a fence was thrown around the site. The same day Fagg telephoned to the Manchester Museum to ask for the immediate secondment of Frank Willett, an archaeologist and art historian who had done recent work in Yoruba country at the site of Old Oyo. Ten days later Willett was in Ife, where he found a team of Hausa well diggers sent down by Fagg from his headquarters at Jos in the Northern Region. He had been at work with them for six weeks and was due to return to England within a few days. Clearly, we had to visit him at once.

When we met him on the site later that afternoon, Frank was at his wits' end. With the aid of his well diggers he had sunk round test pits at ten-foot intervals both inside and all round the building area, revealing numerous patches of potsherd pavement about eighteen inches below the surface and extending over a total area of about seven acres, representing the streets and domestic compounds of an ancient town. In the centre of the building site where the bronze figurine had been found, he had uncovered the remains of a memorial shrine, marked by a line of worn-out grindstones, beside which were found fragments of nearly lifesize figures in terra cotta whose dress and ornaments proclaimed their royal status. At the moment of our arrival the face of one such figure, crowned with a triple diadem, was just beginning to be visible in the partially excavated laterite soil. To clear it for lifting would take several days of patient and delicate work with penknife and paintbrush. In ten days' time Frank Willett would have to return to his post in Manchester, leaving a tidy site with all holes refilled. Tentatively, I suggested that I might be able to telescope my remaining engagements in Ibadan and return to help him. Next morning he telegraphed asking me to do so.

It proved to be one of the most testing weeks I have ever spent. For nine hours a day we worked on hands and knees in the broiling sun. My task was to complete the work on the crowned figure. There was no difference in colour between the terra cotta and the surrounding laterite and only a slight difference in texture. One pressed gently with the penknife until one encountered increased resistance. Then one brushed away the dust and began again. The lady, for such she turned out to be, was worth it. I saw her next at the Royal Academy in London, where she was on loan to an exhibition called "Treasures of Nigeria." And she had a colour plate

Partially exposed terracotta head at Ita Yemoo, Ife, Nigeria, 1958

all to herself in Frank Willett's book *Ife in the History of West African Sculpture*, published in 1967. Regrettably, the original sculpture has since been stolen from the museum.

Frank had his living quarters in a spectacularly placed rest house built by a cocoa research organisation on a conical hilltop two or three miles out of town, with magnificent forest views on every side. There we ate and slept and discussed the archaeology of Yorubaland far into the night, while the crickets screamed outside. And there on January 27, 1958, my family came to collect me at a farewell lunch at which Bernard Fagg was also our guest. It was the first time I had met this outstandingly warm, outgoing, and entirely committed man, and he pressed me somehow to

The same head, after excavation

find time for a brief visit to his headquarters at Jos. He even promised to send me an air ticket from Enugu, through which we were due to pass in a few days' time.

Meanwhile, we continued our eastward course to the ancient city of Benin, which had begun to expand from its village origins around the tenth century and, from the fourteenth until the eighteenth century, ruled a wide empire stretching all the three hundred miles from Lagos to the lower Niger. Our point of contact there was Robert Bradbury, the anthropologist member of Kenneth Dike's historical research project who was studying the elaborate hierarchies of court officials and civil and military chiefs for the light they might throw upon the kingdom's past. Despite the size of the town, there was neither hotel nor rest house, and the Bradburys had only a tiny flat above a chemist's shop. My recollection is that Caroline and Sarah stayed with the Anglican bishop, Dr. Owoloso, and that Christopher and I put up camp beds in a classroom of a secondary school in the cathedral precinct. From such a precarious domestic base did we have to get ourselves tidy enough to spend most of the following day at the palace of the traditional ruler, the *oba* Akenzua II, whose dynasty probably established itself sometime in the fourteenth century.

Bradbury, who was by now familiar with the ways of the court, told us that the oba did not usually receive ladies, so he, Christopher, and I made up the party. The oba, although not wearing any of the magnificent coral regalia portrayed in most books, was still an impressive figure. He looked and was dressed rather like the pope, in a white cassock and with gold-rimmed spectacles. After quite a brief exchange of courtesies he handed us over to the care of a chamberlain to see the sights and said that he would be glad if we would join him for a game of billiards afterwards. The palace was huge, and we walked through many cloistered courtyards, but what chiefly remains in my memory was one given over to the memorial shrines of past kings. Here was, in situ, what we had seen reconstructed in the museum at Abomey and something probably similar to the shrine we had just been excavating at Ife. What was special at Benin were the plaques in cast bronze depicting historical scenes that formed the reredos to many of the shrines. But of course there was nothing at Benin to compare in richness with the little museum at Ife, because Benin had been sacked and thoroughly looted by a British military expedition in 1897. Most of its treasures had been carried off as booty and had been sold by its captors and dispersed throughout the world. One whole department of Dike's research project was devoted to assembling a complete photographic record of the dispersed materials.

Billiards with the oba turned out to be very much a family event. It took place at one end of a large hall, at the other end of which sat perhaps thirty or forty of the palace ladies in threes and fours around small tables, playing cards and chatting. At our end each player was attended by a small boy dressed only in a loincloth who chalked the top of the cue after every shot and stood holding it like a banner until it was next required. The chamberlain kept the score and advised his master on how each shot should be played. None of us performed with any skill, but the oba, who was partnered by Bradbury, seemed to have less luck than the rest, and Christopher and I had some difficulty ensuring that he emerged victorious, but we managed it somehow and carried away with us the memory of his kindly and smiling presence.

From Benin we made our way on January 28, 1958, to Asaba and thence by the Niger ferry to Onitsha, where we stayed for some days under the hospitable roof of John Patterson, then the Anglican bishop on the Niger who was shortly to become the first archbishop of West Africa. I think that it was in talking to him, and to his close colleague Archdeacon Burns, while the evening mosquitoes swarmed in clouds around the house, that I really began to appreciate the difference between missionary life in West and East Africa, at least before the advent of modern prophylactics. Europeans who came to live in this climate, even if some stayed there for many years, never for a moment forgot that they were birds of passage, there just to plant an institution that would pass into West African hands at the first possible moment. Those who stayed tended to remain single, and even those who stayed seldom attained fluency in the difficult tonal languages of the region. They preached, taught, and administered in English or French, relying for their contacts with the unlettered on local intermediaries, today mostly African clergy and teachers but formerly the interpreters who had learned a European language orally in the pidgin lingua franca of commerce.

The pride of Onitsha was its international market, which had been rehoused the previous year in a vast series of concrete hangars on a thirty-five-acre site beside the Niger. It was not in the least beautiful like some African markets, but it now offered all-weather accommodation for three thousand stalls. At first glance the retail activity of the market caught the eye. From early morning until midday the roads and footpaths leading into Onitsha were lined with a steady procession of gaily dressed women, carrying on their heads enormous baskets of yams, maize, peppers, and other foodstuffs from the local countryside. From early afternoon until late evening they returned, laden with their purchases of cooking pots and cotton prints. In the market itself the salespeople, who surprisingly were mostly men, would solicit the passers-by to invest in a gramophone, a hurricane lamp, or a length of cloth. Yet this outward impression of small-scale business was quite misleading. The real significance of this market was that the gramophone salesman with six instruments displayed in his stall could procure the immediate delivery of a gross. The clothier, who in the evening could pack the contents of his stall into a couple of headloads, had access to a thousand more that could be fetched and loaded onto a lorry within the hour.

Onitsha was in fact a wholesale market on the largest scale. From its stalls were supplied the myriad tiny shops and markets of the Eastern Region and much of the Northern Region also. Five hundred miles away by road, a sizable proportion of the visitors at the Jos Museum were, as I was to discover, lorry drivers from Onitsha. Nine hundred miles away, between Maiduguri and Fort Lamy, trucks with Onitsha licence plates ploughed the dust of Bornu. We were given an introduction to the local manager of the United Africa Company who told us that he was utterly baffled by the economics of lorry transport operating out of Onitsha. From July of each year until November, when the Cross River was in flood, the coasting vessels of his company could penetrate some 150 miles inland to the interior markets of the Cameroons. For the rest of the year these markets were supplied, not from Victoria or Calabar on the nearby coast but from Onitsha, along three hundred miles of the worst main road in Nigeria. It was even said that when shortages occurred in the market at Ibadan, a mere ninety miles from the port of Lagos, the news was relayed to Onitsha by telephone and the missing goods supplied by lorries that travelled the three hundred miles of twisting roads overnight. The manager told us that while the full ramifications of this vast system of marketing and distribution remained a mystery, it was known that the brains controlling it were to be found among a small group of rich Ibo women, trusted by the importers for their commercial credit and by the smaller African wholesalers for the taste and judgment of their purchases. He said that the warehouses of his company stretched for a quarter-mile along the river bank, but only a small fraction of the goods contained in them were destined for the company's network of retail stores. The rest would all pass through the hands of the merchant princesses, who arrived with their carriers in the early mornings; each took at least one thousand pounds' worth of goods on credit and returned before evening with payment in cash.

At Onitsha there soon reached me from Bernard Fagg the promised air ticket from Enugu to Jos, and on January 30 I flew the 350 miles for three most memorable days. The significance of the Jos plateau in Nigerian archaeology had been the result of the large open-cast excavations practised by European tin-mining companies on the western side of the plateau that had followed the lines of ancient river valleys where deposits of the mineral had accumulated through hydraulic action. From the 1920s on, miners had been turning in important finds of early stone tools, including Acheulian hand axes uncovered by their digging machinery, and starting in the 1940s there began to be found some examples of a striking and sophisticated tradition of terra cotta sculptures of men and animals, known after the valley in which they were first discovered as the Nok culture. Hence, when Fagg was appointed as Nigeria's first commissioner for archaeology, it was natural for him to make his headquarters in Jos and to set in train the building of a museum to house the artifacts that had been collected. The museum was his pride and joy. He had built it himself with a grant of £6500 from the government using elementary manuals on building construction and borrowing masons from the local Catholic mission. Unlike the Ife museum, where we had been the sole visitors, this one was full of people, and to my astonishment most were women from the local countryside who had called there on their way home from Jos market. They had set down their headloads in neat piles on the grass outside, and they were crowding round the Stone Age exhibits, their voices full of animated interest. As Bernard showed me, these local visitors did not in general sign the book. Among those who did so, a large portion were lorry drivers who gave addresses well scattered through the country but with a heavy concentration of entries from Onitsha.

The class of acquisitions to which Bernard Fagg was giving most attention at the time was, naturally enough, the terra cotta sculpture in the Nok tradition, and we spent most of the following day driving from one tin mine to another in the Nok and neighboring valleys. We had samples from the museum in the boot of the car that we showed to managers and foremen so that they could be properly aware of what to look for. It is interesting to remember that in 1958 the technique of carbon dating was still in its infancy, and the only way to attempt to date the finds of sculpture was by the other artifacts with which they were associated. Because most of the occurrences in the tin mining context had been associated with both stone and iron tools, the working assumption was that the sculptors had straddled the Late Stone and Early Iron ages. Only during the 1960s, when finds of Nok sculpture were at last made in the lowlands to the west and south of the plateau, and always in conjunction with clear signs of ironworking, was it realised how completely finds in the tin mines had been sorted by the action of flowing water, so as to give a totally misleading impression of the real stratigraphy. Since then carbon dating has placed the productions of the Nok sculptors within the period from the sixth century B.C. to the second century A.D. They are thus still ancient enough to have been among the ancestors of other known traditions of sculpture in the region as a whole and give some indication of the depth and strength of an attitude towards ancestors that seems to have been characteristic of western Africa as a whole.

Bernard Fagg's secondary obsession at the time of my visit in 1958 was with "rock gongs," a way of making music that probably originated in Stone Age times. These rock formations tended to occur in and around natural rock shelters bearing signs of occupation by Late Stone Age communities, and they consisted of closely juxtaposed rock faces that were capable of producing bell-like peals of sound when struck with a stone hammer. The search for rock gongs provided the opportunity for a daylong excursion, this time towards the eastern side of the plateau, where we climbed a series of rocky hilltops and ended by paying a call on the Fulani emir of Bauchi, who served us coffee in a refreshingly cool white-domed reception room of his adobe palace. It was my one brief but deeply evocative experience of an outlying province of the nineteenth-century empire of Sokoto. We returned through the dusk to Jos, and next morning Bernard drove me to the little airport, where we sat in his car beside the runway, while he played me recordings of rock gong music until the plane came to take me back to my waiting family in Enugu.

Our evening there was traumatic, for Sarah fell while walking on the garden wall at the rest house and cut her forehead badly enough to need several stitches and a total anaesthetic at the local hospital. We all suffered paroxysms of apprehension as we drove her there through the brief tropical dusk, but we found the most sympathetic attention from the Nigerian staff of the place and an unbelievably kind English doctor was fetched from her home to cope. We told her that we were making for the Cameroon highlands, and to our surprise and relief she advised us to press on next day and get away from the forest and its higher danger of infection.

It took us two days of spectacular but also rather adventurous motoring to get the three hundred miles from Enugu to the little mountain capital of Bamenda. At a place called Abakaliki we left tarmac roads for dirt ones, which continued all the way to Uganda. The first night we spent at a romantically placed rest house perched on a little bluff surveying miles of primeval forest at Ikom. The solitary British district officer flew the flag on one side of us, and the only other building in sight was one of her majesty's more remote prisons. We were very much in the country of origin of Harry Johnston's better cannibal stories. Next morning we descended into the heart of the forest, traversing the Cross River into British Cameroon and from there to Mamfe encountered the only stretch of road that might have proved impassable. During the rainy season it always became so, and this year the rains had lasted longer than usual. But the only alternative route into Cameroon would have involved a northward diversion of more than a thousand miles, so it had to be tried, and in the event we got through with only a little digging. Soon after passing Mamfe we left the main road to Buea and began the long tightly spiralling climb up the densely forested flank of the mountain range, to emerge at last on the lovely, cool, open grasslands that crown the summits at heights of five thousand to eight thousand feet above sea level.

Bamenda in 1958 was a place of character. The district office was housed in a picturesque German fort, high above the town, built in yellowish-brown brick round a central courtyard with bright red poinsettias. The resident's house nearby had a driveway bordered with roses, and there was a rest house with fourteen rooms, colour washed in pink and set in a garden of roses and chrysanthemums, where we spent our first night. Next day we were fortunate enough to be offered the use of an empty house on an agricultural research station ten miles out of town that we occupied for nearly a fortnight. We were now in the country of Gerald Durrell's very funny book *The Bafut Beagles* (1953), but we did not try to call on the *fon* (king) of Bafut or any other local notables. Unenterprisingly, no doubt, we had marked this down as a place in which to rest from the first lap of our journey in preparation for the second and longer one. We spent our mornings writing a half-dozen articles that had been commissioned by the *Times* and the *Manchester Guardian* on various aspects of our West African travels. And in the cool but sunny afternoons we walked in the open pastures behind the house where a mounted Fulani herdsman would occasionally gallop past us, his light cloak streaming in the wind. In these idyllic circumstances Christopher addressed himself to Dante and Sarah's ugly wound began to heal.

At length, on February 17, rested and refreshed, we drove over the crest of the range into French Cameroon. The road was now of laterite, the surface of which had been ground by traffic into a fine red dust, in places nearly a foot deep, which forced us to drive with the windows closed, and even then it came up through the floorboards and soon coated us. It was fortunate that the descent was much gentler on this side than the other, for we slithered and slid for much of the way down to Dschang. It was from there on, as we looked for somewhere to spend the night, that we gradually became aware of the military activity along the route. Our eventual stopping place was at a very basic campsite at Ndikinimeki, which was mainly a military post. There was no catering, but the attendant heated water for us in a cauldron and poured it over our heads, a bucket at a time, through a hole in the roof of the bathroom, after which we opened some of our reserve tins of guinea-fowl stew. In the morning we were awakened by bugles, and it was explained that the army was on manoeuvres. Later in the day the French manager of the campsite in Bafia, where we stopped for breakfast, told us, with obvious fear in her eyes, that a month or so previously a government-appointed chief had been murdered at Ndikinimeki by a hit squad of the left-wing UPC Party, known colloquially as the *Upécistes*, which had been campaigning since 1948 for the reunion of the two Cameroons and their total independence from France as well as Britain. And a few miles farther on we heard sounds of gunfire coming from a wood to the left of the road and felt a small ping, as of an expended bullet, against the side of the car. Needless to say, we had no idea that full independence would be granted to French Cameroon within a few months of our journey, but even as birds of passage it was obvious to us that here, as elsewhere in West Africa, things were on the move. It was an impression that was to be strongly reinforced as we moved on into the colony of Oubangui-Chari, soon to become the Central African Republic. And when we reached the Belgian Congo, our Franciscan missionary hosts working along the south bank of the Oubangui would look grave in answer to our inquiries, and reply, "*Ca pénétre, vous savez, ca pénétre*" (It's spreading, you know, it's spreading).

Meanwhile, however, our journey proceeded without further incident. We ferried across two magnificent rivers, the Mbam and the Sanaga, and entered the northern margin of the great Congo forest. We lunched at the Hotel d'Anjou at Nanga Eboko, where madame the proprietress had adopted a baby gorilla that had lost its mother in a forest fire. It wore regular nappies and giggled helplessly when they were changed. The hotel servants regarded it with deep suspicion, and madame teased them mercilessly for their hesitation in giving it a bottle and even more so when Sarah volunteered to do it. And we spent the night at a lovely comfortable hotel on the outskirts of Bertoua, kept by a French couple who clearly enjoyed living at the back of beyond. They had a schoolboy son who worked in the bar in the evenings. Next day we drove to Bouar, just across the frontier with Oubangui-Chari, along a fearsome stretch of road with a huge pothole every fifty yards. We were now back in the orchard bush to the north of the forest, where the villagers were busy bringing in the cotton harvest, carried by the women by balancing enormous baskets on their heads. Between villages the entire countryside was black from recent grass burning at the end of the dry season. At Bouar there was an inn of sorts, but its clientele of soldiers and *routiers* (truck drivers) was drunk and noisy, so we presented ourselves at a convent of the Oblates of St. Theresa of Lisieux, where the nuns kindly allowed us to camp in their school buildings, bringing us out welcome supplies of pineapples and freshly baked bread.

And so we came on February 22, 1958, to Bangui, destined soon to become the imperial capital of the infamous Jean Bokassa but then perhaps the most attractive little city in French colonial Africa. Its position had been dictated by the narrows of the great river Oubangui, which made it the head of navigation for the big barges plying upstream from Brazzaville in eight days and descending there again in four. Above it much smaller boats could travel on for another week, to Bangassou, but most of the freight proceeded by road, either northwards over the watershed to the River Chari and Lake Chad or else northeastwards to the districts bordering the Sudan. The smarter end of Bangui was

Ferry crossing from Bangui (French Equatorial Africa) to Libenge (Belgian Congo), 1958

built on a bluff overhanging the narrows, with a grande corniche and a moyenne corniche, both commanding splendid views of river and forest that became even more spectacular towards evening as the equatorial sun set directly into the water downstream. At the Hotel Minerva we supped on a vine-clad patio off bouillabaisse made of Nile perch and experienced the unaccustomed luxury of real showers and modern toilets. Croissants for breakfast, of course, after which we wandered out through a town that provided at least its twenty-five hundred expatriate inhabitants with an astonishing range of good shops, restaurants, hairdressing salons, motor car showrooms, and the like. We did not penetrate to the large African township on the flatlands beside the river below the city centre, but our desultory conversations with the local whites constantly reminded us of the apprehension with which the political future was awaited. Some, we gathered, had already sent their families back to Europe, and many more were preparing to leave. But there were others who liked the style of life in Africa well enough to stay on regardless.

That afternoon we crossed by ferry to Libenge on the Belgian side of the river, and there we made our first contact with the Franciscan (Capuchin) missionaries, to whom we had been introduced in advance by Father A. Roeykens, the historian of King Leopold's colonial activities who had worked for many years in the mission there. We had a great welcome from his former colleagues, who put us up for the night in their

197

guest-room, invited us to share their modest table, and entrusted us next day with the letters for their other stations higher up the river on our eastward route. The road, they warned us, would be *pas très fameux* (not too famous), and petrol would be obtainable only at the occasional cotton ginneries and oil palm plantations along the way. There would certainly be no hotel for many hundreds of miles—probably not before Paulis, which was almost on the other side of the country. We were all, I think, feeling a little apprehension at the thought that we had reached the point of no return, and it was certainly a great help to have that missionary mail-bag as our passport on the next and most isolated stretch of our journey.

By the next evening those apprehensions had almost disappeared. We had delivered mail to a happy group of Italian Capuchins at a place called Bosobolo; they offered us their schoolroom for our picnic lunch and brought us copious supplies of iced water to drink with it—"*C'est le whiskey des Franciscains, vous savez*" (The whiskey of the Franciscans, you know). Then, later in the afternoon, we came to a large mission station at Molegbe, where the superior, Father Théodore, greeted us with a beaming "Welcome, my friends, you are just in time for coffee," and, having heard our story, insisted that we should stay, not just for one night, but for two. On such a long journey we must be in need of a day off, and we must have clothes that needed washing and car that should be completely unpacked and cleaned out. So we were shown to a row of simple cells and in due course reported for supper at the refectory table, with maybe ten or twelve Dutch and Belgian priests, to consume the tender meat of a poor young buffalo that had been shot by one of the fathers the previous day. Afterwards deckchairs were placed on a wide veranda for the last recreational half-hour of a missionary day that had started at 4 A.M. All now spoke to each other in their own languages—some in French, many in Dutch or Flemish, a few in Italian. Two old priests, long retired from active work but preferring to live out their days in the sunshine to the cold and regimentation of their Belgian motherhouse, told us in halting French of the hardships endured by missionaries of their generation, when everything not grown on the spot had to be carried in on foot from the nearest river port. Of their working colleagues, all were visibly dog tired, and soon they began to drift away to their rooms.

We did not respond to the four o'clock drum next morning, but we did attend the weekday mass, where we watched from seats beside the altar a seemingly endless procession of children from the junior and senior boarding schools and from the residential courses for catechumens from the surrounding villages, all holding out cupped hands to receive the sacramental wafers. Later Father Théodore took us on a tour of the premises—mission house, convent, schools, farm, workshops, all built of bricks baked on the site. And as we walked, he talked of the future, telling us that the next ten years would see great changes in the country as a whole, *"parceque c'est leur pays"* (because it is their country), and within that time there would have emerged a minority capable of governing it. He recognized that it was mainly through the Catholic Church that nationalism was coming to the Congo, because the educated elite was composed almost entirely of the clergy and of those who had come nearest to joining it. The church had no other option but to back that which it had created. As we shared their meals during the rest of that day, it struck us that these men showed no sentimentality about their work. They did not expect anything very great to come of it. They were just sowing the seed, knowing well the waste and the poverty that was involved in growth but knowing also that a growing crop was not easily eliminated.

Leaving the hospitality of Molegbe with regret, we delivered our final consignments of mail at the Capuchin houses at Banzyville and Yakoma. Here we were close to the confluence of the Uele and the Mbomu, which join to become the Oubangui, and soon we had to cross the Uele, all three kilometres of it, by a ferry consisting of planks laid across four dugout canoes propelled by poles for most of the way and by paddles across the deeper channels. The landing place on the far side was a sand bank, and we had to reach it by driving across two planks that had to be carefully aligned to fit our wheelbase. It had to be done under the eyes of a large and excited crowd of other passengers on foot who contributed advice in many languages, but done it was and we proceeded, with two more ferry crossings, this time across the River Bili, to Bondo and to the hospitality of a different and entirely Flemish-speaking missionary order, businesslike but scarcely forthcoming. Here next morning we had to recross the Uele and climb over a little watershed into the Likati Valley. We were now in the drainage system of the main Congo, and soon, to remind us of our first African journey in 1949, we passed a turn to Stanleyville, which lay just 150 miles to the south. Nearby in the town of Buta we paused to gossip with a Portuguese hotelier who assured us that we would not recognise the Stanleyville of eight years before. Since that time it had grown into a metropolis, where all the former petit blanc storekeepers of the surrounding forest region had now become grand blanc wholesalers, each directing a chain of retail shops with African managers. Everyone, he said, was talking about the rise of nationalism, and in 1958 the world of commerce was already preparing for its advent to power. Like Father Théodore at Molegbe, he prophesied that the next ten years would see even greater changes.

Our road still ran due east, following the northern fringes of the Ituri forest. Much of the way was through orchard bush planted with cotton around the villages, but some was through forest, and as we climbed higher above sea level, we passed signs of recent clearance for plantations of coffee. Titule, a little town scarcely marked upon the map where we were surprised to find a really luxurious hotel, proved to be the local centre of Cotonco, the cotton-purchasing monopoly for the whole area, whereas Paulis, which we reached next day, was the booming capital of coffee, with four hotels, all full to bursting with long-term clients who were waiting for more permanent accommodation. Here, the Dominican Fathers, who ran a large interracial secondary school in the town, obligingly offered us their last two guest-rooms.

At Paulis we learned to our astonishment that a big new road had been cleared straight through the eastern segment of the Ituri forest all the way to Beni, the border post for Uganda. The distance was little more than three hundred miles, and, on freshly graded murram as yet uncorrugated by heavy traffic, we could expect to do it easily in one day. Although rapid, it proved to be a memorable experience, for it gave us a glimpse of what the forest might one day become. For most of the way the clearing extended for a half-mile on each side of the road, and much of it was already laid out in villages with plots of coffee trees extending outwards from the vegetable gardens. All the villagers were of course new settlers in terrain hitherto occupied only by bands of Pygmy hunters and gatherers. At midday we turned off the road to a small convent of Verona Sisters, who showed us into a spotless and attractively furnished parlour where we could eat our sandwiches, and they spoke movingly of their unavailing struggle to make contact with the Pygmies who were all around them and roamed freely through their gardens and farm buildings and who always seemed perfectly happy but utterly detached from the changing world around them.

We slept that night at Beni as planned and the following morning drove down into the Semliki Valley and up through the western foothills of Ruwenzori to our old haunt at the Mutwanga Hotel, which we found had become a centre of international tourism, with a party of rich businessmen from Zurich and Frankfort assembling to climb the peaks. There we bade farewell to the Belgian Congo over a cup of coffee that we could barely afford and continued on our way to the southern shoulder of the mountain and to the Ugandan border. We had travelled four thousand miles since leaving Ghana two months before, and we had achieved a sense of the continuities between one side of Africa and the other that was available to few English people during colonial times.

17

East Africa Revisited
(1958)

From the moment that we crossed the shoulder of Ruwenzori and began our descent into Uganda in 1958, we were conscious of being in a new and different world from that of French and Belgian Africa and one that had changed much since our last visit in 1949–50. Right from the frontier the road was of tarmac, and soon we began to overtake a familiar procession of local people moving their cotton and their surplus bananas down from their little farms to the market town at Katwe. Mostly, they were still doing so by bicycle, but now there were also some small saloon cars with African families inside, likewise on their way to market. But what struck us most vividly, as we gazed out over the splendid landscape encompassing the shores of Lake Edward and the farmlands of southern Toro, was the glitter of corrugated metal roofs on scattered country dwellings, now often rectangular in shape, which eight years previously would almost all have been round with roofs of thatch. Nothing so well depicted the economic progress achieved during the last decade of colonialism in this most fortunate of colonial territories.

To our surprise the road now bypassed Katwe town and took us in a wide detour round to the Kazinga Channel connecting Lakes Edward and George, now grandly bridged at the site of the former ferry crossing. From there we climbed the escarpment leading up to the Bunyaruguru plateau and came to rest at the Kichwamba Hotel, with its unparalleled view westward across the Queen Elizabeth Game Park and Lake Edward to the mountains of Lubero on the Congo side. After a brief pause to unload and refresh ourselves, we still had enough daylight and energy to drive down into the game park and potter past several gently strolling parties of elephant on their way to the lakeshore, where the hippos, with much snorting and blowing, were moving in towards the shallows for the night. It was elating to have once more this access to the world of wildlife, which had all but disappeared from the western African scene. Next day we drove through the high hills of western Ankole to Mbarara, where we paused to call on our old friend Kesi Nganwa, now enganzi of Ankole, who emerged wreathed in smiles from a meeting of his council to greet us. I told him of my plan to return to Ankole for three or four weeks in July to attempt to locate some of the capital sites of past rulers mentioned in the traditional histories we had studied together eight years before. He promised his full cooperation, and we continued on our way to the hospitable home of Eric and Peggy Lanning at Masaka, where Eric was the assistant resident. It was March 1 and we were right on schedule.

My main aim in this part of my study was to explore the area of overlap between traditional history and Iron Age archaeology and, if possible, to get some first-hand experience of archaeological fieldwork. To this end I had been corresponding for a year past with the archaeologist Peter Shinnie, who had recently been appointed as the first director of antiquities in Uganda. It had been my hope to join him in his excavations at the impressive earthwork site at Bigo bya Mugenyi in the Masaka district that had been claimed in some Ankole traditions as the capital of the last of the Chwezi kings of Kitara. Unfortunately, the plan had not worked out. Shinnie, disillusioned by the government's failure to provide him with an adequate budget, had accepted a post at the University of Ghana. He had completed his preliminary excavation at Bigo ahead of time and had already left Uganda by the time we arrived. In his absence Eric Lanning, who knew Bigo well and had for some years been devoting much of his leisure time to the search for related earthwork sites in southern Uganda, was my obvious point of reference, and he was unfailingly generous in sharing his knowledge and experience. It was in Eric's company that I first saw Bigo, with its central mounds and embankments enclosed within seven miles of perimeter trenching, and the nearby sites of Ntusi, which has since proved to have been both older and more densely populated than Bigo, with a history going back to the tenth or eleventh century. And it was he who briefed me about the other earthwork sites at Mubende, Munsa, and Kibengo, all situated in the central grasslands of southern Uganda and all linked by the presence of the same pottery with roughly painted red finger decoration that had not yet been found elsewhere. That brief trip from Masaka was in fact formative for the fieldwork I was to undertake in the following months.

We spent altogether ten days in and around Masaka before going on to Kampala and Makerere, where we stayed in a guest flat in the newly built Institute of Social and Economic Research directed by Audrey Richards. Here we could do our housekeeping in civilised conditions, and we particularly enjoyed the sunset hour, when we could sit out on the patio and watch the herons coming in to roost in the giant fig tree on the lawn below us. They would glide in one by one, their arched necks making them look like flying teapots, until they gently lowered their legs into the standing position as they touched down on the upper branches of the tree. From this agreeable base we renewed our contacts with Makerere, and I think that there were only two evenings during the month we spent there when we did not dine out with old friends. Kenneth Ingham, now a member of the legislative council, still ran the history department and soon asked me to meet his students. His colleague Anthony Low was to be one of my main contributors in the *Oxford History of East Africa*, and we were able to do much useful planning for it together. I called on Kabaka Mutesa, now happily reinstalled in his little white palace at Mengo, and asked for his help in my project to visit the tombs of his ancestors and try to assess their significance as historical evidence. While we were talking, his private secretary entered the room on all fours and from his knees passed him some letters for signature. Sensing my astonishment, Mutesa explained that such was the etiquette of his court but that it did not imply that he enjoyed absolute powers, even in ritual matters such as the royal tombs. He said that I should consult with the *sabalangira*, who was the official head of the royal princes and responsible for the upkeep of the tombs.

The sabalangira, whom I finally tracked down at his country home, was obviously deeply suspicious about my motives, as I should have been in like circumstances. However, he invited me to attend a meeting of the Bataka Council, composed of the ritual heads of the thirty-odd clans of Buganda, over which he was scheduled to preside in Kampala on the following day, so that I could explain my intentions to all of them. I duly attended the meeting, which took place in a little open courtroom just below the Anglican cathedral on Namirembe Hill, taking with me, as always on such occasions, a Ganda student from Makerere who could both vouch for me and act as an interpreter when necessary. I remember it still as quite a formidable experience. These, far more than any educated and semi-Westernised administrative chiefs I ever met, were men of authority in the old tradition. Although most were probably at least nominally Christian, I felt that they nevertheless represented at the same time an older set of beliefs, in which clan heads and royals enjoyed a special access to the wisdom of the ancestors as communicated to them through the spirit mediums living around the tombs. Clearly, what I was asking them to approve was something much more delicate than to take a guided tour around Frogmore, St. George's Chapel, Westminster Abbey, Winchester Cathedral, and the Abbey of Fontevrault in Anjou. It was to inspect the centres of an esoteric cult that was still in daily operation. I never did learn whether they really gave me permission to do so, but in asking for it I had probably done enough to avert active opposition.

As opportunity offered, therefore, we began to visit the tombs, most of which were situated in Busiro County and easily accessible from Kampala. The largest and best known was of course that at Nabulagala, on the next hill to Makerere, where the graves of the last three kabakas, soon to be joined by that of Frederick Mutesa, were housed in a single vast conical thatched mausoleum. But this, we soon discovered, was a nineteenth-century innovation, inspired by the prevailing Muslim and Christian beliefs concerning bodily resurrection. In contrast, the tombs, so called, of the previous twenty-two kabakas, who had reigned from about the middle of the sixteenth century to the middle of the nineteenth, were not really tombs at all but rather shrines or temples representing the palace enclosures of the kings. The only royal remains kept in them were the jaw-bones and umbilical cords of the monarchs. The actual graves were elsewhere, in one or other of two small cemeteries that had been in use at different periods. The cemeteries contained no monuments. They were just plots of uncultivated land, each cared for by a single guardian. But the jaw-bone temples had formerly consisted of large round houses, each forming the centre of a residential complex set within a royal fence. In theory each temple should have been staffed by a circle of women, representing the royal widows, and also by a set of ministers and palace officials, all nominated by the clans of the historical queens and courtiers. In practice the numbers of these attendants had been greatly pared, especially at the older temples, but even the smaller ones were significant enough to be well known to the ordinary people living in the same vicinity. On one occasion, when we were looking for the temple of a certain Kabaka Kigala who had ruled during the seventeenth generation back and therefore presumably during the late fifteenth or early sixteenth century, we stopped to ask the help of a passer-by, who replied at once, "Ah, you must have come to visit our Kabaka Kigala." On another occasion we were visiting the temple of Kabaka Tembo, remembered in tradition as the father of Kigala, and were shown round by a *katikiro*, or prime minister, who spoke throughout in the first person about the deeds of his historical predecessor. "Yes," he said, "I served Kabaka Tembo."

It seemed to me then, and it still does, that whatever the scope for manipulation that is involved in the handing down of oral traditions from one generation to the next, the existence and the continuing maintenance of these temples, staffed by communities of living people who spend their lives personifying the dead, cannot be written off as deliberate and expensive stageplay. Nor, for that matter, can it be attributed to the disinterested service of history. The explanation must lie in the persistence of the living cult of the spirits of past rulers who communicate with their worshippers through those among the widows who practice as spirit mediums. My questions about them tended to elicit the response that they were mostly unmarried women who started in middle life to have dreams that they had been chosen as the wives of this or that past kabaka and who thereupon reported for duty at his temple. Sadly, as a visiting foreigner and with only a month at my disposal I could not hope to get close enough to watch these ladies at their work or to form any sensible judgment about the character of the oracles they delivered when in a state of possession. What was obvious was that the cult was undergoing a brisk revival in the wake of Kabaka Mutesa's return from exile. The traditional round houses at the centre of each complex had mostly been rebuilt in semipermanent materials, with a rectangular ground plan and roofs of corrugated iron, and we were told that the numbers of visiting princes had greatly increased.

I was to write up my conclusions about the royal tombs of Buganda in an article that was published in the *Uganda Journal* early in 1959.[1] Meantime, during April 1958 we made a journey through Kenya, Tanganyika, and Zanzibar, partly in the interests of the *Oxford History* and party in order to make contact with the two archaeologists now employed to conserve the antiquities of the coastal region.

Our first stopping place was with Leonard Beecher, the Anglican bishop of Mombasa who lived in Nairobi and had kindly asked us to stay for a few nights. It transpired that he hoped to interest me in writing a history of the Anglican Church in Kenya, about which I had quickly to disappoint him, but he did not on that account turn us out of the house. On the contrary, I was amazed by the number of hours we spent together talking in his study. He had been thirty-odd years in Kenya, and his wife was a sister of Louis Leakey, the archaeologist. They had been born in Kenya, the children of a missionary family in Kikuyuland, where Louis at least had undergone the rites of initiation into a Kikuyu age-set. These were forward-looking people who saw better than most Europeans the way things were going in the wake of the violent years of the Mau Mau disturbances. I was especially grateful to him for arranging for me to have a day out in the Kikuyu country with Stanley Booth-Clibborn of the Kenya Missionary Council to see the results of the consolidation of landholdings. While in Nairobi I also paid a call on Tom Mboya, whom I had met in London a year or so earlier at a dinner given by Philip Mason at the Athenaeum Club. I reminded him that on that occasion he had said that Kenyan independence would take twenty years to achieve. He replied mischievously, "That was probably twenty years ago, wasn't it?"

We drove out one day to Olorgesaile in the Rift Valley, some thirty miles south of Nairobi, where prehistoric people had lived beside the shores of a now-vanished lake and had left behind them one of the richest known deposits of hand axes and other palaeolithic tools dating, as we now know, to a period about one million years ago. There we made the acquaintance of Merrick Posnansky, today a venerable father of African archaeology but then a young and even younger-looking employee of the Kenya National Parks organisation headed by Louis Leakey. We had already been in touch by correspondence, and I knew that he had just been appointed to the curatorship of the Uganda Museum. With Peter Shinnie unlikely to be replaced as director of antiquities, the immediate future of archaeology in Uganda was going to depend very much on him. Caroline and I were almost equally surprised by the gentle figure with a slight stoop, blue eyes beaming from above a rather long golden beard, that emerged from the official rondavel to greet us. It was a hot, desolate, and dusty spot, and he had been living there in very basic accommodation for more than a year. He gave us our first initiation into palaeolithic tool making and then told us how, a few weeks previously, the governor, Evelyn Baring, and his wife Mary had driven up in their Rolls Royce for a similar initiation and how, on their departure, they had stopped the car two hundred yards down the road and sent the chauffeur back on foot with a packet of sandwiches left over from their lunch. We could understand that Merrick had evoked that kind of concern. Our meeting with him was mainly concerned with his impending move to Uganda, but we also made plans to join up with him for a part of our travels to the Kenya coast. It was the beginning of a long friendship.

From Nairobi we drove the four hundred miles to Tanga, pausing for a few days en route at the home of Henry Fosbrooke, which was gorgeously placed on the lip of Lake Duluti, a crater lake perched among the foothills of Mount Meru. Henry was away in Zambia where he directed the Rhodes-Livingstone Institute, but he had invited us to camp in his guest-house, and we made it our base while we visited the provincial and district archives in Arusha and spent a day out walking among the coffee plantations of the Chagga people on the southern slopes of Mount Kilimanjaro. At dawn and sunset Henry's lovely garden offered almost the best view of the great mountain when it emerged briefly from its encircling clouds. The view southwards from Duluti towards Ngorongoro was hardly less spectacular, with the blue cones of a hundred volcanoes visible across the Masai plains.

At Tanga my business was with Greville Freeman-Grenville, who earned his living in the Colonial Education Service but had devoted his leisure for many years to the history and archaeology of the Tanganyika coast. He was a keen numismatist, competent in Swahili and Arabic, and had made a special study of the written chronicles of Kilwa and some other coastal towns that I, for want of anyone more expert, had helped to examine for an Oxford doctorate during the previous year (1957). He was now engaged to write two chapters for the *Oxford History*, so we had much to discuss. From Tanga Caroline and I made a lightning trip

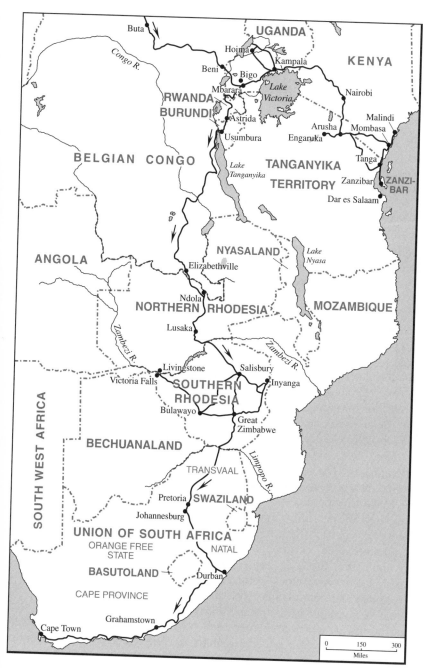

Our second African journey, Uganda to the Cape of Good Hope, 1957–58

to Zanzibar to confer with John Gray, now retired but still living on the island, who was another of my contributors. On our return we received a surprise visit from Neville Chittick, who had recently been appointed as conservator of antiquities in Tanganyika and with whom I was to have the closest contact for the next twenty-five years. The son of a Czech businessman who had settled in England, Neville had been educated at Rugby and Cambridge and had begun his career as an archaeologist in the Sudan Antiquities Department, where he had worked under Peter Shinnie. This was the first time we had met, and it was typical of his dash and spontaneity that he had flown up from Dar es Salaam specially to do so. As we talked, he happened to mention that there was an Iron Age site of some interest that he needed to inspect at Engaruka in the Rift Valley, not far from Ngorongoro, and he suggested that we might go there together. He warned me that it would be no place for the family, and we therefore arranged that after completing my engagements at the coast I would return with my party to Henry Fosbrooke's house at Lake Duluti, where he would collect me in his Land Rover with full camping equipment.

And so we drove in late April up the coast road to Mombasa, where we picked up Merrick Posnansky and travelled on together to stay with James and Dorothy Kirkman at their cottage beside the beach in Malindi. James, like Merrick, was an employee of the Kenya National Parks; his job description was warden of the coastal sites. In practice he was half a research archaeologist and half the conservator of a set of tourist attractions, ranging from Fort Jesus in Mombasa to the pillar erected by the sixteenth-century Portuguese pioneers at Malindi on which he had placed a characteristically worded notice: "Visitors are requested to sign their names on the sheet of paper below, and not upon the monument." The site to which he had devoted most attention was the stone town of Gedi, long abandoned and in ruins, some ten miles south of Malindi. Over five or six years he had excavated most of its main buildings and carefully analysed their contents. From the datable imports he had concluded that it had been founded in the thirteenth century and abandoned four centuries later. It had certainly never occurred to him to doubt that these, or any of the other stone sites in his care, were anything but "Arab cities," founded and occupied by expatriate colonists. "Colonial and comfortable" was his favourite phrase to describe them. What he questioned was the credibility of the traditional histories of the coastal towns, which attributed their origins to the earliest centuries of Islam. Like my co-editor Gervase Mathew, Kirkman believed that Islamic influences had come to East Africa much later, at the same period as their extension to South and Southeast Asia. For many years there seemed to be a cleavage of views between Freeman-Grenville, who defended the earlier dates, and most other archaeologists, who dismissed them. It was resolved only as a new generation of archaeologists led by Mark Horton began to dig beneath the levels of stone building and find the remains of earlier mosques, built in mud-and-wattle, and dating in some cases as far back as the eighth century. Such finds also made it easier to visualise the expansion of Islam among mainly local African people, who were neither colonial nor comfortable but whose descendants later prospered sufficiently to adopt the luxuries enjoyed by their maritime visitors (see Chapter 30).

James Kirkman accompanied us on the first stage of our return journey to Mombasa in order to show us the early stages of his conversion of Fort Jesus from a colonial prison to what he hoped to develop as an archaeological centre and museum for the study of the coastal sites. Some prisoners were still held there at the time of our visit, and we must have been among the first members of the public to scramble among the battlements of the great bastion built by the Portuguese in 1593 to defend their East African settlements from the seaborne incursions of the Turks from the Ottoman province in the Yemen. That afternoon we continued on our way back to Lake Duluti, taking the small country road that ran from Voi round the southern foothills of Kilimanjaro. Chittick arrived next day, and he and I and Merrick set off on the rough hundred-mile cross-country journey to Engaruka. Here, about half-way between Lake Natron and Ngorongoro, a little river plunges over the western rim of the Rift Valley, and for perhaps a mile on either side of it the steep hillside has been terraced with stone walling into little fields once watered by stone-lined irrigation channels leading off the main stream. Almost every terrace plot had a neatly built cairn in one corner, which, although nothing more than a way to pile unwanted debris, helped to create the impression of an abandoned city. It had been suggested by Louis Leakey that the settlement might once have had a population of five thousand. And because it differed so markedly in construction and layout from any modern settlement in the neighbourhood, it had evoked romantic speculations about migrants who had come there from afar.

We stayed at Engaruka two days and took a great deal of exercise, scrambling up and down the steep and stony incline, tracing the courses of the irrigation channels, and plunging with only sandled feet through thorny bush and stands of long grass. My discomfort was increased by my inability to dismiss from my mind the daunting sight we had enjoyed on the drive in, of a large cobra coiled on top of a rock beside the track, its head raised to threaten us as we passed. We stayed long enough for Neville to satisfy himself that, despite its apparent singularity, the place probably represented a response by local people to a special environmental opportunity rather than some unlikely intrusion from outside. In the event, it was only about twenty-five years later, following the patient researches of John Sutton, that enough comparative evidence existed to place Engaruka in the meaningful context of a subsistence strategy common to much of the Rift Valley before the expansion of the Masai, in which the same societies practised both pastoralism on the valley floor and agriculture on the high plateau on the valley's western side and took special care to develop the rare watercourses connecting one milieu to the other.

My business in Kenya and Tanganyika was now completed, and we lost no time in returning to Uganda, where at Makerere the happy news awaited us that I had been appointed by London University to a newly created readership in the history of Africa. It was the vital step in recognition, for which I had been waiting with some anxiety since my abandonment of the opening in Salisbury. Coming to me at the age of thirty-five, it gave me the standing to do many things that urgently needed to be done.

Meanwhile, there were the capital sites of Ankole to be attended to, and on May 9 we made our way to Mbarara and thence a few days later to a spectacularly placed rest house at Gayaza, twenty miles to the south, on the edge of the Isingiro Hills, with a commanding view over fifty or sixty miles of the Masha plain. The accommodation was basic indeed, amounting to four mud walls and a thatched roof, with an outside loo and a kitchen shed, but a subcounty chief had his headquarters nearby and sent us in bananas and eggs and even the occasional chicken. He would probably have sent milk also, but Kesi Nganwa took the duty upon himself, and it arrived each day by bicycle from Mbarara. We had with us a young law student, Andrew Tibamanya, recently returned from a university in India, who acted as our interpreter and public relations man, and, often enough and especially when we had to cross country infested with lion and buffalo, Kesi would join us for the day with attendants armed with guns. It was a great way to practise historical research.

The starting point of my inquiry was Kamugungunu's history of the kings of Ankole that I had read with Kesi Nganwa in 1950 and that had in the meantime been checked and revised for publication by a district judge, A. G. Katate, with the help of an interested and knowledgable colonial administrator, Henry Morris. It was not of course the last word, but the authors claimed that on two subjects at least, the order of succession of the kings and the places where they had built their capitals, there had been substantial agreement among their informants. In theory, therefore, it should be possible to identify a series of sites that were at least roughly datable by reference to the dynastic list. Surprisingly, with Kesi's help, it was always possible to get good directions to such places, even when they were situated in remote and almost uninhabited areas. And usually, when we reached them, there were at least some surface signs of former habitation, in the shape of mounds or dew ponds or sacred groves. Moreover, when the sites were plotted on the map, they made good topographic sense in relation to the known outlines of the country's history. Their positions confirmed that the earliest centre of the kingdom had been in the high hills of Isingiro that looked southwards across the Kagera Valley to Karagwe in the northwest corner of Tanganyika, with which kingdom Ankole claimed a common founder. It was only around the turn of the sixteenth and seventeenth centuries that its rulers ventured northwards into the Masha plain, the classic pastoral country of more recent times, and only in the nineteenth century that they reached the region north of Mbarara.

My best find was a site at Bweyorere, right below the Gayaza rest house where, without putting a spade into the ground, the whole layout of a royal town could be clearly seen. At the top of a small hill was a U-shaped enclosure measuring some 220 feet by 150 feet that was surrounded on three sides by an earthwork bank. This was a characteristic feature of Ankole capital sites in precolonial times, and it defined the area where the king held court. The levelled floor sites of his private quarters were clustered around the U-shaped embankment, and the line of a perimeter

Kesi Nganwa as Enganzi of Ankole, 1958

fence could be detected running in a series of flower petal loops around the crest of the hill. Outside it the lower slopes of the hill were pitted with the levelled house sites of the courtiers, soldiers, and servants, who lived close to the palace but not in it. Interestingly enough, Bweyorere was a site about which the traditional evidence was in conflict. Kamugungunu had attributed it to a king of the seventeenth century, but both the present omugabe and his keeper of the drum believed it to be that of a king four generations later and therefore of the eighteenth century. Merrick Posnansky, to whom I showed the place, returned there the following year and conducted a small excavation that revealed that there had in fact been two periods of occupation, so that both traditions could have been correct.

While Merrick was with us, we paid a quick one-day visit to the great earthwork site at Bigo, which was only some seventy miles north of Bweyorere as the crow flies. It was immediately apparent to us that the two curved embankments in the centre of the site had at one time formed part of a single U-shaped enclosure on the pattern of the royal enclosures in Ankole. Only the great hemispherical mound that formed the third earthwork in the central complex was something quite different and unique. Two years later, in 1960, I was to join Merrick for a part of his excavation there, when he was able to prove conclusively that what had originally been a single U-shaped embankment had been broken up by later occupiers who had used the soil from the break to build the hemispherical mound. When coupled with carbon dates for the original construction going back to the fourteenth and fifteenth centuries, this discovery in effect proved that the royal towns of Ankole were descended from an earlier practice of dynastic building that had flourished in the central grasslands and was associated by oral tradition with the rule of the Chwezi—whoever these may have been (see Chapter 19).

On June 4, 1958, we returned for three weeks to our base at Makerere, partly in order to write up my data on the capital sites for publication in the *Uganda Journal*.[2] I felt that here, as with the royal tombs of Buganda, I had opened up a new line of historical inquiry that people living in the country might be attracted to take further. My next two fieldwork ventures were, by comparison, almost totally unsuccessful. First, I tried to extend my experience of capital sites to those of Buganda, and I spent many warm days walking and climbing over the various hilltops mentioned in the traditions recorded by Apolo Kagwa as the capital sites of the kabakas. It was obvious from the works of the early European explorers that, in the nineteenth century at least, the capital towns of Buganda had comprised many thousands of inhabitants. On the other hand, it was clear from the traditions that most kabakas had built several capitals and that in most cases the period of occupation must have been quite short. Most of the

Search-party for Ankole capital sites, 1958

land covered by these towns would have long been returned to cultivation. Nevertheless, the royal enclosures had always been placed on a hilltop, and these were mostly still uncultivated, so I hoped to find at least some surface evidence in the form of house platforms, fencing lines, potsherds, or middens, but in the event I failed to find any.

Next we tried our luck in Bunyoro. The same omukama, Tito Winyi, who had befriended us on our first visit, was still there, and we had a splendid contact in Sarah Nyendwoha, whom we had met as a schoolgirl in Fort Portal in 1949 and who was now an Oxford graduate, teaching by her own choice in her home district, even though its most advanced school was only a junior secondary one. Sarah knew her way around the local experts in traditional history from the omukama down, but she could do little to help us about capital sites, which had not been well remembered, partly, no doubt, because the older ones would mostly have been in Mubende district in the part of Bunyoro transferred to Buganda following the British occupation. We duly moved our base of operations to Mubende, taking with us the assistant keeper of the Bunyoro royal tombs who was supposed to be well informed but proved quite useless. He said that he could not accompany us without his two wives to cook for him. We bargained for only one wife, but once installed she

213

Hima herdsmen along the way, 1958

announced that she was homesick for the other one. We gave way, and it was indeed a pleasure to see how happily they collaborated, but it did nothing to improve the efficiency of their lord and master. Worst of all, however, in the sharpening atmosphere of ethnic identity that pervaded the years running up to African independence, it was a mistake for me to be seen working in Buganda in association with an official of the Bunyoro government. The rumour quickly got about that we had come to prepare for the restoration of Mubende district to Bunyoro, and we got no cooperation from the Ganda chiefs. All we were able to do from Mubende was visit the earthwork site at Munsa and those in western Bunyoro at Kibengo and in the Bugoma forest that may have been related to Bigo and other sites in the south but that could not be identified in oral tradition. We also treated ourselves to a couple of days at the Murchison Game Park and enjoyed the incomparable spectacle of elephant and hippo browsing with complete lack of concern on the banks of the Nile, while massed crocodiles brushed against the sides of our boat.

18

East to South
(1958)

And now it was time for us to begin our journey south. After a final week at Makerere we had just seven weeks more in which to reach Cape Town for the homeward voyage to England. I was quite sure that the first of these weeks should be spent in Rwanda, where Jan Vansina, who was clearly leading the field in the methodology of collecting and interpreting oral tradition, was now at work as the local *chef de centre* of the Belgian research organisation IRSAC. I had met him at our conference at SOAS in the previous year (1957), and he had kindly offered to place his guest-house at Astrida at our disposal and allow me to look over his shoulder while at work. The essence of Vansina's contribution was that, whereas nearly all the early attempts to record traditions had been limited to the official versions of history preserved and manipulated by states and dynasties, he had set out to collect in addition those of ordinary clans and families. In fact, in his first large research project on the Kuba of the Kasai, he had attempted to interview, at least briefly, every member of the society of seventy thousand people who had any claim to a knowledge of the past, an exercise that had brought him into personal contact with some fourteen hundred individuals. I particularly wanted to see how, in Rwanda, he was adapting his methods to a society of three million.

We drove the 450 miles from Kampala to Astrida in three days, passing once again through the same marvelous scenery of mountains, lakes, bamboo forest, and soaring volcanic peaks that had so enchanted us eight years before. We passed through Goma and Kisenyi, Kigali, and Kabgayi, the names of which were to become familiar all round the world in connection with the terrible events of 1994. The Belgian flag still waved from every government building. There was not the faintest hint that in little more than two years, in advance even of political independence, Hutu would turn upon Tutsi, killing and burning and driving the first waves of refugees into the adjoining districts of Uganda and Tanganyika. At Astrida, soon to be renamed Butare, Jan and Claudine Vansina invited us to dinner on the evening of our arrival to meet the rector of Ghent University who was on an official tour to forge academic links between his Flemish-speaking institution and the newly founded university at Elizabethville, which shared the same language of instruction and catered largely to the children of Belgian colonists. Next morning in Jan's office my indoctrination began.

As we talked, I quickly realised how much it meant to have the resources of a purely research organisation like IRSAC behind one. Jan had been able to tackle his problem of scale by engaging an army of helpers. His principal lieutenants were four highly educated former seminarians carefully retrained as research assistants. The rank-and-file were simple paid informants living in every part of the country whose sole duty was to travel round from one hill settlement to another, inquiring who were considered to be the experts in traditional lore. The experts were next visited by one of the four researchers, who put to them a series of controlled questions designed to elicit the precise nature and extent of their expertise and how they had come by it. The results of these first inquiries were recorded in longhand and sent to headquarters, where Jan selected the most promising for full-length tape-recorded interviews that he conducted himself. The transcription and translation of these oral texts was an industry in itself and formed the main work of the four researchers. It was all very impressive, and, as I began to indicate in Chapter 8, it enabled Jan to offer a very different interpretation of Rwanda history from those based solely on the dynastic traditions recorded by Kagame and his Belgian missionary predecessors. From Jan's more widely dispersed sources it was possible to see far more accurately how the nuclear Rwanda kingdom had emerged from a mutually beneficial accommodation between Tutsi pastoralists and Hutu cultivators in the centre of the country, where the two occupations were practised side by side, and how, in contrast, the areas to the east and west of the nucleus were added by military conquest. The eastern conquests involved the absorption of small predominantly Tutsi kingdoms, the inhabitants of which felt no shame in surrendering to a wider allegiance. The western conquests, however, took place in predominantly Hutu lands, where the resistance to new Tutsi overlords was fierce and prolonged. The process of conquest in these areas had to be repeated in every reign, and even at the time of the German occupation around 1900 it was still far from complete. In that important conclusion drawn from oral history lies the clue to much that has happened since.[1]

We had a great stay with the Vansinas. One day our old friend Alexis Kagame came to pick me up for a drive around some of the capital sites of

Rwanda. He was now teaching at the technical college at Astrida, and he had at last graduated from a motorcycle to a Volkswagen Beetle, which sagged visibly under his weight. Unfortunately, there was nothing to be seen on the surface at any of the sites we visited, except for the circles of fig trees that had grown up from the posts of the boundary fences. On another day Jan drove us into Burundi on a similar mission, where the most striking sight he showed us was the view westwards from our road across a broad valley to the mountain range of the Nile-Congo divide. The slopes of the range had been cleared of forest and were under intensive cultivation up to a height of some eight thousand feet—except in one stretch, where six or seven round groves of forest marked the sites of the royal tombs. The groves ascended the slope at more or less regular intervals from about fifty-five hundred to about seven thousand feet. Each had originally been placed at the edge of the forest at the time of the burial, and subsequent clearance had carefully avoided just these spots. It made the most vivid illustration I have ever seen of the demographic increase of a farming population that had taken place reign by reign over a period of perhaps two hundred years.

It was now August 3, 1958, and we had to move on, as we were expected in Salisbury, Rhodesia, on the twelfth. There was only one feasible route for our two-thousand-mile journey, and it led down the western side of Lake Tanganyika to Albertville and thence west of Lake Mweru to Katanga and the Copperbelt. It was a long drive through the least accessible corner of the Belgian Congo, and there were some stretches of steep mountain country with poorly engineered gravel roads. Some whom we consulted shook their heads and said we should know that only half of those who set out ever arrived at the other end. In the event, we found it not so frightening as we had feared. Burundi, despite the four-thousand-foot escarpment down to Usumbura, presented no problem. Farther south the mountain escarpments were steeper and narrower, but they were marked out into sections, and at the entry to each was an empty fuel drum that one beat with a heavy stick to warn traffic coming in the opposite direction. There was petrol and overnight accommodation available at reasonable intervals of two or three hundred miles. Our main cause for anxiety was that on the second day out the cable of our gear lever slipped in such a way that we could drive only in second or fourth gear. We proceeded in this fashion quite successfully for the next three and a half days until we reached Elizabethville, where in the very middle of the town it suddenly became impossible to drive in any forward gear. At this precise moment Sarah looked out of the back window and said, "*There's* an Austin garage." We were able to reverse into it, using our only remaining gear, and the problem was resolved in half an hour. We were lucky.

It was in Elizabethville that we suddenly became aware of being in a new and quite different African colonial environment than any we had previously experienced. Its most obvious symbol was to be seen in the dress of the African people. All through West and East Africa the people we had met and observed, whether dressed in African or European style, had nearly all given the impression of wearing clothes that they had bought or made up for themselves in colours and designs that suited them. From here southwards, whether in town or country, the vast majority of the Africans were dressed in cast-off European clothing—tattered khaki shorts or sad-looking colourless dresses, giving them an inescapably proletarian appearance. Elizabethville was a provincial capital but also and mainly a mining town, its centre dominated by the rough white mining fraternity. As we sat at a pavement café waiting for our gears to be mended, a car driven by a drunken white man raced down the main street, swerving wildly from side to side and hitting at least ten other vehicles before it finally halted. There were plenty of spectators, but none took any notice. The recently founded university was on vacation, but we were shown over its buildings and saw that it was clearly intended for the education of white students (among other things, courses were taught in Flemish). We had read much of the enlightened employment policies of the mining companies that aimed to create a stable urbanised workforce and that would one day give rise to an African middle class. We therefore made a point of going to see the housing estates that were supposed to be the linchpin of the system and saw row upon row of brick-built pillboxes that scarcely suggested the basis for a civilised family life. It was all much of a piece with that which we were to see farther south.

We had no time to linger in the southern Congo. We were painfully conscious, for example, that we had driven straight through the heartland of a people as important historically as the Luba, who had pioneered the process of state formation in all this part of central Africa and who, as Belgian archaeologists were just starting to discover, had been involved in the first massive exploitation of the copper deposits of the Katanga. But we had to press on, and after only two nights in Elizabethville we crossed the watershed between the Congo and the Zambezi and entered Northern Rhodesia, spending our first night there at the headquarters of an interdenominational mission for migrant workers in the copper-mining town of Kitwe. Next day we reached Lusaka, where we stayed with Henry Fosbrooke at the Rhodes-Livingstone Institute. And on August 12, 1958, exactly as planned, we crossed the Zambezi into Southern Rhodesia, where Walter and Tania Adams had invited us to make an extended stay with them at the university college, so that I could consult at leisure with the members of the history department about the future place of African history in their teaching programme. Our fellow guest in the house was the vice chancellor of my university, Lillian Penson, with whom I was later to have some spirited exchanges in the course of establishing African history as an honours degree at the University of London.

This, then, was the much-vaunted multiracial University College of Rhodesia and Nyasaland, the projected foundation of which had been used to build up political support for the federation of the three countries in Britain in 1953. Now, in 1958, it was painfully obvious that most students were white, and the reason was simply that there was still only one full secondary school for Africans in each of the three territories it served. In comparison with West or East Africa the situation was shameful. In order to achieve even a semblance of African participation the college was having to pile its scarce resources into a big department of education that could admit students at a subacademic level and so circumvent the bottleneck in the schools. Nevertheless, it was clear that in terms of academic quality Walter Adams had succeeded in recruiting staff of high calibre. Eric Stokes, the first head of the history department and a charmingly modest family man, was a distinguished historian of British India, prepared to consider the claims of African history in his syllabus but inclined to concentrate them within the southern African region, so as to allow space for many other elements. His colleague Terence Ranger, recruited with a doctorate in Anglo-Irish history, was rightly impressed by the excellent facilities of the newly established Central African Archives, which would soon lead him to embark on his major work, *Revolt in Southern Rhodesia* (1967), about the great rebellion of the Mashona in 1897. His research interests would guide him to an altogether exceptional range of contacts with the African population of the country and to a strong personal involvement in the local political scene.

It was clear that even on a regional view of African history, Portuguese Africa needed to figure strongly. The Central African Archives had shown foresight in employing the South African historian Eric Axelson to search and photograph the relevant archival material in Portugal, Goa, and Mozambique and was planning to produce a multivolume edition of the archives' contents. The university college, on its side, would soon recruit Malyn Newitt to teach and write about Portuguese East Africa. Meanwhile, there seemed to be an interesting opening into the oral history of the relations between the Portuguese and the Shona empire of the Mwenemutapas in the enigmatic person of Donald Abraham, a former civil servant fluent in Shona who had established relations with the family that had provided the spirit mediums of the Mwenemutapas ever since the foundation of the kingdom some time during the fifteenth century. Donald claimed that the spirit mediums had been the main repositories of traditional history and that he had opened a mine capable of yielding a framework for the precolonial history of the Shona people.

The Rockefeller Foundation had provided the college with the funds to support a research project in oral history. The question was whether Abraham was the right person to run it. While there were obvious risks in employing a self-trained specialist, it looked as though he was.

Finally, in Southern Rhodesia more than in any other African country there seemed to be the possibility of reconstructing precolonial history from the archaeology of the stone monuments, of which Great Zimbabwe was but the best known of many examples. It was an obvious duty for me to see some of these on the ground and to discuss the state of current research with their guardians in the National Museum and Monuments Commission in Bulawayo. Above all I needed to meet Roger Summers, who, with his colleagues Keith Robinson and Anthony Whitty, had just completed a new round of excavations at Great Zimbabwe itself.

The main significance of the 1958 excavations, as Roger Summers explained to us when we met him in Bulawayo late in August, was that they had shown how the main building operations at Zimbabwe had been spread over about four centuries, from about 1050 to about 1450 A.D. and how during this period the skills of the stone masons had improved steadily. It had long been accepted among professionals that the ruins were of Bantu origin and medieval in period. What was not evident was that the masonry skills were local rather than imported and

Beneath the walls of Great Zimbabwe, 1958

that the place had grown from a state of poverty to one of comparative riches before it was overtaken by a sudden decline on the eve of the period of Portuguese contact. It was in fact a story that fitted well with the traditional accounts of the origins of the Mutapa kingdom on the northern side of the Rhodesian plateau at the very period of Zimbabwe's eclipse. Perhaps a single dynasty had moved its capital, or perhaps an older state had been overtaken by a younger rival. The new Zimbabwe dates were among the earliest to be provided by carbon dating. The Mutapa traditions of origin had been recorded by the Portuguese within a century or so of the events. The conjuncture looked reasonably authentic.

Before we parted, Roger Summers took us over the early stone site at Leopard's Kopje and the stone citadel at Khami, both in the neighbourhood of Bulawayo. We then drove through the Wankie Game Reserve to the Victoria Falls and spent a day in the Livingstone Museum, for twenty-two years the headquarters of Desmond Clark, the foremost African archaeologist of our generation. He was unfortunately away, and it was only two years later that I had the chance to get to know him well. Still, we took much consolation from the sight of the falls. They have a spellbinding majesty that no written description has yet managed to capture. "Natural phenomena . . ." Harold Macmillan is alleged to have remarked when taken to see them in 1960, "are not what I . . . left to myself . . . would go out of my way to see. All the same . . . I'm awfully glad you brought me."

From the Victoria Falls we returned southwards and eastwards to Great Zimbabwe, which also has a quiet majesty and conveys a sense of repose in its departed greatness, perhaps the more intense because the remains of the bustling town that once surrounded it have so completely disappeared from view. It is a palace and a citadel but without a city. We had of course read Gertrude Caton-Thompson's 1931 book *The Zimbabwe Culture*, describing her excavations in 1929, and we did not need to be told that most of the stone building at Zimbabwe served the same function as fences and stockades in other parts of Africa. It was nonetheless a great help to have had the guidance of Roger Summers and his architect collaborator Anthony Whitty and to see with our own eyes the successive styles of masonry, which showed how first a modest wall had been built to give privacy to a group of round houses, how further and better-laid walling had then been erected to enclose parts of an adjoining courtyard, and how, finally, a superb wall of carefully dressed stone blocks had been constructed to encircle the entire complex. The hill ruin was sui generis, a case of bespoke tailoring in stone of a summit already littered with gigantic granite boulders.[2]

From Zimbabwe we proceeded to Umtali (now Mutare) near the Mozambique frontier and thence north to Inyanga to observe a quite different kind of stone building, associated with terraced and irrigated

221

agriculture spread across hundreds of square miles of steep mountain slopes. The people who built these terraces lived in dispersed homesteads, each with a stone-lined pit for confining cattle or small stock. It was later discovered that irrigation channels were directed through these pits to carry the manure to the fields below. The most important people in the society seem to have lived on the highest ridges, in stone enclosures, the outer walls of which were sometimes loopholed. For this reason the local Europeans referred to them as *forts*, just as the stock pens were known by them as *slavepits*, although in fact the stone remains of the Nyanga Mountains bear witness to the former existence of a flourishing agricultural economy that can be roughly dated by the affiliations of its pottery to later Iron Age times. The principal mystery, which is still under investigation, is how and why it came to be abandoned (see Chapter 30).

We had now travelled over a great deal of Southern Rhodesia, and it was time to return to Salisbury, pack up, and get on our way to South Africa. All in all we took with us the picture of a university community there that was doing a fine job with its white students but where the teachers were unsettled and restless in the knowledge that the white-driven politics of the country were still moving to the right and increasingly determined to put brakes on the emergence of an African intelligentsia that could penetrate the closed world of white privilege. Many expatriate teachers felt that they had been recruited on a false prospectus and that, if they stayed too long, they would find themselves isolated and trapped. Much as we admired them, we felt relieved that we did not share their predicament.

We crossed the Limpopo River at Beitbridge in early September 1958 and made our first stop in Johannesburg where we stayed with an old school friend of Caroline's, now married to a company director and living in a beautiful house in a prosperous suburb. Like others in the same neighbourhood, the house hid behind a ten-foot wall surmounted by spikes and barbed wire, and every window was heavily barred. Here, as elsewhere in South Africa, we found it almost impossible to avoid controversial topics of conversation. Although Sharpeville was still two years ahead, the apartheid bandwagon had already been rolling for ten years, and it seemed to us as though almost every white South African was troubled in conscience and trying desperately to elicit sympathy and approval. People were immensely hospitable, especially the Afrikaners. Some hoteliers even refused to accept payment from travellers who had been as long "on trek" as ourselves, but always there was the search for approval and identification with their point of view. Among those we met only the academics were different, and what they told us was that the student age group was markedly less racist than its parents. At the University of the Witwatersrand our host was the Portuguese specialist

Eric Axelson, and I spoke to a group of his colleagues about what we were trying to do in African history and met with a friendly response. In Cape Town it was Leonard Thompson, with whom I developed a longstanding friendship. But Leonard was already preparing to leave South Africa, because he felt so strongly that any liberal stance was doomed to failure in his lifetime. We were to meet next at the University of California at Los Angeles, but not before he had recommended to me a young graduate student of altogether exceptional talent who was destined to spearhead the emergence of a whole new school of South African history from a base at SOAS in London. Her name was Shula Marks.

Our journey through South Africa, brief as it was, took us through a great range of varied country, including the areas most intensively occupied by the Bantu-speaking peoples of precolonial times. From Johannesburg we drove the three hundred miles down through the Drakensberg to Pietermaritzburg and Durban, which had been the heartland of the Zulu nation before it became the colony of Natal. We followed the coast road southeastwards to the Transkei and wound our way through the cool and misty hills of the Pondo and the Tembu, sleeping one night at Umtata in the homeland of the Xhosa before staying with friends at Rhodes University in Grahamstown, which until the mid-nineteenth century had been the eastern frontier town of the Cape Colony. Only here had we reached the approximate limits of Bantu settlement, which, as the carbon dating of

Journey's end, the Cape of Good Hope, 1958

early Iron Age sites was soon to tell us, led back to the early centuries A.D. From here westwards, for our last five hundred miles to Cape Town, we were following the lovely coastal plain of the old Dutch colony, much of it occupied piecemeal during the eighteenth century as white stock farmers edged their way into the pastures of their sparsely settled and ill-armed Khoi predecessors. Now the landscape was sprinkled with whitewashed farmhouses surrounded by prosperous-looking outbuildings. We had the sparkling sea on our left and the crenellated scarp of the Tsitsikamas on our right. It was early spring, and madonna lilies grew in profusion by the roadside. As our destination approached, we felt a satisfying sense of completion, which we fulfilled on September 16, 1958, when we drove down the Cape peninsula to the Cape of Good Hope and photographed the good car on a cliff overlooking the Southern Ocean. It had just under twenty-five thousand miles on the clock.

19

Full Throttle
(1958–60)

The sea voyage from Cape Town to Plymouth, which we made in an Ellerman cargo ship with luxurious accommodation for just fifty passengers, gave us seventeen days of precious leisure in which to recollect the experiences of the past twelve months and to plan our return to normality. More than anything else, I think, our travels had left us with the feeling that not just West Africa but all of tropical Africa had reached the end of an era. At a time when most outsiders were still thinking in terms of regions that could be developed at different speeds in order to respect the interests of the various small communities of Europeans who lived in each of them, we were more impressed by the nearly simultaneous growth of political aspirations throughout the continent and of the essential permeability of colonial frontiers to the flow of these ideas. It was not only that in Ghana we had witnessed the euphoric aftermath of a peaceful transfer of power that had been accomplished in just six years of consciously accepted apprenticeship between the colonial authority and its locally elected successors. It was even more the result of our second visit to Uganda, the country we knew best, where we had observed great material progress during the eight years since our previous visit but also a marked deterioration in the relations between the rulers and the ruled. There had been a huge expansion of the civil administration, military and police forces were being strengthened, and British officials no longer trusted their African confidential clerks and were employing each others' wives instead. One had the feeling that from now on every penny of additional revenue would have to be spent on expanding security services. In these circumstances, whatever one's respect for colonialism's past record, it seemed plain that colonialism had nothing further to offer and that it was unlikely to last for even half of the twenty years that seemed to be the official expectation. As for the colonies of European settlement, the

225

thirty-odd thousand Kenya whites seemed to have learned from the Mau Mau episode that they could not expect to be protected a second time by British forces and were modifying their political ambitions accordingly. Tanganyika and Nyasaland would clearly go the same way and probably Northern Rhodesia also. The Central African Federation would surely break up; Southern Rhodesia, with its much larger white population, would perhaps survive without major changes for a while longer. In South Africa, however, we imagined that the white minority government could last indefinitely by the ruthless use of force, and the only scenario for the radical change seemed to lie in outside intervention of some kind.

If our expectations about the probable pace of political change were more than half right, our corresponding assumptions about the economic stability of the independent African countries of the future were certainly more than half wrong. No one at that time had remotely got the measure of Africa's demographic problem. The population of the continent was then approaching 200 million and was thought to have doubled since the beginning of the century. For an underpopulated continent that growth was believed to be entirely healthy and a credit to the colonial system, which had reduced disease and put an end to internal warfare. No one had an inkling that by the end of the century the figure would have doubled and redoubled. Economists like Arthur Lewis and Kenneth Galbraith wrote as if Africa could hope, with only a little outside help in the early stages, to achieve the economic standards of the Western world within the space of a generation. That was an illusion that carried many more in its train and not least for the kind of higher education that it was my business to promote. We assumed that independent African governments would be at least as generous to their young universities as their colonial predecessors and that places like Legon, Ibadan, and Makerere would grow and multiply in the style in which they had been planted, with well-paid professors enjoying security of tenure with half of their time free for research, staff-student ratios of one to ten, and well-stocked libraries subscribing to all the learned periodicals necessary to keep pace with the progress of knowledge. We assumed that before many years had passed, most teachers of African history would be Africans and that the main momentum of new research would be coming from them. Meanwhile, in London it would be our function to gather in apprentices from all over Africa, to train them in the techniques of research, to initiate them into the contents of European archives and collections, and above all to provide them with the opportunity to meet and inspire each other. We assumed that the costs of their overseas training would come, as heretofore, from scholarships provided by their governments.

Such, then, were the assumptions with which I took up my new readership at the University of London, and on the whole I must say that they served me well, giving me the busiest, most confident, and most productive decade of my life. At the start of it Douglas Jones was my only colleague. Robert Hamilton had moved on and we had a vacancy in which John Fage had signalled his interest. He joined us a year later, in 1959. Meanwhile, there were a few research students in their final year, notably Adu Boahen from Ghana and John Flint from King's College, with whom I had been corresponding during my absence, and a few new ones, including my first East African student, Allan Ogot, a Kenyan Luo with a first degree from St. Andrews who subsequently became a professor in Nairobi and a president of the International Scientific Committee for the *General History of Africa* sponsored by UNESCO. I felt enough confidence in Ogot to support him in his desire to work entirely in oral evidence concerning the migration and settlement of the Luo peoples that he proposed to collect in the course of a long year's fieldwork in his native language area in eastern Uganda and western Kenya. This, if successful, would be a methodological breakthrough, but I knew very well that it would be a high-risk venture, at the end of which examiners appointed by the board of studies in history might say that, however impressive, the result was not history as the board understood it. We thought long and earnestly about the Venerable Bede and other medieval chroniclers who had worked by recording and analysing oral traditions, but there remained the question of whether they would have been awarded doctorates of philosophy by the standards of the twentieth century. The crux of the problem was the scholarly convention that the examiner of a thesis should be able to look behind any statement made in it to a cited source that could be verified at will by a visit to a library or archive. In the case of an oral tradition recorded in Kenya in a language unknown to either the examiner or the research supervisor, it seemed that it would be necessary to present, along with the thesis, edited and translated summaries of the field evidence, which was something that no anthropological fieldworker, for example, had ever been asked to do. Nevertheless, I thought it best that Ogot should do all this, even if it meant his taking four years rather than three over his thesis, and it subsequently became the custom among all my students who worked on similar sources.[1]

My literary efforts during that year of 1958–59 were mainly devoted to editing with Gervase Mathew the chapters that had been submitted for the first volume of the *Oxford History of East Africa* and in writing the long chapter dealing with the history of the East African interior from about 1500 to 1850. Although now long superseded, this volume was in its day something of a landmark in the transition from a mainly colonial to a mainly Africa-centered view of African history. At the time of its planning, at least, the archaeological evidence was still thin, almost unsupported by reliable dates, and there was a glaring gap in what would nowadays be called the early Iron Age. The transition from hunting and gathering to the various kinds of deliberate food production was still little understood. My chapter, among others, was marred by a vestigial diffusionism that arose mainly from the telescoping of what are now seen as long drawn-out processes into rather sudden acts of migration and conquest. It was weakest in its failure to deal with the stateless societies, but it did present a picture of the emergence of the larger and smaller states of Uganda and western Tanganyika, which gave later students something to build on. And the second half of the volume, which dealt with the later nineteenth century, showed how even the literature of European exploration could be made to yield a picture far more authentic than the easy generalisations of colonial historians about precolonial times.

Meanwhile, even in advance of his arrival in London, John Fage and I were busily preparing for the launch of the *Journal of African History*, which we were to edit together for fourteen years. In the long run the editorial function in a learned journal becomes mainly a process of selection from the material submitted by contributors. Founding editors, however, have to start by projecting a clear image of what they are looking for, both in articles and in book reviews. In the course of making its supporting grant the Rockefeller Foundation had asked to see specimen tables of contents for the first four issues. We now had to produce the actual contributions from the circle of our professional contacts. We had to persuade publishers to send us review copies of their books. And we had to help the Cambridge University Press to build up the journal's circulation. The members of our first two conferences on African history and archaeology were a great help to us here but so were the librarians of several hundred North American universities and colleges who were prepared to lay out subscriptions in support of a problematical future demand. From the very beginning John and I made it our policy to spread the contents of each issue widely across the whole scope of the subject. We therefore limited the length of articles to ensure that each issue would contain at least six or seven. And we limited the space devoted to book reviews for the same reason. Although it took a huge amount of our time, it kept us, as nothing else could have done, in touch with most of the new work that was being done in the subject all round the world. It was a healthy discipline and one in which we seemed admirably to complement each other. We frequently found ourselves with quite radically different views about the contributions that come in, but we respected each other well enough for a second or third reading to bring constructive reconciliation. We corresponded every two or three days, and we each saw everything that the other was doing. When we at last gave it up in 1973, we both felt the loss.

On my return to London in 1958 SOAS had given me the oversight of the extramural activities by which it sought to interest British school leavers (high school graduates in the United States) in the whole range of its studies in Asia and Africa, and this involved me in lecturing with small groups of colleagues at conferences for sixth formers that we held in different parts of the country. There was little in formal school curricula to point students in our direction, and we had to base our approach on what they had read in the newspapers or heard on radio, for television programmes were still limited. Therefore, we tended to lecture on current affairs, and the exercise helped us to form our opinions as well as put us in touch with a generation of youngsters that was aware enough of the Third World and its problems to volunteer with one of the budding agencies, such as Voluntary Service Overseas (VSO), that provided significant help to Asian and African countries during the early years of their political independence. At this time most volunteers were school leavers with the most slender qualifications, and their contribution was derided by a later cohort as the "Children's Crusade," but at a critical moment it worked a miracle in race relations, both in transforming British attitudes to the Third World and in conveying the idea of outside sources of goodwill in the countries to which they went.

In July 1960 I went with Lionel Elvin, the director of the Institute of Education at London University, to Cambridge to address the Association of Chief Education Officers. Elvin spoke of the need to maintain the impetus of Western education in Africa into the postcolonial period. I said that my view was more apocalyptic and that we were seeing the emergence of a new Africa in which many of the former things would soon have passed away. I said,

I think it is going to make a tremendous difference that in Africa the colonial period is going to fold up after only seventy-five years or so, instead of, say, one hundred and fifty. I think it is going to mean that Africa is *not* going to be incorporated spiritually as well as technologically into the Western way of life. I think it is going to maintain a good deal of its otherness. And I think that, for our education in this country, that means that Africa will present a problem more like Asia than like North or South America. We can perhaps afford to forget the Red Indians, and to treat America in our schools as the projection of our familiar Western civilisation into a different geographical environment. We shall not be able to treat Africa this way. Or at least we shall be failing if we do.

Beyond my strictly academic activities, I tried to respond to a growing number of calls for my help. I remained close to Max Warren, who still headed the Church Missionary Society and often consulted me about problems on the borderlines of ecclesiastical and political affairs. I kept my close contact with Michael Scott and the Africa Bureau, joining the board of one of its subsidiaries, the Africa Educational Trust, which was chaired by Alexander Carr-Saunders, the recently retired director of the

London School of Economics. The trust tried to promote a flow of simply written literature aimed at the emerging class of politically conscious Africans in newly independent and nearly independent countries. The trust's first director was Joan Wicken, who left us to become for many years one of Julius Nyerere's most trusted advisors and speech writers. Under her two successors, Patricia Llwellyn-Davies and Patricia Herbert, it became an organisation largely subsidized by the aid ministries of the Scandinavian countries that cared for the constantly growing number of African students in Britain who were not officially sponsored by their governments.

Again, in 1959 I joined the council of the newly founded Institute of Race Relations. This organisation owed its origins and its initial finances to a group of enlightened mining magnates in southern Africa, and its object was to increase, by research and publication, the public understanding of the problems arising from the interaction of peoples of differing backgrounds and cultures throughout the long span of world history. The director, Philip Mason, I already knew well. He was a man of brilliant gifts who had held high-ranking posts in the Indian Civil Service before his administrative career was cut short by Indian independence and who had since written two marvelous volumes called *The Men Who Ruled India* (1953, 1954). The chairman was again, Carr-Saunders, and the vice chairman was that quite extraordinary man, Kenneth Grubb, who was also the lay president of the Church Missionary Society and a senior member of the World Council of Churches. Oral tradition had it that, after Grubb was expelled from school at Marlborough, his father had sent him to Brazil with £400 and strict instructions never to return. There he had spotted an opening for seaplane travel and was soon running a profitable air taxi service on the lower Amazon. He experienced a religious conversion at the hands of the Anglican chaplain at Bahia. "Poor fellow," he used to say of him, "He was dying of delirium tremens, but he was the minister of the grace of God to me." From then on he combined swelling business interests with evangelism, claiming even to have ridden his mule through the Andes facing backwards so as to be able to discuss the varieties of religious experience with the man on the mule behind. He had concerned himself especially with the treatment of the indigenous peoples and had been appointed by the Brazilian government with a commission to protect their interests. Now in his sixties, and a leading figure in the world of mutual funds, he presented a rather stiff and overly formal image, always dressed in black coat and striped trousers but always remarkably precise and incisive when it came to crucial matters of drafting.

My friendship with Philip Mason went much further than the council table. We corresponded, we telephoned, and we lunched over the institute's business. My first research student, Richard Gray, became Philip's assistant in a large research project on the history of race relations in Central Africa, producing a well-known book, *The Two Nations* (1960), to complement his introductory volume, *The Birth of a Dilemma* (1958). Among the early publications of the institute were two volumes on the early history of the Belgian Congo, *King Leopold's Congo* (1962) and *King Leopold's Legacy* (1966), by Ruth Slade and Roger Anstey, both of whom had previously been my research students. The largest project undertaken by the institute, however, was the investigation into race relations in Britian itself during the decade following the great Caribbean migration of the late 1940s and early 1950s. For this we had to find a great deal of outside money, most of which came from the Leverhulme Foundation and enabled us to employ Jim Rose and Nicholas Deakin for several years to produce the massive report *Race and Colour in Britian*, published in 1968.

In terms of British politics, like so many academics I still lacked a party commitment. Although the Labour Party seemed to have a better understanding of the urgency of decolonisation, I knew that I was not a socialist. The Conservative alternative, though acceptable enough in home affairs, was seriously marred by the Suez fiasco of 1956, which showed so clearly that half the party had not yet come to terms with the realities of Britain's changed status in the postwar world. Here were people who would fight any sensible programme for the decolonisation of Africa. Bill Gorell Barnes, for many years the head of the African department at the Colonial Office, was one of them. He once said to me, "You know, we could have stood up to the Americans . . . and we could have stood up to the Russians. . . . And we could have stood up to the Labour Party. What we couldn't stand up to was the Labour Party *and* the left wing of the Conservative Party." Caroline was by sentiment and conviction a Liberal, and in a rather agnostic kind of way I went along with it to the extent of accepting an invitation to sit on the Liberal Commonwealth Committee, which met at the House of Commons about once a month.

Sometimes I was invited to take part in delegations, organised mostly by the Africa Bureau, to make representations to ministers about African matters. I remember an early occasion, in 1959, when a group of us went to see Alec Douglas Home about the situation in Nyasaland, where the colonial government had reacted with draconian ferocity to disturbances following the return of Hastings Banda to his native land, even to the point of calling in Southern Rhodesian troops and transferring political detainees to Rhodesian prisons. It was the first time I had been in the foreign secretary's room, with its big windows overlooking St. James's Park on one side and Downing Street on the other and its furniture still so redolent of the great Lord Salisbury. As we waited, the private secretary showed us reverentially the place where Lord Halifax used to leave his gumboots after walking across the park from his flat in Carlton Gardens. When we were shown in, Home was frosty and inclined to be sarcastic, until suddenly Violet Bonham-Carter, who was of our number, burst out with all the intimacy to which a daughter of H. H. Asquith was entitled: "Lord Home, I know a young couple in Nyasaland, of whom you, like me, would very much approve—not a kippered old herring like Lord Malvern, and they tell me that it's absolutely frightful there." At last, the ministerial eye brightened and the gold pencil came out. I cannot now remember whether it was before or after our visit that the government sent Patrick Devlin, then a High Court judge, to report on the situation in Nyasaland, which led him to describe the country as a police state. That, at any rate, was the point at which the Central African Federation began to fall apart.

A certain amount of scarcely avoidable journalism came my way at this time. For example, when serious rioting broke out in Leopoldville in 1959, I seemed to be the only available person in England with any first-hand knowledge of the Belgian Congo. So I wrote an opinion piece for the *Sunday Times* and had my first experience of television interviewing, when I sat in one of a row of stalls, with some dancing girls on one side and someone sitting on a log playing a guitar on the other, while I tried to give intelligible answers to fairly inapposite questions. I wrote and spoke with a good deal of misplaced confidence that the Belgians would handle the emergency calmly and intelligently. I did not foresee that within months there would be a parrot cry of *"Pas un soldat au Congo"* (Not a single soldier to the Congo), or that before the end of the year Congolese leaders would be invited to a round table in Brussels to discuss a timetable for independence. Most would attend with the intention of settling for about five years but would find on arrival that their Belgian hosts would be only too happy to settle for a handover period of six months. Again in 1960 I was asked by the BBC to cover Harold Macmillan's African tour for its schools programme. They sent me by special messenger the tapes of his speeches delivered successively in Lagos, Livingstone, Cape Town, and Addis Ababa, and it was in this form that I first saw his outstandingly sympathetic welcome to the newly independent Nigeria, to be followed within a few days by his astonishingly brave warning to the South African parliament about the "wind of change" that had already blown through Asia and would surely sweep through Africa.

A more personal foible that I developed at this time was writing to *The Times*. My exemplar was of course Margery Perham, who did it about once a fortnight, year in, year out, for a quarter of a century. I never attempted it more than about four times a year, but it gave me the kind of thrill that some people get from shooting tigers. To give real satisfaction a letter had to make the top place. If it did, everyone who was anyone would see it. Obviously, it had to be about Africa—I had no standing to write about anything else. It had to be about something of real importance that could be communicated in three densely packed paragraphs. And it had to be completely topical, arising out of the news of that very day. That meant that a whole day's writing time had to be sacrificed to it on the basis of a nearly instantaneous decision taken soon after breakfast. Once posted it could not be retracted, and once in print it was subject to the law of the jungle, which gave no quarter for mistakes of fact or faulty logic. It was an irresistibly exciting experience for as long as the important decisions about Africa continued to be taken in Westminster and Whitehall.

In a domestic way the house in Newton Road still served us well. I worked there for a large part of every day, while Sarah attended St. Paul's Junior School in Hammersmith. On two evenings a week on average Caroline cooked dinner for professional guests. In 1959, as earlier in 1955 and 1956, we took a long summer holiday camping in France, Switzerland, Italy, and Austria. In 1960 we bought a caravan with a view to spending weekends in the country. Before long the caravan became a fixture at Frilsham, where our friends, the Wards, allowed us to keep it in their orchard and to use the basic facilities of their house, which already housed four children at various schools and universities; a score or so of pugs, whose sleeping quarters were stacked at several levels around the kitchen; and a couple of basenjis, African hunting dogs that possessed a highly distorted sense of humour. One of them used to enter the caravan wagging its tail, walk down to the other end of it, and then bare its teeth and snarl at us until we fled in terror.

It was from the caravan in August 1960 that I paid my first and only visit to the Soviet Union. The occasion was a meeting in Moscow of the International Congress of Orientalists to which SOAS sent a sizable delegation. I travelled with John Fage, by now a colleague, in an Aeroflot plane that had red velvet curtains, complete with bobbles, across every porthole. The air hostesses paid us only surly attention, and when we descended the steps at the little airport in the birch trees with no other aeroplane anywhere in sight, the man in front of me turned and said, "My God, it looks like some place we've just moved out of." We were driven through squalid suburbs to the Ukraine Hotel, where we stood for hours in queues while the reception staff argued with each other behind the counter. They tried hard to make us share rooms, but I stood out successfully for a single. Scarcely had I entered it when the telephone rang, and a simpering voice said, "I am a *Finnish* girl. I am not a Russian." And so on. When I returned to the room after the first day at the conference, it was obvious that it had been thoroughly searched.

The congress was attended by some two thousand people, and the number would have been larger but for the six hundred Chinese Orientalists who had cried off at the last moment. It marked the beginning of the political rift between Moscow and Beijing. The African section was a small and peripheral affair that was not even accommodated in the main university skyscraper but relegated to the observatory situated on the edge of campus. Our isolation was aggravated by continuous drenching rain. There were only some sixty of us, including thirty-five Russians and another ten from Eastern bloc countries. Most of the Russians were young "scientific workers" from the recently founded Africa Institute, directed by the senior and genial Ivan Potekhin, whom I had already met and even entertained at my house during his visit to Ghana in 1957. The only other person of comparable standing was the doyen of American Africanists, the anthropologist Melville Herskovits, who had long directed the Program of African Studies at Northwestern University in Evanston, Illinois. This was my first meeting with him, and although he had the reputation of being anti-British, it went like a bomb. We spent an evening together at the Bolshoi, and he invited me, as soon as opportunity offered, to spend a semester teaching in his programme. In Moscow his main ploy, in which Potekhin strongly supported him, was to take the Africanists right out of the International Congress of Orientalists and establish a parallel organisation for African studies that would have its base firmly in the African continent. Only five Africans were in Moscow, all chosen for political rather than scholarly reasons, but thanks to Potekhin and Herskovits, a formal request was sent to Kenneth Dike, as vice chancellor of Ibadan University, to take the initiative in calling an international congress of Africanists, which in the event met under his presidency at the University of Ghana in 1962. John Fage and I were accessories in this transaction but not the prime movers.

Meanwhile, as the rain poured down outside we tried to take the measure of Potekhin's young colleagues. They were not unfriendly, and all spoke either English or French, so there was no problem of communication. They were indeed much better informed about Western publications than we were about theirs. But as they gave their papers, we began to appreciate how far most of them were from Africa and from the primary evidence in their subjects. Only a handful held genuinely academic posts at the University of Moscow, while the recently founded Lumumba Freedom University was not intended to become a place of Africanist scholarship but rather a kind of college of technology for African students, where they could be taught Russian while being inducted into ordinary degree courses in arts and sciences. Most members of the Africa Institute therefore inhabited an ill-defined borderland between journalism, diplomacy, and scholarship. Their stock-in-trade was to study the literature produced in Western countries and to serve it up with an appropriate ideological commentary wherever the demand existed. Sixty percent were Communist Party members as against 30 percent of university teachers in general and 3 percent of the population as a whole. Even so the nearest that most of them could hope to get to African travel was a temporary attachment to a Soviet embassy in an African capital.

One of the nonparty members was brave enough to take me out to a long lunch over which he told me how he had been recruited initially to the Oriental Institute, where he had worked on the French conquest of Indochina and how one Monday morning he had suddenly been transferred to the Africa Institute, where Potekhin had advised him to take as his subject for research African resistance to French imperialism in equatorial Africa. He was expected to attend the institute three days a week for seminars; otherwise, his time was his own. He considered himself well paid, and his wife was earning a good income as a ballerina at the Bolshoi. They had a nice dacha within easy reach of Moscow. During his summer holidays he liked to rent a cabin cruiser and explore the forested region up an easterly tributary of the Volga that was inhabited by Russian Baptists who still lived in stockaded villages by the river but were hospitable to bona fide travellers. As we walked away from the restaurant, he waved to a colleague on the other side of the street and said, "You see that man? He once found a book in the Lenin Library, which no one had ever found before, so he was able to publish quite an interesting article." It gave me a sudden blinding insight into the nature of historical research without access to archives and of research unrelated to any kind of teaching.

On my return from Russia there were perhaps ten days more in the caravan before I was off again, this time to Salisbury, Rhodesia, where Walter Adams had persuaded the Leverhulme Foundation to fund a small conference intended primarily to bring together the teachers of history in the Anglophone universities of Africa. Airlines in those days placed no limit on the number of stopovers, and when offered a long-distance fare, I always made a point of seeing what else could be done with it. On this occasion I decided to take a look at the university college in Addis Ababa that was run by a small team of Canadian Jesuits, invited there by the emperor but on the strict condition that there would be no attempt to evangelise his already Christian subjects. They had on their staff a number of Christian laymen of various denominations, and Robert July of the Rockefeller Foundation had suggested that I might be able to help them recruit a suitable teacher of African history. The Jesuit fathers all dressed in mufti and liked to be addressed as Mister. They lived together in what was known as "the bachelors' residence." During the three days of my visit I saw them often and found their company congenial. They knew the country well, and they foresaw correctly that one obstacle in starting

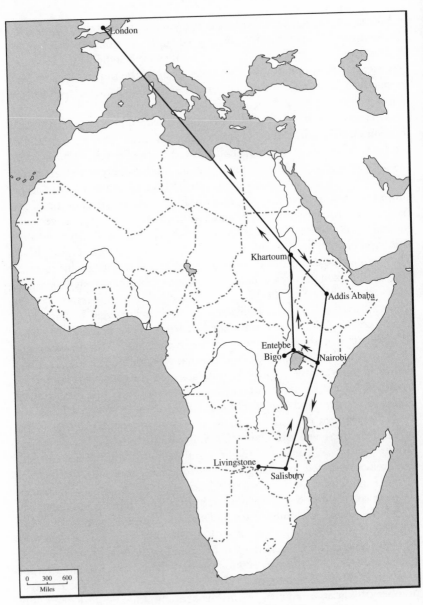

African journey, August–October 1960

any programme of African history would be the deep-rooted contempt of the Christian and Muslim people of the highlands for the rest of the African world around them. African history for them meant the history of Christian Ethiopia, which had, after all, a literary tradition as long as that of any surviving nation of Western Europe. But there would be real difficulty in accepting the need to study the history of "savage tribes beyond the frontiers." So far only the emperor himself had given a lead in the right direction, by reminding his subjects that they too were black Africans. Altogether the Jesuits spoke with much admiration of "the Boss" and in particular of his efforts to free himself from the old guard of corrupt provincial governors and to surround himself with an efficient bureaucracy of younger and better-educated people, typified by the long-serving "prime minister" Aklilu Habte Wold.

On the last day of my visit Father Trudeau, the dean of the faculty, drove me down into the Rift Valley where in the countryside we passed whole companies of brightly dress Oromo horsemen on their way to market and other social events. The horses even had flowers in their bridles, and I had, as nowhere else in Africa, the feeling of having strayed into a scene from the *Canterbury Tales*. I left next day for Nairobi with the uncomfortable sense of having met few Ethiopians, but the university was on vacation and most of its teachers on home leave, so it was probably inevitable. In the event, however, my brief contact with the Jesuits did lead within a few years to the appointment of three expatriate teachers of African history—one Israeli, one Canadian, one American—all of whom had their research training at SOAS and all of whom gave long service. It led also to the award of research scholarships to a succession of four Ethiopians, all of first-class ability, who did their doctorates with us in London. For me the visit was a case of love at first sight, and I confided to Caroline my hopes that something would happen to bring us back there together in the future. As will be seen, in 1966 something did.

The Leverhulme history conference in Salisbury in 1960, to which I now proceeded, stands out as one of the really memorable events of those exciting years. The papers we contributed and discussed there were published in a volume called *Historians in Tropical Africa*,[2] but what stands more clearly in my memory is the cementing of personal relations among those who attended. With only thirty-five participants it was much smaller than any of our London conferences. Nevertheless, every Anglophone university in tropical Africa was represented by the head of its history department. Ibadan, Legon, Fourah Bay, Khartoum, Addis Ababa, Makerere, Nairobi, Salisbury, and Cape Town all were there, together with Hiernaux from Elizabethville, Vansina from Rwanda, the local archaeologists, anthropologists, and archivists from the Central African countries, and three historians from Britain—Ronald Robinson,

George Shepperson, and me. The conference met at a dramatic moment in African history. Vansina arrived there full of news from the Congo, where the army had mutinied in July and Katanga had seceded in August. He told us of Russian money transferred to Patrice Lumumba through Swiss banks and of Belgian arms transferred to Katanga from the NATO base at Kamina. Somalia had become independent on July 1. Nigeria, the most populous country in Africa, was due to become so in October. Even the white Rhodesians were wondering what next.

On the first evening of the conference there was a grand dinner, and I found myself seated next to the governor general of the federation, Lord Dalhousie, and immediately opposite Lord Malvern (formerly Godfrey Huggins), the retired federal prime minister who had recently been succeeded by Roy Welensky. Dalhousie was in a strangely confiding mood. He said he liked Welensky, but he was not sure how well Welensky would do in a crisis. Then, lowering his voice a little, Dalhousie asked me what I thought about "the gentleman opposite" because he rather thought that, if there were a crisis, he (Dalhousie) would have to ask him (Malvern) to return to office. After dinner it was whispered to me by someone that Malvern wished to consult me because he was looking for a biographer, and he bore me away to a remote corner where we talked for a half-hour. He said he admired my book on Johnston and had read it twice. That was endearing, but as I described it in a letter I wrote to Caroline the following day, I had never before met anyone who shifted his ground so constantly in the course of a single conversation. He said that if the Southern Rhodesian government had been given access to the Africans of Northern Rhodesia in 1953, it could have won their support for the federation. But when challenged, he agreed that 1953 would have been ten years too late. As things now stood, he feared that the federation would break up and that Southern Rhodesia would join the Union of South Africa. When I expressed surprise, he said, oh yes, there was no difference between white political opinions in Rhodesia and the Union, "but, of course, the Union would never have us." He then said, "We can go on holding the position in the wrong way—by force—for another few years." I asked, "To what end?" He replied, "To give us time to carry out reforms." I asked whether reforms were politically possible, given the present electorate. He said, "Never mind the political possibilities. Economic development, the full stomach, will do the trick." I asked if that could be done without closing the frontiers of Southern Rhodesia to cheap labour from outside. He said, "The tobacco farmers would never stand for that." And so on. "Not a disagreeable man," I concluded rather primly, "but without principles and bankrupt of ideas." As a potential biographer, I did not feel tempted.

After four days of conferencing for long hours we were all put into a big white bus on the fifth morning and driven for 750 miles around the stone monuments of Southern Rhodesia. We were assured that it was a new bus, but if so, it must have been of the kind designed to convey suburban commuters to their work with the maximum discomfort. On the open road it was noisy, dusty, and unsprung with a wheel span too wide for the narrow tarmac strips of Rhodesian roads. We had to cling to our seats the whole way. Even so, it was always late and left us little time for archaeological sightseeing. Mostly, it was an experience of common suffering, and we got through it, as any group of private soldiers would have done, by singing the equivalent of marching songs. The Southern Rhodesian author and politician Ndabaningi Sithole was of our number and taught us Zulu war cries. These were interspersed with bouts of "Rule Britannia" and Ronald Robinson's favourite number, which consisted of the words "Lloyd George knew my father, my father knew Lloyd George," repeatedly endlessly to the tune of "Onward Christian Soldiers." Jan Vansina stood beside the driver conducting the music.

One aspect of our corporate identity that had been foreseen by Eric Stokes and his colleagues but not at all by the rest of us was that three of our members were black Africans. Because of this the hotels at Great Zimbabwe and Umtali had flatly refused to have us. We therefore spent the first night at the Catholic mission at Gokomere a few miles from Zimbabwe, where we must have consumed several months' supply of sacramental wine. For the second night six of us, including the three Africans, were the guests of Stephen and Virginia Courtauld at their lovely home up a mountain valley to the north of Umtali. They were what were known in Rhodesia as "Government House Liberals," that is to say, they were far too rich and well insulated to care what other white people said about them. Their efforts to make us feel at home were much appreciated but also quite funny. At dinner they sat at opposite ends of a table that would have accommodated forty people, while the six of us were disposed at intervals of about three yards down either side. They talked mostly to each other, and the distance was so great that they had almost to shout. He would say things like "My dear, do you remembered that yacht we had, which we sold to President Tubman?," and she, trying gallantly to broaden the conversation, would turn to her nearest neighbour and say, "Professor Aderibigbe, I expect you *know* President Tubman, don't you?" Then he would try again, "My dear, you remember, when Harold and Dorothy were here, we chartered that plane and flew up to Lake Nyasa?" And she would say, "Well, we *all* know the Macmillans, don't we?" In the morning before we left we all had to sign our names on one of the window panes with a diamond pen, and it was "Dear Professor Aderibigbe, do come and sign your name *here*, next to Roy."

That evening we stayed in the Nyanga highlands where the Troutbeck Inn, one of the great resort hotels of Rhodesia, had actually agreed to have us all. It was the first time they had done such a thing, and they warned us that we must on no account take our African colleagues into the bar, as it was against the law to serve alcohol to Africans. So we all sat drinkless in the lounge, while the other inmates surveyed us surreptitiously over the tops of their newspapers. Soon we realised that the glances were not hostile but friendly and that they came from people who approved of the fact that we would not allow ourselves to be divided from one another by discriminatory legislation. I forget exactly how it happened, but soon we were all in the bar, and no one was objecting. Thus imperceptibly do barriers sometimes fall.

For a day or two more following the return of the white bus to Salisbury, we sat around our conference table. Then on our last day we all climbed into a small chartered aeroplane and were flown to Victoria Falls and the Livingstone Museum. I had done it all two years before, and the excitement of this trip for me was to spend most of the day talking to Desmond Clark. At this point in his career he had been based at the Rhodes-Livingstone Museum for twenty-two years broken only by war service in the horn of Africa. What was chiefly remarkable was that, so far from rusting away, he had used those years in keeping steady pace with almost every publication on the archaeology of the entire continent. He had made his own deeply impressive field researches, especially at the Kalambo Falls site near the south end of Lake Tanganyika where he had established a continuous stratigraphy running from the Middle Stone Age right through to the early Iron Age. But unlike most specialists he had it all in perspective with what everyone else had done. When I stayed with the Clarks eighteen months later in Berkeley, California, I began to learn what had been the contribution of his wife Betty as business manager, linguist, secretary, and hostess in all this great achievement. Later still I was to secure his collaboration as editor of the first, prehistoric volume of the *Cambridge History of Africa*. It was encounters like these that really made the value of all my far-flung travels during these years.

From Salisbury I had routed myself homeward via Uganda in order to spend two weeks in camp with Merrick Posnansky, who was excavating at Bigo along with ten student volunteers from Makerere. Merrick's Ugandan girlfriend Eunice Lubega, who was soon to become his wife, picked me up in Entebbe and drove me out there in a little car that did not look nearly strong enough to cope with the final ten miles of rough bush track that I remembered from previous visits. But Merrick had made friends with the members of a Tsetse Control Unit that was working in the area, and it was now possible to drive right onto the site, where we found him in a large office caravan lent by the Department of

Geological Survey, with a circle of tents for sleeping and an improvised shed of poles and thatch for eating, recreation, and the kind of pot-washing and labelling chores that go on after dark in an archaeological camp. The locally recruited manual labourers, who were used more for bush clearance than for actual digging, had their camp a half-mile away, but otherwise there was no human habitation for several miles around. Working hours were from 8 A.M. until 12:30 P.M. and from 3 till 5 P.M. It was late September 1960, and the equatorial sun was directly overhead. Although it was the dry season, we had papyrus swamps just below us to the north and west, and the mosquitoes came in clouds from sunset till sunrise. Our supply line was long and tenuous. One day the tsetse control people brought us a haunch of bushbuck that gave us a feast. Otherwise, we lived sparely.

On my third evening I wrote to Caroline,

I guess I am feeling somewhat as an archaeologist would feel if I took him along to the Public Records Office and set him down in the middle of a lot of Foreign Office files. It just seems a great mass of incomprehensible detail. This morning I have marked out and started to open up three little trenches, 15' x 3', on top of the central mound. In the course of three hours I suppose we have gone down six or seven inches, taking off the top layer with a hoe, and then forking and shovelling two more layers of top-soil, taking us down to the red laterite of which the mound was built. The only result was half a bag of pottery shards and bones of a goat or small antelope. Next, we shall scrape the surface of the laterite in the hope of detecting post-holes. And I suppose the whole operation will take two or three days for me and two labourers. Still, it is the only way of getting the feel of how these things are done.

By a week later, however, our combined efforts had gone far enough to prove that the central earthworks of this great complex had undergone a fundamental reconstruction, in the course of which the original occupation level, carrying most of the artifactual deposit, had been buried under three to five feet of fresh laterite taken from parts of an older U-shaped embankment (see Chapter 17), so as to make a raised earthen platform in front of the new central mound. That was still only the beginning of the story, which was carried much further after I left, but it made the whole business seem worthwhile. I came away feeling that those two weeks had been a most valuable experience. The mere act of cutting a trench, finding the different occupation levels, sifting the soil, and recording the finds in such a way that someone else could check what I had done made me see the whole process in a new light.

On September 28 Merrick drove me back to Makerere where I found Bernard de Bunsen cogitating his new role as vice chancellor of an independent University of East Africa, with a constituent college in each of the three main territories. That would mean upgrading the Royal Technical College in Nairobi and building a new college from scratch in Dar es Salaam. Seen from my angle, it meant two new history departments to be staffed as soon as possible by qualified African teachers. It began to dawn on me that with the approach of independence, a similar proliferation could be anticipated elsewhere in Africa. The following evening I dined with the Anglican archbishop, Leslie Brown, who spoke of the large number of Tutsi refugees who were entering southwestern Uganda from Rwanda, following the burning of Tutsi houses and the arrest of Tutsi chiefs, to which he was reluctantly convinced that the Belgian administration was party. He thought that in Uganda a poor governor had wasted the opportunities for constitutional development opened by the Hancock mission (see Chapter 13) and that race relations were now worse than they had ever been. He was seriously wondering for how much longer it would be possible for the Anglican Church to have an expatriate as archbishop. My last few nights were spent with old friends in the secretariat who fully confirmed these views.

On my way home to England I stopped off to spend two nights with Neville and Lillian Sanderson in Khartoum. It was my first visit to the university there, and some Sudanese research students came to us at SOAS as a result of it. I was also, like most first-time visitors, deeply impressed by the unself-conscious friendliness of the Sudanese whom I met there. But the combination of heat and humidity in Khartoum in early October had to be experienced to be believed. I do not remember any air-conditioning on the university campus, and it seemed to be accepted that no work was possible between midmorning and late evening, although tennis might be played for a half-hour before sunset. We slept of course on the roof. It did much to reconcile one to the prospect of an English winter.

20

Spreading the Word
(1960–62)

In the three years after October 1960 our postgraduate research work in African history at SOAS really came of age. We took in five new doctoral students in each of those years, and they came from ten countries. Only two of the fifteen were British. Of these David Birmingham came to us with a first degree from the University of Ghana, where his father Walter Birmingham was a professor. While in Ghana David had been fired with an interest in Portuguese sources for West African history, and he soon settled down to work on the sixteenth and seventeenth centuries in Angola.[1] He later became our colleague for several years before going to a chair of modern history at the University of Kent at Canterbury. The other British recruit, Tony Hopkins, came to us from Queen Mary College in our university, where the Tudor historian S. T. Bindoff had advised him to "try something new, like African history." Hopkins was a delight to initiate because, having had no previous contact with the subject, he insisted on reading almost everything before committing himself to study the emergence of African merchant families in nineteenth-century Lagos. He was the first of our English research students really to bury himself in African family papers, which he located while living in a hired room in a Yoruba family compound, studying the inscriptions in the cemeteries, and following up the names in the local telephone directory. He made his early career at the University of Birmingham and wrote a famous book, *An Economic History of West Africa* (1973), on the economic history of West Africa before becoming the Smuts Professor of Commonwealth History at Cambridge.

Of the three recruits from outside England in 1960 one was Shula Marks, who came to us from Cape Town University. After working on the so-called Bambatha rebellion of 1905 in Natal, she stayed with us to rebuild the whole concept of research into South African history,

243

becoming a professor in London and a distinguished successor of Keith Hancock's as director of the Institute of Commonwealth Studies.[2] A second was Bertin Webster, a fiery Canadian from Vancouver who worked on the independent African churches of Yorubaland, collecting his own sources like Tony Hopkins and later teaching at Ibadan and heading the department of history at Makerere before settling at Dalhousie University in Halifax, Nova Scotia.[3] The third was Isaac Akinjogbin, who worked on eighteenth-century Dahomey and made a long career at the University of Ife in his home country of Nigeria.[4]

The next two years, 1961 and 1962, brought us three delightful Ghanaians, Kwame Daaku, John Fynn, and Kofi Darkwah, all steered in our direction by John Fage's successor, Graham Irwin. Daaku learned Dutch and spent a full year in Holland working at the archives of the Dutch West India Company concerning seventeenth-century trade and politics on the Gold Coast. This led him to the significant conclusion that the warfare that raged in the Gold Coast hinterland at this period was caused not by the European merchants at the coastal forts seeking slaves for export but by the competition between Akan states in the interior to corner the gold production of the forest region.[5] Fynn learned Danish and used it, along with English, to work on the Asante kingdom in the eighteenth century as seen through the intelligence networks of the coastal traders at Accra and Cape Coast.[6] Kofi Darkwah came to us briefed to specialise in the history of another African region and set to work on nineteenth-century Ethiopia, producing a useful and respected book on the emergence of the kingdom of Shoa.[7] The plan of his department at Legon was that he would teach the history of eastern Africa and that he would receive regular travel leaves to immerse himself more deeply in his field of study. By 1965 we had trained four Ghanaian teachers of African history for the University of Ghana, and there were more research students in prospect, both from there and from the new University of Cape Coast. It seemed that we had established an almost idyllic academic relationship that would grow firmly with time. We could not possibly have imagined that within a few years Daaku would die from an illness that should have been curable, Fynn would endure long periods of political detention at the hands of the Nkrumah government and its military successors, Darkwah would feel compelled to earn his living in African countries other than Ghana, and even Adu Boahen would undergo one detention and live under the constant threat of more.

Our remaining recruits of this period came from all parts of the world. They included an Indian, B. S. Krishnamurthy, who had tired of teaching English at the University of Madras and who put his savings into training for a completely new career; he worked on the early colonial history of Nyasaland and subsequently taught, first in Nigeria and then for many years at the University of Zambia. A Guyanan, Walter Rodney, learned Portuguese and wrote an outstanding thesis on the Upper Guinea coast between the fifteenth and eighteenth centuries before going to teach at the University of Dar es Salaam,[8] where his radical political beliefs inspired him to write a second and widely read book, *How Europe Underdeveloped Africa* (1972). He died while still in his thirties, by political violence in his own country. A Canadian, Gerry Caplan, wrote on early colonial Zambia before returning to teach in Toronto.[9] A Ugandan, Matthias Kiwanuka, represented the first fruits of Makerere's honours degree programme; he undertook a critical study of the oral traditions of Buganda as collected by Kagwa and other amateur historians during the early years of this century.[10] An American, Suzanne Miers, was born in the Belgian Congo, educated in Belgium and England, and married a British army officer with whom she had lived in Singapore and Kenya. She now was tragically widowed with two young children to support. She researched and wrote on African slavery during the late nineteenth and early twentieth centuries.[11] She made her subsequent career at the University of Wisconsin and Ohio University. Thirty years later, when I had been seven years a widower, we were to link our lives in marriage.

For us at SOAS the great innovation of these three years lay in the planning and implementation of a first degree programme, B.A. honours in history with special reference to the history of Africa. For this we had a pattern to follow that stemmed from the existing programmes for Middle Eastern, South Asian, Southeast Asian, and Far Eastern history taught by our colleagues in the Asian sections of the department. It required us to teach compulsory outline courses in two long periods of African history, each covering the entire continent, and an appropriate selection of optional and special subjects dealing with smaller areas in much greater detail. In this way the larger part of the entire three-year degree programme could be taken in African history, with the remainder drawn from the existing university syllabuses in English, European, and Middle Eastern history. The most difficult hurdle to overcome was the availability and cost of staff, for it was reckoned that to teach such a syllabus year in, year out would require five people, whereas with Douglas Jones and John Fage we were only three. I managed to get a fourth position created for my former research student Richard Gray, who was now teaching in the University of Khartoum. In the event, however, he arrived only just in time to replace John Fage, who effectively left us in September 1962, first on a visit to the United States and later to found the Centre of West African Studies at Birmingham University. We had also interviewed Humphrey Fisher, a graduate of Harvard who had recently completed a doctoral thesis at Oxford on the Ahmadiyya movement in West Africa and seemed to be well qualified to develop the study of Islam and sub-Saharan Africa, but he wished, before doing so, to work for two years in Arab refugee camps in Jordan. He was expected to join us in 1963. Meanwhile, like many another small business in the start-up stage, we had to make do with a lick and a promise.

More dangerous than the practical hurdle, however, was the ideological one. Our proposal had to win the support of the full board of studies in history, and I feared that among its sixty or seventy members, at least half of whom were concerned solely with short periods of English or European history, there would be many who still could not bring themselves to believe that African history could offer a comparable alternative. There would be powerful voices among them, to whom the rest would respond on the day of judgment, and none would be more powerful than that of Lillian Penson. A former chair of the history board and a former vice chancellor of the university, she was now an active member of the Inter-Universities Council for Higher Education Overseas and spent most of her vacations visiting the African universities on the councils on which she served. If she spoke against me, many would surely follow. Bernard Lewis, who was now the head of my department, strongly advised me to go to see her and ask for her support. I did so, and it did not seem to go at all well. "Young man," she said, "Now that Doctor Nkrumah is not in the room with us for once, let me tell you . . ." And what she told me was, in effect, that while African history might be all right for the Africans, it was certainly not all right for the British. I have often thought about this encounter, and it seems to me in retrospect that what she was expressing was the residual prejudice of most of the generation older than mine. I was full of foreboding when I left her, but on the day of battle she did not speak against me. In presenting my case to the board I remembered the well-chosen phrases of the Book of Common Prayer on the subject of Christian marriage, and I said that after twelve years of preparation in the service of the university my proposal could not be said to have been undertaken "lightly or wantonly, but reverently, discreetly, soberly and advisedly," duly considering the purposes for which history honours had been ordained. That seemed to put everyone in a happy mood, and the proposal passed without a vote.

Our business with the board of studies was completed in the autumn of 1960, and it committed us to begin our undergraduate teaching in September 1961. Meanwhile, I had received an attractive invitation from the Free University of Brussels to spend some months there as a visiting professor, and SOAS kindly allowed me to accept it from January until early May 1961. The invitation had its origin in a close friendship I had formed a few years earlier with a Brussels professor, Jean Stengers, when I was working on Johnston and he on the Nile policy of King Leopold II. We had helped each other with the archival sources in our two countries, and the acquaintance had matured into a firm friendship between our two families. He was, and is, the most learned man I ever knew, with an insatiable curiosity that ranges over the whole field of modern European history and politics. He lived with his wife and three children in a large house with six floors in the Avenue de la Couronne, with his parents and two aunts next door. Most of both houses, however, was occupied by Jean's library, which filled every spare room and corridor and overflowed onto the staircases, so that it was possible to use only the central eighteen inches of each step for its original purpose. Starting from his interest in King Leopold, Jean had become a recognised expert on the partition of Africa and the subsequent history of the Congo region. Although he had never been to Africa and never intended to go, he was a leading and respected figure in the Académie Royale des Sciences d'Outremer, and he felt strongly that his university should be participating in the development of African history as an academic subject. He hoped that my visit would help this forward and thought that its centrepiece should be a course of formal lectures in French on the precolonial history of Bantu Africa that would be open to staff members as well as students from all the relevant disciplines. From my side, I realised that there could be no better way of preparing for what I had shortly to begin to do in London, but I also knew what a vast difference there was between speaking another language for ordinary social purposes and trying to be a little eloquent in it. It was Jean's kindness in reading and commenting on all my scripts, often at short notice, that made all the difference to my sense of satisfaction in the job.

Having missed a summer holiday that year, we treated ourselves to Christmas in the Austrian Alps at Hochsölden before installing ourselves in the comfortable modern flat that had been leased for us in the Rue Meyerbeer in the Brussels suburb of Uccle. Two days later, feeling distinctly nervous, I gave my inaugural lecture, "The Search for African History," to a large audience that included most of the top brass of the university. I was told that I got through it with only a single small mispronunciation. I soon learned, however, that fully scripted lectures, far from being a reasonable precaution for a foreigner, were in fact an almost indispensible part of the local teaching system. All examinations here were oral, and they were conducted by the teachers of the courses. The first rule was that no question might be asked that had not been fully dealt with in our lectures. Although not actually compulsory, the sporting thing for teachers to do was to reproduce the texts of their lectures and to offer them for sale at cost. This virtually eliminated the need for the students to read anything else. I gathered that regular teachers took considerable pains to keep their lectures up to date but that most were less successful in eliminating old material in order to make room for the new. In these circumstances the older teachers would start by circulating last year's text and then give an oral commentary upon it—"Page six, paragraph two, very important" and so on.

All this Caroline and I learned from the congenial parties for students that we gave at our flat on Friday evenings. We also learned how much better for relations between teachers and students was the British system of written examinations, set by a board and submitted in anonymous answer books, as against the oral examinations conducted solely by the teacher, which was the norm in most universities on the continent of Europe. The first system enabled the teacher to pose as the ally of the student against the unknown and unidentifiable examiner. The second presented the teacher in the role of a potentially hostile judge from the first encounter. In Belgium in 1960 such fears could be carried to bizarre lengths. For example, the University of Brussels was "free" in the sense that all teachers were required to affirm belief in the duty to teach and publish the truth as they saw it without reference to higher authority of any kind. At that time such an affirmation effectively excluded the employment of any Catholic teacher. Nevertheless, as we quickly discovered when we tried to serve meat at our Friday dinners, a great many students were Catholics, and some told us that they had to go to great lengths to conceal their beliefs from their teachers, even to the point of looking up and down the street before entering a church.

My public lectures apart, the seminar teaching in which I took part with Jean Stengers and one or two other colleagues involved only fourth-year students. They spent most of their final year pursuing individual research projects that would be discussed in common in the presence of teachers and doctoral candidates. The projects had been chosen by the students from a list I sent before I arrived of problems connected with the initial establishment of European colonies in tropical Africa—revenue and expenditure, law and justice, trade and transport, resistance and rebellion, and so on. We also discussed the recently published report of the royal commission chaired by Walter Monckton on the future of the Central African Federation. Great emphasis was laid on the oral presentation by students of the results of their studies, and I found the whole exercise impressive in comparison with what might have been expected from the hard-driven third-year students of British universities. As Jean Stengers explained to me, most of these students were destined for high school teaching in small towns up and down the country, and this kind of training would enable them to carry on with some kind of research activity, in local history or whatever, that would enliven their performance as teachers.

My own great opportunity, practised in the intervals of French composition, was to master the literature bearing on the precolonial history of the Congo basin that I found in the splendid libraries of the Ministry of the Colonies and in the Congo Museum at Tervuren. Our daughter Sarah, now twelve, returned to London for most of the Lent term, staying with friends and relations who lived within reach of St. Paul's Girls' School. Caroline and I, feeling for the first time in our lives extremely well paid, were able to spend some enjoyable weekends in Paris and The Hague, where we found the little Mauritshuis, stacked with Vermeers, the most enchanting of all picture galleries. At Easter Sarah rejoined us, and we drove up to Denmark to stay with a dear friend, Britta Holle, at her flat in Copenhagen and later at the country cottage she was building in the pretty farmlands adjoining the shores of the Kattegat. At the castle of Helsingør, the Elsinore of Shakespeare's *Hamlet*, there hung a map of Denmark's world empire in the eighteenth century depicting Danish Greenland, Danish West Indies, Danish settlements in West Africa, Danish enclaves in southwestern India, Danish Andamans, and Nicobars. I began to understand the economic rationale of all those copper domes in Copenhagen and all those unpretentious but comfortable country houses scattered through the beechwoods of Fünen and Jutland. I remembered that a thousand years earlier the Danish empire would have looked more concentrated and would have included southern Sweden, all of Norway, and two-thirds of the British Isles. Indeed, I have long supposed that my Oliver ancestors were sturdy Danish Olavs who crossed the North Sea to settle in the delectable Scottish borderlands of upper Teviotdale.

Our stay in Brussels ended in early May 1961. I thereby escaped having to conduct my oral examinations, but the texts of my lectures circulated and Jean Stengers kindly performed this last duty on my behalf. The university in due course sent me an enormous medal, and I was soon afterwards elected a corresponding member of the Royal Academy of Overseas Sciences, but it could not be said that my visit gave rise to any more long-term result. The circumstances of Belgian disengagement from the Congo were too traumatic to permit any increased funding of African studies. Most Belgians wanted to forget about the Congo, and they had never been interested in any other part of Africa. Louvain managed for a time to keep the contact with its daughter institution at Lovanium, but even Louvain was unable to find a place for so distinguished an alumnus as Jan Vansina, who thus came to make his subsequent career in the United States. The archaeologist Jean Hiernaux, who had been the rector of the State University at Elizabethville, was a Brussels man and a regular attendant at my lectures, but he too soon left Belgium for a post at the Centre National pour la Recherche Scientifique (CNRS) in Paris. In fact, it was only when a much younger man, Jean-Luc Vellut, returned from Lovanium to Louvain-la-neuve in the late 1970s that African as distinct from colonial history achieved any kind of take-off in Belgium.

Meanwhile, on my return to London I found John Fage well advanced with preparations for the third and last of our large conferences on African history and archaeology. It proved to be much the most interesting of the three, because it had as its leading theme the idea that the emergence and proliferation of African language families could be explained largely in terms of the evolution of strategies of food production appropriate to various types of environment. The idea came from a work of originality and importance published in 1959 by a cultural anthropologist, George Peter Murdock, of Yale and later Penn State, called *Africa—Its Peoples and Their Culture History* (1959), which attempted a classification of African peoples according to what they grew and ate. In particular Murdock stressed the limited number of indigenous food plants available in the moister forested regions of Africa and therefore the great importance to be attached to the patterns of diffusion of the food plants imported into Africa from Asia and the Americas. His broadest hypothesis was that food-producing populations had their origins in the savanna belt to the south of the Sahara, were able to penetrate the equatorial forest only after receiving the yams and bananas of Southeast Asia, and developed dense populations there only after these crops had been augmented by the maize and manioc of Central America. Such ideas sparked immediate interest, not only among historians and archaeologists but also among historical botanists and comparative linguists. At last, we seemed to be within reach of an acceptable alternative to the military migrations of predatory pastoralists and blacksmith-armourers that had dominated so much of the earlier thinking about the distribution of African populations.

In London this period coincided with that in which my colleague Malcolm Guthrie had more or less completed his immense comparative work on the Bantu languages and when he was at last prepared to start thinking about its implications for African history. What he saw, or thought he saw, was on the one hand a cradle of the entire family stretching across the whole region to the south of the equatorial forest from the Atlantic to the Indian Ocean and, on the other hand, a primary division of that protolanguage into western and eastern dialects from which the modern Bantu languages all descended. Against such a conclusion there was that of the American scholar Joseph Greenberg, who held that the Bantu languages as a whole constituted one subgrouping of a much wider family of Niger-Congo languages that had its main base in the forest region of West Africa and in the savanna belt to the north of it. Roland Portères of the Natural History Museum in Paris argued the case for an independent cradle of agriculture in the region of the upper Niger, and it was tempting to equate this tentatively with the heartland of the Niger-Congo language family. If so, the speakers of these languages would have built up their numerical predominance on the basis of savanna food plants like dry rice and pearl millet. The question, then, was how these populations spread into the forest environment to the south.

There was substantial agreement that this had to be on the basis of the yam and the oil palm, both plants of the forest margin but possible to cultivate in forest latitudes once primary forest had been cleared. Murdock had proposed that virtually all the edible yams were of Asian origin, and therefore of relatively recent introduction, but most experts present thought that there were enough indigenous yams in West Africa for their cultivation to have been an independent and early development. The next question was why the cultivation of yams did not appear to have been widespread among the Bantu speakers of the Congo forest. Guthrie, who held that Bantu was an independent language family with its kernel in the savanna to the south of the forest, saw was no great problem here. He acknowledged a tenuous connection between his nuclear Bantu and some "pre-Bantu" ancestors who had migrated from eastern West Africa. When asked how he imagined such a tenuous connection to have occurred, he suggested that a few parties of fishermen might have paddled their canoes down the Sangha tributary of the Oubangui from the northern savanna and up the southern tributaries of the Congo to the southern savanna, where they could have planted the seeds they had brought with them. It was all highly speculative, but the nature of the discussion illustrates the kind of intellectual scenario in which we were operating at the time. At least, it could now be said that African history was acquiring an African baseline.

The conference was held at SOAS in early July 1961. It was attended by about 150 people, including representatives from all the African universities, France, Belgium, Portugal, and a sprinkling of Americans, reflecting the foundation of African studies centres in Boston, New York, Los Angeles, and Wisconsin. This time John Fage and I edited and published a selection of the papers in a special edition of the *Journal of African History* that appeared early the following year.[12]

Appropriately, it was during the month of the conference that Mortimer Wheeler wrote to me announcing that the British Academy had finally been successful in securing treasury funding for a British school of history and archaeology in East Africa and inviting me to join its governing council. Its name was later changed to the British Institute in Eastern Africa, and, outside of SOAS, it was to be my largest academic interest for more than thirty years, my main point of contact with archaeologists, and the focus of most of my later travels in Africa. Among the council's earliest actions was the appointment of Neville Chittick as its director in East Africa, a post he held for eighteen years, initially from a base in Dar es Salaam but later from Nairobi, where he built up and trained a locally recruited staff, including a chief clerk, secretary, librarian, archaeological assistant, draftsman, and driver-mechanic, all of whom remained with the organisation for many years. The assistant directors changed more frequently but included many who became well-known scholars, such as Merrick Posnansky, Robert Soper, David Phillipson, Peter Robertshaw, and Justin Willis. The first president of the council was Laurence Kirwan with whom I worked closely and happily and whom I ultimately succeeded.

Meanwhile, John Fage and I spent an intensely busy summer vacation, during which we wrote most of the Penguin *Short History of Africa* that in the course of the next thirty years was to go through six editions and be translated into twelve languages, with total sales running into several hundred thousand. The request had come in April from Ronald Segal, who had been commissioned by Penguin to edit an Africa series and who asked for a text of sixty thousand words, for which he promised an initial printing of thirty thousand copies. It seemed too good an offer to refuse and, seen in this modest compass looked like something John and I, working together, should be able to produce almost straight out of our heads. We talked up the 60,000 words to 100,000 and then agreed to take ten short chapters each, with John covering West and North Africa and I the East and South. We aimed to write a chapter a week each, and we nearly succeeded. Putting the two halves together took much longer than we had anticipated and involved much redrafting, but by the end of the year it was nearly done, as indeed it needed to be, for in mid-March 1962 I was scheduled to leave on my first visit to the United States and would be away from home for six months.

I am astonished in retrospect to remember that my chapters of the Penguin *Short History* were written in our modest caravan parked between the apple trees in the Wards' orchard at Frilsham. There was just room in it for three narrow sofabeds. One faced the entrance, whereas the two at the other end were separated by a folding table on which I could write or type when it was not in use for meals. But I rather think that most of my manuscript drafting was done on a clipboard on my knee. There was a narrow shelf above each bed, where I may have kept a half-dozen books for daily reference, but the larger part of my active sources consisted of my lecture notes from Legon and Brussels. I have always been an agonisingly slow writer, with an average output of two paragraphs a day. During this brief emergency I may have raised that to three paragraphs. But we did not go without our tennis, country walks, or evening chatter around the Wards' kitchen table. We were indeed increasingly sure that here, among the woods of beech and oak overlooking the valley of the little river Pang, was where we longed to find that gamekeeper's cottage or whatever that would begin as a weekend retreat and gradually become our permanent home. It must have been at the end of this summer that our dear friend and neighbour Katherine Blanford suggested that, if planning permission could be

Back cover photo for the Penguin *Short History of Africa*, 1962

obtained, she might be willing to sell us a woodland acre on the edge of her park, a mere three or four hundred yards from our camping site.

The autumn term of 1961 brought our first cohort of undergraduate students. That we achieved our target of ten guinea-pigs we owed to S. T. Bindoff of Queen Mary College who invited us to give five "missionary lectures" on our subject to his first-year intake, on the understanding that we would teach the African elements of the programme to any converts, while he and his colleagues would teach the European elements to our direct recruits. My memories of that first group are almost entirely happy. Pioneering perhaps demands greater effort all round than routine operations, and it breeds a pleasant camaraderie. Because of the little-worked state of the subject we had to plunge those students straight into areas of controversy and conflict that have long been pushed to the borderlines of more established fields of study. How little comprehensive literature existed at the time can be quickly glimpsed from the "Suggestions for Further Reading" at the back of the Penguin *Short History*. It meant that students had to read more, not less, and they had to be prepared to read French as well as English. One member of the group, who later became a successful chartered accountant, told me in after years that he felt that we had given him an excellent education for that job because we had taught him to look at a lot of ropey evidence and to write comprehensibly about it. The difference this had made in his profession was that, instead of being sent to check the books of one ordinary firm after another, spending a day or two at each, he had soon found himself chosen for the kind of three-week assignment that precedes a take-over bid.

Again, for small numbers it was possible to make special arrangements. I went to see Andrew Cohen, at that time permanent secretary at the Ministry of Overseas Development, with the suggestion that he might make it possible for some of our undergraduate students to be exchanged for a term with an equal number from a West African university, and for some years running he did so. Most of our first cohort went to the University of Ghana, where they were looked after by Adu Boahen and his colleagues, and during the following long vacation they made their way home in twos and threes by a variety of enterprising routes. One lot hitch-hiked north to Timbuktu and west from there to Dakar. Another lot got to the Central African Republic and canoed down the Oubangui to Brazzaville. The future chartered accountant crossed the Sahara in the back of a lorry carrying a cargo of young camels from Niger to Algeria. Strangest of all was the adventure of two women who hitch-hiked in one articulated truck more than three thousand miles from northern Ghana to Khartoum. Somewhere on the borders of Chad and the Sudan the truck broke down and remained for five days by the roadside while help was fetched. By this time it had accumulated about fifty other unofficial passengers, mostly pilgrims travelling to Mecca. All these now camped beside the truck and slept under it at night. The driver gallantly surrendered his cab to the two white women, and the pilgrims shared their food with them. The only interpreter available in the party was a small Arab boy who knew a little French. The whole story says much about security in remote parts of Africa during the early years of postcolonial independence.

The autumn term over, I flew with John Fage to Dakar, where Daryll Forde, as director of the International Institute, had organised an international seminar on ethnohistory at which a certain number of Anglophone and Francophone historians were to meet and discuss questions of methodology with some anthropologists who had done historical work. Although I viewed this exercise with some foreboding, it would be my first foray into western West Africa, and I keenly looked forward to visiting the capital city of the former French West Africa federation, which had controlled the affairs of its constituent colonies of Senegal, Mauritania, Guinea, Ivory Coast, Soudan (Mali), Upper Volta (Burkina Faso), Niger, and Dahomey (Bénin). The federation had been, more than anything else, a means of compelling the more prosperous colonies to subsidise the more impoverished ones. It could not survive the introduction of democratic majority rule in its richer member states, and an independent Senegal had thus been left, as windfalls, with the governor general's palace, and all the grand offices of the now-defunct federal ministries, including the university, the archives, and the headquarters of the organisation for scientific research, the former Institut Français d'Afrique Noire, now cleverly renamed the Institut Fondamental d'Afrique Noire, so as to retain the same acronym of IFAN. It seemed clear that, with all these advantages, Dakar was likely to be the point of entry for any future research in the area by our students and that the more contacts I could develop there the better.

And so, having spent a night in Paris, John and I embarked at Orly airport, along with several other conference attenders, on a freezing foggy morning in early December. The pilot taxied briskly towards the runway, took a right-hand bend much too fast, and came to a shuddering halt with the undercarriage buried in the mud. The lights went out, and there was a deathly hush among the passengers, until a familiar voice said, "*Eh bien, nous sommes tous provisoirement vivant*" (So, we are all still alive, for the time being). It was Hubert Deschamps, the recently elected professor of African history at the Sorbonne who was paying his first visit to Senegal since his retirement as the French governor there some years before. While we waited interminably to be rescued, he walked up and down the aisle, beating his breast and saying, "*Oh, la France, oh, la France. Après l'Irlande, c'est la nation la moins sérieuse de l'Europe*"

255

(Oh, France, oh, France. Except for Ireland, it is the least serious country in Europe). Eventually, ladders were brought and we climbed out and were driven back to the airport building. We left again, more successfully, at midnight. At Ngor airport to greet us in the dawn sunlight there was the ever-smiling face of Raymond Mauny, still the chief archaeologist of IFAN but soon to be nominated to a second chair of African history at the Sorbonne. And soon we were bowling down the spectacular clifftop road to central Dakar, with only the two rounded hills known popularly as *les mamelles* (breasts) blocking the view to the westernmost point of Africa at Cape Verde. I was greatly impressed by the bay of Dakar, with its immense vista of ancient Wolof settlements stretching away to the south, and with the island fortress of Gorée, two and a half miles offshore, where long before the colonial occupation of the mainland a succession of French and British companies collected slaves for shipment across the Atlantic.

The conference, which filled most of our days, was tedious in the extreme. Plenty of relevant and able people were present. Jack Goody had come from Cambridge and Dan McCall from Boston, V. L. Grotanelli from Rome, Ivor Wilks from Ghana, Jacob Ajayi and Colin Newbury from Ibadan, Allan Ogot from Makerere, and Donald Abraham from Salisbury. Fortunately, we had all submitted our papers in advance, and from them Jan Vansina as editorial secretary was later able to compile a fairly useful volume.[13] But seated round a table our minds failed to meet, and all attempts at fruitful discussion were frustrated by the need to translate from French into English and vice versa in the interests of our African participants. Most of the interpretation was done by Vansina, while Mauny, who sat beside him, kept filling up his glass with white wine. This brought a wicked glint into his eye and an ironic tone into his voice that were frequently amusing but destructive of sustained concentration.

But there were also, as I had anticipated, the uncovenanted benefits of being in this place with these people at this time. At the university were those like Denise Bouche and the two Brasseurs who went out of their way to invite us and show us round. And there were others, like the head of the department, de Bien, who received us in his office and explained that the university was still paid for out of the French metropolitan budget and that, so long as this was so, the syllabuses taught there had to conform to those laid down by the French Ministry of Education. We went on down the corridor to call on his two African assistants. Both, I think, were Guinean refugees in Senegal. One, Boubakar Barry, later came to us as a visiting lecturer at SOAS. We called also upon the ex-federal archivist Moreau, who was clearly someone who was out to encourage foreign researchers. We lunched with the great Théodore Monod, who had just returned after crossing the Mauritanian desert on a camel. There were those who maintained that Monod would surely have walked, leading the camel so that it did not get too tired, and others who thought that he would probably have carried the camel. His wife told me that it was his habit to rise at 4:15 A.M. and to work fasting until 1 P.M. After a light lunch he went back to work until dinner at 7:15. The most interesting topic we discussed at his table was the horror, which he obviously still felt profoundly, for the attempted invasion of Dakar by the British and the Free French in 1940. It was an attitude I had to learn to understand with Deschamps also, because his initial inclination to Vichy had been occasioned by the British air raid on his hometown of Noyon in an attempt to destroy the main German U-boat base used in attacks on Allied shipping in the Atlantic.

After the Dakar conference I was in England for only eleven weeks before I set off to the United States in response to an invitation from Mel Herskovits to spend the spring quarter as a visiting professor at Northwestern University. This gave me just time to teach the Lent term at SOAS, correct the proofs of the *Oxford History*, and put the final touches to the text of the Penguin *Short History*. In London, following the independence of Tanganyika in December, our friends Sam and Sarah Ntiro had been setting up the new high commission, and February 1962 saw the conference called to discuss a constitution for the approaching independence of Kenya, when we lent our house to the Africa Bureau for an evening party for the African delegates. They arrived late in Newton Road, fly whisks and all, having been closeted in a private meeting with the colonial secretary, and at once crowded round our radio to hear a broadcast by their leader Ronald Ngala. Ten o'clock struck, and the BBC announcer said, "We regret to tell you that the talk which was to have been given by Mister Ronald Ngala will not now take place." From the back of the circle came the voice of Colin Legum, in obvious imitation of a Kenya settler: "Oh, these bloody Africans." It brought down the house.

21

New World Awakening

(1962)

My first visit to the United States began, oddly enough, on the Pacific Coast. My temporary appointment at Northwestern had brought in its train several invitations to lecture at other U.S. universities, among them a pressing one from Jim Coleman, the founding director of the African Studies Center at the University of California, to visit the campuses at UCLA and Berkeley. It fitted best to do this on my way to Evanston, where Caroline and Sarah would join me later. And so, on March 17, 1962, having circled on foot a still-frozen Round Pond in Kensington Gardens, I caught the midday plane to Los Angeles. From one side of the world to the other it happened to be a perfectly clear day, and it gave me the best visual geography lesson of my life. The icy mountains of Labrador glistened in the sun. On the St. Lawrence and the Great Lakes the winter ice was just breaking up into long floes; only Lake Michigan was clear. The prairies were still under snow all the way across to the Rockies, beyond which the Painted Desert and the Grand Canyon threw up their vivid colours of rusty orange and cobalt blue. At last we were flying low over Los Angeles, an apparently endless tropical suburb, its streets exactly criss-crossed, the houses tiled in brilliant colours, the unfenced gardens with their freshly watered grass and pale blue swimming pools. It was still only six o'clock, and waiting to meet me was Leonard Thompson, our host at Cape Town in 1958, now transplanted as one of the founders of African history in the United States.

Leonard was the perfect initiator into the American scene. As a recent migrant he knew the things I needed to be told. In particular he knew the whole bundle of ignorant prejudices about American education that European academics tended to bring with them and the insufferable patronage with which they would air them in front of justifiably outraged hosts. "Of course, I understand that in America you can get a B.A. in hairdressing and needlework." And so on. He taught me the all-important fact that the slightly looser structure of U.S. undergraduate degrees made it far easier to introduce a new subject like ours than it had been in Europe. In a climate of expansion the history department of an average American university would not only accept but welcome the appointment of a properly qualified historian of Africa, whose two or three courses would be added to the general mix and, if adequately supported by student enrollments, would quickly become established. Once the bandwagon got rolling, there would probably be vacancies for five hundred specialists in the field. Altogether, there was much to be learned by a visitor from a country with forty universities and about the same number of colleges of advanced technology, enjoyed by perhaps 2 or 3 percent of the population, and one with four hundred universities and eighteen hundred colleges of higher education, attended by more than a quarter.

I was impressed by the manner in which this university, like others in the United States, handled its short-term visitors. I gave a public lecture to an audience of perhaps two hundred on a general topic that assumed no prior knowledge of the subject and addressed a seminar of around thirty postgraduate students on the research topics being pursued at my university. I lunched with the teachers of history. I was taken to see the performing dolphins at Wonderland of the Pacific. I was dined by the Thompsons at a beach restaurant in Santa Monica with the Leo Kupers and the Mike Smiths. I had dinner with Jim Coleman at the Bel Air Hotel, and we had one of those long, unhurried, wide-ranging conversations that perfectly illustrated the genius of his leadership in building up the whole programme of African studies at this large and important university. I had to ask myself whether a visitor to my university would have been so well used and so well treated. I was to revisit UCLA briefly in 1967. Meanwhile, it remained firmly within my horizon of regular contact as a place where African history was well rooted in the precolonial past and effectively buttressed by both archaeology and historical linguistics. Over the years its output of doctoral students in African history must have rivalled that of Wisconsin.

On March 21, 1962, I flew up from Los Angeles to San Francisco and caught the helicopter across the bay to Berkeley, where another recent migrant, Desmond Clark, was beginning to do for African archaeology in the United States what Leonard Thompson was doing for African history. Clark was waiting by the landing pad, and soon we were on our way to his house at Orinda, a country village in an apple-green valley beyond the hills that ring the eastern side of the bay. There was as yet no specialist in African history at Berkeley. A few years hence this role would fall to the historian of Madagascar, Raymond Kent, an early product of the Wisconsin stable. Meanwhile, the modern side of African studies was represented by the political scientists David Apter and Carl Rosberg, to both of whom Desmond quickly introduced me. I gave a public lecture next day but was saved from any further formal engagements by the appearance of a rival speaker in the person of President John F. Kennedy, who came to give the Charter Day address on March 23. It was the only time I ever saw him in the flesh and heard his crisp and invigorating oratory. On the two weekend days that followed, the Clarks took me sightseeing, first in the vineyard country east of Orinda and then in the redwoods north of the bay, near which we saw the rare sight of a California mountain lion sniffing out the bushes on the opposite side of a little gully from our picnic site. It was a memorably happy visit, and it let to many years of professional collaboration.

On March 26 I flew from San Francisco to Chicago and so arrived in a rather roundabout way at my main destination in the northern suburb of Evanston, some fifteen miles up the western shore of Lake Michigan. After the glory of the California spring it did not look at all prepossessing. The snow had just melted, leaving every blade of grass blackened by the accumulated dirt of winter. The trees were still bare, and great blocks of dirty ice were piled up along the lakeshore. Every other day at least, the north wind blew relentlessly, and people scrambled from their heated houses to their heated motor cars and thence to their heated shops and offices. For the first two weeks, while I waited for Caroline and Sarah to arrive, I lived alone in two dowdy rooms in a residence for married students. The whole building had that smell of centrally heated and air-conditioned dust peculiar to North American hotels in which no window is ever opened, winter or summer. Access to the apartment was not made easier by the fact that the authorities had arranged for the staircase to be painted simultaneously with a major overhaul of the lifts. I found it best to use the fire escape.

As soon as I reported for duty the following morning, however, things started to look up. The history department had done its homework, and sixty-five undergraduate students were inscribed on my lecture list. I was expected to assign enough written work to enable me to report on them and place each in one of four "grades" before the end of the term. Since this was to be the first comprehensive outline course ever given on the history of Africa, it provided a good illustration of how quickly an innovation could be put into viable practice in U.S. academe. Still more impressive, the members of my graduate seminar had each already written, typed, and circulated a twenty-five page paper on one or other of the topics I had sent ahead of my arrival. In general I found that U.S. students expected to be told in some detail what they were to read but would show much more energy and initiative than all but the best British students in finding and reading what had been recommended. It was symptomatic that the university library was open until 2 A.M., seven days a week, and staffed outside office hours by student helpers.

The animating figure in African studies was of course Mel Herskovits, who had joined the staff of the university in the early 1930s and was now within a year of his retirement. His long service had helped the library to build up the best collection of Africana in the country. He had watched his opportunities and had been among the first to secure government and foundation funds for the establishment of a multidisciplinary programme that he now directed from Africa House, a pleasant frame building on a residential street at the southern edge of campus. Access to it was controlled by an imposing lady called Anne Moneypenny, who would beckon one to her desk and whisper conspiratorial information, such as "Six calls to Washington already this morning." Mel had his office on the bedroom floor, and he had placed me in the adjoining room, separated only by the former family bathroom, through which he would come charging whenever he had anything to discuss. It was a happy arrangement that gave me a feeling of great support in all the small problems that beset a visitor in a strange land. "You'll need a car," he said. "Let me see what I can do." A few days later a glamorous canary-yellow Chevrolet Impala, almost new with a roof that went up and down at the touch of a button, was delivered to my door at a nominal rent of $300 for the duration of our stay, not just at Northwestern but for an extended summer holiday to follow. "You'll want to see a bit of the country now that you're over here," said Mel's friend in the motor trade. "Take it anywhere you like. Just bring it back to me before you return to England." It was fun to go and meet Caroline and Sarah in Chicago on April 12 with transport worthy of a filmstar, and I enjoyed driving Sarah to school in it on my way to Africa House.

Northwestern had been more than accommodating in scheduling my formal teaching between Mondays and Wednesdays so that it would be possible for me to travel to engagements elsewhere during the second half of each week. My first such escapade was to Boston University, which had been on the front line of federally supported African studies programmes. I stayed there with the founding chairman, Bill Brown, on April 25 and talked to his staff and graduate students on the following day. Two African historians were already in post, one of whom, Norman Bennett, was almost of my vintage. The other, George Brooks, was just beginning and was to make his main career at the University of Indiana. It was in their agreeable company that I had my first sight of Boston Common and of the harbour where the celebrated tea party took place in 1773. That evening I crossed the Charles River to Cambridge to spend the night with old and dear friends from Bletchley days, Barbara and Joe Eachus. In the morning they put me on the Greyhound bus to Northampton, where I was to speak at a faculty dinner and seminar of the Connecticut Valley colleges—Smith, Amherst, Mount Holyoke, and the University of Massachusetts—at Smith College. There I spent the afternoon with that great and heroic woman Gwendolen Carter, who had made a triumph out of life on crutches, heading the department of political science at Smith, travelling over nearly all of Africa, and publishing prolifically on the politics of newly independent states. She had just been approached about the possibility of succeeding Mel Herskovits at Northwestern. We sat discussing it in her lovely country garden with its long views of the Connecticut River Valley, and I wondered how anyone so disabled could contemplate leaving such a place for the suburbia of Evanston and the administrative pressures of running a programme. Although it was our first meeting, I ventured the comment that it would represent the triumph of ambition over common sense. She did not accept my advice, but it was the beginning of a long warm friendship that was renewed in places as far apart as Evanston, Dakar, Addis Ababa, and Frilsham.

Over the first weekend in May we made a family expedition in the canary-yellow motor car to the University of Indiana at Bloomington, where a programme of African studies was being developed under the direction of Gus Liebenow, the anthropologist of Liberia. With the arrival of George Brooks from Boston and Phyllis Martin from SOAS it too would become a place of importance for African history. In 1962, however, our dinner companion with the Liebenows was the professor of police administration. Very different was our experience the next weekend at the University of Wisconsin at Madison, where we stayed with the Vansinas and visited with the Curtins and where I lectured and met a research seminar in what was already a flourishing school of African history that was setting standards of training that were perhaps unique in the world. Phil Curtin was a vigorous and vocal critic of British practice in relation to the doctoral degree, which put the whole emphasis of three or four years' work into the production of a thesis that was, as nearly as possible, complete and ready for publication as a definitive contribution to knowledge in one small and specialised corner of the field. This, he maintained, was to throw upon the market for academic employment people who were quite unqualified to teach across the broad range of the subject. For him the most important part of doctoral training was the two years of attendance at formal courses in four relevant fields of history, which students had to complete before undertaking any original research. This was the norm in American universities, and in many of them it was followed by a thesis that could be completed within a single year and was regarded as an exercise in scholarly competence rather than an original contribution to knowledge. In addition, Curtin demanded from his graduate students that they have a working knowledge of two foreign languages, one of which should be African, and that every thesis be based partly on fieldwork undertaken in an African country. Conscious that such a commitment of time would run far beyond any ordinary scholarship or private pocket, he was successful in obtaining foundation grants sufficient to top up the emoluments of his *corps d'élite* to the point where it could be said that the best Wisconsin doctoral graduates were the best-trained entrants to the profession from the late 1960s on. Not many were Africans, and not many of the others worked for any considerable time in African universities, but their collective contribution to research in African history and to the establishment of the subject in the major universities of North America was to be preeminent.

My final sortie from Northwestern was to New York, where Robert July had arranged for me to spend two days of consultation with his colleagues at the Rockefeller Foundation. It was an interesting assignment. The officers, he told me, were trying to develop a strategy to assist the new nations of Africa to secure a sense of national identity, which would "combine an appreciation and utilisation of their traditional culture with the best that is available from the West and elsewhere." They foresaw that there would a need for national histories, based on something more than romantic yearnings after a glorious precolonial past and coupled with a calm reappraisal of the changes wrought by Africa's relations with Europe during the past four hundred years. They wanted my thoughts on the directions that research and training in African history might best take during the next several years, both inside and outside Africa, and they sought my help in identifying both the Africans and the expatriates from Europe and North America through whom departments of history in African universities might be helped to grow and prosper. I still have the notes from which I spoke to them, and in retrospect I find that they illustrate quite well the effect of my U.S. travels on my professional outlook.

I suggested that the proper aim for universities in Africa was to make African history as naturally the centre of historical education as American history was in U.S. universities—dominant but not exclusive. I said that in my belief this aim was already accepted by universities in Anglophone Africa, and its implementation depended entirely upon the supply of teachers with the necessary skills, whereas in Francophone Africa not even the aim existed. My travels in the United States, I said, had left me with the impression that African history might expect to achieve the same kind of attention nationwide as, for example, Latin American history. One might expect a large number of universities to make a single appointment in the subject, but research training would be best concentrated in a handful of larger centres like those at Wisconsin and UCLA. It seemed to me that the best contribution Rockefeller could make to history in the African universities would be likely to come from encouraging these few centres in ways that would help them to attract research students from African countries by providing fellowships on a scale generous enough to permit the holders to spend a part of their time in fieldwork in Africa. Needless to say, I did not fail to remind them that the largest and best established of these key centres was to be found at SOAS, where we were already deeply involved in the training of both African and North American academics.

The details of our discussions during those two days are probably no longer of interest, and I have no idea how far anything I said may have influenced the policy or actions of the foundation. The significance of the visit for my story is simply that, whereas in 1948 I had been a lone voice crying the cause of African history in the wilderness, here I was in 1962 on the forty-second floor of the Rockefeller Building, discussing a strategy for the development of African history on three continents with a group of highly intelligent people with the resources to greatly influence academic decisions throughout the Western world. These were the people who had already helped with the launching of the *Journal of African History*, who had provided Allan Ogot with the fellowship to carry out his pioneering study of oral traditions among the Luo, and who had provided the university college at Salisbury with the means to sponsor Donald Abraham's researches on the medieval kingdom of the Mwenemutapas. I left them with the optimistic feeling that the current initiative would turn out to be much more than a gleam in the eye.

From New York I returned to Evanston in time for commencement exercises, a curious phrase used in most U.S. universities for the final graduation ceremonies held at the close of the academic year. It was scarcely an exciting experience, but it seemed the proper way to say goodbye. I was sorry, however, to have missed Sarah's graduation from Haven Junior High School, which had taken place the previous day, when, as Caroline described it, little boys in bow ties and little girls all in white walked hand in hand into the future, while the congregation of proud parents sang, to the music of Schubert's Unfinished Symphony,

> Led by a distant voice,
> We're leaving childhood's carefree pleasures,
> We seek the greater joys
> Of learning and of life's great treasures.

There was, she said, not a dry eye in the hall. We had in truth, all three of us, become attached to this midwestern community, which we had found friendly, tolerant, and immensely hospitable. At the end of three months there were a score of colleagues and their families with whom we had come to feel real friendship. Among the graduate students were four or five with whom we kept contact, including Steve Feierman, who was to become one of the stars of Phil Curtin's team at Wisconsin before settling in at the University of Florida at Gainesville. In my lecture class were a couple of State Department recruits, of whose total involvement with the subject one felt no doubt. Among them also were at least twenty African Americans, which was considered a large number to find in any enrollment list at a private university. One of my colleagues said, "They must be very good at football; they wouldn't be here otherwise." But as I discovered, that did not mean that they were poor students. What I learned from them was that the forty million African Americans were an important factor in the general acceptance of African history on this continent. I suppose that of all the books I have published a very large proportion has been bought and read by African Americans.

My last chore before leaving the university was to grade my students, and I marvelled at the simplicity of the operation. In a British university I would have drafted a question paper that would have been shown to an external examiner and conned over by a committee before being printed and issued to the candidates in a specially invigilated three-hour session. The answer books would have been marked by two examiners, checked by a third, and amalgamated with other marks awarded for other courses by a full board of examiners, which would have argued solemnly about the borderline cases for an entire day. Here, I simply announced that the next lecture hour would be devoted to a written examination, set and marked in whatever form I pleased and without any attempt to conform my standards with those of other teachers. The answer papers were returned to the students, complete with my marks and remarks, and they were quite free to come and argue about them and even to burst into tears while doing so. I reported the marks to the dean, who would in due course record them in a final transcript, the student's academic passport for employment or further education. It was looser and more impressionistic than the British system of rigid classification but much more economical in teachers' time and much less invidious for the recipient. Again, it did not have the confrontational element induced by the oral examinations of continental Europe. Its results were probably as close to the mark as any academic results awarded at a particular arbitrary moment in a person's life have any right to be.

At length, on June 20, 1962, we three Olivers set off westwards for our great adventure in the splendid yellow car. It was midsummer and time, so we thought, for the mountains. Our broad aim was to drive the Rockies from south to north in July and then in August to cross Canada from west to east. We had booked homeward passages by sea from Montreal at the end of that month. The first leg of our journey, then, was across the prairies to Denver, and we did it by easy stages in three days, discovering as we went the basic comfort and the extraordinary good value of U.S.

country motels. Not many British people were travelling on holiday in the United States at that time. There were exchange controls and niggardly allowances of foreign currency for private travel, and the real cost of crossing the Atlantic was much higher then than today. We were fortunate in having earned and saved some dollars, and we were astonished at how far they went. On our second day out we crossed the Mississippi at Hannibal and the Missouri at St. Joseph and spent the night at Smith Center, half-way across Kansas and allegedly the geographical centre of the United States. It certainly did not appear that it could have any other claim to fame. At Denver we joined forces with our friends the Eachuses and next day drove south in tandem to the attractive little mountain resort of Taos in northern New Mexico. It was our farthest south.

From there northwards we tried to keep as close as possible to the watershed line known as the Continental Divide. While at Taos we picnicked by the Rio Grande, which in its lower reaches forms the boundary between Texas and Mexico. Near Buena Vista in central Colorado we stayed beneath Mount Harvard, beside the main source of the Arkansas, which flows right across the prairies to join the lower Mississippi. Next day we crossed the divide to the upper waters of the Colorado River, which drops down through Utah to the Gulf of California in northern Mexico. In Estes Park and again in Yellowstone we were right on the divide, among mountain streams flowing, some eastwards to the Missouri, some westwards into the Snake and Columbia rivers in the states of Idaho and Washington. In Montana, where we made our longest stay beside Lake Macdonald in Glacier National Park, we were on the western side of the range. In Canada, from Banff and Lake Louise northwards to Jasper, the ice-clad crests were just to our west, and from the hot springs at Miette we gazed out to the north over country draining to the Mackenzie River and ultimately to the Beaufort Sea. Throughout this mountain trail, extending over more than two thousand miles of roadways, we found our lodgings in log cabins in national parks, nearly all of them scenically placed and many of them comfortably furnished. We stayed happily for two or three days at a time, walking higher into the mountains by day and using the admirable footpaths provided. Only at Yellowstone did we feel oppressed by the numbers of other tourists and the obtrusive behaviour of the local bears, which spent their time rummaging in the dustbins and parading round the campsites with Coca-Cola cans on their noses. In general the farther north we went, the more exquisite the scene became, with a crispness of air and a clarity of atmosphere I have never experienced elsewhere.

Our crossing of Canada was by comparison a disappointment. On leaving the mountains we entered a belt of heavy rain that travelled with us all the way to the Quebec border. We pressed forward in the hope of outpacing it, but it caught up with us again while we rested at night.

Almost all that I remember of northern Alberta was our surprise at seeing the many domed Russian Orthodox churches built by migrants from the Ukraine during the early years of this century. Of Saskatchewan I remember the bizarre fact that all the doctors were on strike against some piece of legislation introduced by the Social Credit Party. Of Manitoba I remember the skyscrapers of Winnipeg looming above the horizon of a flat grey landscape. We did not stay there but drove straight on to Port Arthur on the northwestern shore of Lake Superior, where we found lodgings with a family of recent immigrants from Finland who showed us with pride the sauna they had constructed beneath the sitting-room. We were now on the Canadian shield, which stretches all the way to Hudson Bay, where the basement rocks are covered by only an inch or two of soil and every slight depression is filled by a shallow lake, making the whole area an angler's paradise, nowadays increasingly accessible through the use of small pontoon-planes. We found an attractive small hotel at a place with the name, memorable to us, of Roland's Lake, the proprietors of which made the best part of their living by flying holiday makers to a network of otherwise inaccessible fishing camps. Here we paused for a few days of gentle canoeing before moving on, in two more travelling days, to the home of my cousin Betty Price in Como, on the Ottawa River, within commuting distance of Montreal.

From the Prices we made one more tour to the east and south. At Quebec we attended the changing of the guard on the Heights of Abraham, all very British, with an incredibly smelly mascot goat leading the parade, and later mingled with the crowd of French-speaking Canadians taking their Saturday evening exercise on the wooden walkways suspended on the side of the cliff. There were parents and children in their best clothes and teenagers swinging along four abreast in single-sex groups, eyeing their opposite numbers and exchanging jokes with them over their shoulders as they passed, in just the same way as teenagers in Normandy and Brittany of the 1930s. Beyond Quebec we followed the north shore of the St. Lawrence estuary as far as St. Siméon, where we ferried across it to the Rivière du Loup and continued right round the coast of the Gaspé Peninsula. We were now in the rural heart of French Canada, with villages dominated by white-painted Catholic churches and in the gardens elderly women knitting as they swung gently to and fro in the family *balançoirs*. It was a France that had never seen a revolution. From the Gaspé we crossed New Brunswick by the shortest route into Maine to stay for a few days with old friends Julian and Carola Peck, who spent their summers by a lake near Farmington, and from there returned through Vermont to Como.

We had by this time driven the yellow motor car more than twelve thousand miles, and our last expedition in it was to return it to its owner.

We took it first to Niagara Falls, from where Caroline and Sarah took the train back to Montreal, while I drove on alone across Michigan to Evanston, said my thanks to Frank Katzen, who had made our journey in it possible, and enjoyed a last meal with Mel Herskovits, whom I was to see only once more and that briefly at International Congress of Africanists in Accra. Soon after he died suddenly in 1963 during the first year of his retirement. I flew to join the others in Montreal, and soon we were embarked in a Greek liner, the *Homeric*, bound for Southampton. We had had a wonderful introduction to North America. My academic invitations had given me quite a representative picture of the burgeoning interest of the universities of the United States in an Africa liberated from colonialism, and if our holiday travels had been rather targeted on natural phenomena, that too had contributed to our sense of scale and proportion. The only sadness in it had been that during these six months Caroline had suffered the first severe attacks of the rheumatoid arthritis that was to encompass the last twenty years of her life in an ever-more remorseless grip of pain and progressive disablement. It was not a matter to which she ever willingly referred. When people asked her how she was, she replied, "Fine, thanks." Within the family, however, it became the main fact of our lives for many years.

22

The Crest of the Wave
(1962–63)

In 1963 I would be forty years of age, and SOAS decided to celebrate the event by asking the University of London to create a chair of the history of Africa and at the same time submitted my name as its preferred candidate for the post. It was to be not a personal chair but an established chair, that is to say, it would create a strong moral obligation on the university to keep it in being and to keep it filled whenever a vacancy should occur. It therefore constituted a considerable degree of recognition for the subject. The procedure for dealing with such a request was to submit it to a panel of nine assessors, four of whom would be chosen by the school and five by the university, two of them from other universities. The assessors were consulted initially in writing, and if all agreed the proposal was accepted. If any of the nine expressed doubts about the suitability of the preferred candidate, the post would be publicly advertised, and the assessors would consider the applications and conduct an interview. I was fortunate enough to have my name subscribed in the postal ballot. The public announcement was made only in April, but I had known for some time that it was on the way. It made for a happy homecoming.

During the years following my promotion the problem of recruiting suitable colleagues seemed to vanish. The readership I vacated was won, in open competition with several strong contenders from all over the world, by Richard Gray. That left Douglas Jones in the third place, and Humphrey Fisher, who had now joined us after his service to Arab refugees in Jordan, as the fourth. Anthony Atmore, a graduate of Cape Town University who had worked briefly in the Colonial Education Service in Malawi, came to SOAS to take a second undergraduate degree in the history of the Near and Middle East and completed it with first-class honours in 1963. Bernard Lewis thought highly of him and suggested that we might appoint him as a specialist in the history of Muslim North

Africa. It was no part of my nature to look gift horses in the mouth, and soon I was preparing the case for a specialist in South African history also. We looked at some candidates already teaching in South African universities but decided that Shula Marks, who had taken our in-house courses in African history as qualifying papers and was now well advanced with her doctoral thesis, would be the best choice. By 1964, therefore, there were six of us, and during the three following years we were able to recruit David Birmingham as a specialist in western Central Africa and Richard Rathbone for contemporary history. We were then by far the largest and best-balanced team of African historians in the world, and so we remained until the middle of the 1980s—long after the special circumstances attending our growth had ceased to exist.

There was plenty to do immediately. Our undergraduate programme was building up to full strength, with three annual cohorts on the books at any one time. In our research supervision the middle years of the 1960s brought us many of our best doctoral students who later carried the subject to new centres all round the world and helped by their publications to fill out its scholarly literature. Significantly, the United States was the largest beneficiary. Hollis Lynch and Marcia Wright went on to make their careers at Columbia University in New York. Ned Alpers did the same at UCLA, Suzanne Miers at Ohio University, and David Cohen at Johns Hopkins and later Northwestern and the University of Michigan. Richard Caulk was the only one of our American students to work for any length of time at an African university, in this case Addis Ababa. Donald Crummey, in origin a Canadian, was his colleague there for several years and later moved to the University of Illinois. The British contingent was smaller. David Ross, after a period at Fourah Bay, went to Vancouver. Sean O'Fahey, after starting at Khartoum, settled at the University of Bergen in Norway. Only Richard Rathbone remained at SOAS throughout his career.

Among our African research students the pendulum was now swinging from West to East Africa. We took on two more Ghanaians in addition to the three who were still completing. But Nigeria was by this time almost self-sufficient in postgraduate training, and only a few Nigerians now came our way. We had Martin Njeuma from Cameroon and Omar Nager from the Sudan. But our closest links were henceforward with Uganda, Kenya, and Ethiopia. From Uganda Mati Kiwanuka was now followed by Sam Karugire, and from Kenya Allan Ogot was succeeded by Godfrey Muriuki and Gideon Were. From Ethiopia we were joined in 1964 by Taddesse Tamrat, the first and the best of a succession of four outstanding research students to come to us from that country. Not quite in Africa though near it, the Hebrew University of Jerusalem sent us Nehemia Levtzion and Mordechai Abir, who were to be the precursors of several others from Israel.

The supervision of such a large and varied group of research students was excellent for the morale and the breadth of outlook of the staff members who now shared it, and our weekly seminar developed a reputation that attracted many more than its formal members. We were by this time trying hard to practice the recommendations of the 1961 conference in regard to the use of African sources. The three East Africans were all working on the traditional evidence available in their own languages and spending the second year of their courses collecting and interviewing in the field. David Cohen was demonstrating that in four years it was possible, with great industry, for someone with no previous knowledge of an African language to achieve enough proficiency to collect, transcribe, translate, analyse, and interpret spoken texts embodying the oral traditions of more than a hundred clans in Busoga, Uganda.[1] Nehemia Levtzion was employing his excellent knowledge of written and colloquial Arabic to interview Muslim clerics and rulers in northern Ghana on the spread of Islam in that area.[2] A Canadian research student, Gordon Haliburton, was following out on the ground the astonishing progress of the Liberian Prophet Harris, who had acted as the informal precursor of European Christian missionaries right across the southern Ivory Coast and western Ghana.[3] In Uganda Michael Twaddle was tracing the career of the Ganda warlord Semei Kakungulu, who during the early colonial period built up a small empire around the foothills of Mount Elgon with the connivance of British colonial officials who still lacked the resources to subject the area themselves.[4] There was also, however, the case of Taddesse Tamrat, who brought his own already sophisticated understanding of medieval Ethiopian history to the study of historical texts in Ge'ez and Amharic captured or copied by Europeans and now scattered around libraries in Britain, France, and Italy. For him the problem was to learn European languages sufficiently to master the findings of three hundred years of Ethiopianist scholarship, and he did it so well that his thesis, *Church and State in Ethiopia—1270–1527*, was pronounced by the best informed of his examiners to be "the second most important book ever written about Ethiopia." Published by the Clarendon Press in very nearly its original form, it has stood the test of time.[5]

Beyond the work that we carried out on the premises, however, these years in the middle 1960s gave us unprecedented opportunities to travel in Africa and to observe what was happening to our subject on the ground. External examinerships were the best source of fares, and in those days of circular tickets and unlimited stopovers the secret of the game was to see how many other places one could visit on the outward and return journeys. My first trip to Africa after my visit to North America was

271

to the inaugural meeting of the International Congress of Africanists, held in Accra in December 1962. This was the organization initiated at the International Congress of Orientalists in Moscow two years earlier, the prime objective of which was to assert that African studies should be based in Africa and give due prominence to African scholars. And, viewed in those terms, the first meeting was a considerable success. Of the 450 people who attended, 175 were Africans and they came from every part of the continent. Moreover, they assumed quite naturally all the leading roles. Kenneth Dike, now vice chancellor of the University of Ibadan, was the president, and Aklilu Habte of the University of Addis Ababa was his deputy. Francophone Africa had no comparable institutional figure, but it was effectively and gracefully represented by the Senegalese writer and intellectual Alioune Diop who, together with Léopold Senghor, had in the early 1950s founded the journal *Présence Africaine* in Paris. Joseph Ki-Zerbo, an outstanding historian from Upper Volta, was a brilliant and authoritative chairman of the history and archaeology section. A. C. Jordan, formerly of Cape Town university, chaired the linguistics section, and Humpate Ba of Niger chaired that on religion and philosophy. Kwame Nkrumah came to open the proceedings amid the most portentous precautions for his security. Our programme told us only that we were to be addressed by "a representative of the Ghana government." But as we walked up Legon Hill together to the great assembly hall, Adu Boahen pointed out that a great many policemen were disguised as gardeners demurely trimming the shrubberies by the roadside, and indoors a great many more were disguised as delegates and wearing conference badges. Soon there was a flurry of motorcycles accompanying a long line of official cars, led by the beflagged Rolls Royce inherited from the former British governor. This was now used only as a decoy, while the president travelled in a bulletproof limousine farther back in the procession. He emerged, a godlike figure in a gorgeous kente cloth, read a long and unremarkable speech, and then withdrew.

It was not of course to be expected that a conference of this kind would produce many contributions or formal discussion of real academic distinction. It was, as I remarked in a broadcast talk I gave on my return to England, rather a kind of initiation rite, in which Africa was laying claim to a cultural liberation to match its political independence. Hitherto, most Europeans and most Africans had imagined that cultural liberation had been achieved by the intellectual elite of colonial Africa in the measure that it had shared, through education, in the cultural heritage of Western civilization. Educated Africans had mastered the civilization of their colonizers. They had become citizens of the world. The very last thing that educated Africans were thought to require was any knowledge of Africa. They had turned their back on all that. The study of African languages, religion, anthropology, history, fine art, music, and drama were felt to concern only a few specialists scattered around the world at large. They were not thought to be connected with the progress of Africans towards intellectual or cultural liberation. It was only as political independence was achieved in West Africa, and was seen to be impending elsewhere, that there came a sudden sense of cultural nakedness that had to be covered, a lack of identity that had to be made good. In the case of some of the brasher participants, who seemed to come mostly from Anglophone Africa, this could go so far as the claim that African studies should be the monopoly of African scholars. The Francophone participants were noticeably more cosmopolitan. Alioune Diop was indeed so sure of himself that he could afford to be generous in his outlook. He was the cultured man of the world, gently pointing out that Africa had some riches to share with the rest of us, while freely acknowledging that it was the West that had supplied Africa with most of the instruments for its self-expression. It was with relief that I heard that he had been chosen to succeed Dike as the next president of the organization.

On my own account, I remember the Accra conference first and foremost as my opportunity to revisit Ghana and renew my contacts with the university with which we had so many professional dealings. The vice chancellor now was Conor Cruise O'Brien, the brilliant Irish diplomat whose previous appointment had been as the United Nations representative in Kinshasa (Leopoldville), in which capacity he had played a leading role in mobilising international intervention to end the secession of Katanga. He had come to Ghana as the personal nominee of Nkrumah and was believed to be advising him regularly and drafting his speeches on foreign affairs. In the university O'Brien was personally liked and respected, even though he made no attempt to conceal his opinion that its generally elitist image stood in need of change. Many more students would need to be recruited, without any corresponding increase in staff, and the Oxbridge style of collegiate building would need to be greatly simplified. I do not know how willingly he was associated with the most radical change of all, whereby the university was henceforward to admit students on the basis of the West African school certificate to a preliminary year and so in effect to take over from the schools the responsibility for all the sixth-form teaching of the country. But certainly this was the main cause of dismay among the long-serving expatriate staff members who had hitherto felt that they belonged in the same league as their opposite numbers in British universities, with the same opportunities for research and writing and with the standing to compete for vacant posts at home. Now they felt that, if they stayed, they would be downgraded, and with the exception of those who had married in the country, they were nearly all trying to leave.

The head of the history department, Graham Irwin, was at this moment away, negotiating a future career at Columbia University, and his next two senior colleagues had declared their intention to leave at the end of the academic year. Though we did not yet see it clearly as such, it was in fact an example of the stealthy erosion of earlier academic standards that would soon sweep across the length and breadth of the continent. It was not only, or even mainly, the expatriates who were affected. It made nonsense of the research training that we in the outside world were giving to the African academics of the future, as so many of them returned to their countries to find that they would never again have the chance to join in the advancement of knowledge through research, because they were overwhelmed by the numbers and the generally lower quality of the students pressing in upon them from the schools.

I spent much time in Ghana with the longest serving of the expatriates, Jack Lander, who was soon to migrate to Canada. I spent more with Adu Boahen, who as the heir apparent to the exodus might have been expected to rejoice at the prospect of early promotion. But, characteristically, that was not the way he saw it. He was still seeing his first book through the press and was anxious to get on with a second, concerning his home region of the former Asante empire. He did not want the responsibility or the distractions of running a department, and all he pressed me for was to help him in the search for another expatriate to succeed Irwin. I also had long talks with the attractive and radical political scientist Thomas Hodgkin, recently recruited from the Oxford Extra-Mural Delegacy to head a new Institute of African Studies that was intended to become the spearhead of postgraduate education on the arts side. With his colleagues, who included the historian of Asante Ivor Wilks and the Ghanaian musicologist Nana Nketia, Hodgkin had devised a really interesting programme of courses leading to the master's degree that looked as though it might attract plenty of international as well as local customers. By the time I left, my overall picture of the place was by no means gloomy. Lander's view was that Adu Boahen would end by accepting the succession to Graham Irwin and that he would do the job well.

Back in England in January 1963 there seemed at first to be graver dangers to African universities from the interference of arbitrary governments in Central Africa than in West Africa. From Eric Stokes in Salisbury there came a string of urgent letters concerning the deportation from Rhodesia of his deputy in the history department, Terence Ranger, by the newly elected Rhodesian Front government of Ian Smith. No one had suggested that Ranger's presence in the country was a security risk. He was merely an outspoken critic of white minority rule, the editor of a mimeographed newsletter, and the organizer of peaceful demonstrations against the colour bar. The deportation order was therefore the arbitrary

274

act of a government seeking to curry favour with a minority white electorate. The faculty members of the college were quick to see the threat posed to academic freedom. They realized that from now on it would be difficult, and perhaps impossible, to recruit teachers from abroad and that pressures would increase to break the federal character of the college by founding separate universities in Nyasaland (Malawi) and Northern Rhodesia (Zambia). "The crisis," wrote Stokes, "will have demonstrated the urgent need to build bridges in our rear across the Zambezi. A university in Lusaka has become a necessity of policy." In Salisbury the principal of the university college, Walter Adams, had issued a strongly worded statement of protest in which he said, "We shall not be deterred from continuing to be a centre of free discussion, or, as individuals, from exercising our civil liberties." Eric was hoping that we at SOAS would join the public hue and cry. This, my director decided, we could not do, but we did manage to cable to Ranger an offer of alternative employment, which reached him before he left Rhodesia. I felt quite proud of the speed of our gesture, even though in the event we were outbid by the new university college at Dar es Salaam, which offered him its chair of history.

During the spring of 1963 I undertook, on behalf of the Council of the Royal African Society, a modest inquiry among those teachers in United Kingdom universities who were engaged in any branch of African studies—mainly anthropologists, economists, geographers, historians, and political scientists—with a view to seeing how many would care to form an African Studies Association along the lines of that which had been established two years earlier in the United States. I corresponded with about 200 individuals, 125 of whom accepted an invitation to an inaugural meeting at the Commonwealth Institute, while 65 others, who could not be present, expressed interest in the project. I still have the notes from which I addressed them, and I find that their interest today is in the optimism with which most of us then viewed the future, both of our studies and of the long-term relations with the African universities that would result from them. I estimated that at least 250 more Africanists could be found among the British teachers already working in African universities, and I quoted an estimate made by Alexander Carr-Saunders for the Inter-Universities Council for Higher Education Overseas that a further 5,000 expatriate teachers would have to be recruited to meet the needs of the African universities between then and 1980. I hazarded the guess that of these at least one-quarter would be Africanists who could be expected to serve on average for ten years in Africa and would then return to posts in United Kingdom universities, where they would prove a powerful force in helping to break down the European parochialism of most of our existing academic disciplines. Of course, in the event I was to be proved quite wrong. The African universities, under independent

African governments, would be quite unable to maintain the standards of pay and conditions necessary to recruit expatriate staff. They would offer two-year contracts that would not be attractive to people of the calibre to command subsequent appointments at home. And they would exact low-level teaching duties on a scale that would preclude any attempts at serious research. But all this lay, for the present, below the horizon of our expectations.

On a more personal level, with the Penguin *Short History* and the *Oxford History of East Africa* now behind me, I faced the problem of how to focus my personal research and writing. John Fage and I were agreed that we did not wish to collaborate in another larger work of general synthesis, although we were prepared to think that at some time we would undertake the general editorship of a Cambridge history of Africa in several volumes, which had already been suggested to us by Philip Harris of the Cambridge University Press. Meantime, it seemed to me that I should be looking for a smaller topic that would involve the use of primary sources but that would yet have a wide significance. Just when I had reached this stage in my thinking, I was approached by George Sinclair, at that same time a member of Parliament but previously a colonial civil servant who had been a senior official of the Gold Coast during its transition to independence as the state of Ghana. Sinclair's former chief, Charles Arden-Clarke, had recently died, and his family and friends were looking for a biographer. The great attraction of Arden-Clarke as a subject was that, when he joined the Colonial Service in Nigeria in 1919, he was posted to a newly created subdistrict in a remote area to the north of the middle Benue River that had until then not been administered at all. At one end of his career he had therefore been responsible for instituting colonial rule and had lived with all the problems of a pioneer administrator, while at the other end in Ghana he had spent eight years winding it down and handing it over to African rule. Nothing could better illustrate the extraordinary brevity of Africa's forcible initiation into the modern world. However, the feasibility of such a biography would obviously depend on the scope and quality of the private papers and of the other sources to which I might get access. I could only say that I would look at the papers and form a judgment.

During that summer of 1963 the Arden-Clarke papers filled most of my leisure moments. They accompanied us to Frilsham, where we spent the weekends and the long vacation in the caravan planning the house that was to be built for us on the woodland plot farther down the road. The collection proved to include two veins of rich material, the first of which concerned his early years in Nigeria when he was a young bachelor living as a lone European in a bush station and representing a distant government with the support of a dozen lightly armed Hausa police. Every Sunday he wrote to his mother, describing in detail his daily doings, from the pursuit and punishment of insubordinate tax defaulters to the occasion when, visited by another white official on tour, the two young men spent the evening dancing foxtrots to the gramophone while keeping their pipes in their mouths as a gesture to propriety. And his mother kept his letters. But then, on his first leave, he married. His wife took over the Sunday letters, and his mother failed to keep them. There followed fifteen years of happily married life during which he rose through the ranks of the Nigerian civil service and was promoted to be the resident commissioner, first of Bechuanaland (Botswana) and then of Basutoland (Lesotho). For these years the papers contained little of significance. The second rich vein began only when he was appointed in 1947 to be governor of Sarawak. His wife did not accompany him, and therefore he wrote her long marvellous letters about his tours of inspection, travelling mostly by canoe and often in the company of Malcolm Macdonald, who was the high commissioner in Southeast Asia. It was Macdonald who recommended him in 1948 as a man with the strength and wisdom to handle the political crisis that had been developing for two years past on the Gold Coast, and from 1949 until 1957 his base was at Christiansborg Castle on the outskirts of Accra. There Georgina Arden-Clarke joined him for about six months of each year, and for these months the private papers had little to offer. During her absences, however, Arden-Clarke wrote to her usually three times a week, and these letters, written in the early mornings on ordinary blue airletter forms, were the pick of the collection. Despite the long intermissions, they afforded the outlines of a very fascinating picture of developing relations between Arden-Clarke and Nkrumah that started with the abrupt arrest and imprisonment of "our local Hitler" and ended with Arden-Clarke's fighting Nkrumah's cause against a reluctant colonial secretary for an early date for independence. "Yesterday," he wrote to his wife on September 16, 1956, "the Secretary of State surrendered with the words 'I feel you have left me no alternative.' He was right, I hadn't." And then he went on,

I wish you could have been there, darling. It is the culmination of seven years' hard work, anxious and exciting work, and I couldn't help a thrill of triumph and achievement. If I could feel like that, I wonder how Nkrumah will feel when I tell him tomorrow afternoon, and how the Assembly will behave when the announcement is made in the House on Tuesday morning. . . . I shall have to see to it that my children do not smirch their record, or throw their Freedom away, between now and Independence Day.

There were many more such tempting morsels, and the brief autobiography called *Ghana*, published by Nkrumah in 1957, was also illuminating. But when I added up the score in September 1963, it did not look encouraging. I knew that I should get no help from the public records, which under the legislation then prevailing would remain closed for fifty years. So far as Ghana was concerned, I hoped that Nkrumah might be prepared to allow me a sight of some of his papers and those of his party, the Convention Peoples Party (CPP). But for the long years spent by Arden-Clarke in southern Africa, the only chance was that the local administrations in Botswana and Lesotho might be more flexible than their masters in Whitehall. Because I was scheduled to go to Salisbury as an external examiner in November, I decided to route my outward journey through Accra and Johannesburg and to spend a couple of weeks sizing up the archival situation at the high commission in Pretoria and the protectorate capitals at Maseru and Mafeking. On the return trip I planned to make stops in Zambia, Dar es Salaam, and Nairobi for other business.

At least as I experienced it, the act of settling into a professorial chair was both undramatic and long drawn out. For a year beforehand everyone around me knew it was going to happen and treated me accordingly. Six months beforehand it was announced in the press, and the letters of congratulation flowed in. On the day itself I merely reported for duty as usual. But a month or so after that the vice chancellor of London University gave a dinner for all the newly appointed professors on the one hand and all the recently retired professors on the other. And in his speech after the dinner he got the two lists reversed, so that he first thanked me and my peers for our loyal service and wished us well in our hard-earned retirement and then went on to welcome our venerable elders to their new and exciting duties. There now remained only one further ritual act to be performed, which was the so-called inaugural lecture, addressed not to one's students but to one's historian colleagues from all over the university. It was expected to be both serious and amusing, memorable enough to merit publication and at the same time light enough to be endurable by people with different specialties from one's own. I realised that it was one of the things I needed to be thinking about while on my forthcoming travels.

I flew to West Africa on November 17. By a strange coincidence the vice chancellor who had entertained me the previous week was in the next seat. He was going to represent the university of London at the ceremonial inauguration of the former university college of Ibadan as an independent university, free from its former special relationship with London. It was his first trip to Africa, and he spent most of it reading Dickens's novel, *Barnaby Rudge.* When we were somewhere in mid-Sahara, he glanced out the porthole, turned to me, and said, "Well, Oliver, you must admit, the Almighty made a bad job of that!" I tried to tell him that if we had been

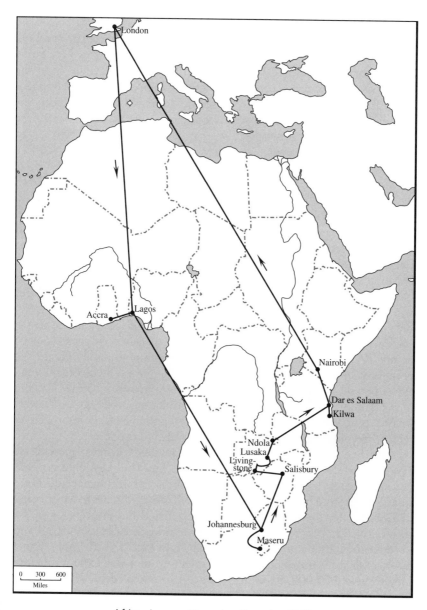

African journey, November–December 1963

making the journey six thousand years earlier, when the rain belts were differently disposed, we would have been looking down on a parkland full of grazing animals, including herds of domestic cattle kept by Late Stone Age pastoralists who had left their paintings and engravings upon the local rocks. He looked at me with incredulity, but fortunately Kenneth Mellanby, the distinguished botanist and zoologist who had been the founding principal of the university college at Ibadan, was also on the plane and came to my support. We parted at Lagos, and I flew on to Accra, where the O'Briens had invited me to stay with them in the vice chancellor's lodge at the top of Legon Hill.

I found Conor O'Brien greatly changed in his outlook since my visit of the previous year. On the day of my arrival in 1963 Radio Monrovia had announced in its news bulletins that he had resigned the vice chancellorship following a difference of opinion with Nkrumah. It was untrue, but it led him to tell me that here, no less than in Smith's Rhodesia, academic freedom was in peril. In this case the threat came from the ideologues of Nkrumah's CPP who were talking of the Marxist concept of the political party as a nation-building institution. At the universities the government was proposing to introduce a citizenship training programme that would be a compulsory course for all students and would be examined in the same way as their other subjects. This Conor had refused pointblank to accept, saying that the citizenship training programme could operate as a voluntary extracurricular activity but nothing more. The ideologues had thereupon set to work in the senior common rooms of the university, and it was Conor's belief that promises of promotion, privileges, and even cash transactions had been made to the programme's supporters, along with corresponding threats to those who failed to cooperate.

Clearly, the circumstances were not propitious for my request to see Nkrumah's side of the Arden-Clarke relationship. The question was put to him on my behalf by Nana Nketia, the chairman of the Higher Education Board, but he told me that Nkrumah refused to even discuss it. My mission to Ghana therefore failed in its main objective. I did, however, spend a memorable afternoon with Adu Boahen visiting the new industrial and harbour town at Tema, which I had known in 1957 as little more than a fishing village. It now had 50,000 inhabitants, and was expected before long to have 250,000. Its industry was to be powered by the electricity from the Volta Dam and would be based upon a gigantic aluminum-smelting operation in which Ghanian money would be matched by foreign investment. An oil refinery, financed half from Ghana and half from Italy, was already functioning. The cocoa export of the interior would mostly pass through its harbour, which would also be the base for a fleet of fishing trawlers. Our guide was a former school friend of Adu's now a senior Ghanian civil servant who was in charge of the resettlement of population from the rural areas flooded by the Volta Dam. He was no party man, but he was totally committed to the project and clearly believed in its future success. At the time all this looked like sound development. It was not yet obvious how far Nkrumah would overcommit the country's resources on the one hand and deter foreign investment on the other.

On November 21, 1963, I flew to Johannesburg and early next day took charge of a rented car and drove the forty-odd miles to Pretoria, where the British high commissioner still exercised the dual role of a diplomatic representative with the South African government and the administrative chief of the three British protectorates of Bechuanaland, Basutoland, and Swaziland that lay within or adjacent to South Africa. It was here that I hoped to find Arden-Clarke's official correspondence with his superiors and so do something to fill the ten-year hiatus in his private papers. The staff of the high commission could not have been more helpful. They gave me full access to the files and registers and even produced a colleague, called Lawrenson, who had worked close to Arden-Clarke in Bechuanaland. In a couple of long days I was able to see most of the relevant material and to grasp the essential picture of Arden-Clarke as a resident commissioner, doing his work with tact and assiduity but communicating as little as possible with headquarters. It was clear that the detail of his activities would have to be recovered, if at all, from the archives of his former residencies at Mafeking and Maseru.

In 1963 South Africa was in the full grip of "grand apartheid"— the maintenance of white supremacy was attempted by the imposition of police-state methods, such as the widespread use of spies, infiltrators, agents provocateurs, telephone tapping, and above all, detention without trial for ninety-day periods that could be indefinitely renewed and gave the police every opportunity to use torture to obtain evidence and confessions from those arrested. While I was in Pretoria, the so-called Rivonia treason trial was under way; it resulted in sentences of life imprisonment for Nelson Mandela and other leaders of the militant wing of the African National Congress. The interesting point in retrospect is that, from the British High Commission downwards, everyone at that time assumed that such methods would be successful and that the only possibility of major change would come from outside intervention, prompted perhaps by some act of hideous repression by the regime in power. Meanwhile, the South African government would pursue its declared policy of forcing its African population into ethnic "homelands," dissidents would flood into the protectorates, and for security reasons the republic would try to gain political control of them. And Britain would not be well placed to protect them.

It was with such a sombre perception of current trends that I set off on November 23 to drive the 250 miles to Maseru. I paused to replenish the petrol at the little town of Kroonstad in the Orange Free State, and it was there that I learned from the garage attendant of the assassination of President Kennedy. "Some bloody nigger lover done this," was his inconsequential comment. In Maseru I had a great reception from the government secretary, Hector, who lost no time in telling me that Prime Minister Henrik F. Verwoerd's drive to capture Basutoland from the inside was real, serious, and might well succeed. His game, both here and in Swaziland, was to win the traditional ruling groups by promising to entrench them in their privileges and to help them to gain the support of their people through full bellies and somewhat enlarged frontiers. Hector said that South African agents came and went the whole time and that there was nothing his government could do about it. He was firmly persuaded that, if the British simply tried to hold on, they would lose and that only strong political and economic counterattractions could win the day. And with that introduction he told me that he would be spending the next two days attending the legislative council and that I was welcome to use his office and filing clerk to help me in my work.

Despite all this help, I found Arden-Clarke as elusive in Maseru as I had in Pretoria. Undoubtedly, he had presided over an administrative revolution in Basutoland, and I had the impression of an executive officer of character and drive who carried out the instructions that came to him from his successive high commissioners, Lord Harlech and Evelyn Baring, with the minimum of words and these more often spoken than written. At the end of the second day a telegraph arrived from Pretoria that put an end to my work there. Hector's opposite number in Mafeking had consulted the Colonial Office about my access to his archives and had received a reply saying that the fifty-year rule must be strictly adhered to. There was clearly no point in my going to Mafeking, and I spent what remained of my time in Maseru visiting the small nucleus of a university college that had been founded by Canadian missionaries farther up the valley at Roma and talking in my hotel to Professor Cowan, formerly of Cape Town University and later of Chicago, who had prepared a draft constitution for an independent Basutoland, to be achieved within two years and to be supported by massive external aid, which would embarrass the South African government by planting a fully independent African state in its midst. The document was under debate in the local legislative council.

On November 27 I drove back to Johannesburg and the following day flew on to Salisbury for a week of blinding work as external examiner. As I see from a letter I wrote to Caroline at the end of it, I marked forty-two honours scripts, spending forty minutes on each, attended two long faculty meetings, gave a talk, had individual discussions with twelve undergraduates, with each of the history teachers, and with the principal Walter Adams. I found the place deeply shaken by recent events in Central

African politics. The federation was breaking up. Nyasaland had already stopped its contributions to the university budget. Northern Rhodesia had announced that it would do so as soon as it could implement its plans for a new university at Lusaka. The Rhodesian Front government was hostile to the college and was giving scholarships to white Rhodesians to attend South African universities. Walter Adams was showing signs of wear and tear and would soon move away to become director of the London School of Economics. In the history department Terence Ranger's deportation was soon to be followed by Eric Stokes's appointment as Smuts Professor in Cambridge and by Richard Brown's move to the University of Sussex. When I asked how they would be replaced, I was told that it would probably come down to recruiting the local schoolmasters. With Nkrumah at one end of tropical Africa and Ian Smith at the other the outlook for higher education was beginning to look threatening. At the same time, with so many new institutions emerging, it did not look to me as if the role of SOAS need be a diminishing one.

I had planned to spend my last day in Rhodesia with Donald Abraham, interviewing the spirit medium of the founding ruler of the Mutapa dynasty at his headquarters in the Zambezi Valley. To my lasting regret the trip had to be cancelled on account of heavy rain, but in recompense I had the pleasure of spending the next few days travelling in southern Zambia with Brian Fagan, then the Iron Age archaeologist at the Rhodes-Livingstone Museum in Livingstone. I had met him briefly in 1960 in the company of Desmond Clark. Fagan was now twenty-seven and still unmarried, radiating fitness, activity, and enthusiasm for the job. He took me to see the mound sites that he had been excavating on the Batoka plateau where, because of waterlogged conditions, early Iron Age farmers had built and rebuilt their villages on the same sites, and where the stratification of their middens showed they had progressed from a stage where most of their animal food had consisted of wild game to nearly all of it coming from domesticated goats, sheep, and cattle. Carbon-dating laboratories in those days were still rather thin upon the ground, but Brian already had enough dates to show that the Iron Age settlement in central Zambia had extended over most of the first millennium A.D. We spent the night at Kafue and on the following day descended into the Zambezi Valley, driving by rough tracks up the northern bank between the Otto Beit Bridge and Kariba. All along this stretch Tonga villagers, whose lands had been flooded by the artificial lake above the Kariba Dam, had been resettled, and a pumping station had been built to supply them with piped water on a riverside bluff called Ingombe Iledi. A storage tank had been sunk into the summit of the bluff, and here the engineers had stumbled across human skeletons accompanied by rich grave goods, including gold beads, copper bracelets, ingots of smelted copper, tusks, and the remains of woven cloth. It looked as though Ingombe Iledi had been at some time a chiefly capital, dominating a trading crossroads between the Indian Ocean and the upper Zambezi and between the copper belt to the north and the Zimbabwe plateau to the south. The earliest carbon tests suggested dates around the eighth century, but after considerable controversy, much of it fought out in the *Journal of African History*, dates in the fourteenth and fifteenth century were eventually accepted. It was hugely helpful to me to have seen the actual site.

Brian Fagan left me in Lusaka on December 10, and I spent a useful day prospecting in the archives for materials that might be used by future research students; then I caught the local plane to Ndola, about 170 miles away. It was there, at the Rhodes Hotel, that I received from Caroline a cutting from the *Listener* of November 28 with the text of a televised lecture by Hugh Trevor-Roper, on "The Rise of Christian Europe." His opening sentences said,

It is fashionable to speak today as if European history were devalued: as if historians, in the past, have paid too much attention to it; and as if, nowadays, we should pay less. Undergraduates, seduced, as always, by the changing breath of journalistic fashion, demand that they should be taught African history. Perhaps in the future there will be some African history to teach. But at present there is none: there is only the history of the Europeans in Africa. The rest is darkness, like the history of pre-European, pre-Columbian America. And darkness is not a subject of history.

There was more in the same vein. If it were true that all history was equal, then indeed we Europeans might neglect our own history and "amuse ourselves with the unrewarding gyrations of barbarous tribes in picturesque but irrelevant corners of the globe; tribes whose chief function in history, in my opinion, is to show to the present an image of the past from which, by history, it has escaped," Trevor-Roper said.

As I read it, I realised that the subject of my inaugural lecture had been determined for me. Trevor-Roper was Regius Professor of Modern History at Britain's oldest university, so his remarks could not be ignored or dismissed in an amusing aside. Everyone who heard or read my lecture would know what he had said. I would have to address Trevor-Roper's comments head on by showing that what had been developed thus far, mainly as a contribution to education in Africa, had now reached a stage where it had some significance for the study of history as a whole. My lecture would be called "African History for the Outside World" (1964). As I waited for the international flight to Dar es Salaam next morning, I began to write it.

The plane, when it came, was full of southern African dignitaries on their way to Kenya independence celebrations, with Joshua Nkomo resplendent in a hyena-skin hat. My host at Dar el Salaam was Terence Ranger, who had recently arrived to take up his post as head of the history department. Our business was to discuss his syllabus proposals and other professional matters, but in the evening he and his wife Sheilagh told me something of what they had endured in Rhodesia in the way of threatening telephone calls, abusive letters, and actual manhandling by white thugs. Next day I was carried off by Neville and Helen Chittick to their seaside cottage at Bagamoyo, where we could watch from their garden small very unmilitary-looking squads of Mozambican "freedom fighters" drilling farther down the beach and using wooden sticks in place of guns. Neville was now director of the British School of History and Archaeology in East Africa, and he had undertaken as his first large research project the excavation of the medieval stone settlements on Kilwa Island that I had last seen in their utterly neglected state during my journey down the coast in 1950. His digging season there was already finished, but somehow he and Terence had managed to borrow the government's six-seat presidential aeroplane to fly us down there for a day, and we duly set off with Neville seated beside the pilot, trying hard to persuade him to land on the beach beside the ruins and not at the official airstrip on the mainland opposite. To my great relief the pilot refused to consider it, and we crossed to the island safely, if slowly, by dhow.

The great discovery of the season was a ruined palace with an attached warehouse complex more than a mile from the main town settlement. It was built on a low cliff at the northern tip of the island, commanding the entrance to the safe roadstead between the island and the mainland. It was approached from the shore by a flight of steps cut into the rock that led up past a fine octagonal bathing pool to an open air reception area, the walls of which were pocked with many niches for lamps. Beyond the pool were the private apartments of the merchant princes who ruled here, building up their wealth by offering an entrepôt and port of transshipment for the rich coastal trade between the Red Sea and Persian Gulf to the north and the ivory, copper, and gold of the Zambezi and the Limpopo to the south. As we walked to it and round it in the blazing midday heat, Neville explained that, unlike the town, which had grown and changed through at least four centuries, the palace was visibly all of a piece and datable to the late twelfth or early thirteenth century. It would take him several more seasons to finish his work there and bring it to publication. Meanwhile, and especially because the place was so difficult to reach, I felt privileged to have seen it again.[6]

In December 1963 Tanganyika had been independent for just two years, and I am interested to see from my final letter to Caroline that the government already was showing that it had a dictatorial side. "Dar es Salaam Club, worth perhaps £150,000, was taken over without compensation a week or two ago, and there have been some ugly, political reversals of judges' decisions. But at least Julius Nyerere refuses to have his name spattered over every street and university, and has recently sent round a wonderful circular on 'Pomposity in public servants.' " In retrospect one can see that it was the frightening away of foreign investment by doctrinaire acts of nationalisation that was to be the financial undoing of the country. At the time, most of us in Europe were accustomed to the expansion of the public sectors in our countries, where its results were scarcely revolutionary because socialism was merely nibbling around the edges of well-established capitalist systems. We did not appreciate how much more lethal state socialism had to be in countries where the main problem was not how to control corporate enterprise but how to arouse it.

The last stopover of my tour was in Kenya, which had been an independent country for all of three or four days. My business there was to discuss the teaching of history at the recently upgraded Royal Technical College, which was now a constituent college of the University of East Africa and would soon become the fully independent University of Nairobi. Things there were temporarily in the hands of an English colleague, A. J. Hanna, on secondment from the University of Southampton, but it was already known that in a year's time they would pass into those of my former student, Allan Ogot, who would move there from Makerere as professor and head of the department. He later told me how, on the eve of Kenyan independence, he had been rung up at Makerere and offered first the ambassadorship in Delhi and then that in London. He had steadfastly refused both and had been roundly criticised for his lack of cooperation. I found his sense of priorities inspiring, but in retrospect they could be seen as hard-headed also. Ambassadorships in new states have tended to be more precarious than university chairs, and the position of an ambassador appointed at thirty and fired at thirty-five is not necessarily one to be envied.

I reached home after five weeks' absence on December 21, 1963. I already knew that for most of that time Caroline had been suffering severe attacks of arthritic pain. She had taken the best advice and had been told that, while there might be remissions, she could not hope for a lasting cure. It was plain to both of us that her future would be increasingly circumscribed.

23

The Start of the Marathon
(1964–65)

The year 1964 began for us with the excitement of building at Frilsham. We had been working on the site by ourselves for more than a year. During my absence in Africa a bulldozer had carved out the course of a driveway winding down the steep upper slope of the hillside and cleared the dense thicket of thorn trees growing on the natural ledge where we meant to build. Hitherto, the outlook from it had been a matter of guesswork. Now we could see the view that we would soon have from our windows, and it proved more splendid than we had dared to hope. Two more days with the bulldozer sufficed to broaden the ledge and throw out the spoil in two levels, one for the house and terrace and another for the surrounding lawn, both overlooking the adjoining parkland, which falls away gently into the valley of the little river Pang. We had already designed the house, which was to be prefabricated of Canadian cedar shingles and was to have two French doors opening onto the terrace and three large oriel windows facing the view. With the exact position of the house fixed, a local firm needed only to install the drainage, lay a concrete raft for the floor, and build one brick chimney. The house was delivered on a single articulated truck and erected in about ten days. It then needed to be decorated and furnished. The astonishing thing in retrospect is that it could all be done on about three years' savings from an academic salary. It could certainly not be so done today.

We called it Frilsham Woodhouse, and the possession of it gradually changed our lives. We seldom missed a weekend there, and during school and university vacations it became our main base. After Sarah left school, the weekends became longer. A great many people came to stay with us there, especially professional colleagues and graduate students from overseas. I did virtually all my reading and writing there, at first in the old caravan, which stood on a spur of the drive, but soon in a garden room built of the same cedar shingles as the house, to which I gradually transferred most of my books and papers. Increasingly, we went to London for only three or four days in the middle of each week to teach and administer in the university and to keep in touch with the big world.

My regular activities outside the university at this time included the councils of the Institute of Race Relations; the British School of History and Archaeology in East Africa, soon to be renamed the British Institute in Eastern Africa; the Royal African Society; the Africa Educational Trust; the African Studies Association of the United Kingdom; and the Africa Centre at Hinsley House, Covent Garden. Around such council tables— even those with the most academic interests—I met and gradually came to know well a wide circle of fairly senior people in government and diplomacy, banking and commerce, the armed forces, the churches and aid charities, and the media. It always interested me that people who had spent their mornings and early afternoons managing thousands of people or millions of pounds should suffer themselves to be driven, on the way home, to some little meeting about the publications programme of a research institute or the affairs of a club for foreign students. I came to understand that they did it, at least partly, in order to see and be seen by others. They were doing good, but they were also networking. So, I suppose, was I.

Frilsham Woodhouse, newly built, 1963

288

The most agreeable and in many ways the most useful form of networking that came my way was a dining club that came to be known as the Africa Private Enterprise Group. It emerged gradually from a nucleus of business supporters of the Institute of Race Relations, and it was chaired for many years by Philip Mason and afterwards by Michael Caine. Its city members did most of the hosting and were directors of the big banks and the trading, mining, oil and agribusiness companies working in Africa; it also included one or two parliamentarians, two or three senior civil servants from the Foreign Office and the Ministry of Overseas Development, two or three academics, two or three journalists and broadcasters, and a representative or two from the aid charities. It met three or four times a year. Guest speakers, usually of great distinction, were encouraged to confine their remarks to fifteen minutes, as a focus for the general discussion that followed, but mostly we came to use the company as a sounding board for our speculations about the present and future problems with which we were wrestling in our different kinds of work.

There was still much travelling to be done, and April found me once again in West Africa, primarily to attend a seminar of Anglophone and Francophone historians and social scientists organised by the International African Institute at the University of Ibadan. This brought me some new friendships, especially with the brilliant geographer, anthropologist, and film-maker Jean Rouch, who spent his summers in Paris at the Musée de l'Homme and his winters directing the work of the branch of IFAN at Niamey, where he had made a first-rate study of the oral traditions concerning the early history of the kingdom of Songhay. It also gave me the opportunity to renew contact with my many Nigerian friends and former students and to appreciate the dispersion that was taking place in higher education as the more recently founded universities at Lagos, Ife, Nsukka, and Zaria began to compete for academic staff with Ibadan.

None of my African travels had as yet taken me to Sierra Leone, but I now had the opportunity to do so in style, as Desmond Crawley, our close friend and neighbour in Newton Road, had recently been appointed high commissioner there. I travelled via Ghana, where I stayed once more with the O'Briens and found them fully embattled against a government that they now recognised as hopelessly dictatorial. During the interval since my last visit, the government had sent in thugs from the Young Pioneers of the party to invade the university campus and terrorise the students into participation in the Citizenship Training Programme. In one form or another, and sometimes repeatedly, this was to be the experience of almost every university in independent Africa. The single-party governments created by the independence leaders were afraid, above all else, of their students, because students tended to be the most articulate critics of the abuses of single-party regimes. Students read foreign books and newspapers. They were taught by foreign teachers. They took every opportunity to travel abroad. They understood the workings of democracy in Western countries, with freely functioning opposition parties, independent and powerful trades unions, a free press, and judicial systems that were effectively protected from government interference. Therefore in West and East Africa, just as much as in white-ruled South Africa, universities were regarded as places that must be penetrated by police informers and regularly reminded of the forceful methods available to the party and the state. In 1964 Ghana looked like an aberration, but within a year or two it became clear that it was merely the precursor in a general trend. African universities would mostly cease to be places in which any kind of social research, including the search for oral history, could be freely practiced. And that would affect not merely the future of international recruitment of academic staff but the development of those subjects as a whole.

Meanwhile, I flew on to Sierra Leone, where at Port Loko an airport official stood by the steps of the aircraft asking each alighting white male passenger if he was Professor Oliver. I was conscious of being the scruffiest candidate for the honour, indeed the only one dressed in shorts, but I was nevertheless borne away to a special shed, given a drink, and then escorted to a waiting Land Rover emblazoned with the royal arms beside the tarmac. The driver explained that Port Loko was separated from Freetown by a wide creek that I would need to cross in the high commissioner's launch. But that scarcely prepared me for the almost destroyer sized vessel that was moored at the dockside with a smartly uniformed crew that solemnly saluted and led me to the only seating accommodation available, a canopied throne standing on a high dais amidships. I sat trying to look as dignified as my shorts and sandals would permit, while we ferried across to a private dock on the other side, where Desmond's town car awaited me.

In 1964 Sierra Leone was in its second year of independence, and the British high commissioner, though housed in a modest enough residence on the hillside above town, had inherited some of the more impressive trappings of the former colonial governor. In some other respects, however, as the Crawleys explained to me, the furnishings of a high commission residence were very different from those of a Government House. The Foreign Office in its wisdom had already learned that no diplomatic purpose was to be served by inviting Africans to formal sit-down meals, because one never knew how many people would be present on the day. No one would refuse an invitation, but only a few would signify an acceptance in advance. Many more would come without accepting, and some would feel free to bring their friends. The stand-up buffet had therefore become the normal form of entertainment. That seemed to me good sense and to correspond with all my experience of African ideas of hospitality, according to which the most important thing is to keep an open door.

I stayed only a few days with the Crawleys but long enough to make contact with the University of Fourah Bay, which was the oldest institution of higher education in tropical Africa and the only one to be linked, for historical reasons, with the University of Durham rather than that of London. I already knew the vice chancellor Davidson Nicol. John Hargreaves, the founder of the history department, had recently left to take up an appointment at the University of Aberdeen, and his place had been taken by Peter Kup, who was to make his future career at Simon Frazer University in Vancouver. There was also a young American, John Peterson, who was to write a distinguished book on the history of the country, *Province of Freedom* (1969). The great treasure house of the place was the national archive, miserably housed on the university campus but competently arranged, thanks to the labours of a former archivist, Christopher Fyfe, who had proceeded to a post at the University of Edinburgh. My warmest contact, however, was with Arthur Porter, a Sierra Leonian and a friend since the Leverhulme conference in Salisbury who had just been appointed as the first vice chancellor of the University of Nairobi. In the early evenings the Crawleys took me driving through the old historic villages of the Sierra Leone peninsula, where the early Creole migrants from England and the New World, and the West African slaves freed by the ships of the British Anti-Slavery Squadron during the early nineteenth century, had been established in settlements with very English names like Gloucester and Worcester but with architecture more reminiscent of the Caribbean and the American South than of anything either European or African.

Back in London my next outstanding engagement was the delivery of my inaugural lecture on May 13, 1964. I was confident about the script, which I had drafted with much care but also in high spirits. Caroline had sent it during my absence to Keith Hancock, whose judgment had been enthusiastic: "I saw the gaffe of the Regius Professor (Hugh Trevor-Roper) in the *Listener*. He gave Roland a good opening and I'm glad he has taken it. I think it a splendid inaugural lecture. . . . It explains what has been done, what is being done and what is likely to be done. And why. I found all this most satisfactorily informative and very interesting." On the day itself it all went like a dream. Margery Perham came from Oxford to take the chair, which enabled me to refer quite early on to the views of her Regius Professor. Happy chuckles of anticipation came from all round the room. The audience was obviously going to be sympathetic. Trevor-Roper had said in his broadcast that the purpose of history was to enable us to discover how we have come to where we are. From this I did not dissent:

My worry is that he seems to regard himself as only about the fourteenth Mister Trevor-Roper whose existence needs to be historically explained, whereas if he would only take a slightly long view of his own genealogy, he would discover that his relationships are worldwide, and that the struggles of his brother man, even in the most picturesque corners of the globe, are not as irrelevant as he seems to think.

I explained how the study of African history had sprung from the needs of higher education in Africa and how the University of London had become the main centre of research training in the subject. But I pointed out that our lead was being increasingly challenged, and I predicted that in the future fewer research students would come to us from overseas. That meant that within a few years our reputation would stand or fall by our success in teaching the subject on a broad basis to undergraduates, most of whom would be British. I described the pattern of our first degree syllabus, the first victims of which would be taking their final examinations in a week's time. I said that, so far from being a case of seduction by the changing breath of journalistic fashion, my wooing of the University of London had been pursued over twelve years and should have satisfied the most exacting standards of middle-class morality. I quoted the eighteenth-century slave trader Alexander Dalzel, who wrote in the introduction to his *History of Dahomey* (1793) that "to arrive at a just knowledge of human nature, a progress through the history of the ruder nations is essentially necessary." "You notice," I remarked through a swelling gale of laughter "how much more humane is the outlook of the eighteenth-century slave trader than that of the twentieth-century Regius Professor."

I concluded by saying that I had two distinct ambitions for our teaching of African history at SOAS.

The first is that our undergraduate school shall attract a sufficient number of British students to make some contribution to what our American colleagues describe as "the globalisation of history." Because, call it what you like, there is no doubt in my mind that this is the next great stride which historical education has somehow got to accomplish, in this country as in others. And my second ambition is that our postgraduate school should remain, as I believe it is now, almost wholly cosmopolitan, a group in which Africans and Americans, Asians, and Europeans can feel completely at one on the study of man in Africa.[1]

During the rest of 1964 and much of 1965 all my writing effort went into collaboration with Anthony Atmore on a book called *Africa Since 1800*. This was the brain-child of Philip Harris of the Cambridge

University Press, who had helped so much with the founding of the *Journal of African History* and who was to be the key figure in sponsoring the *Cambridge History of Africa*. The book with Atmore was conceived as a textbook suitable for the upper forms of secondary schools in Africa, but in the event it found its main market as an introductory text for courses in African studies at American universities and colleges. First published in 1967, it enjoyed steady and satisfactory sales and a fourth, revised edition appeared as recently as 1993. When we first discussed it in June 1964, Harris said that in his experience literary collaborations worked best when there existed a clear difference of status between two authors and when they agreed from the start that one would be responsible for the first draft and the other for the final text. Anthony Atmore, with his earlier experience of schoolteaching in Malawi, seemed an ideal partner, and so indeed it proved. We both worked at a tremendous pace throughout the long summer vacation, and half the book was in Harris's hands by November. Although it lacked the excitement of original research, I could do my part of it in the peace of Frilsham, and it gave me the satisfying sense of making the kernel of my undergraduate teaching accessible to wider numbers.

I took one negative decision in 1964, which was to break with the quadrennial sequence of conferences on African history and archaeology, held in 1953, 1957, and 1961. At a time when so much effort was being made to centre African studies in Africa, it seemed to me inappropriate for SOAS yet again to occupy the centre of the stage, and this was also the hesitation that I tried to express in reply to French soundings about a proposal to hold a fourth conference under the auspices of the Musée de l'Homme in Paris. Instead, I suggested that we might organise a small and specialised symposium, somewhere much less accessible than central London to keep the riffraff out, to study the problems of chronology in precolonial Africa. On the archaeological side its primary task should be to examine side by side all the carbon dates obtained from Iron Age sites throughout the continent, with a view to determining such questions as where and when ironwork had begun in Africa and the routes by which the practice spread from one region to another. On the historical side the most crucial question to be addressed would be the value to be attached to the genealogical evidence remembered in oral traditions. What were the criteria for distinguishing the authentic from the spurious? How did the average length of a dynastic generation vary according to the systems of royal succession practised in different societies? And what means could be used to mesh the genealogical record in neighbouring and interacting societies? How far might it be possible to test genealogical evidence by archaeological means? And was it possible that the astronomical record of solar eclipses might be used to supply at least a sprinkling of absolute datings?[2] During much of 1965 my African history seminar busied itself with the preliminary research on these matters. The conference took place at Moor Park near Guildford the following year.

It was in the early months of 1965 that John Fage and I finally committed ourselves to be the general editors of the *Cambridge History of Africa*, to be completed in eight substantial volumes of 250,000 words apiece. We had been discussing the project in a desultory way with Philip Harris for three or four years and always on our side trying to postpone it until the field of potential contributors had become somewhat larger. Now he told us in no uncertain terms that the time for a firm decision had come. There was a UNESCO project, which was likely to be backed by large subventions of international taxpayers' money, and unless we acted promptly the potential contributors would all go in that direction. The question has often been asked why, when we had been so complaisant about the location of international conferences on African history in Africa, John and I nevertheless decided to compete with a UNESCO project instead of joining it. The first answer would be that in fact we were not presented with any such choice. The UNESCO project had at the time got no further than preliminary discussion meetings, and we had no idea what part in it might be offered to either of us. The Cambridge proposal therefore stood by itself. It came from the press of our old university, which had made a great success of publishing the *Journal of African History* and had behind it a long record of collaborative histories that had become standard works of reference throughout the world. Philip Harris had made it quite clear that the press was determined to proceed with an African project and that if our response was negative, he would look elsewhere. He did not need to add that in this case we would risk losing our lead in the subject in our country. We knew that the Cambridge proposal would be a huge and long-lasting responsibility, but our answer was never really in doubt.

The first of our tasks was of course that of planning the spread of our eight volumes across the centuries, and—as a result of our earlier collaboration on the Penguin *Short History* and of our continuing partnership in editing the *Journal of African History*—our minds were so well in tune that it took us no more than a single afternoon to reach agreement on the broad outline. Our guiding principle was to maintain a steady widening of focus from the pinpoint aperture bearing on early prehistory to the broad beam playing upon recent times. We decided that the first volume would be written by archaeologists and Egyptologists. It would be concerned with human origins and with the ages of Stone and Bronze. A large part of it would be devoted to the history of ancient Egypt, seen for the first time in its African context. The second volume would run from the fifth century B.C until the tenth century A.D. and would deal with the Iron Age of sub-Saharan Africa as well as with Greek and Roman imperialism and the early spread of Christianity and Islam through the northern regions. The third volume would be concerned with the emergence of states and kingdoms between the eleventh and the sixteenth centuries, when the dominant external influences were mainly Muslim. The fourth volume would cover the period from the sixteenth to the eighteenth centuries, when European influences began to be felt alongside the Islamic ones. The fifth volume would deal with the first three-quarters of the nineteenth century, when almost the whole of the continent became connected in some way with outside influences while remaining for the most part politically independent. And the three final volumes would focus on the events of the past century, beginning with the partition of Africa by the European powers and ending with the evolution of the modern nation-states.

Our next task was to identify and nominate our volume editors, and here we were much influenced by the lore about other collaborative histories sponsored by the press. The most obvious rule of the game was that a volume progressed towards completion at the pace of its most dilatory contributor. Furthermore, there would always be some contracted contributors who would fail to produce anything at all. From this it followed that the most serious duty of a volume editor was not to edit but to engage in rescue operations of a last-minute kind. The worst problems arose from the fact that the laggards would almost never admit to their failure and offer to withdraw in time for a satisfactory alternative to be found. They simply gave up replying to reminders and, if contacted by telephone, would assure the caller that everything was in hand and would be ready next week. Every publisher is familiar with the condition. It was accurately described by a lawyer friend as "debtor syndrome," and as we discovered, not even volume editors were immune from it. For all these reasons John and I were anxious, perhaps a little too anxious, that our volume editors be people who were close to us, by long association if not by geography. All were in fact British, although two were employed at universities in the United States and Canada. It may be that, as a result, our contributors, though much more widely dispersed around the globe, were nevertheless recruited too much from a similar background of training and experience. That this was helpful to the coherence of the finished product there can be no doubt.

Of course, both John Fage and I realised from early on that the *Cambridge History* would prove a major commitment through most of the time that we would spend as university teachers. The press had warned us that to assemble, edit, index, provide maps for, and finally to print and publish the materials for a single volume of such a series must take at least five years. In practice we found that it took ten and that this was very much in line with the press's experience with its other collaborative histories. The notional timetable for the first five volumes envisaged their publication at yearly intervals from 1971 until 1975, but in the event the first appeared in 1975 and the fifth in 1981. We had anticipated from the first that there would probably need to be an interval between the precolonial and the colonial parts of the series. After all, in 1965 the process of decolonisation was still far from complete in the southern third of the continent, and it was reasonable to imagine that serious ideological differences might develop between African and non-African contributors to these later volumes, as well as between their African and non-African readers. The three final volumes therefore were not commissioned until 1973, and they were published between 1984 and 1986, which, as it happened, was to be the year of my retirement.

In June 1965 my grandmother died in her ninetieth year. Through fifty-one years of widowhood she had been the linchpin of a large family that had grown from her five daughters to include ten grandchildren and twelve great-grandchildren. She kept them all in her mind, not bothering to remember their birthdays but watching their progress through schools and universities into careers and marriages, accepting unquestioningly their spouses and descendants, and, at least during the last twenty years of her life, planning and replanning the eventual distribution of her many beautiful possessions among them. She put them up when they passed through London. She bade them to meals, so that they should meet each other. Whenever they were absent abroad, she plied them with bright, cheerful, gossipy letters written in her strong, easily legible hand. It was always said in the family that she kept a small stock of purple paper for communications with the seriously erring, but, if so, it was seldom used. She spent the last two years of her life in a kindly Catholic nursing home in South Kensington but maintained her Presbyterian prejudices to the end. "Yes," she would say, with the corners of her mouth turned right down, "it is nice enough, but, you know, they are *all* Roman Catholics, and they are *always* out at mass." I visited her often and was there even on her last day, when she only had the strength to say my name but, as always, with affection.

For the rest of that summer we were at Frilsham, where I was still working at *Africa Since 1800*, but in September I was invited by Terence Ranger to a conference in Dar es Salaam, which gave me the opportunity to revisit Uganda and Kenya as well as Tanzania. The two years since my previous visit had seen significant changes, starting with the revolution in Zanzibar, that had toppled the sultanate and driven out the Swahili Arab element in the population, causing Julius Nyerere to declare a political union of Zanzibar and Tanganyika under the new name of Tanzania. The wider effect of the disturbances in Zanzibar had been to stimulate political ambitions in the armed forces of all three East African countries, which had led to mutinies serious enough to require British military help in their suppression. It had been a humiliating experience for the political leaders, all of whom determined to avoid any repetition by strengthening the outreach of their ruling parties and making it increasingly difficult for any kind of opposition to find expression. The new political atmosphere was strongly nationalistic. Though similarly motivated in all three countries, the repression drove each further into separate compartments, to the point where it became difficult for a citizen of one to be employed in either of the others.

In the longer run such developments could not augur well for the universities. For the time being, however, these still looked in rude health. At Makerere there were many new faces. Bernard de Bunsen had departed the previous year and had been succeeded by a Ugandan, Y. K. Lule, a political nominee who was said to be supplying the college kitchens from the produce of his farms. I paid him a formal visit, but we had only a guarded conversation. Of the former long-serving expatriate professors, I think that the geographer Kenneth Baker was the only survivor. But the painter Sam Ntiro was back at the art school after his spell as Tanganyikan high commissioner in London. Jim Coleman, the former doyen of African studies at UCLA, was there under Rockefeller auspices, heading a new department of political science, and my host Noel King had migrated across the continent from Ghana to found a lively and popular department of religious studies. History had lost its old leaders, but my recent doctoral pupil, Mati Kiwanuka, had returned to fill the place left vacant by Allan Ogot. As I wrote to Caroline,

It is curious, the function of a visitor in these places. Senior people, who have argued themselves silly in faculty discussions, come to grope for one new idea that can help them. Then there are the lonely young, whose professors are too busy to talk to them about their research. There is a history master from Budo, with a hare-brained plan for a thesis he will never write. And a young philosopher from McGill, who had been attending to Southern Sudanese refugees in his spare time and wants to write a Penguin Special on the situation there. And a Mombasa Arab, with a traditional Islamic education, who wonders how to adapt it to teach the history of Islam in Africa to non-Muslims. And so it goes on. I suppose it is a good way to learn.

After just two years in Dar es Salaam Terence Ranger had gathered around himself a handful of talented young historians, the nucleus of those who were to become known around the world as "the Dar School." They included two recent doctoral graduates from Cambridge—John Iliffe, who had researched on the period of German rule in Tanganyika, and John Lonsdale, who had worked on the Nyanza Province of Kenya in early colonial times. John Sutton, an Iron Age archeologist from Oxford and one of the earliest students of the British Institute in Eastern Africa, was also a member of the team, which would soon be joined by Walter Rodney, the Guyanan trained in early West African history at SOAS. Only several years later were they joined by the first two Tanzanians to gain doctoral degrees—Isariya Kimambo from Northwestern and Arnold Temu from the University of Alberta.

The conference held there in September 1965 has been described by Jan Vansina in his autobiography as the most important ever held in African history, and he presents it as the occasion when African history, as taught in Africa, broke free from the apron-strings of SOAS.[3] This is not quite how I remember it, but the record is there for all to read in the volume of proceedings entitled *Emerging Themes of African History*.[4] Several papers focussed on early manifestations of African resistance to the imposition of colonial rule and showed, amongst other things, that "primary resistance" often amounted to much more than a blind desire to drive out the newcomers and restore the status quo ante, and that African cult leaders in particular had frequently shown a power of innovation and a capacity to bring about "enlargements of scale" spreading far across earlier ethnic and linguistic boundaries. All this was interesting and valuable but hardly earthshaking. Ranger had indeed already aired most of the leading ideas in his book *Revolt in Southern Rhodesia* (1967). What he and his colleagues now added to that was the idea that African history should be useful history, concerned with the lives of ordinary people and a source of inspiration to African political leaders engaged in the work of nation building.[5]

As I sat just across the table from President Nyerere at the opening dinner, I remember wondering how far people of his sort really stood in need of this kind of inspiration. After all, when he had needed a historical justification for his move to a single-party state, he had produced a telling, even if largely mythical, picture of precolonial Africans discussing their political problems under the shade of a big tree, with the chief listening until all had spoken before giving his decision, after which there was no further talk, but people jumped to obey. On this occasion Nyerere seemed totally relaxed, impish, and amused, and when the principal of the university, Cranfield Pratt, explained to him that, in deference to his many pleas for economy, only beer would be served at the meal, Nyerere replied, "My dear principal, you must guard your academic freedom." When we had finished eating, the president's speech of welcome was delivered into his hands by Joan Wicken, the sometime secretary of the Africa Educational Trust who was now Nyerere's confidential secretary and speech writer. It was outspoken on the subject of the deputation of

Chinese historians that had been expected and had failed to turn up. We were to forget all about them in our forthcoming discussions.

Terence Ranger had been diplomatic in inviting Allan Ogot to chair the conference, and I reported to Caroline that he had been a telling chairman

unloading gruff Luo acerbities on white and black alike. . . . All the same I sense a growling undertone of African impotence and frustration at the fact that outsiders are still so obviously writing most of the books, and there has been some only half-joking talk of putting down an embargo on all books written by foreigners on Africa. "We can't do without you, and yet at the same time can't you leave us alone?" is what it seems to be saying.

It was a feeling with which I could sympathise, even as one of the main offenders. In retrospect it seems surprising that I had never encountered it before.

On October 2, 1965, I flew with Allan Ogot to Nairobi, where he and his wife Grace invited me to stay with them at their new house on the Kabete Road. From there I gave an address to the Kenya Historical Association, an organisation dating from colonial times, of which Allan was now the president. I visited his department at the university, and I remember his serious concern at a recent circular from the Ministry of Education encouraging all schools in the country to collect and record the oral traditions of their neighbourhoods. He feared that it would result in nothing but the contamination of the sources. Last, I visited Neville Chittick at the new headquarters of the British Institute, which was now established at the Mansion House, Chiromo. Built originally as a private house standing in its own large park on the edge of the city, it had become the property of Nairobi University, which would one day build all over the site. Meanwhile, and thanks largely to Allan's advocacy, the house had been let to the institute at a peppercorn rent. There Neville had his offices, surrounded by a growing library, the storerooms in which he kept his archaeological finds and equipment, and the garages for the Land Rovers used in fieldwork. Soon he would be joined there by Robert Soper, who would concentrate on the Iron Age of the East African interior, while Neville pursued his special interests at the coast. It had all come a long way from Gervase Mathew's early dreams in 1951.

24

The Lions of Judah
(1965–66)

Back in London for the autumn term of 1965, I soon faced a considerable extension of my job at SOAS. My director, Cyril Philips, had planned a fundamental reorganisation, whereby the departments divided according to disciplines would be balanced by the creation of five "area centres" that would be concerned with the development of interdisciplinary studies and teaching programmes dealing with Africa, the Middle East, South Asia, Southeast Asia and the Far East. I was invited to become the first chairman of the Centre of African Studies. It involved, first and foremost, the responsibility for devising and implementing a programme of one-year master's courses in which students with an appropriate first degree would be taught in seminars rather than lectures, each taking three seminar courses and submitting one long essay embodying an element of original research. The success of the venture would depend on the richness and diversity of the whole programme and therefore on the number and quality of the teachers who could be persuaded to take part. We had some seventy Africanists on the staff of the school at that time, and there may have been another twenty scattered around other colleges in the university. I made it my business to meet them all individually, and on the whole I marvelled at the generous response of the busiest people to the suggestion that they might take on what, in terms of teaching, preparation, and assessment, would probably amount to an additional day's work each week for no tangible reward. Ironically, it seemed to be those with the lightest teaching duties, such as those responsible for languages for which there was little or no student demand, who were the least inclined to search their experience for what they might usefully contribute.

The master's programme in African area studies that emerged from these consultations proved to be both attractive and relevant. The generation of students that graduated in the later 1960s, in Europe as also in

North America, included many who had caught the Africa bug. Some had taken part in the Children's Crusade of youngsters who had spent a year teaching in Africa between leaving school and going up to the university. Increasingly, however, the voluntary aid organisations that sponsored these activities were seeking graduate recruits and a somewhat longer commitment, and it was among returning graduate volunteers that we found some of our best master's students. Here, we hoped, were the kind of people who would carry their African interests into British secondary education and help to broaden its outlook. The new degree also attracted some excellent recruits from the United States and Canada, where it was normal practice to take a master's degree on the way to a doctorate, and to some it was advantageous to do so at a European university, especially when tuition fees were high in the United States and quite nominal in most European countries. Altogether, the introduction of master's degrees added greatly to the school's profile as a teaching institution and could have done so even more radically had the British government been more generous with its scholarship grants for this level of university education. Soon the government would start to apply the brakes to our international recruitment also, by forcing us to raise quite drastically the fees we charged to foreign students. While it was clear that something had to be done to curb the overall number of foreign students in Britain, which at this time was approaching 100,000, it always seemed to me short-sighted not to draw a line between undergraduate and postgraduate recruitment.

Above all, however, it was the changing image of Africa that marked the beginning of a new era for African studies in Britain at this time. Ian Smith of Rhodesia led off the dance with his Unilateral Declaration of Independence of November 11, 1965. The British government was not prepared to take the risk of using force against him, but our friends in the Foreign Office assured us that it would all be all right, as they had prepared a worldwide system of sanctions that would bring the Rhodesians to heel within six weeks. With the manifest failure of these sanctions Britain became the immediate target of diplomatic action by the independent African states, many of which actually broke off relations, while others were restrained only by the fear of losing British aid. And then, in an atmosphere already fouled by the Rhodesian situation, there began the long series of military coups that dominated the African scene in 1966 and 1967. A fortnight after Smith's declaration, Colonel Joseph Mobutu used the army to seize power in Zaire. In January 1966 Tafawa Balewa, the greatly respected federal prime minister of Nigeria, was assassinated by army officers who proceeded to set up the first of many military governments, which in the following year would lead the country into a full-scale civil war, fought between different sections of the army but claiming the lives of a million civilians also. In February it was the turn of

Kwame Nkrumah, who was deposed by a military coup while on a visit to China. He was initially given sanctuary by Gamal Abdel Nasser in Egypt but later moved to the hospitality offered him by Sékou Touré on an island off the coast of Guinea. Meanwhile, in Uganda Prime Minister Milton Obote, a northerner, was preparing to use his largely northern army, commanded by General Idi Amin, against Kabaka Mutesa of Buganda who was also the constitutional president of the whole country.

Altogether some seventeen African countries experienced military interventions during these two years. It did not mean that civil chaos prevailed in all of them for any length of time. But it drastically reduced the areas of Africa in which research could be planned and prepared for with the confidence that it would be carried to completion. In my inaugural lecture I had expressed the hope that research directed from outside Africa would always be seeking to fill the gaps between what was being done from inside, but things did not work out that way. The countries without research bases of their own tended also to be the worst governed and those where the security risks were the greatest. More and more of the outside research was being channelled into a diminishing number of safe countries. Again, despite the continuing need for expatriate teachers, it was becoming steadily more difficult for African universities to provide the conditions that would attract them. Countries under military rule were countries with frequent roadblocks manned by armed soldiery, sometimes with drink taken and sometimes with their hands out for bribes. With so many weapons so widely dispersed through the community some inevitably found their way into the hands of criminals, so that the police needed to be similarly armed, and civilians had to live with the sounds of shooting, especially at night. In these circumstances our former export trade in expatriate historians for African universities almost dried up.

In July 1966 Caroline and I were visited at Frilsham by Mordechai Abir, a former doctoral student now working at the University of Addis Ababa as the dean of arts. He told us with a certain amount of mystery to expect some kind of glad tidings from Ethiopia that would require our presence there during late September and early October. Meanwhile, he needed to check with me the biographical details of a citation he had undertaken to draft. In August came the official announcement from the Haile Selassie Prize Trust that I had been selected to share the annual Award for African Research with Henry Pereira, a British solar physicist and later chief scientific advisor to the British government who was at that time director of the Agricultural Research Council of Rhodesia, Zambia, and Malawi based in Salisbury, Rhodesia. The award was substantial, and it would be presented, together with a gold medal, by the emperor at a ceremony to be held in Addis Ababa on October 3. Caroline was invited as an official guest, and for me the biggest thrill of the whole episode was that, although she had now been painfully ill for three years, she was absolutely determined to make it, and in some miraculous way her health started to improve day by day until, by the time of our departure, the active symptoms of her arthritis had virtually disappeared.

And so at the end of September we flew to Addis Ababa, where I had to be, for a few days, a public person. There were press photographers at the airport, and I was interviewed on Ethiopian television, which at that time had just five thousand viewers—all of them, I was told, were aristocrats unable to manage the knobs for themselves and had to engage specially trained servants to do it for them. At the university I lectured to an audience of more than one thousand students and afterwards faced a barrage of naughty questions that centred on whether it was historically acceptable to believe that the Ethiopian monarchy was descended from King Solomon and the queen of Sheba. I paid a call on Taddesse Tamrat's father, a senior cleric in the Ethiopian Orthodox Church who thanked me gravely for being "the father" of his son. We were taken to see the tomb of the Emperor Menelik, high up on Entoto Mountain, and the nearby Church of the Holy Trinity where he worshipped, its surrounding walls honeycombed with hermits' cells. We were shown over the Gibbe, the former royal palace on the outskirts of the town, where only a decade later Emperor Haile Selassie was to be imprisoned and then murdered.

Most of our time in Addis Ababa, however, was spent at a weeklong conference, "Africa and the World," which had been organised by the prize trust as a setting for the presentation ceremony. The participants came from Ethiopia, Egypt, Kenya, Uganda, Cameroon, Nigeria, and Ghana, among African countries, and—outside Africa—from Britain, France, East Germany, Israel, the Soviet Union, and the United States. There were a happy mixture of academics, administrators, journalists, and writers, and they met under the chairmanship of Robert Gardiner, the distinguished Ghanaian who was directing the United Nations Economic Commission for Africa (UNECA), which had its headquarters in Addis Ababa. Most foreign guests were lodged along with us at the Ethiopia Hotel. Some, like Basil Davidson, Gwen Carter, and Colin Legum, were already old friends, so that the atmosphere of the dining-room soon became that of an agreeable house party. Twice in the week we were taken on expeditions outside the capital, the first southwards to the lakes of the Rift Valley, with their incredible profusion of aquatic birds, and the second westwards to the famous fourteenth-century monastery of Debra Libanos, perched on the craggy lip of the Blue Nile gorge, where it flows southwards from Lake Tana towards the Sudanese frontier. I think that nearly all of us had been expecting to see a medieval stone building, and it was disconcerting to be confronted with a glaringly modern concrete church surrounded by a collection of thatched rondavels nestling among

At Haile Selassie's reception, Addis Ababa, 1966

copses of thorn trees and differing from those of an ordinary African village only in the little wooden crosses that topped each conical roof. It was moving to think that such a place could have survived through five centuries as a centre of liturgy and literacy and with the spiritual power to beget establishments all over the southern regions of an expanding Christian kingdom.

The conference met under the shadow of the military coups of the previous few months, and Colin Legum gave the opening address, which was attended by the prime minister and fully reported in the local press. He said that no one should be in any doubt that Africa's standing in the world was lower than it had been in 1960 and, more important, that Africa's standing in its own eyes was much lower than it had been then. He went on to point out that, while nearly every African country was increasingly preoccupied with its internal problems of national unity, it was futile for Africa, however united in its attitude, to talk as if it was capable of altering the power structure in Rhodesia, let alone South Africa, by itself. Africa had to study the forces operating in the outside world and make use of them. It was remarkable that such a speech could be made in the capital of the Organization of African Unity (OAU) and even more so that Robert Gardiner, speaking from the chair, should follow it with the suggestion that, since Africa must learn to address its problems, both *colonialism* and *neocolonialism* should be treated as unmentionable words. Not even Ivan Solodovnikov, our rather ponderous Russian colleague soon to be appointed Soviet ambassador to Zambia, was disposed to object.

In retrospect the most interesting feature of the conference was the emphasis laid on surviving ethnicity as the most essential problem of Africa in 1966. It was the very small size of the ruling elites capable of thinking in national rather than ethnic terms that had made parliamentary democracy unworkable and so had given the military juntas their opportunity to seize power. It was ethnicity that was forcing even the most emancipated and forward-looking politicians to turn away from earlier pan-African or regional concerns in the more urgent attempt to contain the centrifugal forces within their national borders. It is interesting that nobody, not even the economists from the UNECA, made any mention of overrapid population growth as a factor in Africa's increasing poverty and instability. Instead, most of the talk was about the need for industrialisation and for the creation of economic units large enough to sustain developed industrial markets. There was some rather frightening discussion of the role of education in strengthening national ideologies, which was most persuasive as argued by the strongly Zionist educator Don Avni, who came from Bar Ilan University in Tel Aviv. But it was clear that in Africa the success of such projects would depend on the rapid development of secondary education, using English and French as the languages of wider communication. And there—as Dudley Seer, the chief planning official of the British Ministry of Overseas Development, was quick to warn us— the countries of Africa would find themselves increasingly caught up in an international competition, whereby they either had to reward talent and skill at the international standards or lose them to the developed world. Patriotism, he said, was the only cure, and patriotism depended to a large extent on good government.

Finally, on October 6 came the presentation, held in the recently completed Africa Hall built by the emperor as a permanent meeting-place for the OAU. Of seven awards, six were for various kinds of service to Ethiopia, only one of which went to an Ethiopian, Tsagay, for his contributions to Amharic literature. The award for public service was given to an English nun, Sister Gabriel Cubitt of the Little Sisters of St. Vincent of Paul who had built up a large orphanage and leper colony at Nazareth in the Rift Valley. The award for agriculture was won by an Italian settler, Guido de Nadai, who had developed a citrus estate near Asmara to the point where its products were exported all round the Red Sea and the Mediterranean. That for industry went to the Dutch director of the Wanji Sugar Corporation. The prize for Ethiopian studies was awarded to an Italian botanist, Rudolfo Picho Sermolli of the University of Genoa who was renowned as a specialist in the botany of virgin tropical forests, a man of formidable physique and courage who had travelled the equatorial regions of the world alone, walking for up to eighteen hours a day and spreading a sleeping bag wherever he needed to rest. Last came the award for African research that I shared with Pereira. Pereira's citation referred to his worldwide reputation for his work on agricultural meteorology, soil physics, and water use in East African conditions. Mine spoke of my part in developing a new approach to African history as the history of peoples rather than as the disjointed story of periods of foreign intervention.

The emperor's arrival in the hall was almost clandestine. Suddenly, the trumpets sounded. The lights went on over the dais, and there he was, his little Chihuahua dog sitting heraldically at his feet. One by one we stood while the band played our national anthems and while our citations were read in Amharic and English by the vice chancellor of the university. Then one by one we walked to one side of the emperor's chair and bent low while he hung our medals on ribbons round our necks. Afterwards we returned to our places and made brief speeches of thanks. Before I left England, Taddesse Tamrat had written down for me an Amharic phrase of gratitude and had coached me in its pronunciation, and I used it to end my little speech of thanks. Afterwards, while the prize winners were waiting on the steps outside the hall for an official photograph to be taken, I was suddenly aware of the little dog in front of me, and a still small voice at my side was saying, "And how many years have you lived in Ethiopia, Professor Oliver?" It was the emperor, and since he spoke in English, he perhaps was teasing me. I will never know. After the photograph he disappeared as silently as he had come, and the rest of us moved across the street to the Jubilee Palace for a reception. A pair of tame cheetahs with gold collars and chains, each held by a uniformed attendant, sat on either side of the door. Inside we gathered in a long reception room, and once again the emperor was silently disclosed, standing on a low dais at the far end, alone except for his little dog. Then came the only moment of high drama, when the doors were thrown open, and there entered in a column of threes a procession of some twenty footmen, each holding high a silver tray with champagne glasses already filled. They were led by a butler who carried an opened bottle in one hand and a small tray with two glasses in the other. The procession halted in front of the dais. The official taster came forward and drained one of the two glasses, after which the emperor was served the other, while the footmen distributed their loads among the guests. In due course some of us were summoned singly to the dais to meet him. I have some rough notes of his remarks, which were in French:

How did you come to take up these studies? For how many years have you been working on the history of Africa? Ah, if you have been working for twenty years, that is indeed something. It is easy to begin but difficult to continue to the end. . . . If you have worked for twenty years, it is altogether my pleasure to give you this prize. . . . Will you continue with these studies after your return home? In that case this prize will serve to encourage you. . . . How many Ethiopian students have you taught? Two is very little. . . . I hope there will be many more.

I carried away with me a lasting memory of his bright penetrating eyes and kindly smile, but he seemed lonely in his majesty.

Next morning, our last day in Addis Ababa, Pereira and I were invited once more to the Jubilee Palace, to see the imperial lions. We had no idea what might be in store for us as we followed an attendant round to the back of the building, and we were taken quite by surprise when he opened the door of a large cage built against the palace wall and signed to us to enter. The door was then locked behind us, and we found ourselves alone with a party of smallish lions with unusually grey coats. They were obviously used to visitors, and two or three of them came right up to us and rubbed themselves against our legs, just as cats might do when introducing themselves. Pereira looked at them with disgust. He had spent his visit to Addis Ababa declaring his admiration for all things Rhodesian and earning among his conference colleagues the nickname of "In Rhodesia we." Now he turned to me and said, "If lions ever got into this state in Rhodesia, we'd shoot them."

Next day Caroline and I flew home through a sky so clear that we could see both shores of the Red Sea and its northern bifurcation into the gulfs of Suez and Aqaba. She was still well, and we spent the journey planning how we might one day return to Ethiopia. I was particularly eager to travel in the southwestern part of the country, where there were reported to be many earthwork sites and trenching systems marking the boundaries of small states that had existed there before the Ethiopian conquests of the late nineteenth century. Unfortunately, it was not to be.

Meanwhile, in March 1966 I was invited by Harvard University to serve as a visiting professor for the spring semester of 1967. Although not yet noted as a centre of African studies, the outstanding repute of the place was tempting, and I judged that, after five years' absence, my picture of African history in the United States must need refurbishing. From my previous experience I guessed that once there I would receive many invitations to pay short visits to other universities and that I would be able to travel to them just as easily from Harvard as from any of the more established centres. After consulting my employers, I negotiated for a shorter spell there, from early February until early May. This would enable me to be present at my university for the first and the last third of the academic year.

There was indeed much to be done at home, first in launching our new Centre of African Studies, with its highly experimental programme of multidisciplinary master's courses in which students were in effect to teach each other by preparing papers written around a common theme proposed and guided by the teachers. There was some initial fumbling, but Richard Gray and David Birmingham soon provided the ideal prototype by offering a course on trade within Africa in precolonial times, a subject for which there was at that time virtually no secondary literature but for which there existed a wealth of easily accessible primary sources in the works of the nineteenth-century explorers and missionaries. Their students succeeded so well that, between them, their course papers made a thoroughly useful volume, published two years later by the Oxford University Press under the title *Precolonial African Trade* (1970). But there was also the question of how such courses should be formally assessed. In North America it would have presented no problem. Teachers would simply have assigned marks for the coursework submitted. But British academic rigidity required a formal three-hour written examination for each course, with the answers assessed by an external examiner. In a very British way we submitted to the outward form but modified the practice by requiring candidates to answer only one question and by ensuring that every question was addressed to the special interests of one particular candidate.

The list of our research students working for doctoral degrees at this time shows clearly how the weight of our contribution had shifted from West to East Africa. Michael Twaddle was completing his thesis on the Ganda warlord Semei Kakungulu,[1] following which he would teach for several years at Makerere. David Cohen, after a preparatory year in London, was already engaged in fieldwork in the Busoga district of Uganda and was sending me regular and convincing accounts of his progress.[2] Ahmed Salim, a Mombasa Arab with a first degree in Arabic, was in Kenya doing both archival and interview work for his study of the Swahili-speaking peoples of the coastal province during the colonial period.[3] Two new arrivals had taken their first degrees at Makerere. One of them, Samwiri Karugire, was the tall and dashing son of a county chief in Ankole. He had spent his boyhood with the cattle herds and had consumed nothing but milk until his eleventh year. He was ideally suited to carry on the search for the oral tradition of his people and to bring its interpretation to a new level of sophistication.[4] His fellow recruit from Makerere was Godfrey Muriuki, a Kikuyu from the Nyeri district of central Kenya who was likewise to make a distinguished contribution to the history of his people in precolonial times, using for his sources the genealogies of the *mbari* kinship groups and the sequence of age-grades arising from the initiation system.[5] Socially, they were untiring as sparring partners, and I remember hilarious weekends at Frilsham, when the "peasant cultivator" scored points off the "lordly pastoralist" as they helped me in my garden, while the advantage went the other way when we went striding over the Berkshire downs. Muriuki and Salim would in due course become the twin pillars of the history department at Nairobi, while Karugire would go to join Kiwanuka and Twaddle at Makerere. Romilly Turton, who was researching on the trade and politics of the Kenya and Ethiopia borderland, would go on to teach for eight years at the new University of Zambia. And Rex O'Fahey, who had worked on the history of the Darfur sultanate, would serve for a time at the University of Khartoum.

Another of my preoccupations during the autumn and winter of 1966–67 was the launching of a charitable organisation that was to grow into the Minority Rights Group. In May 1965 I had been approached by David Astor, the editor and proprietor of the *Observer* and the close friend and financial supporter of Michael Scott. He spoke of his sincere and deeply held belief that the most crucial issue of the later twentieth century would concern the treatment accorded minorities throughout the world. He told me that he was interested in founding an organisation for the defence of oppressed minorities worldwide. He envisaged a specialised research body, on the lines of Amnesty International, that would collect information and feed it to a chosen circle of quality newspapers based in several of the larger countries. His basic idea was that, even though the worst cases of persecution tended to occur in countries that did not have a free press, the diplomats of those countries nevertheless studied and reported on the press of the countries to which they were accredited, and their governments might respond to international criticism if it reached them from many different quarters simultaneously. He was also interested in a technique described as "the higher blackmail," which consisted of using the threat of widespread publication as a spur to remedial action. He envisaged that, as soon as funds permitted, there would be a director who would be a former journalist or newspaper executive and who would report to a widely representative council that would include both journalists and academics with special knowledge of different regions of the world. He was already in touch with several likely people who knew me well, including of course Michael Scott, but also my friend and former neighbour David Kessler, the proprietor of the *Jewish Chronicle*, and Jim Rose, who before undertaking his 1967 survey, *Race and Colour in Britain* for the Institute of Race Relations, had spent ten years as director of the International Press Institute in Zurich and was therefore uniquely well informed both about newspapers and the state of press freedom in different countries. David Astor asked me whether I would consider becoming the chair of such a group. It was a large proposition, and I took time to think it over and to consult my employers, but finally I undertook to try to guide it through its early stages.

I suppose that the birth pangs of any organisation are likely to be painful and protracted. We could do nothing in a practical way until we had the funds to employ a director and to subsidise an initial programme of investigation and publication. We had therefore to begin by gathering a council of individuals with the weight and reputation to convince likely donors, and we had to bring its members to a common understanding of what most needed to be done. Our early meetings were held at monthly intervals over a sandwich lunch provided by David Kessler in his flat over the offices of the *Jewish Chronicle*. David Astor, Michael Scott, and Jim Rose attended from the start and were soon joined by Max Warren, now a canon of Westminster; Robert Birley, the well-known former headmaster of Eton and Charterhouse who had spent the first two years of his retirement at the University of the Witwatersrand; and Jo Grimond, the former leader of the British Liberal Party. Together we tried to categorise the different types of minority situations and to short-list those that might benefit from attention in the world press. We thought of the Aboriginal populations of North and South America and Australasia whose homelands had been overrun by migrant colonists from Europe and whose already shrunken areas of refuge were under threat from majority governments eager to exploit their oil, minerals, timber, or fisheries. We thought of the minorities created all over the New World by the forced migration of Africans during the period of the Atlantic slave

310

trade. We thought of the minorities stemming from more recent colonial rule, composed partly of European colonists but also of the client groups, mostly of Asian origin, recruited as labourers on sugar plantations or in the construction of railways and like projects all round the tropical world, whose descendants had stayed on as artisans, clerks, merchants, and managers and whose livelihoods were increasingly threatened by the majority populations of the new national states. We thought, finally, of the minority situations arising from the period of rapid economic growth in the industrialised world during the 1950s and 1960s that had brought West Indians and Pakistanis to Britain, Mexicans to the United States, Algerians to France, Moluccans to Holland, Turks and Yugoslavs to Germany, and Greeks and Maltese to Australia. These were migrations by some of the poorest people of the world into the midst of some of the richest, and it seemed that, here if anywhere, the media of the host countries could, if properly informed, play a useful and constructive part.

Gradually, we began to see that our immediate objective should be to sponsor a series of situation reports, aimed primarily at the quality press and therefore written mostly by journalists with experience as foreign correspondents and then submitted for verification to experts with a long-term commitment to the region concerned. Most of the work could be done on a commission basis, but we would obviously need a small central office to devise the programme, find the right investigators, and develop relations with the supporting newspapers. Our press members were always definite that newspapers, though they might use our reports, would not be prepared to contribute to their cost. Some of us thought that wealthy members of the richer minorities might help to fund us, but we soon discovered that few were inclined to look beyond their own communities. Peter Benenson came to share with us his experiences in funding Amnesty International, but we did not think that his method of enlisting a mass membership of small subscribers would work in our case. It seemed that our best hope was to win the support of one or two of the great foundations and to build our way from there into the long-term confidence of some smaller charitable trusts. I hoped to begin the process during my coming visit to the United States.

25

Scholarly Wanderings
(1967–68)

I flew with Caroline to Boston on February 2, 1967. Sarah, now seventeen, stayed with our tenants at Newton Road but joined us for the Easter holidays. Cambridge wore a very different look from the summery scene I remembered from my first visit in June 1962. The Charles River was a frozen waste, and snow lay piled by the side of the streets, burying the cars that had been parked there overnight. In one of the longest winters on record it was to snow every alternate day until we left. Every pavement was encrusted with ice, every road deep in slush. Students arrived at lectures stamping the snow from their boots and removing sodden anoraks. Harvard lecture rooms had a special line in central heating pipes that groaned and clanged throughout the day. It was not the best weather for Caroline's damaged joints, but fortunately we had leased the most comfortable apartments in Bradbury Street, belonging to a patrician professor of history, H. Stuart Hughes, who had collected some beautiful furniture as well as a splendid library comprising the historical and literary classics of four European languages. Here she could rest and read, and let the best of Harvard come to her.

And the best of Harvard, so far as we were concerned, were the undergraduate students, brilliantly selected with the help of teams of alumni working all over the country. Here were the products of the most prestigious New England prep schools, like Choate, Groton, and Andover, but also bright youngsters from Iowa and Idaho and a fair sprinkling of African Americans. Students from Harvard and Radcliff were mostly mature and friendly, and they also *looked* good. A Saturday evening performance at the campus theater, full of young men and women turned out in their best, could give one quite a lift. My lecture class reflected the surging attraction of the Peace Corps for well-educated young Americans of that time. Half my audience had already been to Africa, and most of these had actually worked there for a year or two. At the end of each lecture I would be surrounded by friendly questioners and borne away to drink coffee with them at some drugstore in the square. They were easy to invite home to the apartment, and Caroline enjoyed them as much as I did. I also had an excellent graduate seminar, but its participants all came across the river from Boston University, for there was no ongoing graduate work in African history at Harvard.

In contrast to the students my colleagues on the faculty at Harvard made no attempt to mount the kind of welcome we had so much appreciated at Northwestern University in 1962. Our countryman John Parry, whom we had known as principal of Ibadan University and who now occupied the chair of oceanic history at Harvard, was friendly and hospitable. Otherwise, the only professorial home we entered was that of a classic historian who invited us for tea. On the campus the history department did its business over a fortnightly lunch at the Faculty Club, but these were scarcely sociable occasions. After the first course had been served, the chair would ask the graduate assistants to leave, as there was business to discuss. A little while later he would invite the assistant professors to withdraw so that the confidential business could be settled. Finally, the associate professors would be dismissed in their turn, leaving the innermost group of full professors in a huddle at one end of the table.

On one occasion the chairman invited me to meet two or three of his senior colleagues over dinner in order to discuss the future of African history at Harvard. They made it clear that they were thinking in terms of a single appointment, and one of them asked me who was the best man in the world at this subject. I tried to explain that all the potential contenders for such a title, whether in North America, Europe, or Africa, were already leading teams of four, five, or six specialists and would be unlikely to leave those positions in order to be a one-person band. The questioner replied, "But this is Harvard," and it seemed to me to express very well just what was wrong with the place. In the event, the question was soon resolved because, as Nigeria moved inexorably towards civil war, Kenneth Dike, an easterner, fled from his vice chancellorship at Ibadan and came to the United States to prospect for alternative employment. He settled for Harvard and, no doubt with John Parry's help, he soon secured the establishment of two junior posts as well. In retrospect Dike's migration should be seen as much more than the beginning of African history at Harvard. It also marked the start of the sad drain of scarce intellectual talent from black Africa to the United States in search not so much of financial reward as of security and freedom. As Dudley Seers had remarked at the Addis Ababa conference in 1966, patriotism is largely a product of good government.

For the rest, our 1967 stay at Harvard was mostly memorable for our travels to other places. We had rented the Stuart Hughess' small motor car along with their apartment, and our first excursion in it took us down slippery roads to New Haven, where the colonial historian Robin Winks was our host, although an appointment in African history was already in view. There I gave a public lecture and talked to graduate students. The following week I spent two days in New York, soliciting the Ford and Rockefeller foundations on behalf of the Minority Rights Group. Ultimately, Ford was to be by far our largest supporter. Immediately, Ford officials told me merely that they liked our idea but needed more confidence in our ability to carry it out. Meanwhile, our application would be placed on the back burner of projects that were reconsidered at regular intervals, and they advised me to let them hear from us at least every three months and always report some genuinely new development. Ford helped those who helped themselves.

Early in March I flew to the West Coast to speak at a summer school organised by the African studies program at UCLA. Leonard Thompson was still in charge of African history there, although he was out of town at the time of my visit. In 1968 he would move to Yale, and his place would be taken by Terence Ranger from Dar es Salaam. Meanwhile, the fort was being well held by Ned Alpers, a recent doctoral graduate from SOAS who was to become well-known for his masterly study of the ivory and slave trade of East Central Africa in precolonial times,[1] and by Bob Griffeth, a young Arabist historian of West Africa who had been a member of my graduate seminar at Northwestern in 1962. A recent arrival in the program was Merrick Posnansky, who since leaving Makerere in 1963 had served for a brief spell as professor of archaeology at the University of Ghana, where most of his future research was to be based.

Sarah joined us from England for most of our last month at Harvard, and during the spring recess in early April we all three set off southwards in search of the sun. We paused for a night in New York, where I had been invited to lecture at Columbia by Graham Irwin, who was now installed there as professor of African history, and the following day we drove down the peninsula of northern Virginia, crossing the mouth of Chesapeake Bay by bridge and tunnel and staying in the vicinity of the museum town of Colonial Williamsburg. Spring had reached Virginia, and the Daughters of the American Revolution, who guided us through the reconstructed Georgian houses in their eighteenth-century fancy dress, were pleasing to the eye, as were the horse-drawn carriages that plied the well-shaded unpaved streets. Next day we drove to Jefferson's fabulous villa at Monticello, set amid massed daffodils on a spur of the Skyline Ridge with sweeping views to the east and north. I remember the singular position of Jefferson's bed, set in an alcove carved out of the dividing

314

wall between a rather grand reception room and a book-lined study, presumably so that he could enter or leave it from one side or the other as circumstances required. We spent that night in Charlottesville and next day drove the northernmost section of Skyline Drive on our way to Washington, D.C., where we stayed for a few days with our former neighbours in Newton Road, John and Helen Scott who were now working in an editorial capacity for the World Bank. It was the season of the cherry blossom, and Washington was looking its best. I just felt that it needed a few more great monuments to keep company with the Lincoln Memorial. I think it must have been the Scotts who first told us the charming story of the two British midshipmen who were being shown around the town by an American guide who kept referring to the occasion in 1812 when the British had burned Washington. At last, one of the midshipmen said, "God, did we really do *him*? I knew we did Joan of Arc." We returned to Massachusetts by the lovely valley of the Susquehanna, spangled with villages of prosperous-looking white-painted frame houses, and turned eastwards at Binghamton to cross the Hudson at Albany.

During our remaining month at Harvard I paid short visits to the University of Illinois at Champaign-Urbana and to the University of Wisconsin at Madison. At the first my host was Brian Fagan, now an enthusiastic migrant to the United States, where he would soon settle permanently at the Santa Barbara campus of the University of California. He had undertaken to collaborate with me in writing a difficult chapter for the second volume of the *Cambridge History*, on the making of Bantu Africa between the notional dates of 500 B.C. and 1000 A.D., and this was our first opportunity to discuss the outline of its likely contents. It was a partnership that was to continue in our joint authorship of a volume called *Africa in the Iron Age*, published by Cambridge University Press in 1975. It was, however, my visit a fortnight later to Madison that remains forever burned into my memory. The African studies program there had grown vigorously since my previous visit in 1962. It was now strong, not only in history but in anthropology, political science, and linguistics, and I was told that between its various disciplines it had 140 graduate students in training. For my public lecture there I had been asked to take as my theme the problem of the Bantu expansion, on which I had recently published an article in the *Journal of African History*.[2] In this I had tried to construct a scenario of population growth that would fit the linguistic classification of Bantu by my colleague Malcolm Guthrie.

It was not in fact such a bad scenario. It proposed an expansion of the Bantu-speaking peoples as a result of the transfer of food plants and agricultural techniques from the savanna margins north of the equatorial forest to the similar savanna country to its south, passing through the forest latitudes in the hands of mobile fishing communities that practised some riverside agriculture. Following Guthrie's analysis of the incidence of common word roots, my article postulated a rapid build-up of Bantu-speaking populations on the southern margins of the forest, followed by a dispersion northeastwards, southeastwards, and southward from there. Its gravest shortcoming was my uncritical acceptance of the assumption, shared by Guthrie with most of his predecessors, that the languages with the highest proportion of common roots were also the oldest, whereas more sophisticated linguists had long realised that the oldest members of any language family were to be found in that part of the habitat where neighbouring languages had become most different from each other. Judged by this criterion, the oldest languages in the Bantu sphere were those spoken in the northwestern quarter, while the youngest were those spoken in the east and the south. When I had completed my exposition to a packed audience, an unknown voice at the back of the hall, since identified as that of Joseph Miller, gently inquired whether I did not think that in any coherent language family the highest incidence of common roots was most likely to be found around the geographical centre of the habitat; borrowing might be a more likely explanation than paternity. It was a question that had never occurred to me, nor had it been suggested by any of my linguistic mentors at SOAS, and I just did not know how to reply. There was a long and deeply embarrassing silence before the chairman decided to take the next question.

After my return, duly chastened, from Wisconsin we had only a few days left before our departure for England, and on one or two of them the sun at last came out, and the grassy bankside of the Charles River was suddenly crowded by a student "love-in." There were flower people offering blooms to the passers-by, and there were wigwams with notices reading "Please do not disturb." It was all very colourful, good-natured, and orderly, but it was nonetheless a protest against the war in Vietnam and a precursor of the really massive demonstrations that were to build up during the next few years and to become the U.S. counterpart of the period of unrest among students that was to afflict European countries at the same time. As Vansina and others have noted, it was to be an important factor in the nationwide growth of interest in African studies, for a high proportion both of those who taught and those who studied these subjects were actively involved in the protest movement. Caroline and I observed it as a curiosity, without at all appreciating its significance.

At home in London and Frilsham I was plunged into the usual maelstrom of teaching, administration, editing, and committee work, all of which make up the stuff of academic life but do not stand retelling. These were Sarah's last months at school, and we had been hoping that during the interval between school and university she might be able to join us on a research trip to southern Ethiopia in 1968. Our plans for the expedition were already quite well advanced. SOAS had granted me the necessary leave of absence. The Ethiopian authorities had given permission. Tom Huffman, today a well-known professor of archaeology at the University of the Witwatersrand but at that time a graduate student of Brian Fagan's at the University of Illinois, was lined up to accompany us. We had close friends at the embassy in Addis Ababa who would have taken care of Caroline if her health had prevented her from travelling deeper into the country. Unfortunately, a series of domestic problems compelled us to seek a postponement, and in the event the opportunity never recurred.

Meanwhile, in December 1967 the Pan-African Congress of Prehistory and the International Congress of African Studies had arranged to meet in successive weeks at the University of Dakar, and I was fortunate enough to attend both and to do so from an idyllic base at the Ngor Hotel, perched above its beautiful little bay ten miles to the north of the town. My quarters were a chalet in a casuarina grove that I shared with Brian Fagan for the first week and with John Fage for the second. Over the intervening weekend I and the Griffeths, who were on research leave from UCLA, drove to St. Louis, the oldest of the French possessions on the coast and built on an island at the head of the Senegal estuary, some two hundred miles north of Dakar. Here French merchants had settled from the late seventeenth century onwards, building substantial houses for their local wives and families and sending Wolof trading agents up the river to the interior markets. During modern colonial times the island had housed the governments of both Senegal and Mauritania, as distinct from the federal capital of French West Africa at Dakar. What I had not previously realised was how sharply the river marked an ecological boundary between tropical Africa and the Sahara. We had driven north from Dakar through agricultural country but on crossing from St. Louis to the north bank of the river we entered a desert scene in which sitting camels were being loaded for a departing caravan, while tired-looking minivans came rattling in from places like Nouakchott, Tabermakounda, and Matam.

It would be difficult to imagine two conferences more different in character than those I was attending. The first was a conference of archaeologists in which I was the only historian. Desmond Clark was the president, and everything worked with the precision one might have expected. There were papers ready in French and English, and a time table that was strictly observed. My objective was to get to know as many of those working on the Iron Age as possible, and my efforts ended in my being asked to chair a concluding discussion on this topic in which West African and Bantu African specialists mingled in a really worthwhile exchange, the unexpected conclusion of which was that the most important developments connecting the two regions were probably

317

attributable to the very late Stone Age rather than the early Iron Age. It was a conclusion that has been borne out by much of the more recent research. During such time as he could spare for me, I spoke earnestly to Desmond about the *Cambridge History* and about my hope that he would undertake to edit the prehistoric and Egyptological volume, which he finally agreed to do. The social event of the week was a champagne party given by President Léopold Senghor in his splendidly decorated palace, guarded by the celebrated corps d'élite of *spahis* dressed in scarlet cloaks and holding drawn scimitars before their faces. The master of the house sat on a sofa upholstered in gold damask at one end of the drawing-room, conversing easily in English as well as French to those who were brought to sit beside him. I was told at the British Embassy that he spent much of his leisure time in Shakespeare studies, to the point that the British Council had been asked to appoint a representative competent to advise him on the subject.

The meeting of the International Congress of Africanists, held the following week was in contrast a rout so pitiful that it was astonishing that the organisation survived it. I wrote to Caroline,

We are now in the third day, and there are still no papers, no list of members, no firm programme. Whole national delegations, including even presidents of sections, have failed to turn up. No Boahen, no Ogot, no Ki-Zerbo. So we limp along from improvisation to sheer invention, and the only compensation is that there are only enough interpreters for two sections out of six to function at any one moment, so that we get plenty of spare time.

In retrospect I see more clearly than I did at the time that it was not just the failure of Alioune Diop and his circle in Paris but a reflection of the deteriorating economic and administrative situation in Africa as a whole. Many countries were suffering from political disorder, and everywhere universities were beginning to be strapped for cash and particularly for foreign exchange. The result was a gathering held on African soil but attended in overwhelming numbers by North Americans. It was in Dakar that I felt the first intimations that African studies was going to have only a limited future in Africa itself and that the real powerhouse and place of opportunity, even for African scholars, was destined to be the United States.

On my return to England I was met with the good news that Sarah had been offered a firm place at Somerville College, Oxford, for October 1968 and also that she wished to spend the intervening nine months doing something useful in Africa. She left us in February for the highly reputed girls' secondary boarding school at Gayaza in Uganda, run by missionaries of the CMS. There she shared a bungalow (and a maid!) with two other young volunteers and taught history and mathematics to the two junior forms. Uganda was at this point in the second year of Milton Obote's first presidency, when the government was nominally civilian but existing by the favour of a rough northern army, which was making its presence felt in the capital. But Gayaza was out of town and fairly well protected, and life there was undisturbed by the rent-a-crowd elements, including students at Makerere who were throwing stones at the British High Commission because of the British failure to make war on Smith's Rhodesia. She was close enough to know that these things went on but not in danger. It seemed to us a good way for her to be spending the first half of her nineteenth year.

At the end of March 1968 I flew to Chicago to take part in the most groundbreaking and significant research seminar I have ever experienced. It was organised by Brian Fagan with the backing of the Wenner-Gren Foundation, and it brought together just fifteen people—four linguists, six archaeologists, four historians, and one all-important historical botanist—to discuss the problems of Bantu origins. No formal papers were submitted, but my 1966 article was circulated with the invitations, and my colleague David Dalby brought with him the proofs of the two relevant volumes of Malcolm Guthrie's great work on comparative Bantu, for which Dalby acted as spokesman.[3] To that extent he and I were in the dock, but it was, as Vansina has written, a cosy conference, and its fundamental significance lay in a constructive comparison of the archaeological and linguistic evidence. According to my notes, there was general agreement that the dispersion of Bantu languages had to be seen in terms of a dramatic growth of population resulting from some form of food production, but also there was a common view that the whole process could not have taken place within the comparatively short span of the Iron Age. Desmond Clark was emphatic about the evidence for the existence of dense population on the southern margins of the equatorial forest towards the end of the Late Stone Age. David Dalby was equally insistent that the degree of differentiation now existing between the Bantu languages could not be accounted for within the period of two thousand years. It was also stressed that, whereas there was plentiful evidence of predecessor languages to Bantu in the form of surviving pockets of non-Bantu speech across much of eastern and southern Africa, there was no such remnant language to be detected anywhere in the northwestern quarter of the Bantu sphere. There was thus a strong disposition, much encouraged by the botanist Jack Harlan, to see the proto-Bantu as Late Stone Age fishermen and vegeculturalists, growing beans, cowpeas (black-eyed peas), yams, and oil palms in and around the equatorial forest and later spreading outwards from there. "All in all," I concluded, "it looks as though Iron Age technology cannot be held responsible for the first settlement of the Bantu in the southern woodlands, though it may well account for the outward spread of Bantu populations from there." While more evidence was still to come, notably when Bantu linguists began to work out genealogies based upon relative linguistic distance rather than numbers of common word roots, it can be said that in Chicago in 1968 we were getting somewhere near the historic reality.

In 1968 I made one other journey, which began with an external examinership at the University of Ife. The Nigerian civil war was still raging around the peripheries of Biafra, but Colonel Odumegwu Ojukwu's forces had been driven back from their early dare-devil advances across Benin and Yorubaland, where evidence of hostilities was mainly confined to the numerous military roadblocks along all the main traffic routes. The car sent from Ife to meet me at the Ikeja airport failed to show up, but I was offered a lift to Ibadan, which would be within fifty miles of my destination. There, on asking for Jacob Ajayi, I was shown into an examiners' meeting over which he was presiding. The room was full of old friends, including Adu Boahen and Terence Ranger who were there as external examiners, and with the marvellous spontaneity of Africa I was provided with coffee and a mark sheet and invited to join in. Reaching Ife that evening, I buried myself for four days in students' scripts. As an old hand at the game I knew the special characteristic of African examinations, which was that, while nobody did very badly, hardly anybody did very well. This, I knew, was primarily because African students habitually did their private study in groups of four or five, sharing the recommended reading and relying on each other to supply summaries and conclusions. Consequently, in examinations they tended to say much the same thing in much the same words. The competitive spirit was rare and not much admired where it existed. Commonly, a degree was described by students as a meal ticket, meaning a passport to some kind of indoors employment. Teachers and examiners were all well aware of the situation, but there was nothing that an external examiner could do to help. It was, however, possible to detect from the scripts where teaching seemed to have been defective, and I concentrated my efforts in this direction.

My principal host in Ife was Isaac Akinjogbin, a former doctoral student at SOAS and now the head of the history department and a figure of high authority, to whom well-mannered students genuflected when he passed. One day, when the examinations were over, he took me to see his home village at Ipetumodu, where he had recently completed building a family house. We set off down the main road to Ibadan and after eight miles turned down a track that appeared to lead through virgin forest with tall trees heavily interlaced with creepers. This, however, proved to be nothing but a kind of defensive screen, for we soon entered a huge clearing, inhabited, so he told me, by twenty thousand people. It had ten churches, three mosques, electricity, and piped water. Isaac's new house stood on

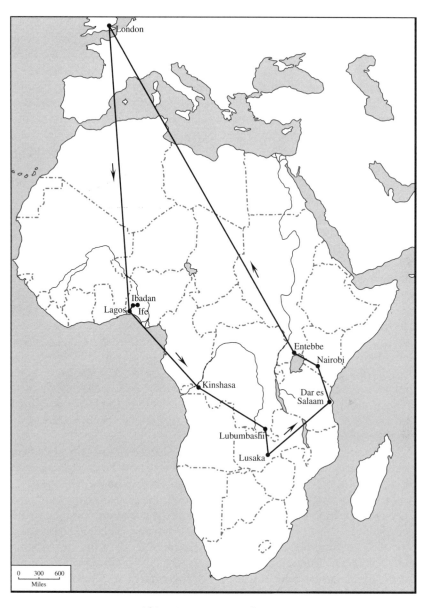

African journey, June–July 1968

the edge of the town. It was built in the ornate Afro-Brazilian style with ten rooms, and it looked quite ready for occupation. As we settled down to a picnic lunch on a generous balcony, I asked him when he would be moving in. He replied that he had no intention of leaving the university campus. Following Yoruba custom, he had laid out his first savings on a house that was for the use of any members of his extended family who might be in need of it. He had built it large enough to accommodate several sets of relations, but, as it happened, all his siblings were doing well, so for the present it was empty. If he were to live in it himself, life would be intolerable, because every morning there would be a queue of people seeking favours of one kind or another, and in Nigeria it did not do to send such people away empty handed. It gave one to think much about the social and economic status of university teachers in what was still overwhelmingly a peasant society.

One evening I drove with the entire staff of the Ife history department to an evening party in Ibadan given by the Ajayis to celebrate the departure of my former student Bertin Webster, who had just been appointed to the chair of history at Makerere. There was a buffet supper for sixty in the garden, followed by Hi-Life (a dance), which continued late into the night. "What a country," I wrote to Caroline, "where the great men and their wives are still so young and gay." On my return journey to Lagos I spent two nights with the Websters in Ibadan and found him already full of plans for his new post. I felt that the much-needed cross-fertilisation between universities in different countries of Africa had begun. During the next years it was to be carried much further but for the most part by political refugees. The recently founded University of Zambia was to be one of the early beneficiaries.

In Lagos I saw much of my old friend Ade Aderibigbe, who had been my very first African doctoral student. He was now head of the history department at the University of Lagos, where Saburi Biobaku was the vice chancellor. After showing me the campus, he took me for a long drive through new and old Lagos, ending up at the palace of the hereditary ruler known, like the ruler of Benin from whose dynasty he claimed descent, as the oba. The building in current use was quite modern but nevertheless full of interest. The audience chamber, which also contained the grave of the oba's father, was laid out on ordinary days as a schoolroom for his children. They filled three classrooms, separated by movable screens, and these of course were only the young ones. It was explained that the ruler's title meant 'father of all,' and the present one clearly was trying to live up to it. The old palace, which still stood just beside the new one, was alleged to be three hundred years old, and certainly it was built in the traditional style in a series of small courtyards, each surrounded by a cloister, with the living-rooms behind. The main courtyard contained a shrine housed in a gigantic safe, which was opened for us, the attendant knocking three times on the door before opening it to reveal what looked like a miscellaneous collection of the possessions of former rulers. We walked through several other courtyards built in the same style, some of them tiled with Delft and looking cool and attractive.

Naturally, throughout my visit to Nigeria I was taking every opportunity to inform myself about the war and in particular about the rights and wrongs of the Ibo claims for an independent Biafra. It was indeed a difficult question and became more so as the Ibo moved from their original position as the initiators of the war into that of a beleagered minority heroically defending its homeland and seeking by every means to enlist the sympathies of the outside world. The Ibo were more uniformly Christian than other Nigerians, and the missionary lobbies of every denomination felt a responsibility to support them. Moreover, Ibo Christians were mostly Catholic and were served by Irish missionaries who nursed the memory of their country's secession from a larger state. The missionaries brought in the help of the aid charities, which flew in food and medicine and kept open airports that were also used for the supply of arms. The nurseling Minority Rights Group could hardly avoid cutting its teeth on such a problem. And yet, as I stayed on for a few more days in Lagos with friends in the employment of Shell, I was made increasingly aware that Biafra had other less attractive friends—French oil interests prepared to give financial aid in the expectation of winning concessions away from their Anglo-Dutch rivals; all the arms traders of the world, eager to peddle their wares; colonial Portugal, only too willing to provide the line of communications to a scene of African discord; a gaggle of small economically unviable Francophone African states, delighted at the dismemberment of a giant neighbour. But for me the decisive issue was the growing perception that Iboland and Biafra were not identical in territory or in outlook. As I wrote in a letter to the London *Times* soon after my return to England,

I think that the Biafran secession must now be seen in retrospect as a gambler's throw, based upon the premise, which events have proved to be a false one, that all the peoples of the former Eastern Region would fall in behind a new, Ibo-dominated state. The Ibo leaders of the secession were, in fact, seeking to retreat from the position of a successful and therefore disliked and persecuted minority within the state of Nigeria, into the position of a dominant majority in a smaller unit.

And I concluded, "I happened to be in Nigeria at the time of Lord Shepherd's recent visit, and I think that his message to the Federal government was well understood, that Britain would cease to supply arms if those arms were not used with the greatest possible restraint and responsibility. So far as my information goes, General Gowon's record justifies such a measure of trust." (Shepherd was a minister of state in the Foreign Office, and Gowon was head of the federal military government.)

In 1967 I had accepted as a research student a rather celebrated Zairean, Thomas Kanza, who had been one of the earliest graduates of the Congolese university at Lovanium and had gone on to be the first ambassador of the independent Congo Republic (Kinshasa) in London and Washington before transferring his political allegiance to the dissident "Stanleyville government" of which he had been the foreign minister with a working base in Uganda. One way or another things had not worked out well for him, and he had come to Britain as a political refugee. It was Thomas Kanza who had suggested to me that, since my travels were taking me in any case from Nigeria to Zambia, I should pause en route at Kinshasa and try to establish an ongoing relationship with Lovanium. His sister Sophie was minister of education in Mobutu's first cabinet, and his brother-in-law, Marcel Lihau, was president of the Court of Appeal. They lived on the campus at Lovanium, and they arranged for me to be invited to visit briefly and lecture. On June 26 I therefore flew the fifteen hundred or so miles from Lagos to Kinshasa, supposedly for three nights but, as it turned out, for seven. I was lodged in a rather monastic guest-house but with access to the staff club and swimming pool, and the Lihaus were endlessly hospitable. The rector of the university was a Congolese, Monseigneur Tharcisse Tshibangu, with whom I had talks about the potential role of the University of London in training Congolese research students. He was quite enthusiastic, though he made it clear that Britain would have to pay for them as well as train them. Behind him, however, there was an éminence grise in the person of Monseigneur Luc Gillon, a dynamic Belgian priest and nuclear physicist who had been the founding rector and had stayed on after Congolese independence as director of development. To my great regret I did not meet him until much later, and then only glancingly, because it was he who had built the *colline inspirée* (hill of inspiration) and given it so much of its atmosphere, its shape an elongated oval with student residences at one end, professorial housing at the other, and library, lecture rooms, and university church in the middle. Jan Vansina had long warned me that when Gillon appeared at the pool in his purple swimming trunks, it was customary for other staff members to withdraw while he dived in and swam his accustomed number of lengths. Jan also had a prime story about how, when staying in Gillon's house as a visiting lecturer, he had bought a dead puff adder in the market and arranged it late one night in the bathroom that they shared. He heard the monseignoral alarm clock go off at 4:30 A.M. He heard the bath water running, followed by the sounds

324

of vigorous scrubbing. He heard Gillon depart for mass at precisely his usual hour. The two men breakfasted together, but no word was spoken about the snake.

Lovanium in 1968 was just ten years old, and despite the intermittent attentions of Jan Vansina its teaching of African history was strongly regional and markedly premodern. The seniors in the history department were Father François Bontinck and Canon Louis Jadin, both of whom had done good work on the sixteenth- and seventeenth-century history of the kingdom of Kongo as described by the European missionaries of that period, but they were still a long way from any conception of an Africa-based interpretation of the history of the continent as a whole. There was, however, a young layman, Jean-Luc Vellut, who had taken his doctorate at the Australian National University and who was starting to work actively on the more modern history of the Congo-Angola borderland and with whom I felt an instant rapport. He was destined to supply the next generation of leadership in the subject, both in Zaire and later in Belgium, where he settled at Louvain-la-Neuve.

I had originally been invited to give a public lecture in the town of Kinshasa, but the authorities concerned had failed to notice that the date for it coincided with the Day of National Independence, when the capital would be full of visiting heads of state and there would be processions and celebrations of every kind. So I was able instead to deliver my set-piece to a mainly student audience at Lovanium. I was a little relieved, because I had come with a well-travelled script, called "A Historian's View of Africa," which I had first composed for the Imperial Defence College in London and I had put into French as *"Un historien face à l'Afrique."* I had used it in Addis Ababa in 1966, as well as at several universities in the United States, and I set some store by it, as a test of integrity, to use exactly the same words to a range of differently composed audiences. But I had been a little apprehensive about its suitability for Kinshasa. At Lovanium, I knew, it would be all right. I also gave a seminar on the current ideas about the Bantu expansion. Then, my work done, the problem was how to get to Lusaka, a thousand miles away, in time for the conference on Central African history for which I was expected the next day. Once again it was the Day of National Independence that enforced a last-minute change of plan, because the entire fleet of Air Congo had been hijacked to transport the president's guests, and the offices of the company remained firmly closed throughout the holiday period. Moreover, there was no working telephone line between Lovanium and Kinshasa, fifteen miles away. The Belgian Fathers on the campus greeted my predicament with gales of good-humoured laughter, but I worried about the University of Zambia, which had paid my fare. People in midcareer are so self-important, and I fear that I was no exception.

In the event, I reach Lusaka in time for the last two days of the 1968 conference, the main purpose of which was to establish the identity of a recently founded history department at a university that was still only two years old. Its head was John Omer-Cooper, the historian of the nineteenth-century Zulu diaspora who had previously worked at the University of Ibadan. He had chosen for the second appointment my former Indian student B. S. Krishnamurthy, who had served his African apprenticeship at the University of Zaria and was to remain in Zambia for two more decades. My more recent research student, Romilly Turton, had just arrived, and there was also a temporary research fellowship in Zambian history, held by Andrew Roberts, in which I was closely interested, since it was a joint appointment with SOAS, funded out of the British development budget. The incumbent was to spend three years in Zambia, followed by a fourth year with us in London. Andrew had been trained by Jan Vansina at Wisconsin and had worked in depth on the oral history of the Bemba. He was better qualified for this type of research than anyone else in Britain, and I hoped strongly to find the means for SOAS to be able to attract him permanently. And so indeed it worked out. He was to become an editor of the *Journal of African History*, a volume editor of the *Cambridge History of Africa*, and in due course one of my successors as professor of African history at the University of London. The only Zambian citizen who was at that time in sight of a history post at the national university was Mutumba Mainga Bull, whom I had examined for her first degree at the University College in Salisbury. She was now working on the oral history of the Lozi kingdom, and I undertook to act as her official advisor for the external doctorate of London University. I gave her some technical help and saw her successfully through her examination, but when she next wrote to me, it was on her official notepaper as the minister of health in the Zambian government.

My two colleagues, Anthony Atmore and Shula Marks, who worked on the history of southern African at SOAS, were also present at the Lusaka conference, and on July 6 we started to make our way home together. We paused for a couple of nights in Nairobi, where I stayed with Neville Chittick and spent a long day out with Godfrey Muriuki, driving round the Kikuyu villages in the foothills of Mount Kenya where he had spent his youth. At last he brought me to his mother's house, surrounded by a small banana plantation eight miles from Nyeri. After we had talked to the old lady, it occurred to me to ask him at what age he had seen his first white man. After some thought he replied that he must have been eleven, when a white missionary had come to inspect the school he was attending. I then asked him how old he had been when he first realised that his country was being ruled by white men. He said that that had been much later, when he was at the secondary boarding school in Nyeri during the Mau Mau emergency, when the school buildings were protected by white soldiers. I was astounded by both his answers. I had thought of Kenya as a colony in which white settlement had been the dominant characteristic and in which Nyeri was one of three or four leading settler towns. Yet whites had hardly figured in his youthful perspective. It was a useful corrective, which I have often had occasion to quote.

From Kenya my party moved on to Uganda, about four hundred miles away, where I spent my first night as Sarah's guest in her missionary bungalow at Gayaza. Next day we all drove off for a long weekend in the Western Province, revisiting Masaka, Mbarara, Fort Portal, and Mubende and archaeological sites along the route. My party flew home to England on July 15, 1968. Sarah followed on August 23 to prepare for undergraduate life at Oxford in October.

26

Revolting Students

(1968–72)

In the autumn of 1968 the general climate of student unrest, which had erupted violently in France the previous May, spread rapidly through the rest of Western Europe. I do not know whether any careful historical inquiry has been made about its origins and aims, but as it hit us in one small college of a large university, it was more like a virus than a revolution. It affected undergraduates much more strongly than postgraduates, and it was characterised by a kind of euphoria that caused its adherents to feel that all initiative and all decision making should henceforward belong to persons aged eighteen to twenty-one. Older people were members of "the Establishment" and were the dupes or the conscious collaborators of the military-industrial complex. By bringing about the resignation of President de Gaulle, French students had shown what could be achieved in other countries also. With only a little marching and waving of banners the walls of Jericho would crumble. In particular the undergraduate students of this age group felt that the universities belonged solely to them. Although their stay was for only three years, they felt that it was they who should decide what subjects were "relevant" and who should appoint the professors best suited to teach them. The fount of rightful authority was the Students' Union, the almost daily meetings of which should naturally take precedence over other, merely academic, engagements.

In retrospect I think that the reaction of the academic staff to the new situation was rather creditable. Most of us did not get angry or bluster. We took the students as seriously as possible and gave them every opportunity to talk to us in small groups. My diaries for that academic year and the four that followed are peppered with the word *forum*. It meant an open meeting held at the end of the teaching day for those inscribed in the same degree programme. We set the agenda and we set it on the principle that those who wished to change things had

328

better understand in some detail how the existing system worked. Why degrees? Why syllabuses? Why lectures? Why examinations? Why boards of studies? Why academic boards and governing bodies? Why universities, and what of their functions, not merely in transmitting knowledge but also in preserving and extending it? We went on talking and listening until everyone agreed that they had had enough, and I think that the exercise, although extremely time consuming, did serve a purpose. The key was to talk to small groups and to avoid the general confrontations that the leaders were always trying to provoke. At the end of the day, our students, like those at many other British universities, achieved modest representation on the governing body and the right to express formally their individual views on the performance of their teachers. In several continental countries things went much further. France institutionalised dissent by dividing the Sorbonne into twelve universities, some of which consciously recruited staff members on the basis of their political beliefs. In Denmark and Holland significant numbers of older academics came to feel so harried that they left the profession.

In England the sharp edge of student unrest fell primarily upon the heads of institutions, who could not avoid direct encounters with the hard core of troublemakers and who had to take difficult disciplinary decisions in the knowledge that, while the public and the press demanded strong action, the police and the law courts took the view that students were now adults and entitled to the same immunities as unionized employees. It was the heads of colleges who had their offices forcibly occupied and their confidential filing cabinets broken open. The rest of us mostly faced nothing worse than crossing picket lines on days when students were on strike. All the same, like many others of my generation I look back on the five years of student estrangement as an unhappy period, when I wondered if I had taken up the wrong profession. I was conscious of a great deterioration in morale and discipline. Students looked increasingly bedraggled and unkempt. They came only erratically to lectures. They failed to submit their written work. They responded to criticism with looks of pitying contempt. As I moved about London, I was aware that university education was falling steadily in public esteem, to a point where employers wondered what was to be gained by recruiting graduates and where governments knew that university budgets could be pared without fear of losing a single vote.

Although it had its comic side, a good example of the harm that students could do to the cause of higher education occurred in November 1972, when Edward Heath, then prime minister, came to lunch at the school. He had made it known that he wished to exchange ideas with a few specialists in the different regions of Asia and Africa, following a tour that he had recently made in the Far East. It was intended to be a private occasion, and none but the actual participants had been told of his coming. In the event, the appointed day coincided with a memorial service in Westminster Abbey for the famous yachtsman Sir Francis Chichester, at which Heath had agreed to read the lesson. He instructed his staff to warn us that he would be a half-hour late for lunch. Most unfortunately, the Downing Street telephone exchange looked up the wrong number and connected the private secretary with the astonished president of our Students' Union, who thus had nearly two hours in which to organise a really noisy crowd, complete with a squad of mobile demonstrators dressed in motorcycling gear who drove up from the London School of Economics. When the prime minister arrived, he had to be escorted through a shouting mob waving placards inscribed with "Heath Out" and other unendearing slogans. The luncheon party went well enough, but it took place behind drawn curtains and against background noise, after which our guest had to be spirited away through a back door. When some three months later I was his guest at an official dinner, he greeted me in heavily ironic tones with "Well, your students gave me a fine reception," and although he was greatly amused when I told him why, it was obvious that the episode had rankled.

Above all, we did not know then that in the end the student unrest of the late 1960s and early 1970s would all blow away as suddenly as it had come. By the fifth year it looked more like an irreversible change in the landscape, and had it not been for our graduate students, we should have felt like relics from the past. At least in African history, however, these years were the most prolific of any in the training of doctoral students. We had six members of staff with enough experience to be actively involved in supervising research, and our reputation was well enough established to assure us of a flow of good students. Of forty doctoral candidates whose names appear in my engagement books for this period, twenty came from African countries, including five South Africans, four Zimbabweans, three Nigerians, two Ugandans, two Ethiopians, two Zaireans, one Gambian, one Sierra Leonian, one Cameroonian, one Sudanese, and one Zambian. Of the rest, ten came from Britain, four from the United States, three from Canada, two from Israel, and one from Guyana. Of the forty, all but two managed to do some part of their research in an African country, and all but a handful went on to teach, at least for a time, in universities in Africa. In this part of our work, at least, my colleagues and I could still feel that we were doing something of real value.

One organisation with which I had been closely connected for fifteen years fell victim to the student malaise. In 1969 Philip Mason retired with honour from the Institute of Race Relations, which he had directed so fruitfully for sixteen years. Under his leadership it had produced a steady flow of dispassionate studies, culminating in the massive 1967 report *Race and Colour in Britain* by Jim Rose and Nicholas Deakin and in Mason's 1970 volume of reflections on race in world history called *Patterns of Dominance*. As his parting legacy he persuaded the Ford Foundation to make a handsome grant of $400,000 to enable the institute to engage a team of temporary research fellows to report critically on the racial policies being pursued by governments, both in Britain and the wider world. Under the permissive leadership of Hugh Tinker, who succeeded him as director, these young men, who in any university context would have had the standing of graduate students, were encouraged to spend their time reforming the government of the institute. One went so far as publicly to describe his employers as "spies for the government" and an "obstruction in the struggle of black people for freedom, justice, and a better life," for which he received a caution but not a dismissal. Sides were quickly taken, and the entire institute neglected its work to fight the internal battle. New members were enrolled who were thought likely to join in replacing the director and council, and after a year of misery the council was defeated by a narrow majority at an extraordinary general meeting. The trustees thereupon cut off the funds, and the victors were left to pursue their radical policies under the direction of the former librarian from a new address in Pentonville. It was a classic example of how easily an organisation with a small membership could be taken over and its whole character changed by a little deliberate recruitment.

It was some comfort to me that, while the Institute of Race Relations was ailing, the Minority Rights Group (MRG) was at last springing from a set of ideas shared by a few friends into something more durable that also would be able to carry on in some measure the aims of the institute's founders. The key development was the recruitment as director of Lawrence "Laurie" Gander, the courageous editor of the *Rand Daily Mail* who had placed the considerable reputation of his newspaper solidly behind the tiny Progressive Party, even when it was represented by only a single member in the South African parliament. Laurie, at the time we contacted him, was standing trial for alleged offences against the security laws. His passport had been seized, and we knew it was certain that his mail was being opened. We were lucky enough to have as intermediary Philip Brownrigg, a London director of the Anglo-American Corporation of South Africa and a member of the council of the Institute of Race Relations who knew Laurie intimately and was able to arrange for the secure transmission of correspondence. Everything had to be done with the utmost secrecy for fear of prejudicing the outcome of the trial, but we shared our intentions with the Ford Foundation, and it was undoubtedly influential in securing our first substantial grant of $72,000 over three years, which was awarded in December 1968.

It took Laurie almost a year to extract himself from his legal entanglements, but as soon as he arrived in London things began to happen. He established the right size, format, and level of academic or journalistic competence for our reports, which would both convince the thirty-seven world-class newspapers that had agreed to study them and also look attractive in serious bookshops, where they could be sold to the general public. He drew up a programme for the first six reports, all to appear in 1970, starting with one on the treatment of religious minorities in the Soviet Union by Michael Bordeaux and two of his assistants at the newly founded Centre for the Study of Communism and Religion in Canterbury. It was followed by a really impressive analysis by Harold Jackson of the *Guardian* of the dual concept of a minority in Northern Ireland, whereby Catholics balanced their resentment against minority status in the province by cultivating their sense of belonging to the majority on the island as a whole, while Protestants sharpened their attitudes of dominance by the thought that, at a broader level, they were the real minority. The same is of course true of the Arab minority in Israel, which consoles itself with the thought that it represents the majority population of the Middle East, while the Jews overassert their majority standing in Israel because of their minority situation in the region round about. The four remaining reports dealt with the relations between the northern and the southern Sudan, the predicament of the Asian communities in East and Central Africa, the Crimean Tatars, and the blacks in Brazil.

With such a crisp take-off MRG was up and away, but its very success demanded a rapid increase in its pump-priming funds, and I felt that this required a chairman very much better known than I. Therefore I resigned in the autumn of 1970 to make way for Jo Grimond, with whom I worked closely as deputy until 1975, resuming the chair on his retirement and holding the main responsibility for a further fourteen years. Laurie Gander soon found himself unbearably homesick for his native South Africa and stayed with MRG for only two years. Before leaving, however, he had found an able assistant in Ben Whitaker, a former Labour member of Parliament for Hampstead who succeeded Laurie as director in 1971 and was to remain in post for seventeen years.

In our family life the years from 1969 till 1972 were more unsettling than any others we experienced. In the spring of 1969 Caroline's health took another sharp downward turn, to the extent that I was seriously wondering whether it would be possible for me to continue in my profession. Later on we learned that the only way to cope with a progressive disease was progressively, by holding onto the main pattern of one's life while making constant small adjustments in the knowledge that in six or twelve months still further adjustments would be necessary. Above all, it was important for the breadwinner to go on winning bread to pay for the additional help that would be needed. At this stage of things, however, we were still naively looking for a permanent solution and wondering whether we could not find a climate that was kinder than the British one, with lower taxes and cheaper labour, where a premature pension and a little private means might suffice. And so we went in September 1969 to stay with old friends in Malta, where it had been suggested that all these conditions might be met. In the event, quite a short visit served to convince us that the island was rather unattractive and that its political future was far too uncertain to risk settling there.

Soon after our return from Malta Caroline's right knee began finally to collapse, and by Christmas it had become clear that she would need major orthopaedic surgery and that in the longer term we would need to move from our little house in Newton Road, with its three storeys and its steep stairs. In January 1970 we went to see David Evans at the Westminster Hospital who said that he could remove the joint and fuse the two bones into a stiff leg on which she would be able to walk with a stick. The operation was fixed for early March, and my director Cyril Philips gave me compassionate leave for the month of February so that I could take her to Tenerife. There we stayed in a clifftop hotel overlooking the little rocky cove at Santiago, and there we had our joint initiation in the operation of wheelchairs. It was difficult at first to feel ourselves the objects of so much pity from other guests, but we learned to do it with a certain amount of speed and even panache, which soon eased the tension. Out of doors the sun shone and the sea sparkled. We hired a car and drove all over the island, admiring its wonderful seascapes. There followed for Caroline almost three years of unrelieved discomfort, with her leg in plaster from hip to ankle as the bones failed and failed to fuse. The operation was repeated in February 1972, and only nine months after that was success achieved.

Meantime, I had been through another period of professional restlessness. In May 1970, soon after Caroline's first operation, I wrote to consult my brother-in-law Hugh Linehan, who had a printing firm in Dorchester, about the possibility of a part-time involvement in some small business that would enable me to give Caroline more help and enable us to spend the worst of the winters in a warmer climate. I also sought the advice of Michael Caine about the likelihood of my being able to fill a consultancy role with one of the larger companies trading in Africa. He generously took the time to enter right into my problems, and I think that it was he more than anyone else who convinced me that it would be better to try to carry on within an academic framework. We therefore went ahead with the sale of our Bayswater house, replacing it with a modern flat in Southampton Row just across Russell Square from the school. From here it was possible to combine teaching with housekeeping during the middle days of each week. With Sarah now at Oxford we were able to spend regular long weekends at Frilsham, where I now did all my writing and editorial work. Caroline too was a voracious reader, both of nineteenth-century novels and of the literature of African travel. She had already written a distinguished essay on the African career of Richard Burton for a volume edited by Robert Rotberg, and now she was slowly assembling the materials for the five biographical essays that she was to publish in 1980 under the title *Western Women in Colonial Africa*.[1] She was able to walk with the help of a stick from one room to another, but steps were a great difficulty for her, and she did not often go out. She would make valiant efforts, however, to accept the grander invitations that sometimes came our way. I became quite expert at the preliminary staff work and was greatly impressed by the evident eagerness of all concerned to do everything to make it possible. "Four steps and a hand rail," they would say. "You can use the private lift, and we'll tell the policeman to let you park by the door."

Even at the height of my middle-aged madness it had never been my intention to abandon the study and writing of African history, and in fact during the two worst years of it I was very much employed in writing, with Brian Fagan, a short book called *Africa in the Iron Age* (1973), which was to be the introductory volume of the trilogy commissioned by Cambridge University Press, of which *Africa Since 1800* had been the first to be published. It was, as I remarked in the preface, the fruit of a good friendship that had begun within sound of Victoria Falls in July 1960 and had continued not only at international conferences but on archaeological sites and in each other's homes. Brian had entered into the partnership with some hesitation, because, as he constantly reminded me, archaeologists tended to be "little men in little holes" who did not like their holes to be compared with other people's holes in the interests of broader synthesis. But we were both attracted by the challenge of crossing disciplinary boundaries, and in the performance it was literally true, as we claimed, that every chapter, every paragraph, and almost every sentence had been written at least twice and sometimes more often. Rereading it after a lapse of twenty years, I find many small areas, and a few larger ones, where it has been overtaken by later research. There is perhaps to be detected a certain residual tendency to diffusionist interpretations, though not on anything like the scale of the early editions of the Penguin *Short History*. All in all I feel that it deserved better than its modest success. Certainly, it was not helped by the fact that Cambridge University Press took three years to publish it. As I warned them at the time, it was a field in which knowledge was advancing so rapidly that revised editions should ideally appear at three-year intervals. But the largest reason for our failure to keep it up to date was a tragic fire in Santa Barbara in

1977, which destroyed Brian's house, his library, and every note he had made in twenty years of study. His response to the situation was to renounce his ambitions as an African specialist and to broaden his base by a comparative approach to his subject. With characteristic generosity he made over to me his interest in the book's future. However, since it was the archaeological rather than the historical evidence that was being added to fastest, I could not do what was necessary by myself, nor could I easily ask another archaeologist to take responsibility for Brian's contribution to our joint effort.

In June 1972, leaving Caroline in the safe hands of a congenial retired district nurse who lived in the next village, I made my first visit to Africa in nearly four years. Its main purpose was to act once again as an external examiner at the University of Ife, but I took the opportunity to travel there by way of northern Nigeria, where Michael Crowder had invited me to stay with him in Kano and to visit the two fairly recently founded universities, there and at Zaria, which served the Northern Region. Despite the region's size and its demographic predominance over the rest of the country, the colonial respect for Islam had caused Western education at every level to come much later to the north than to the south. Only with the advent of political independence had the Muslim elite of the north begun to appreciate that its future influence would depend upon its catching up with the southerners in both secondary and tertiary education. Now, in the aftermath of the civil war, four more northern universities were in prospect at Jos, Maiduguri, Ilorin, and Sokoto, and the politicians were deeply concerned that all these institutions should be staffed by northern scholars as soon as possible. While these were in training, the authorities were looking to expatriates to fill the gaps, lest southerners entrench themselves in permanent appointments. On both counts it seemed that here was a scene in which SOAS could play a useful part.

The summer rains had not yet reached Kano, and the temperature when I landed there was well over 100 degrees, but Michael, after more than twenty years in West Africa, knew all about tropical comfort. He met me in his air-conditioned car and soon whisked me off to his rather charming cottage on the edge of the old colonial quarter, ten miles from the university campus, where he lived a very private life attended only by a cook, a driver, and a pair of basset hounds, and bathed in a continuous flow of European classical music. There was just time for a drink before the northern and Muslim vice chancellor came alone for an informal dinner, after which Michael withdrew to a garden annex where he slept and worked. He warned me that I should be breakfasting alone, since it was his custom, come what might, to rise at five o'clock and to write from then until half past ten, after which he would drive to the campus to teach,

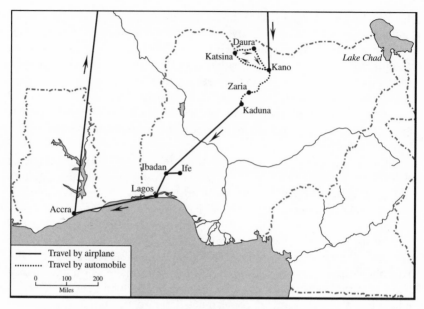

West African tour, June–July 1972

administer his department, and be all things to all people for the rest of a long working day. I saw and greatly respected the discipline that had enabled him to maintain a steady output of highly articulate publication from a sequence of pioneering posts in Nigeria and Sierra Leone, each of which he had cheerfully vacated as soon as an African successor was available to take over.

Michael had tactfully arranged for me to spend my first day in Kano in the company of a former doctoral student at SOAS, Adamu Fika, now a lecturer in Michael's department but soon to leave the academic profession in order to head the bureaucracy of the new northern Nigerian state of Borno. Adamu had written his thesis on the modern history of the Kano emirate, which he was now actively revising for publication,[2] and there could have been no more appropriate companion and guide for a 250-mile drive through the Hausa countryside, where every peasant's mud-walled compound looked like a walled city in embryo. We passed many groups of pastoral Fulani that had been grazing their herds on the stubble of the Hausa farmers' previous harvest and were now driving the animals northwards again to free the fields for sowing as soon as the new season's rainfall allowed. We paused for some hours in Katsina, now, like Kano, the capital of a Fulani emirate established during the *jihad* of the early nineteenth century but previously the seat of a much more ancient

336

Hausa dynasty. But even the older parts of Katsina seemed to be groaning under the weight of modern lorry traffic, and Adamu's friends in the local administration kept trying to divert us to look at mosques built by the Public Works Department in the 1930s. Consequently, our next stopping place in the little town of Daura, close to the Niger frontier and away from the main routes, gave me a much better picture of a Hausa capital in pre-Fulani times. Its streets lined by high mud walls and its open spaces planted with shady trees seemed cool and welcoming even in the intense heat of early afternoon. There were saddled horses waiting patiently for their riders, and pedestrians proceeding at a dignified pace who showed no glimmer of surprise at our presence among them. Daura had been the capital of the Hausa kingdom of Gobir, where the jihad was first declared by the Fulani cleric Usuman dan Fodio in 1804. Long before that, perhaps as early as the eleventh century, it was, according to some Hausa traditions, the earliest stronghold of a horse-owning military elite that gradually imposed its ascendancy over the surrounding population of Hausa peasants and incorporated them into a series of small kingdoms in which the military caste ruled from walled citadels and took tribute in food and raw materials from the villagers in return for security and protection.

Daura, one might say, represented the first stage in the formation of city-states in Hausaland, and it was a great help to have seen it, when on the following day another of Michael Crowder's colleagues, John Lavers, took me on tour of old Kano, which represented something much more complex—something still concerned with military protection but even more so with trade and industry. We visited first the square-mile of market, my dominant memory of which is of the tap-tap and knock-knock of several hundred workers in metals, wood, and leather who were fashioning their wares in full view of the customers. The weavers at their looms were out of sight, working in private premises all round the old town, but their cotton textiles were much in evidence beside those imported from Europe. We visited the pits, where much of this cloth was dyed in various shades of indigo, and nearby them were camels loading for the Saharan trails. I was reminded that all this commercial activity had begun at least as early as the fourteenth century, when merchants from the empire of Mali settled here, bringing with them their industrial skills and their teachers of religion and literacy. Last, we climbed the hill of Dala, an inselberg of ferriferous granite thrusting up from the plain, from the summit of which we could see the whole of the old city standing within its sixteen miles of defensive wall, which also enclosed a wide segment of unbuilt agricultural land where the citizens could plant emergency vegetable gardens in times of siege. According to the earliest traditions recorded in the Arabic chronicle of the town, Dala Rock was the sacred dwelling-place of the priest-kings of pre-Islamic Kano, known by the title of *tchunburburai*, who descended from the rock only once a year to show themselves to the people and claim their loyalty. Shortly before our visit an archaeological dimension had been added to the place by the discovery of an iron-smelting furnace, dated by carbon to around 630 A.D.

That night, June 6, the first rain of the 1972 season fell in Kano, and in the morning there was a faint hint of green in the landscape as we set off southwards to Zaria. The distance was little more than a hundred miles, but as we travelled we noticed that the guinea-corn in the fields beside the road, only just visible in Kano, grew taller and lusher until around Zaria it stood waist high. The Fulani herds, which we had passed two days earlier on our way to Daura, had in fact been moving north about a week ahead of the rain belt. I felt happy to have witnessed at first hand one of the greatest underlying rhythms of West African life and history.

Ahmadu Bello University in Zaria was for me a place of great interest. The department of history there had been founded by Charles Smith, the most Nigerianized of all the British expatriates. His guiding principle had been that Nigerian academics should be trained from start to finish in Nigeria, free from the corrupting influences of Europe. Charles was by this time half retired, and the department was in the able hands of Robert Gavin, but here were his academic progeny, comprising six or seven bright young lecturers who had come all the way to doctoral degrees without leaving their country. I spent a couple of days talking to one after another and looking at their theses, which seemed to be well up to standard. But I thought I did detect in these people a consciousness of having missed out on a necessary experience of international competition, which they felt when they encountered their southern Nigerian peers. My visit was also memorable for an afternoon out with a young Yoruba archaeologist, Ade Obayemi, who took me to an inselberg site at Dumbi and taught me how these rocky prominences had attracted early Iron Age settlement by reason not only of their ferriferous composition but also because of the springs of perennial water that percolated to the surface around their bases. In the proliferation of northern universities Abuyemi was to be the head of the department of history and archaeology at the University of Ilorin, while another of the Zaria team, Elizabeth Isichei, a New Zealander married to an Ibo professor of medicine, was to occupy the corresponding position at the University of Jos.

After spending two nights with the Gavins at Zaria, I was driven to the capital of the Northern Region at Kaduna, and it was here that I began to be aware that Nigeria was still under military rule—soldiers now constituted a substantial and visible interest group in the state. The streets were full of highly polished chauffeur-driven staff cars with military officers inside. We drove into town behind a car with *L* (for

338

learner) plates, in which a young woman was taking a driving test with her uniformed husband or boyfriend seated in the back. "That young woman will *pass* her test," said my companion with a smile. And at the airport I found my plane to Ibadan had been diverted to Lagos in order to transport a party of senior officers to their destination. All the same this government headed by Major General Gowon did not seem at all like tyranny. Politicians had disappeared from the stage, but people still talked politics and felt no need to lower their voices when they did so in public places. The departments of central and local government were still run by civil servants, and the military governors confined themselves to the role of inspectors. There was an inspection by the military governor while I was at Ife. The authorities took him to see the new sports stadium, where he interested himself in the composition of the running track. They told him that it had been imported from Australia in barrels. He demanded to know at what cost and issued orders that on the next occasion a Nigerian substitute must be found. The professor of geology was summoned and told to get working on the problem. It seemed quite a reasonable contribution to come from a major general.

All in all I was well impressed by the evident progress made by the history department at Ife since my visit four years previously. In particular the variety of educational experience and the spread of research specialisation represented in the staff seemed to be exactly what an African university should be aiming at. Of its eight members, all Nigerian, three had taken their higher degrees at Ibadan, three more with us in London, one in Moscow, and one in Washington. Only two were specialists in Nigerian history. Two more had worked on Francophone West Africa, one on North Africa, one on East Africa, one on the USSR, and one on the United States. Moreover, the Rhodesian archaeologist Peter Garlake, a refugee from the Smith regime, was at the Institute of African Studies. Together they formed a lively and argumentative group with the alumni of Moscow and Georgetown in the lead as sparring partners. It was obvious from the examination scripts that the undergraduate teaching was being well carried out. Several of them, however, talked to me about the practical difficulty of reconciling their academic ambitions with the economic circumstances and social customs that surrounded them in West Africa. All were members of extended families that made heavy calls on their time and their pockets. Their houses, even those of the bachelors, were full of women and children who operated at a level of noise and interruption that made it unthinkable to work at home. Even in their offices, visitors called unannounced from early morning on, and it did not do to plead that they were busy; all had to be politely received and listened to at length. In these circumstances they might just manage, in five years or ten, to bring a thesis to the stage of publication, but the second book could normally be achieved only by those who sought an appointment overseas. I believe that these considerations were genuine and that they were common to all young African universities that I visited. Gradually, one had come to realise that, once the staff of a university was substantially Africanised, its ethos and daily practice had to move closer to that of the society within which it was set. The founders' dreams of reproducing Oxbridge in tropical Africa were politely returned to the world of dreams.

I completed my 1972 West African tour with a brief visit to Ghana, where the civilian government led by Professor Kofi Busia had been evicted at the beginning of the year by a second military junta headed by General I. K. Achiempong. By all accounts the difference between the two regimes was minimal. Both governments subsisted by overtaxing the farmers who were thereby discouraged from producing the all-important export crops. Both deterred foreign investment by squeezing the mercantile and mining firms surviving from colonial times. Both tampered with the judiciary and used emergency powers to suppress their political opponents. Foreign debt had risen to a level at which further loans were unobtainable, and the civil service and the army could be paid only by printing money and driving up inflation. It remained only for the situation to be compounded by the oil crisis of the following year, when the cost of the country's most essential import would soar by a factor of six.

These were not favourable conditions for the University of Ghana. Of the four Ghanaians we had trained at SOAS, one was dead, another had left the academic profession, and a third explained to me that, with a family of four children to support, he would probably need to seek employment in a more fortunate African country. Only Adu Boahen, reinforced by seniority and a certain international reputation, retained his indestructible ebullience. We spent a happy afternoon together, walking over the plot of land he had just acquired atop the escarpment at Mampong, twenty miles inland from Accra, where he planned to build a weekend retreat for reading and writing. Reluctant as ever to assume administrative duties, he had persuaded the authorities to recruit yet another expatriate as head of the department of history—Alastair Lamb, a veteran of the University of Malaya at Kuala Lumpur whose love of adventurous travel had led him to arrive by car across the Sahara. His wife Venice had developed a consuming interest in West African textiles, and she built up a collection that was to become internationally known. I spent four enjoyable days as their guest, but it did not seem likely that they would stay there long. We were still at that time operating an annual exchange of undergraduate students between SOAS and Legon, and I was able to meet the British participants and hear of their experiences. But gone were the days when they could expect to travel freely across

West Africa on their homeward journey as their predecessors had done, and it seemed unlikely that we would be able to continue with the project for much longer. Ghana held so many pleasant memories for me that it was sad to leave it now with foreboding.

Soon after my return to England in 1972 there came the news from Uganda that General Idi Amin, who had seized the presidency from Milton Obote in a military coup the previous year, had ordered the summary deportation of the entire Asian population of the country, numbering some seventy-four thousand, to be completed within ninety days. Although the decree was later amended to exempt those who had opted at the time of independence for Ugandan rather than British citizenship, it quickly became obvious that citizens and noncitizens alike were being terrorized into departure by rough northern soldiery licensed to assault, rob, and confiscate. Until the very last moment these unfortunate people had no idea where they might go. The British government sought the help of its Commonwealth partners, especially India and Canada, and finally took responsibility for about half the total. The refugees were allowed to take only £55 each, and most lost even this at roadblocks on the way to the airport. The resulting emergency impinged directly on our family, because the refugees were brought immediately to a reception centre at Greenham Common, only a few miles from us at Frilsham. Sarah, who had just completed her education at Oxford, spent that autumn and winter as a volunteer worker at Greenham, teaching the womenfolk English and helping to care for them in other ways.

For Uganda the expulsion of the Asians meant the loss of most of its skilled artisans, traders, and businesspeople, and the start of a rapid decline from prosperity to poverty and indebtedness that in turn cut off most of its contacts with the outside world. Among the Europeans a few brave missionaries stayed on, but the flow of replacements ceased. It was the same at Makerere. The history department lost Bertin Webster, its Canadian head, and the three other expatriate members of staff. There was some brave talk of "Ugandanization," but the reality was that three young and inexperienced men were left trying to do the work of seven. They recruited one promising recent graduate and sent him to me at SOAS to work for a higher degree, but by the time he had completed it, all three of his colleagues were in exile, and he did not dare to return home. As serious from my point of view was the fact that Uganda, which had been such a key area in the development of precolonial history on the eastern side of the continent, now joined the growing list of African countries that were effectively closed to research. In archaeology, as in history, the hiatus was to last for more than a decade.

27

Filling in the Gaps

(1973–78)

During the 1970s, and indeed right up until my retirement in 1986, my scholarly life as a teacher, writer, editor, and supervisor of research was increasingly interrupted by the calls of college administration. Following on four years as chairman of the Centre of African Studies, in which my main preoccupation had been the establishment of new master's degrees, I was appointed in 1971 as the senior tutor at SOAS, which gave me the oversight to the whole of the teaching programme of the school. The appointment came at a significant moment. Hitherto, student numbers had been limited by the size of our accommodation to around seven hundred. Now, with a large extension of our building nearly completed, it was possible to think in terms of raising our total numbers, in the course of ten or fifteen years, to as many as two thousand. Such a transition would involve a radical change in the composition of the student body. Hitherto, all but three hundred of our students had been postgraduates whose numbers could not be expected to increase significantly beyond their existing level of around four hundred. It was clear, therefore, that our projected expansion would have to be built mainly around our undergraduate programme, and the recruits would have to come mainly from British schools. As things stood, all we could offer them was a long list of single-subject degrees, half of them with the Asian and African dimensions of the main arts and social science subjects and the other half in Asian and African languages, of which only a handful of British school leavers would even be aware. The fundamental problem here was that, although half our staff members were language specialists, they could make little direct contribution to our expansion. The additional teaching would fall mainly on the rest, who would need to share the load as equally as possible. In these circumstances it seemed plain that we would need to take a long step in the direction of the American system of modular degrees in which

342

students choose their courses from two or more compatible disciplines. My early activities as senior tutor were spent in discovering how far along this path my colleagues were prepared to go.

There were already a few well-established precedents at British universities, notably the Oxford degree in philosophy, politics, and economics and the Cambridge practice of dividing degree courses into two parts that could be taken in different subjects. The 1960s had seen the emergence of a good many more such degrees, particularly in the new universities, where it was easier to experiment. But most honours degrees in Britain were still awarded in a single subject, examined in one fell swoop at the end of three of even four years, and the assumption prevailing among most of our teachers was that, as the sum of knowledge increased, so honours degrees would inevitably become more and more specialised and take longer and longer to study. Four-year degree courses were proliferating, and five-year degrees were deemed by many to be just round the corner. With government scholarships available for all who gained admission, teachers had no occasion to consider the financial implications of their academic aims. In such an atmosphere combined degree courses studied in only three years were regarded by most teachers with great suspicion, a sure road to lower standards. There was much contemptuous talk of "the cafeteria system," and we were often reminded that the adjective *multidisciplinary* was merely the Latin for *polytechnic*.

Nevertheless, the various committees set up to explore the problem finally reported in favour of combined degrees available in variable proportions, and we proceeded with the long fight to secure their acceptance by the heads of departments, the academic board, and the relevant boards of studies of the university. But mortifyingly, no sooner were we successful than the government decided to limit expenditure on student grants by forbidding all universities to increase their student intake. So, although we had the programme and the teachers and the space, we were prevented for something like fifteen years from recruiting the students who could benefit. It was a classic case of the essential clumsiness of government tinkerings with university funding that was to plague us increasingly during this period.

Fortunately, my administrative duties did not preclude my continuing activities as a research supervisor in African history, and I have said (Chapter 26) that the 1970s were a period when my colleagues and I were at our busiest in this field. My own following of research students included many of the most interesting and gifted who had ever came my way. There was Merid Aregay, a gentle and self-deprecating Tigrean from the University of Addis Ababa with an already mature knowledge of Amharic and Portuguese sources who took for his subject the sixteenth- and seventeenth-century history of the Christian kingdom. There was

343

John Tosh, an Englishman with a first-class degree in modern history from Oxford who went to Uganda to work with distinction on political leadership among the Lango during precolonial and colonial times. There was John Lamphear, a warm and courageous New Englander with four years' service in the Peace Corps in Tanzania who came to us to read for a master's and stayed to do a doctorial thesis on the traditional history of the pastoral Jie of northeastern Uganda. There was Owen Kalinga from northern Malawi who worked on the traditional history of the Ngonde kingdom. There was Daniel Bimanyu, an immensely able and likable Zairean, who had worked his way from a village school in the Lubero Mountains to the west of Lake Edward to the University of Lovanium and thence to London, choosing for his thesis topic the Swahili-influenced Manyema community of northeastern Zaire that led resistance to the colonial occupation of King Leopold in the late nineteenth century. There was Gervase Clarence-Smith from Cambridge and the Sorbonne, already trilingual (English, French, and Portuguese), who worked on the peoples living in the hinterland of Mossamedes in southern Angola. There was Tim Matthews, who came to us as a political refugee from the University College in Salisbury to finish his interrupted bachelor's degree and stayed to research on the Tonga of the Zambezi Valley. And there was Neale Sobania, an American from Hope College in Michigan who came to us after four years with the Peace Corps in Ethiopia and studied the interethnic movements of the peoples living around the eastern shores of Lake Turkana. Although my visits to Africa were by this time much curtailed by Caroline's health, it made me feel full of muscle to be directing the research effort of such a varied and talented group.

In January 1973 I was invited by the Ethiopian organising committee to chair the historical section of the Third International Congress of Afrikanists to be held in Addis Ababa in December. It looked like an easy assignment in which my main duty would be to review the papers submitted by participants in advance of the conference and to arrange them in intelligible groupings for discussion and subsequent publication. In practice, despite the circulation of three successive announcements of the event by the organising committee, the response was thin. By the end of July only a handful of papers had come in, and only six were from African universities, including three from Addis Ababa itself. It was only by appealing to personal contacts wherever I had them that we managed to assemble a reasonable scatter of contributions from the various regions of the continent. When it came to the search for travelling expenses, it was apparent that foundations and government agencies were notably less prepared to help than on the two previous occasions and that UNESCO was the only large outside supporter. Even in the richer non-African countries, would-be participants were finding difficulty in persuading their employers to cover their expenses. In contrast with the Dakar conference of 1967, only some twenty-five Americans were able to be present. None of the delegations from Western European countries numbered more than ten. The Russians sent just three. Thanks mainly to UNESCO, nearly one hundred delegates came from African countries, with Anglophone countries much better represented than Francophone ones, and African predominance was assured by the presence of another hundred participants from the host country.

Come December I arranged my journey to Addis Ababa to give me a brief stay in the early medieval heartland of Ethiopia around the pilgrimage centre of Lalibela, built, or rather chiselled, out of the living rock by the Zagwe kings of the twelfth and thirteenth centuries. The rockhewn churches of Lalibela are of course world famous, and I had long been familiar with the illustrations of them in published works on Ethiopian history. But no photograph or drawing can begin to convey an adequate impression of subterranean architecture, which cannot be viewed in any kind of perspective. On the surface there is nothing to be seen save a bare hillside set in glorious mountain scenery. Without a guide one might walk the hillside for a week without stumbling on the excavated areas. When one gets to them, one can only stand on the edge and look down into the narrow courtyards surrounding the small churches, their outside walls honeycombed with hermits' cells and ancient tombs. It is precisely this invisibility that is the key to the magic of Lalibela. These churches were never intended to accommodate ordinary worshippers but only the actual celebrants of the liturgy—priests, deacons, cantors, musicians, and drummers—and the small numbers of lay communicants, composed mainly of the very old, the very young, and the very sick who alone were encouraged to receive the sacraments of the Ethiopian Orthodox Church. In contrast the mass of worshippers at Lalibela were the pilgrims who came in from the whole surrounding countryside for the great feasts of the church and camped out on the hillside, performing their devotions within sound but not within sight of the chanting and drumming that rose from the caverns below.

I spent my first day at Lalibela on the churches. On the second I hired a mule called Desta and a guide called Kalemu who brought his English-speaking schoolboy son for the first half-mile or so in order to tell me that his father was a poor man and that those who blessed the poor would find blessing. I was afraid that the recitation would continue all day, but at last he took charge of his father's cloak and departed. After that Kalemu and I got on splendidly by repeating the slogan that Desta was a good mule and Kalemu a good guide. The scenery was breathtaking, and Desta improved on it by walking on the outside inch of every precipice as we climbed to the steep mountain ridge to around ten thousand feet above sea level. On the top were pretty, almost Alpine, farms with wheat growing strongly and hay being harvested with sickles, while the children pastured the sheep and goats. After a final desperate scramble on foot up the last crag we came to a stone church set among rocks and to a tiny village, where a charming old man tried to sell me manuscript pages from his family Bible. It was hard to believe that, less than a hundred miles away, the eastern slopes of the same mountain chain were in the grip of a drought so disastrous that the crops had failed and the cattle were dying, while the human population had fled on foot to camps along the only motor road by which emergency supplies could be brought to them.

I reached Addis Ababa on December 6, 1973, and plunged at once into final preparations for my section of the congress. Whatever the defects in their advance planning, the Ethiopians had done much better than the Senegalese in the day-to-day logistics. Delegates were met at the airport and guided to their hotels. Transport to the conference hall worked admirably. There was a clear timetable, and even the last-minute communications were duplicated and distributed with the utmost efficiency. The emperor came to open the proceedings on December 10, and I was among those detailed to take leave of him afterwards. He had aged visibly during the seven years since I had met him, but I remember the strong grip of his hand upon my arm as we parted, and I remember the little dog waiting for him with affection on the seat of his car. The formal sessions of the conference went well, and thanks to UNESCO there were capable interpreters available at all of them.

The final Saturday and Sunday were free of formal engagements, and I jumped at the kind offer made by Richard Caulk, our former research student now on the staff of the Addis Ababa history department, to take me on a lightning visit to the southwestern corner of the country, where I had hoped to do fieldwork some years before. The third member of the party would be a Dutch Lazarist missionary, Father Jan de Potter, whose order had a station at Bonga, the administrative headquarters of the Kafa province, where we could all spend the night. Our outward journey was for me a valuable experience, as we followed, more or less, the track of the conquering migrations of the pastoral Oromo who in the sixteenth and seventeenth centuries invaded the southern provinces of the Christian empire and established a line of predatory pastoral states dividing the Christian agriculturists of the north from those of the southwest. Crossing the watershed between the Awash and the Omo rivers, our route followed the Gibbe Valley to Jimma and thence through heavily forested mountainous country, across the Gojab River, and upwards again into Kafa. The mission was hospitable, but our time was limited, and on the following day we had to retrace our steps to Jimma, where we hoped to visit the descendant of the Oromo sultans, Abba Lukas. Unfortunately, we had a breakdown, and it cost us most of the day. We limped into Jimma towards evening and consigned the car to a garage, which had to work on it through most of the following morning. In this way we missed the luncheon banquet given by the emperor for the congress delegates. But at least we had an unhurried interview with Abba Lukas in his picturesque wooden palace on the outskirts of town. Richard Caulk knew enough to arouse the old man's interest, and he finally produced a manuscript chronicle, beautifully written in Arabic, that detailed the succession of his forbears from the time of their separation from the main body of the Oromo in the Arusi highlands to the east of the Rift Valley.

Back in Addis Ababa, the lively and agreeable British ambassador Willie Morris and his Canadian wife Margaret had made early touch with me to ask what they should be doing about the congress. I had suggested a party for the delegates from Commonwealth countries, which duly took place on the final Tuesday with thirty or forty guests from Nigeria, Ghana, Kenya, Zambia, Britain, and Canada sitting down to a friendly lunch at tables set under the shade trees by the sunlit embassy lawn. None of us who took part in that peaceful scene could have imagined that within three months the imperial government would be overthrown by a communist-inspired coup d'état and Addis Ababa subjected to a reign of terror of peculiar frightfulness.

Next day I returned to Frilsham and to Caroline, who had been attended during my absence by our retired neighbour Nurse Robbins. Sarah, who was now teaching in Germany, arrived to join us for Christmas 1973.

The years from 1973 until 1977 stand out in my records as those in which John Fage and I were most intensively preoccupied by the general editorship of the *Cambridge History of Africa*. In 1973 we felt that the time had come to commission volume editors for the three final volumes, which would be concerned with the colonial period and after. The intellectual and ideological hiatus between African and non-African historians in relation to this period, which we had foreseen as a possibility in 1966, had not really developed significantly enough to pose an editorial problem. More relevant now was the practical issue that the parallel UNESCO series, with its large injections of international funds for travel, conferences, authorship fees, and subsidised publication prices, was to our certain knowledge attracting some of the authors whom we were trying to enlist. We had a head start in actual production, and we needed to exploit it to the full. The first of our volume editors to turn in a completed assignment was Richard Gray. He had been skillful but also fortunate in that only one of his authors had let him down at the last minute. John Flint, who had been intended to precede him, had been much less lucky, having had to find three substitute authors at short notice and to help all of them to a great extent himself.

It was in working on the typescripts and page proofs of these two volumes that John Fage and I had to make the myriad decisions about format, orthography, maps, bibliography, and indexing practices necessary to establish consistency throughout the series. They were finally published in 1975 and 1976. Next came the two volumes that John and I were handling as volume editors and that cost each of us the usual amount of time in securing satisfactory second drafts and making good the failures of some of our contributors. Our largest problem, however, was caused by Desmond Clark, who in 1976 sent us a draft of his volume at double the length for which he had contracted. Both John and I were utterly disconcerted. We felt that the whole proportion of our series would be upset by it. But the head of Cambridge University Press, Michael Black, had been through it all before. "The alternative solutions we have found," he wrote to us, "are (1) to insist that it be cut, (2) to publish in two parts, (3) to acquiesce. One tends to go through these alternatives in that order." We put much effort into trying the first alternative, even to the point of sending a forty-page letter with our detailed suggestions for abbreviation, but it was time wasted. Desmond had already congratulated his authors on their contributions, and he now refused to budge. If historians cared to produce "childrens' encyclopaedias," that was their affair. Archaeology demanded the full panoply of scholarship, complete with the footnotes appropriate to a research publication. We had thus to face a volume of 1,150 pages, priced beyond the range of any but institutional purchasers. We left it to Michael Black to conduct the surrender.

In 1975 I resumed the chairmanship of the Minority Rights Group, where my first duty was to acknowledge a handsome grant of $60,000 from the Ford Foundation, bringing its record of support for us to a total of $200,000. Under Ben Whitaker's direction the flow of reports was developing steadily. By the end of the decade we had produced about fifty, embracing almost every corner of the globe—"Eritrea and Tigray," "The Crimean Tatars," "The Basques and the Catalans," "The Chinese in Indonesia," "Europe's Gypsies," "Canada's Indians," "The Kurds," "The Palestinians," "The Untouchables of India," "Nomads of the Sahel," "Indian South Africans," "Aboriginal Australians," and "Hungarians in Rumania," to name but a few. In Britain, at least, I met many people in public life who told me how much they appreciated the reports, and the fact that they achieved overall sales of some 250,000 argued strongly that we must be achieving a significant educational impact, which was in line with our status as a registered charity. What worried some members of my council was whether we were doing enough to bring direct pressure on the responsible governments to improve things. Michael Scott in particular, supported as always by David Astor, felt strongly that we were not on the way to becoming another Amnesty International, as they had hoped, and that we never would be so long as Ben was in charge. They lost no opportunity of lobbying me to bring about a change of directors.

Given their expectations of the organisation, there was a sense in which Michael and David were right. I knew very well that Ben Whitaker had no ambition to build MRG into another Amnesty. He wanted to do a limited job, taking less than the whole of his time, for which he was long content to be paid a mere pittance. Within those limits he was doing a fine job. He was choosing the right subjects for investigation and usually choosing good authors for them. He was also raising, with little help from the council, the funds necessary to support his operations so long as they could be carried on by himself and two assistants from a couple of rooms in a mean street. To have entered the business of applying direct pressure on governments would have involved recruiting and paying for staff of the same order as Amnesty's 150. It would have meant the attempt to build a mass international membership, and it would probably have been necessary to forgo, as Amnesty had done, the many advantages of charitable status. Most of our existing support was dependent on our retaining that status, and I found that most members of the council felt that Ben had earned the right to go on doing things his way. But Michael, no longer in the best of health and prone to feel that all his ventures were being undermined by his successors, went on fighting his corner for more than two years, to the point that he was making it difficult for the council to do its regular business. In the end he left, taking David Astor and two others with him. When it happened, I could only feel relief, but it was a source of great personal sadness to me to lose the friendship and respect of someone whom I had formerly admired so greatly.

Late in 1974 there took place the revolution in the Portuguese armed forces that brought to an end the long dictatorship of Antonio de Oliveira Salazar and Marcelo Caetano and that resulted in the quite sudden dissolution of the Portuguese empire in Africa. In January 1975 I was invited to take part in a seminar organised by the Gulbenkian Foundation in Lisbon, the main purpose of which was to advise on the changes in higher education most likely to be needed in newly independent African countries. So far as I can remember not a single African academic was invited, but there were perhaps ten or a dozen scholars from Britain, France, and the United States who had some experience of the consequences of decolonisation in universities in Anglophone and Francophone Africa. The Portuguese representation consisted on the one hand of the leading figures in Portuguese colonial studies and on the other of some young, bright-eyed, and smartly uniformed members of the staff of the military government. Along with the other visiting civilians I wondered what to make of this miliary presence in our midst. The cold war was at its height and the promoters of the coup d'état were generally supposed to have been inspired from the Marxist left. And certainly the graffiti painted on every blank wall in the city reinforced the impression that the country must be trembling on the brink of a second and more overtly political revolution. But the officers' wives who joined us each day for lunch spoke more freely than their husbands, and their problems seemed to centre around the difficulty of finding good domestic servants and seasonal labourers to harvest their family vineyards in these difficult times.

In the formal meetings the military observers listened but spoke little, and the main dialogue was between the visitors and the home team. Trying to contribute from their experience the visitors stressed that students in newly independent countries wanted and needed to know much more about their African neighbours and much less about their relations with the former colonial power; the problem was that of Africanising, so far as possible, the content of higher education. Our Portuguese colleagues did not like this at all. Their dominant concern seemed to be mainly with the preservation of the Portuguese language as the medium of education and communication. At all costs, they said, they must avoid a repetition of what had happened in Brazil where, a mere century and a half after decolonisation, language change had gone so far that Portuguese books now needed to be republished in Brazilian editions. It was clear that we were talking across a gulf that would be bridged only when there had been time for some corresponding experience to emerge. Meanwhile, only the officers of the Gulbenkian Foundation seemed to appreciate the urgency of setting in hand the training of some African academics for the universities of Angola and Mozambique, which had hitherto served only the needs of the Portuguese colonists, most of whom had now fled to Portugal or Brazil.[1] Naturally, I hoped that the foundation might provide scholarships for some Angolans and Mozambicans to study African history in London, where my colleague David Birmingham was admirably qualified to supervise them and where they could work in the company of students from other African countries. It was the internal conflicts in both countries, exacerbated by outside contestants in the cold war, that brought these efforts to nothing.

In 1976 Cyril Philips, who had been the head of my department during my first ten years at SOAS and then for nineteen more years director of the school, reached the age of retirement. After much careful thought and discussion with Caroline and a handful of close friends, I decided to offer myself as a candidate for the succession. As I wrote to Keith Hancock, who had agreed to support me, "I know that it is going to be a difficult time, with universities unpopular with the public, with government anxious to cut expenditure, with a country less and less conscious of the world

350

outside Europe, where there are many people who might think that this School should be allowed to run down." In retrospect I am pleased to see that I also said, "There are three or four people inside the School who could pull this off, and we all get on exceedingly well with each other, so it does not really matter who gets it. We will close ranks behind whomever is chosen, and it will work." For so, in the event, it turned out. My friend and colleague Jeremy Cowan, professor of the history of southeast Asia, was appointed, and I served him happily for ten years, first as dean of students and then as head of the history department. We agreed about most things, and certainly never exchanged a cross word.

In June 1976 I paid what proved to be my last visit to Nigeria, to act for the fourth time in sixteen years as external examiner at the University of Ife. It was good to see the history department there operating happily, with no staffing difficulties and with improving results in undergraduate education, although there was still little sign of ongoing initiative in research. These were the great days of the Organization of Petroleum Exporting Countries (OPEC), when Nigeria, as a major oil producer, was among the few African countries to be on the winning side, but it did not seem that the universities were getting any share of the increased revenues. A small indication, but one that was repeated at both my later ports of call, was that all the guest suites built for official visitors had been taken over to house regular staff. At the University of Ibadan staff accommodation had become so inadequate that newly appointed teachers had to be billeted with their families in night clubs and other equally unsuitable places while waiting their turn for housing on campus. Two of the best of my former students were so treated and as a result failed to settle into their jobs. This impression was strongly reinforced when I went on to stay with Michael Crowder, who was then serving as a research professor at the University of Lagos, where his old friend and literary collaborator Jacob Ajayi was now the vice chancellor. It seemed a perfect appointment for someone who had been so devoted to life in West Africa for more than twenty years, but he told me that, sadly, he would soon be leaving, because he had come to the conclusion that no Nigerian university would be able for much longer to justify the employment of an expatriate in such a senior and prestigious post. I began to realise that, despite the huge proliferation of universities in Nigeria, the role of expatriate teachers was fast diminishing. The vast majority of the new posts being created would be filled by local candidates with little postgraduate training.

Nothing took me to East Africa during the later 1970s, but I was much aware that in Uganda there was a crisis at Makerere that deepened with every year of Idi Amin's disastrous dictatorship. In August 1976 my former research student, Mati Kiwanuka wrote from Nairobi to say that he had fled Uganda following the murder of a close relation by Amin's soldiery on the Makerere campus. His wife and young son, who had tried to follow him, had been picked up by the security police and had spent six hours in the torture chamber on Nakasero Hill. They had then been released, but the family house had been seized and all their possessions stolen. They went into hiding and eventually escaped from the country to join him, but for nearly a decade they were refugees, moving from one short-term appointment to another, and one by one their colleagues followed in a similar course. Among my other former students, Sam Karugire took refuge in Zambia and Patrick Kakwenzire in Nigeria. By the time of my next visit, in 1982, all the properly qualified members of the department of history had left, and their places had been taken by young students with local master's degrees.

My travels during these years were mostly to Zaire in connection with the International Congress of Africanists, of which I was now a member of the permanent bureau. They began with the shortest journey I ever made to Africa, when I found on arrival in Kinshasa that the meeting of the bureau had been cancelled the previous day for fear that UNESCO would not pay the cost. It was then that I learned the meaning of the curious French expression *"On vous a posé un lapin"* (You have been faced with a rabbit). I suppose that the English equivalent, "You have been stood up," is just as curious. James Coleman, who was then the representative of the Ford Foundation in Kinshasa, treated me to a long mollifying lunch, and the Belgian anthropologist Luc de Heusch insisted on opening his last bottle of champagne for me before I caught the next plane home. The real hero of the episode, however, was the philosopher and dean of the arts faculty Valentine Mudimbe, who moved heaven and earth to secure my reimbursement and on his next visit to Europe came all the way to Frilsham to place the cheque in my hands.

The next meeting of the permanent bureau, in December 1976, was somewhat more successful. It was held at Nsele, the so-called *cité du parti* of President Mobutu's Mouvement Populaire de la Révolution, spectacularly situated beside the eastern shore of Lake Malebo (formerly the Stanley Pool), just where the great river Congo enters the lake. At sunset the lake gleams in marvellous shades of pink, and when darkness falls the lights of Kinshasa and Brazzaville sparkle across the water from thirty miles away. Here during the late 1960s a team of architects and engineers from Taiwan had embanked some two miles of lake frontage with a magnificent electrically lit promenade dominated by a presidential palace and seven luxurious villas for the most important class of visitors. Ranged in a semicircle behind were some twenty low buildings, each comprising seven "studio suites" with bedroom, bathroom, sitting-room, and outdoor terrace. Behind this again were dormitory blocks capable of housing several hundred people for large conferences. There was a central building with a vast canteen, large and small assembly halls, conference rooms, and a VIP wing with a dining-room and an expensively furnished salon. The whole complex was set in a huge experimental farm, with cattle introduced from Brazil and irrigated plantations of citrus, pineapples, and other crops new to the area.

The place had been planned as an inspiring conference centre for party workers, but in practice I gathered that it was little used. Access was difficult, and it was too far from the city lights to appeal to any large number of Zaireans. Though admirably set up for important visitors and their retinues, it was too far from the capital to be useful even for them. Moreover, now that the Taiwanese had departed, it was proving impossible to keep it in decent running order. In the studio suite assigned to me, half the lights were out of action, the bathroom was quite unlit, the loo had no seat and was not working, the telephone had been cut off, the large refrigerator was broken, and the sheets were filthy. Drinking water had to be begged as a favour from the VIP bar and carried away in a hastily rinsed beer bottle. Indeed, the only part of the installations that seemed to be functioning perfectly was the Voix du Zaire propaganda network, transmitted through thunderous loudspeakers set up in every corner of the grounds and active from eight in the morning until midnight. Altogether, it was a good example of what can happen to foreign aid in a patrimonial state.

In this rather strange mixture of splendour and squalor we had our meetings. Of the twelve non-Zairean members of the bureau, the French anthropologist Claude Meillassoux and I were the only ones present. Jacob Ajayi, our treasurer, made heroic efforts to reach us from his previous engagement in Khartoum but arrived only after the meeting was over. Our Soviet member cabled to say that he had not received his ticket. Several others were expected but just did not come. So, with Monseigneur Tshibangu, our president, and Valentine Mudimbe, our secretary, we were four official members, with my former research student Daniel Bimanyu as recording secretary, and we met amid the gold plush and chandeliers of monseigneur's villa, with various beautiful women hovering around to answer the telephone and ply us with drinks. The first beer of the day was served at ten o'clock. Nevertheless, we worked hard and efficiently for seven hours on the first day and for three more on the second to formulate a viable programme for the next meeting of the full congress, which was to be held two years later in Kinshasa. The third day I spent with Daniel Bimanyu.

I had always found this man particularly congenial, but never so much as now, in his own country. He had recently returned from England with his doctorate and had been expected to join the staff of the now-unified National University of Zaire, the arts and social science departments of which had been relocated seven hundred miles from the capital at

Lubumbashi (formerly Elizabethville). The campus there was, he told me, riddled with police informers, and he had opted for a less prestigious post at the Institut Pédagogique, the training college for secondary school teachers in the comparative anonymity of Kinshasa, where his wife, a Muslim *arabisée* from Kisangani, was able to supplement the family income by informal trading across the river to Brazzaville. Even so, life was precarious. The population of Kinshasa was growing faster than the food supply, and many hours a day were consumed in walking on foot from one market to another. On this occasion he had borrowed a car, and we drove some forty miles upriver to see a hydroelectric plant and a steelworks, where a friend of his was a junior manager who showed us round and gave us lunch. The friend made no attempt to disguise from us the fact that the whole enterprise was crumbling. The electricity, which was supposed to be supplying the Katanga copper mines, was getting no farther afield than Kinshasa. The steel was costing ten times that of the world market. Seen through the eyes of these two highly educated young men, Mobutu's Zaire existed to serve a parasitic and ever-expanding capital city, where wealth was concentrated in the hands of two to three thousand presidential protégés who monopolised the import and export licenses of the entire country.

Three more meetings of the permanent bureau were scheduled during the two years before the congress. Two were cancelled at the last minute for lack of funds. The third was convened in Paris at only a few days' notice, because Tshibangu and Mudimbe were passing through. As a result, the fourth congress, when it took place in December 1978, was overwhelmingly a Francophone gathering, with upwards of 100 representatives from Zaire itself, 52 from other Francophone African countries, 46 from France, 14 from Belgium, and 5 from French-speaking Canada. Only 15 delegates came from the United States, 5 from English-speaking Canada, 4 from Nigeria, 3 from Ghana, 3 from Sudan, 2 from Uganda, and 2 from the United Kingdom. There were small groups from the two Germanies, Poland, Bulgaria, Brazil, Chile, Korea, Sweden, and Denmark. The Soviet Union was unrepresented. The programme worked out in some detail at Nsele in 1976 was finally circulated only in May 1978. Consequently, the handsome portfolios handed out to delegates in December contained only fourteen short summaries of papers submitted from all disciplines. We had to hastily reduce the five working sections to two. Of the thirteen experts in simultaneous translation provided by UNESCO at a cost of $30,000, only six were actually needed. As so often in Africa, the general capacity for *viva voce* improvisation proved surprisingly high, and several working sessions were of great interest to those who attended them. But although an invitation to hold a fifth meeting of the congress in Nigeria was accepted by the bureau, it was difficult to believe that international funds should any longer be so ineffectively deployed, and henceforward it was the American African Studies Association with its annual conference that provided the most effective focus for these studies. The geographical displacement from Africa was unfortunate, but it reflected the reality of where most of the serious research on Africa was now based.

My remaining African journey, undertaken in March 1978, was to Cameroon, where the University of Yaounde had invited me to make a short visit under the auspices of the British Council. The head of the history department there, Martin Njeuma, had taken his doctorate at SOAS, and his wife Dorothy, who was a distinguished animal geneticist trained at Queen Mary College, was now the vice minister responsible for higher education. As a result, I received royal treatment and was sent to live at the luxurious Mont Febe Hotel some ten miles out of town, the only drawback to which was that President Félix Houphouet-Boigny of the Ivory Coast, who was paying a state visit, was being entertained in an official guest-house in the same village. Whenever he left it, the only road to the capital was closed for several hours, lest his howling and flashing motorcade be impeded by other traffic. I remember long spells of enforced idleness and am surprised to find from my official report that in fact I was able within about ten days to give six lectures to undergraduate students, speak to a staff seminar, have individual meetings with five graduate students and several members of staff, and give an evening lecture open to the public, "Cameroon—The Bantu Cradleland," which was followed by interviews with the local press and radio.

The special interest of Yaounde University was that it served a country using both French and English as languages of wider communication. Its declared policy was that teaching could be given in either language and that all students should become capable of understanding lectures in both. There was a flourishing school of interpretation, and the hope was that the university would develop a special role in mediating between two traditions of higher education. In practice some relief was expressed when I offered to give my lectures in French, as it was thought that more students would understand them that way, but staff and research students, at least, seemed to be genuinely bilingual. In history and social sciences the most curious lack was of teachers with any knowledge of German, for here was a country whose early archives and ethnographic literature were mostly written in German, and yet no one I met could read them. More generally, it was instructive to see an ex-colonial university of French foundation and to compare it with its Anglophone equivalents. First, there was no campus. Most staff and students lived scattered through the town and came to the university only to teach or be taught. There were no common rooms or recreational amenities. The university library was totally inadequate to

355

the needs of anything more than a junior arts college. And, above all, the ratio of students to staff was about double that of the Anglophone African equivalents. There was the typical case of one junior lecturer charged with six courses running simultaneously on colonial America, the social and economic history of Cameroon, historical methodology, Europe since 1945, and the economic history of the United States since 1783. I talked to several teachers about how they coped with the written work of students, and it appeared that most were supposed to read about five hundred essays a term, which would have taken them about twenty-five hours a week on this task alone. In practice most teachers seemed to have second jobs. One senior professor was running a private school in the town. Another owned four taxis. A third was engaged in retail trade. Several more were in real estate, using their supposedly secure public sector salaries as collateral for bank loans. It gave me a glimpse of the way in which universities in other African countries would go as they lost their privileged late colonial status and descended to the economic standards of the societies in which they were set.

My last weekend in Cameroon was spent in an entirely delightful way, as the guest of the Njeumas. We flew two hundred miles to the coast at Douala and motored from there through the massive plantations of rubber trees and oil palms dating to the German colonial period to the former German capital at Buea, built at some five thousand feet above sea level on the southern slopes of the eleven-thousand-foot Cameroon Mountain, which is by far the highest mountain in western Africa. Below the German fort there nestles the Bakwerri township of the same name, where Martin had his family home. From it on the following day we drove by Jeep to the summit of the mountain, which was, alas, enveloped in cloud, and afterwards descended to sea level to visit the coastal town of Victoria, so named by the Baptist Missionary Society, which planted its first station there in 1858. From Victoria we looked out at "Johnston Island," where my early hero had built his Oil Rivers consulate in 1885. Far away, across the Bight of Benin, we could discern the volcanic cone of Fernando Po. I felt that another corner of the map of African had come alive for me.

28

In Tenebris Lux

(1979–83)

When I returned from Kinshasa in December 1978, I found Caroline very unwell and Nurse "Robbie" Robbins at the end of her tether, having had problems by night as well as by day. She soon made it clear that she would not be coming to us again. Throughout January 1979 Caroline, though she struggled up to London with me during the week, grew visibly worse. At the end of the month she had a fall and was carried off to the Battle Hospital in Reading with violent inflammation of the shoulder muscles and a serious infection of the lungs. For two and a half weeks she lay there, practically unable to move and in nursing conditions that could only be described as scandalous. It was the house doctor who warned me that, if she was left there any longer, the prognosis would be very bad indeed. England was under snow, and the ambulance service was on strike, so we loaded her into our car as best we could and drove the twenty-five miles of icy roads to a private nursing home at Edgecombe House to the west of Newbury. There a wonderful transformation took place, the result of comfort, care, tempting food, and brilliant physiotherapy. In early March I was able, with the help of a skilled private nurse, Julia Coble, to bring her home to Frilsham. But in April Caroline suffered a cruel attack of shingles, the residual pains of which never left her. In June a gastric ulcer caused severe haemorrhages that had to be treated in hospital. In September she fell and cracked a femur. The John Racliffe Hospital in Oxford decided that Caroline would not stand an operation, and she was transferred to the Nuffield Orthopaedic Hospital, where she remained for three and a half months, supposedly waiting for the crack to heal itself. There were said to be forty physiotherapists in this world-famous establishment, but they were not allowed to lift patients singly and never could any two of them be found free to try to get Caroline onto her feet. In January 1980 they abandoned their efforts altogether,

357

and in our desperation we turned once more to Edgecombe House, where the single visiting physiotherapist managed to repeat her miracle of the previous year, to the extent of making it possible for Caroline to walk the necessary few steps from one room to another by leaning on the arm of one helper. This made it possible for her to live for nearly four more years at home.

Everything, however, depended on the availability of that helping arm. From Thursday night until Monday evening it could often be mine. On Saturdays and Sundays there was help from Sarah, who was now working at the headquarters of Amnesty International in London. But essentially we had somehow to arrange for an uninterrupted succession of resident helpers with some nursing experience. It was not easily achieved. The first stayed a month but then decamped without any notice at all. The second gave notice after three days and left after ten. We tried an agency, which aimed to send us people for four weeks at a time, but they did not always last that long. Some did a fine job and even made us enjoy their company. But there were some who drank and some who stole, and it was sometimes necessary to leave Caroline in their sole care for three days at a time while I did my inescapable London duties. The year 1981 brought us some longer runs of luck than 1980. An aunt of mine put us in touch with Gloria Blake-Mahon, a sometime nursing sister with the Franciscan missionaries in Bengal. She was supposed to be sixty-five but confessed on arrival that her real age was seventy-eight. She served us wonderfully for three months, until she strained herself and had to leave. There followed nearly six months more of constant changes, ending up with the proverbial friend of a friend, who proved to be an alcoholic so serious that she would borrow money from me nearly every morning so that she could spend the whole middle of the day at the local public house and so make herself incapable of further work when she returned. It took us several weeks to get rid of her, as she had literally nowhere else to go. Our experiences gradually taught us that we must aim to employ only the young and the strong, and since the dependable British young were likely to be engaged in more rewarding occupations, it seemed best to look among visitors from abroad, who might be either students of our language or young adults from Australia or New Zealand working their passages round the world. With our London flat to offer at weekends we had the makings of a viable proposition. A search of the registers of new arrivals at the London offices of the Australian states brought us three splendid cheerful young women, each of whom stayed with us for a couple of months or so. They were succeeded by a young German from the Rhineland who, though moody and eccentric, did the job successfully enough for eight months on end. With this kind of continuity life could begin to seem almost normal again.

Our last two helpers might have been providentially chosen to suit the terminal stages of Caroline's long ordeal. The first was Inger Aasa, a twenty-year-old Swede from Luleå on the northern shores of the Baltic, just below the Arctic Circle. Having spent a year of voluntary service with the Swedish Lutheran mission in northwestern Tanzania, she was now a student at Uppsala University, where she had attracted the attention of our old friend Bengt Sundkler, the sometime bishop of Bukoba diocese and subsequently professor of missiology at Uppsala. It was Bengt who suggested that, since African history was one of her subjects of study, she might consider spending a year helping in our household. In September 1982 she arrived with her guitar, radiant, caring, and gentle, and became at once a member of our family, as we did of hers. Within weeks her younger sister came for a visit, and I remember them singing together as they swept the leaves from the drive. A week or two later it was her young man, Richard Marklund, to whom she had been informally engaged since they first met at a Bible camp when they were both fourteen. He too had worked in Tanzania and was now reading theology at Uppsala in preparation for a career in the Swedish Lutheran ministry. They hoped to be married in June 1983, and Inger would therefore want to leave us by the end of April. Meanwhile, Caroline would enjoy all the love and attention that her deteriorating condition demanded. On February 17, 1983, on my return from a midweek in London, Inger said to me, "There have been *three* of us here while you were away. Of course, there always are, but this time I have been more aware of it." Next day our doctor warned me that Caroline had infected sinuses in her back that were not susceptible to any antibiotic. It was only a matter of time before the infection spread into the tissues and the bloodstream. Pending the inevitable collapse, he though she would be in every way better off at home with Inger than in hospital. There would be daily visits by the district nurses.

With Inger scheduled to depart in two months' time we needed to search for a successor, and Caroline's eye fell upon an advertisement in the personal column of the *Times* by a young German man, Peter Süssenbach, who was seeking to work for a year in England. It seemed to me improbable that our predicament could appeal to him, but Caroline insisted that I write. To my amazement he responded at once, saying that he had just finished his national service working in a nursing home for old people and that our problem seemed to be just what he was best qualified to help with. He said he could be available on April 11, which happened to be the precise date that Inger had independently marked down to allow for a proper handover, including "a practice day off" at our London flat. He would be prepared to stay until January 1984. And so, on April 11 I met him at Newbury Station. He had a small suitcase in one hand and a big bunch of flowers in the other. He understood from the first that it was a terminal case, and he was not dismayed by it. He told me that at his old peoples' nursing home the average length of stay had been four months, so he had watched many people die. In June he said, "Either it goes the short way or the long way. The long way might take six months." It was a remarkably accurate estimate.

Right up to this point, and even a little beyond, Caroline managed to remain her warm, sociable, and uncomplaining self. Neighbours visited her regularly, some looking in almost every day. Though we could no longer put them up in the house, students and former students, colleagues, and visitors from overseas came down from London for the day. Suzanne Miers wrote her long, very funny letters about the impact of her British nanny on a small midwestern university town. Except for the weeks of Wimbledon, Caroline did not spend much time watching television. Instead, she read and reread her favorite nineteenth-century novelists— Jane Austen, The Bröntes, Mrs. Gaskell, George Eliot, and increasingly, Anthony Trollope. At the beginning of her confinement at Frilsham she was still putting the finishing touches to her book of biographical studies called *White Women in Colonial Africa*. I did the proofs and the index for it in 1982, when she could no longer write more than a few words at a time herself. It arrived in published form in time to give her a real sense of achievement. Of the five characters portrayed in it, the two with whom she felt most affinity were both single missionaries from humble homes. The first was Mary Slessor, the Scottish mill hand who took her Presbyterian faith to the Efik fisherfolk of the Calabar estuary, achieving such a degree of natural authority among them that she was gazetted as an honorary magistrate by the first British commissioner of the Oil Rivers protectorate, whom she was apt to address as "Laddie." The second was the wonderful Irish Franciscan, Mother Kevin, who was the dynamic founder of a flourishing order of African nuns, the Little Sisters of Mary, whose members radiated from a motherhouse in Buganda across much of East Africa. Her personality is best conveyed in an anecdote of John Gray's about how he called on her on the day that the ecclesiastical authorities forbade her nuns to practise midwifery, and how, consumed with Hibernian rage, she had said, "I tell you what, Sir John: the pope and all his cardinals is a lot of blithering bachelors!"

Caroline's studies of these two great women might be taken as a statement of her own Christian sympathies. She was the daughter of a Scottish Presbyterian mother and an Irish Catholic father, and she had worshipped happily enough in the Church of England during the thirty-six years of our marriage. She was in fact as unsectarian as it was possible for anyone to be, and the fact that she decided at the end to leave this world by the Roman road is not to be seen as a dramatic deathbed conversion. We had both felt close to the Catholic Church throughout our married life. She had shared my early enthusiasm for St. Francis, and in the 1950s we had made the pilgrimage to Assisi. We had stayed with Catholic missionaries all over tropical Africa and lived much with Catholic friends in England. Above all, our hearts had kindled at the reforms set in motion by Pope John XXIII and the leaps in ecumenical endeavour that had followed them. Several of our nursing helpers were Catholics of this ecumenical sort. The first, Julia Coble, accompanied me one Sunday to the Anglican church in the village and, to my unspoken astonishment, took the Sacrament. We never discussed it, but I felt sure that it was the invitation I needed to do the same thing in reverse. It all proved much easier than I had imagined, and the experience of it seemed to me to be transforming. By little and by little I found myself alternating between the two altars, and this was the situation when in April 1983 Caroline decided that she would like a visit from one of the monks at the nearby Benedictine abbey of Douai. It was the prior, Father Leonard Vickers, who came. He was the broadest minded and least ecclesiastical of men, destined to be the next abbot and to die an untimely death in his first year of office. He came on a day when Caroline was very sick and stayed only long enough to leave her with the comfort and reassurance she needed. He came again in August to anoint her and once more to bring Holy Communion for both of us, before she entered the shadowy world of heavy pain-killing drugs. He was bound for a yearlong assignment in Washington, D.C., but his colleague Gervase Holdaway took over from him and visited her faithfully every week. She died, still at home at Frilsham, on the evening of December 7, while Sarah, Peter, and I were all present in the house.

Looking through my engagement books for the years from 1979 to 1983, I find myself astonished at how far it was possible for a profession to be carried on against the background of so much anxiety and disruption of domestic life. But I had at last learned the lesson that the right reaction to the life-threatening illness of a partner is never willingly to abandon the breadwinning process. In grave sickness one has to seek many different kinds of trained help, and most if it has to be paid for. And at the end the survivor needs to have as many ongoing interests as possible.

Obviously, the work that could be done at Frilsham was the most easily managed. In 1979 Anthony Atmore and I completed *The African Middle Ages, 1400–1800*. It was the last of the trilogy of introductory textbooks that had begun with *Africa Since 1800* and continued with *Africa in the Iron Age*. It was published by Cambridge University Press in 1980, along with a third revised edition of the first one. During 1981 and 1982 I was much engaged with the *Cambridge History of Africa*, overseeing with John Fage the seventh and eighth volumes, edited by Andrew Roberts and Michael Crowder, respectively, but also reviving the sixth volume, which had been abandoned by its volume editor while he wrote another book. Some chapters had been sent in by diligent contributors two or three years previously, but their receipt had never been acknowledged, and one had even been published by its justly irate author in another place. Other chapters were long overdue, but no steps had been taken to remind the defaulting contributors, one of whom had died and not been replaced. It was a delicate and deeply embarrassing task simultaneously to coax the righteous into revising what they had written three years previously and the defaulters into a belief that it was never too late to make a start.

I still managed to get to London every week in term time where, since 1978, I had been head of the history department at SOAS. With thirty-one members it was one of the largest in the country, and its interests extended from Senegal and Morocco to the Philippines and Japan. There had been a time, a decade earlier, when it had been responsible for the education of half of the students in the school, including 150 of the school's 300 doctoral candidates. Now postgraduate numbers were falling sharply, partly because our work in training university teachers for Asian and African universities had been largely accomplished but partly also because the British government was forcing us to charge dramatically higher fees to overseas students, who were therefore seeking places in more outward-looking countries such as the United States and the USSR. Simultaneously, within Britain history as a first-degree subject was losing ground to the social sciences. It was clear that we could no longer expect the same generous allocation of the school's resources that we had enjoyed before, and in practice this meant that when vacancies occurred, we were not allowed to fill them. This was economy applied according to the luck of the draw, and as a result some sections of the department, notably that which dealt with China and Japan, were reduced to near impotence. It seemed to me that, far from increasing the range and specialisation of our degree courses, we now had to reduce and simplify them, so that they could be taught by fewer teachers and in the context of combined degrees. It was a hard doctrine for British university teachers, accustomed to ever-increasing specialisation, to accept.

In my personal capacity I remained of course a teacher of African history, and the African section of the department was more buoyant than most others. Shula Marks was still in the full flush of her remarkable career as a supervisor of research on southern African history, and Michael Brett, who had joined us in 1970 as replacement for Anthony Atmore, was beginning to establish our first firm foothold in the history of North Africa. We still had some thirty research students between us and were making a large contribution to the master's and undergraduate programme, so when our West Africanist colleague Douglas Jones died in 1979, we were able to replace him with Gervase Clarence-Smith, and when David Birmingham left us for his chair of modern history in Canterbury, we were able to appoint Susan Martin. But instead of having ten to fifteen research students on my books, I now only had three or four, and I felt that my firepower had been correspondingly reduced. The African history seminar, in which I had always felt so much pride and joy, was still well enough attended, but it had fewer African members and fewer people working on precolonial subjects. I had always hoped that I would live to see a generation of African academic historians that would record and publish the traditional evidence of their native language areas, but the impulse to do so was fading fast. More and more of Africa was being closed to research by political insecurity. The Sudan, Uganda, Ethiopia, Somalia, Zanzibar, Mozambique, Namibia, Angola, the People's Republic of the Congo, the Central African Republic, Chad, Libya, Algeria, and Mauritania were all effectively closed to any kind of research that involved the questioning of people, and many other countries placed difficulties in the way of those who wished to do so, even in the case of their nationals. Historians were being driven out of fieldwork and back into the archives and so to limit themselves to modern history.

Furthermore, as I looked round the seminar room, I worried increasingly about how many of the present generation of research students would find jobs. Already in 1977 I had given a talk at University College in which I predicted the impending collapse of the "African history mushroom." I said that, whereas in 1947 there had been only a single academic practitioner of the subject, thirty years later there were at least one thousand in university posts around the world and probably another thousand aspirants. Most of the overproduction had occurred in the United States, where Philip Curtin, for example, was warning all his graduate students that most future openings would be in establishments with only a single teacher who would in most cases be expected to teach another non-African course as well. In England there were at this stage somewhere around ninety posts scattered across about fifty universities. With few exceptions they were occupied by people who had begun their careers teaching in African universities during the 1950s and 1960s, but this line of approach was now closing down, and there was no reason to think that all those places, when they fell vacant, would be regarded as sacrosanct to Africa.

By this time of my life I was, frankly, bored by undergraduate teaching. I believed in the value for lecturers of having to prepare lectures, of having once a year to bring them up to date and to present them to an audience that might catch them out if they had not done so. But I was perpetually disappointed by the quality of the audience, which so often appeared as an inert mass that had somehow to be energised. I consulted the university's experts on visual aids, and they told me that the disembodied voice was generally easier to listen to without the distraction of having to watch the expression of a live speaker. They told me that, in the days of radio, audiences had been able to listen with concentration to talks lasting thirty-five to forty minutes, whereas, with the coming of television and the speaker's face on the screen, it had been found that three or four minutes marked the limit of full attention; hence the television practice of alternating speakers, even on simple news programmes. I therefore tried the experiment of recording my lectures on tape and of spending the contact hours in free discussion with those who had already listened to them that way. The result seemed to me an improvement, although it did not suit everybody.

Above all, however, my use of taped lectures opened my eyes to the possibilities of shared teaching by different institutions and different countries. For example, I had always been conscious of the complementary strengths and weaknesses existing between our school of African history and that of the University of Paris. They had many more specialists in West and West-Central Africa than we had, and we were correspondingly stronger in East and South Africa. An annual exchange of taped lectures, supplemented by occasional visits by the teachers themselves, might greatly strengthen the interest in our courses. And, far beyond this, my imagination ran on to what might be achieved by the regular exchange of taped teaching materials between European and African universities. That would of course require a separately funded administrative organisation to set it up and run it, perhaps under the auspices of the European Community, which had large unspent balances for educational and cultural development that had accumulated under the Lomé treaties. (Under the Lomé treaties former British, French, and Belgian colonies had special tariff and trade arrangements with full members of the European Community.) Between 1979 and 1984 I made several visits to Paris and Brussels in aid of these two projects. Our French colleagues were as friendly and welcoming as ever, but it gradually became clear that, because of the tight control exerted over first-degree syllabuses by the French Ministry of Education, effective cooperation could only be practiced at the postgraduate level. In Brussels the problem was that Lomé funds could only be spent in response to specific requests by African governments. For a project to be successful, the Commission for Development needed to drum up requests from several governments simultaneously. After quite a promising start they failed to do so. In retrospect I see that the technology available at the time was probably too clumsy for the job of recording, copying, and distributing large numbers of tapes to and from Africa. It was a development that would have to await the Internet.

Sometime in May 1979 there dropped through our letter-box at Frilsham an impressive-looking envelope embossed with the royal arms. It carried an invitation from the lord steward to the state banquet to be given in honour of President Daniel Arap Moi of Kenya on June 12. It arrived when Caroline was temporarily out of the hospital, but there was, alas, no question of her being well enough to attend, and, however reluctantly, I had to accept for myself alone. On burrowing farther into the envelope Sarah found an enclosure in the form of a chauffeur's dinner ticket, which she insisted on appropriating for her own use. So, come the day, we set off together from the London flat, were directed by the police into the central courtyard of Buckingham Palace, parked, and were sniffed out and passed as safe by an amiable police Labrador, whereupon I made my way to the grand entrance and she to the staff dining-room. Naturally, I had feared that I would know no one, but as 177 guests assembled in an anteroom for cocktails, I found plenty of old friends and, notably, Conor O'Brien, whose wife Moara was in hospital in Dublin following a serious motor accident. We went through the evening together, alternately separating and joining up again to compare notes. At dinner, which was indeed served on gold plate, I found myself beside the deputy master of the household, Colonel Blair Stuart-Wilson, who talked engagingly about his job of keeping an essentially peripatetic court in a state of equilibrium, whether in London or Windsor, Sandringham or Balmoral, on the royal yacht or in some guest-house or embassy abroad. Over dessert he said that perhaps he ought to tell me that, when we moved through to the drawing-rooms, I would be on the queen's short list of guests to be presented and that if I had anything at the front of my mind to tell her, I should do so without waiting for her to make the running. That was how she liked it. Further conversation was obscured by the entry of a group of young soldiers in kilts who rushed round the tables playing their bagpipes and then took up a static position immediately behind us. Good tribal fun, I suppose.

As we left the dining-room, an equerry standing by the door said, "Professor Oliver? We're trying to spread people out a little. Would you go straight through to the door at the very end. There'll be someone to take care of you there." I did so and found myself in a long drawing-room, the near end of which was occupied by a clutch of high commissioners from the East African countries, many of whom I knew. But before long another equerry approached to say that he would take me to the lord chamberlain. We threaded our way though the middle of the room, where Margaret Thatcher in a white evening dress was holding forth to a circle of cabinet ministers, to the far end, where we halted beside a man holding a long white wand. I suddenly realised that the queen, in an emerald green evening dress and diamond tiara but with no other decorations, was standing talking to another guest only a yard away. "I'm afraid we're going to have to talk to each other for a little bit," the lord chamberlain said. "One never knows quite how long these things are going to take. . . . Now, you see this wand? Well, actually it's telescopic. I can fold it up and take it with me in a taxi quite easily. You see, like this." He began to demonstrate the procedure but suddenly stopped, grabbed me by the arm, and introduced me, "Professor Oliver, your majesty." Her smile was dazzling, but she mostly looked straight ahead as we talked.

The conversation that followed was gentle, slow, almost meditative. We talked about London University, where the queen mother was intending to relinquish her role as chancellor when she reached the age of eighty in the next year. We talked about East Africa, wild animals, and early man. We talk about the Seychelles and their role as a place of confinement for high-level political prisoners, including most recently Archbishop Makarios of Cyprus. She said, "You know, it's really rather awkward for someone in my position, when you're not allowed to mention somebody's name one day, and the next day they come and tell you that you should have them to lunch." It seemed a good professional reflection. I saw her hand clench and realised that it was the signal for the next actor to be brought on scene. There was no farewell. The lord chamberlain simply moved straight across in front of me, forcing me to step back. Soon I was fetched away again to the room beyond to be introduced to President Moi, who was holding court there in the same fashion, attended by the duke of Northumberland. I reminded the president of his visit to my house in Newton Road at the time of the Kenya constitutional conference in 1962. He was polite but no spark flew. For the rest, this room seemed to be occupied only by the very grandest people. The queen mother was standing alone in one corner. The archbishop of Canterbury was in another. Prince Charles buzzed in and out. Soon the queen passed through, and I guessed that she was doing her vanishing act. The party in the next room went on some time longer, until all the royals had worked through their lists. With enough friends there it was hugely enjoyable.

When we finally departed, Sarah swept up to the grand entrance with due aplomb, and as we drove home I asked her about her party downstairs. She had encountered only one problem, which was that the chauffeurs of the great, when they meet, always begin by asking each other whom they are driving, and the conversation develops from there. She had parried it by saying that she was driving someone they would not have heard of. They had probably concluded that I was the head of the secret service. But she had also learned the most important fact in a chauffeur's life, that it is not mainly about driving but about waiting around for one's passenger. No one could predict at what time any guest at that party would leave. Therefore all drivers were required to sit in their cars from ten o'clock on. And I had emerged at eleven thirty. They also serve who only sit and wait.

In Tenebris Lux (1979–83)

In 1981 Larry Kirwan retired from the presidency of the British Institute in eastern Africa, and I was elected by the governing council to succeed him. It was an honorary post but far from an honorific one. It was to take a great deal of my time and attention during the next twelve years, but it was time gladly given. It gave me a foothold in ongoing research that would last beyond my retirement from the university. And it gave it to me in the part of Africa I knew best and in the period of history that most interested me. At a time when so many historians were retreating into recent history, I was glad to be in regular touch with work of Iron Age archaeologists who seemed to be increasingly prepared to move forward in the direction of precolonial history. The institute by this time was firmly established in its base at Nairobi. It employed two European archaeologists, as director and assistant director, and they were assisted by a locally recruited staff, consisting of an editor, librarian, administrative secretary, draftsman, archaeological assistant, driver-mechanic, secretary, storekeeper, messenger, and a team of night watchmen. The senior staff were engaged solely in research and publication. They each had projects of their own, and they were supposed to actively encourage and assist research by others. As president it was my duty to chair the council in London, make executive decisions with the other officers between council meetings, and in general know enough about the work going on in Africa to represent it accurately to our sponsors and donors and enough about the British background of research funding to advise the director in the field about which things were possible and which were not. The indispensible condition for doing the job properly was to make an annual visit long enough to see at first hand both the headquarters work in Nairobi and the fieldwork in progress, wherever that was taking place.

I made the first such visit, thanks to teamwork by Sarah and Inger at Frilsham, in December 1982. It was, before all else, a farewell visit to Neville Chittick, who had occupied the post for the previous eighteen years and was scheduled to retire, aged sixty, the following May. The fact that we were both contemporaries and old friends made it quite different from all my later journeys, and it was a delight to stay with him, as I had so often done before, and to talk about the past as well as the future. I found him in fact quite upset at the prospect of his coming retirement. He had parted from two wives, the institute had become his mainstay, and he had no clear idea where he was going to live after he left it. Professionally, he had been unfortunate in that the large-scale excavations at Aksum, which should have crowned his achievements as an archaeologist, had been closed down after only two seasons by the Ethiopian revolution. He had made several attempts to write up his findings there but had found it impossible to do anything definitive without more evidence. Year by year he had waited for a change in the political situation, but it had not come.

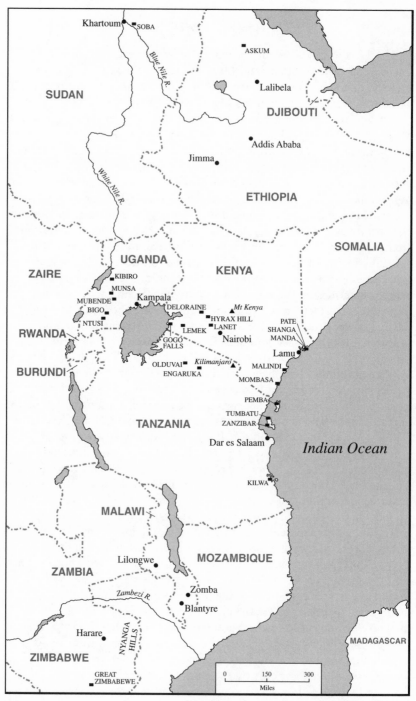

Archaeological sites referred to in connection with the British Institute in Eastern Africa, 1981–92

368

Without it his hopes of returning to a senior academic post in Europe or the United States were unlikely to be fulfilled.

Naturally enough, he was a little sensitive about my need to prepare the way for his chosen successor, John Sutton. The University of Nairobi had recently asked us to vacate at short notice both the office building and the two staff houses that we had long occupied on its campus, and I needed to discuss with the vice chancellor and others how they thought relations with the institute should develop in the future. It was the same with the National Museum, where relations with the director, Richard Leakey, who controlled permits for archaeological excavation, had not been altogether easy. It was embarrassing to have to insist on doing some of these things without his presence, but it was the only way to get plainspoken opinions. For the rest, Chittick and I called together on the British high commissioner, Leonard Allinson, and found a sturdy friend, who after his retirement served for many years on the Institute's council. As it happened, he had on his desk a request from the Foreign Office for an opinion on the institute's usefulness, and he sent along to us a young member of his staff, who had taken a degree in African history at the University of Birmingham, to check that he had the facts right. I went to see the vice chancellor of Nairobi University in company with my friend Godfrey Muriuki, now a senior member of his staff, and the upshot was that the institute would move off the campus but only after the new director had had an opportunity to size up the alternatives. I spent a couple of days as the guest of Allan and Grace Ogot, both of whom were now close to the political leadership of the country. They helped me greatly in assessing the political risks involved for the institute in maintaining Nairobi as its base.

The talk of the town during my 1982 visit centred upon the serious rioting that had taken place a few months earlier, when a group that was trying to organise a military coup had begun operations by combing the poorer districts of eastern Nairobi with loudspeaker vans, inviting the inhabitants to sally forth then and there and loot the homes and shops of their richer neighbours on the western side of town. Thousands responded to the call, and for twenty-four hours a wave of looters rolled remorselessly westwards to do just that. A contraflow developed of demure African women carrying away beds, sofas, and television sets on their heads, while the shabbier car owners of all colours helped with the logistics of removal. Grace Ogot, who owned a boutique in the centre of town, was one of those who lost their entire stock. President Moi, who was touring the northern province, rather bravely flew back to Nairobi just in time to rally the forces of loyalty before parallel demonstrations were to be unleashed in Mombasa and Kisumu. The police in due course gathered courage to loot the looters, and the wave of crime was rolled back. But it had been an ugly incident, and the better-off of all races were left acutely aware of how easily it could be repeated. It was the Ogots who advised me that the institute, if it left the university campus, would have no difficulty in finding suitable accommodation in the western suburbs but also that it would be wise to direct its search to the areas west of State House, where military protection would be concentrated. Since then I have often reflected that it is salutary for those who live outside Africa to remember the circumstances in which autocratic government is apt to develop and the widespread support that, at least in the early stages, it can enjoy.

Midway through our affairs in Nairobi Neville took me for a brief trip to the Lamu archipelago situated off the northern extremity of the Kenya coast, where four years previously he had conducted a fairly large excavation on the island of Manda, the results of which he was still preparing for publication.[1] We drove to Mombasa and from there flew north in a small aeroplane, from which, sitting beside the pilot, I could see the whole width of the coastal plain in some detail—Kilifi Creek, the Sabaki River, the ruins of Gedi standing between the sea an the lagoon behind it, the mouth of the Tana, and then the three main islands of Lamu, Manda, and Pate. Lamu at that time had no motor traffic, and its narrow streets were thronged with stately pedestrians in Arab dress. We stayed in the little house that Neville rented in the Arab quarter of the town. There were already some European and American tourists to be seen, but I was far more conscious of the presence of Islam, recognizable in demeanour, clothing, gait, and manners. Here were people who despised and abominated the rule of the *Wa-Afrika*, the Western-educated Kenyans from the interior who occupied the local government offices by day and moved into the bars to drink alcohol and listen to pop music late into the night.

Neville had many friends in the town and took me to call at a number of the older houses, built typically with their kitchens over the front gate, leading to a garden, and then to the main house with an open baraza (veranda) for daytime sitting in front, sleeping quarters in the middle, and bath and storerooms behind. The larger rooms were always long and narrow, the width determined by the length of the mangrove beams that supported the roof. It was a feature of traditional architecture up and down the coast, as also of the towns of Arabia and the Persian Gulf, which imported East African mangroves for this purpose. As we were to see next day, the waterways of the archipelago were lined with mangrove forest, and the waterfront of Lamu town was littered with *bariti*, carefully assembled stacks of mangrove beams, awaiting shipment in the Arab dhows that sailed northwards on the summer monsoon. We visited the local boat builders in the creek to the north of the town. Here again I was struck by the significance of the mangrove in a generally treeless part of the world. There was one fullsize dhow on the stocks, but the mainstay of the industry lay in the production of *machua*, the much smaller seagoing sailboats used by the Swahili and neighbouring peoples for fishing and in coastal trade. It seemed to me suddenly significant that these were the northernmost of the Bantu-speaking peoples, and therefore probably the first to adapt to an intercontinental trading economy, and that it was perhaps their role in the coasting trade that explained the remarkable diffusion of their Swahili language, first as the lingua franca of the coast and later as that of the caravan trade with the whole of the East African interior. Next day we sailed northwards in a machua, crewed by three Swahili fishermen, to the north end of Manda Island. We walked from there to Neville's site, a stone harbour town of the tenth century, remarkable for its massive seawall, with houses built on bastions projecting into the water. On the return journey the wind was behind us and I steered the machua, while Neville, dressed in a *kikoi*, the skirtlike cloth worn by Swahili men, sat in the hold, reading Darwin's *Voyage of the Beagle* with the aid of a goldrimmed monocle. It is almost my favourite memory of him.

Soon after our return to Nairobi Neville and I flew together to Khartoum to visit the excavation then in progress under the institute's auspices at Soba, some twelve miles up the Blue Nile from the centre of the city. This was the site of the capital of the ancient kingdom of Alwa, the southernmost of the three Christian kingdoms of Nubia that flourished from the seventh century A.D. until its conquest by the Muslim dynasty of the Funj in 1504. The site was in danger of encroachment by the expanding suburbs of Khartoum, and Larry Kirwan had chosen it as suitable for the institute's attention and negotiated a concession from the Sudanese Department of Antiquities. There had been a brief survey in the previous year by Charles Daniels, professor of archaeology at the University of Newcastle who was now returning with a team of six European colleagues to complete his survey and to excavate the largest of several mounds that were now the only visible features on the surface of the site. A nearby house had been rented for the use of the visiting team, and they were joined every morning by some seventy cheerful Sudanese labourers who had been recruited in the neighbourhood.

Khartoum itself presented a sorry spectacle in 1982 compared with my last visit in 1960. The country had suffered from years of increasingly corrupt military rule and persistent civil war in its southern provinces. More recently, it had been hit even harder than most African countries by the oil crisis, which had drained its foreign currency reserves to zero. There were long queues at petrol pumps, and the sand blowing in from the desert was forming into small dunes in the streets, while pools of sewage

371

from blocked drains filled every depression. The Anglican cathedral had been converted into the Museum of the Revolution. Neville had reserved rooms for us at the Sudan Club, once the acme of colonial comfort in the capital, where the water taps now produced at best an uncertain trickle and three-quarters of the electric sockets lacked bulbs. Taxis were hard to find, and we had no means of communication with the site, so that the best plan seemed to be to walk to the Department of Antiquities, which was housed in the National Museum, and hope that our people would come and look for us there, as in the end they did.

The essential feature of the site at Soba was that all the main buildings of the town had been built in an extremely durable kind of thin, square, kiln-baked brick, which later Muslim inhabitants of the area had systematically pilfered to line their tombs. The opportunities for excavation were therefore limited to the foundations of the original buildings and to the objects buried beneath their floors. To a large extent it was the archaeology of the ground plan. At the time of our visit the team, led by Daniel's chief assistant Derek Welsby, was already at work on the great mound and uncovering the semicircular outline of what had clearly been the apse of a Byzantine church. Further investigation was to reveal that it was indeed the apse of a five-aisled cathedral of similar shape and dimensions to the metropolitan church of the northern Nubian kingdom of Makurra at Faras, the marvellous wall frescoes of which are exhibited in the National Museum in Khartoum.[2] Neville and I spent the day driving round the whole site with Derek Welsby and stayed overnight with the team in the excavation house, which I remember as even dirtier and more uncomfortable than the Sudan Club. It was a brief enough visit, but it served to change many of my preconceptions abut the operation, which was absorbing, for the time being, the lion's share of the institute's research funds. It had been presented to the council as an urban site covering one square mile, the excavation of which might take a decade. I came away from it with the impression, which appeared to be that of the team members also, that one further season should suffice for what most needed to be done, after which the institute would be justified in resigning its concession. After that, the place being so accessible, it might become a training site for the archaeology department of the University of Khartoum. I spent my remaining two days in the Sudan talking to the antiquities authorities and those of the university along these lines, and it seemed to give satisfaction to both.

29

The End of the Marathon
(1984–85)

The year 1984 found me sixty years old and a widower, but with Sarah still living at home, both at the London flat and in Frilsham on weekends. That helped greatly to soften my grief and mitigate my loneliness. So did the letters that flowed in for several months as the news of Caroline's death percolated to friends around the world. For many weeks almost every moment of spare time was occupied in answering them, and I realized for the first time how important a part of mourning is achieved by the largely repetitive act of responding to the sympathy of all sorts of people, some of them the merest acquaintances who had remembered something about her that they admired. "How *nice* Caroline was, intelligent and brave." "What courage and intellectual vigour Caroline has had, continuing from her couch to participate in this world much more than most of us do on our feet." "Our memories of her will be of laughter and of her particularly lovely voice, talking with so much animation and understanding both about people and things. She simply radiated vitality and hope." "*Une rare qualité morale, dont le contact enrichit le coeur, donnant si généreusement son amitié, et attirant l'amitié*" (A rare moral quality, contact with which cheers the heart, radiating friendship and attracting it in return). "When I first came to America and the children were at their most difficult, I took heart from the thought that I could write to Caroline, and she would see the funny side. There was no one else I could write to in the same vein." "*Et lux perpetua luceat eis* (And may light eternal shine upon them), but Caroline had quite a lot of light on her when she was still alive."

Soon some of our oldest friends took the occasion to renew relationships long held in abeyance by our enforced immobility at Frilsham, and the social network gradually reconstructed itself. It was the same even with our neighbours in Berkshire. Apart from a few close neighbours who had continued to visit in ones and twos, our social life had almost

373

lapsed. Now kind friends took steps to revive it. Among them, a group of ecumenically minded people from Douai and the surrounding Anglican parishes, assembled by Gervase Holdaway, made a deftly timed proposal to spend a day at my house discussing the scale and distribution of aid to underdeveloped countries. It came at the beginning of an interesting little local movement, known as the Mid-Kennet Ecumenical Group, which did much to transform relations among the churches in our area. It was to lead me into the company of many congenial people and to be one of the major interests of my retirement. Again, widowerhood made it possible to build something of a relationship with my mother, now in her mid-eighties and living in a retirement home in Kensington quite close to her former address. Over the years she had found it difficult to accept that the health problems of a daughter-in-law could take priority over hers, but now my visits could be more frequent and less hurried. I used to take her little meals on my way down to Frilsham that we would share in her room, as a change from those of the communal dining-room. It helped to moderate her pent-up feelings of neglect over the years, but I am afraid that our efforts at conversation were not brilliant. Right to the end she thought that employment as a university professor must resemble that of a shop assistant, which she understood much better. "What time do you get out?," she would ask. And once, when I attended a weeklong conference in Germany, she said, "I have reread your entry in *Who's Who*, and I cannot see anything in it to explain what you could have been doing in Germany."

Editorial work on the *Cambridge History* was in its final stages. I finished the final editing of Volume 8 in May and went on to deal with the proof stages of Volume 6. But the end of this marathon was now in sight, and I was beginning to consider what should follow it when, appropriately, the publishing firm of Weidenfeld and Nicolson came back to me with an invitation, first made a quarter of a century earlier, to contribute an African volume for its series on the history of civilization. The idea appealed to me because it was to be aimed not at a specialist audience but at highly intelligent readers who had not previously read anything significant about Africa—"la haute vulgarisation," as George Weidenfeld described it. In all the general works I had attempted thus far it had seemed necessary to have a mainly regional breakdown of chapters. Now the challenge was to take a set of themes, such as the growth of food production, the historical significance of language relationships, early trade and transport, the nature of traditional warfare, slavery in African societies, the growth of government systems, and the diffusion of Islam and Christianity, and to treat all these things as nearly as possible within the framework of the entire continent. I took some time over the decision and did much general reading about the history of other continents, but by the autumn of 1984 I was committed. The result would be entitled *The African Experience*, and it would occupy most of my writing time until the close of 1989.

For the rest, 1984 was marked for me by many interesting journeys. In May I went with Gervase Clarence-Smith to Paris to keep in touch with our colleagues at the Sorbonne. Christopher MacRae, who as a young man had accompanied our family on our trans-African journey from Ghana to Uganda in 1958, was now head of chancery at the British Embassy in Paris, where he not only put me up at his flat in the "gate house" but also gave a formal and much-appreciated dinner party, attended by Henri Brunschwig of the Institut des Hautes Études, Jean Devisse and Claude Perrot of Paris I, Catherine Conquéry of Paris VII, and Jean-Paul Chrétien of the Centre Nationale pour la Recherche Scientifique.[1] It made the perfect introduction to two days of intensive visiting and discussions at these several institutions, which cemented relationships, even if they failed to lead on, as I had hoped, to the regular exchange of teaching courses.

From Paris I went on to Brussels in order to try to promote my project for an exchange of taped teaching materials between European and African universities with the Development Commission of the European Economic Community. It was my first initiation into the workings of the EC's international secretariat, and it left me wondering how anything ever got done there. At the time the EC consisted of eight member states speaking five different languages, but the work of the Commission for Development concerned essentially relationships with the fifty-three "associated states" composed of the former British, French, and Belgian colonies in Africa, the Caribbean, and the Pacific that enjoyed special trade and tariff arrangements with the full members, formalized in the so-called Lomé treaties. The Development Commission derived large revenues from the tariff remissions on the trade with the associated states, but it could spend them only in response to requests emanating from those states, and the resulting bureaucratic intricacies had led to the accumulation of huge unspent balances. At an individual level the officials whom I met could not have been more welcoming and helpful, and I felt that they genuinely wanted my application to succeed. But I quickly became aware that within the secretariat there were English-speaking and French-speaking sections working in parallel and not always in harmony and that the same divisions were replicated among the diplomatic missions of the associated states. My mentors advised me that, for my project to fly, it would be necessary to drum up support from both French-speaking and English-speaking African countries, and the key figure in this respect would be the Mauritian ambassador, Monsieur Charles, who, although representing a former British colony, was both French-speaking and black and frequently acted as the intermediary between the Francophone and

Anglophone missions. We went to call upon him at his embassy, and he was both charming and intelligent, but it was clear to me that we were still only at the beginning of a long process of canvassing, which it would not be easy for someone fully employed at a university in London to sustain.

By July 1984 I was at last ready to take a long holiday, and I decided to take up three longstanding invitations from close friends in Scandinavia. Despite the considerable distances involved, I determined to keep full local mobility while there by driving my car. Taking ship from Harwich to Esbjerg, I drove across Denmark to the little wooden house near the Kattegat, where our friend for thirty-five years, Britta Holle, now lived in a nominal kind of retirement, writing prize-winning manuals on the education of disabled children and travelling all over Scandinavia, teaching primary schoolteachers how to recognize the symptoms in time for treatment to be effective. We knew each other quite well enough to say that we wanted to read our books in the mornings, while in the afternoons we would walk for three or four hours, either through the beechwoods around Helsinge or else among the forests of conifers planted by King Christian V to stabilise the sand dunes deposited across the north of Zealand by a freak storm in 1673.

On August 1, 1984, I crossed the straits to Hälsingborg and drove through the "endless forest" of Skåne to Jönköping and thence up the western shores of Lake Vättern towards the mining town of Örebro and so to my next port of call, with Bengt Sundkler, at Uppsala. Once more I was in the company of an old friend who had frequently visited us at Frilsham, and he was now putting what were intended to be the finishing touches to a history of the Christian church in Africa. This was certainly the impression that I formed of it as I read the typescript on the balcony of his lovely flat. Unfortunately, as he grew older, he sought advice from far too many people and kept amending his text to meet their conflicting criticisms, with the result that at his death in 1995 it was twice the length and still unpublished. He had engaged to help him a young Englishman, Christopher Steed, recently graduated with a master's degree from SOAS, whom he generously freed for a week or so to accompany me on the next stage of my trip, which took us through the lovely and sparsely inhabited mountain valleys of central Sweden to Östersund and so down into Norway. We spent a day in Trondheim, with its forbiddingly dark fourteenth-century cathedral, the only building of its kind in Norway, and with its old wooden warehouses with living accommodation above, clustered along the landward side of an offshore island from which Hanseatic merchants had conducted the international trade in furs, skins, and fishery products with the small communities of hunters and fishermen living on the northern mainland. The parallels with the offshore islands of the Swahili coast were not lost to us.

From Trondheim we drove north again and turned eastward over a high pass into Sweden at Frostvikken. We were now in Saame (Lappish) country, with herds of reindeer grazing the mountain plateau of the Stekkenjok, until at last we descended into a land of lakes and birch forests stretching away eastwards to the Baltic coast. For most of our trip Bengt had arranged through his network of former theological students for us to be able to use some kind of church accommodation—here a retreat house, there a parish flat for visiting preachers, somewhere else a school building where the pupils were still on holiday—and now at the end of it we were bidden to stay in Umeå by his sister, Inger, and her husband, Stig Hellsten, a former bishop of the diocese of Luleå, which covered the whole northern third of the country. Unlike the younger pastors of the Swedish church, who mostly spoke English and looked to American Lutheranism for their outside sustenance, Stig's generation had been educated in German theological literature, and we had to converse in my increasingly rusty German. But he impressed me greatly and particularly by his insistence that, even in Arctic winter conditions, a bishop visiting his diocese would always travel either with his wife or else alone, for only thus could he establish the right relations with his clergy and their families. The moment there was a chaplain or even a driver involved, the hierarchical atmosphere was unavoidable.

From Umeå, Christopher returned to Uppsala by train, while I continued northward to the small town of Skellefteå, near which Inger and Richard Aasa-Marklund had their summer cabin beside a birch-fringed lake. Both were still students at Uppsala University, but they were spending the summer vacation in the midst of their families. Richard's mother lived in Skellefteå, beside a grand baroque church that, like many others in northern Sweden, was half encircled by a church village of old log cabins built by farmers from the surrounding countryside so that they could spend the weekends within reach of Christian worship. On the Sunday of my visit the huge church was packed to the doors with fifteen hundred youth leaders assembled for their annual conference, and it gave me a sense of the vitality of the Christian life still subsisting at the northern end of this notoriously irreligious country. Inger's mother lived in Luleå at the northwestern corner of the Baltic coast, and in due course we stayed a few days with her there. But the highlight of the whole trip was the visit we paid to the ancestral village of the Aasa family at Juoksengi on the great Tornio River, which flows southwards to the northeastern Baltic and forms the boundary between Sweden and Finland.

Juoksengi, as I remember it, was a straggling village of perhaps two hundred homesteads, each of which was set in a long narrow strip of farmland only six or seven hundred yards wide but running back three or four miles from its river frontage into the forest behind. Only the first half-mile of each strip was cultivated, carrying the crops that could thrive within a growing season of ten to twelve weeks of nearly perpetual daylight, above all, potatoes, turnips, oats, and barley. The rest was summer pasture, consisting of lightly forested land climbing the sides of the valley where cattle, living most of the year in barns attached to the houses, could be turned loose to graze during the short summer months. Farming in these latitudes had always been a precarious business, and Inger and Richard told me that, although the imagination of the summer visitors tended to focus on the discomforts of winter cold and darkness, the really abiding fear of every northern family before the advent of modern transport had been whether last summer's harvest would last until the next growing season.

We stayed in Juoksengi with Ester Aasa, the eldest of Inger's many aunts, who lived in one of these traditional farmhouses, which she shared with her brother Lasse and his wife. Ester was not only the head of the family but also the churchwarden, and her standing in the community was reflected in her post office box number, which was 1. Within the household she presided over the *pörte*, the big family living-room that contained both the kitchen range and the huge tiled stove by which the house was heated. It was furnished with only a long dining table and chairs in the centre and by a fitted wooden settle running right round three walls, on which, between meals, people would sit either alone or in small groups, some talking, some reading, some telephoning to relatives in distant parts of Sweden. The main traditional use of the settle, however, was that here those whose private quarters did not adjoin the great stove or its chimney would bring their bedding and sleep in cold weather.

Inger had prepared me to meet in Ester one of those rare, marvellous, comprehending, soft-spoken women who understood more about life than other people and to whom everyone brought their problems. Unfortunately, she spoke only Swedish and Finnish, but we did not lack for interpreters, and when she started to tell me about the past of her remarkable family, I listened to as good a piece of frontier history as one could hope for from any continent. The Aasa family, she said, had been small farmers like everyone else, but they had also owned the village store and traded in reindeer skins with the Saame from the surrounding forests. Her father, Allan Aasa, growing up in the 1890s and early 1900s, had received nothing more than a few years of primary education but had used them to so much better purpose than his contemporaries that he became the village letter writer, a part-time occupation that gave him valuable access to the innermost thoughts and business affairs of his neighbours. Again, in his capacity as storekeeper, he used his superior literacy to study the advertisements and the operating manuals about plumbing and electricity, simple farm machinery, bicycles, and eventually motor cars. He bought the first examples of these novelties and learned how to service and fix them. Only then did he begin to purvey them to his neighbours. He became well enough off to send all of his eight children to secondary schools, which meant boarding them in Luleå and other towns of the Baltic littoral. Most had become primary teachers, and their children, of whom there were twenty-three, had nearly all succeeded in getting to universities and were aiming to become high-school teachers, nurses, ministers, or missionaries. It was a great improvement story, and what was perhaps most remarkable was that, of Allan Aasa's thirty-one descendants, only one had died, while all the survivors were still fully in touch with each other, keeping their loyalty to the northern province for all the harshness of its climate and taking their holidays in a circle of family visits, of which Juoksengi was still the centre. There on the summer pasture Lasse Aasa had built with his own timber and his own hands a cluster of summer houses large enough to accommodate them all. It had become the symbol of a way of life that they were still concerned to honour.

I was to return more than once to Juoksengi in future years. Meanwhile, it was mid-August 1984, and Sweden was girding for its winter's work. We stayed briefly with Inger's mother in Luleå and then made a swift return to Uppsala, driving the 550 miles in a single day. There Bengt had arranged for me to spend a day in Stockholm visiting the officials of the Swedish International Development Authority, which had for many years been a major donor of scholarship funds to the Africa Educational Trust, and which I now hoped to interest in the foundation of a Swedish branch of the Minority Rights Group. I was fortunate to be accompanied on this mission by Bengt's colleague and successor Carl Frederick Hallencreutz, who was to become the first chairman of the group's Swedish council. Next day I resumed my homeward journey, crossing Sweden to Oslo and thence over the high mountain plateau to the Hardanger Fjord and Bergen. The western fjords of Norway were at their most captivating in the late August sunshine, and I vowed to return there again and again.

Back in England after my Scandinavian holiday I buried myself for the autumn of 1984 in the necessary but mostly unmemorable activities of a senior academic. I made the last proof corrections to the *Cambridge History*. I prepared a completely new series of introductory lectures on the sources of African history. I fought my corner among the other heads of departments and secured the creation of a new chair in Chinese history and a new readership in the economic history of Japan. Then, early in December 1984, I left for two months of intensive travels in East Africa. It was now two years since I have been able to inspect the work of the British Institute on the ground, in addition to which I hoped to visit all the East African universities and try to drum up support for my project for the exchange of taped teaching materials. Independently of this the EC officials in Brussels had encouraged me to investigate what demand there might be for retraining fellowships for academic staff in midcareer who had been prevented by the continuing political and economic crises in the region from studying abroad and keeping up with the progress of knowledge in their subjects. For such retraining they were confident that funds would be readily available. For my part I welcomed this opportunity to come close to the universities and to discuss the work of a whole range of arts and social science departments. I thought it would also be in the interests of the British Institute that I should do so. It had now been seventeen years since the institute had been able to do any research in Uganda, and even in Tanzania its activities had been much hindered for about ten years by the poor relations existing between the governments of Tanzania and Kenya. It would be timely to show our faces again in both countries but to do so in Uganda was still quite an adventure. Amin had been overthrown, but the second Obote government was still fighting for its existence, and conditions were said to be fairly chaotic even in the capital. No one was going there for fun.

Celebrating the completion of the *Cambridge History of Africa* with John Fage (*left*), and Michael Black (*center*)

I began my tour in Kenya in December 1984. It was the first time I had seen the institute since its move from the university campus into the leafy suburb of Kileleshwa, where it occupied what had formerly been a fairly roomy private house with a little cottage for guests in the garden beside it. Here I could stay and cater for myself, with easy access to the institute's library and transport without disturbing the new director, John Sutton, and his family in their house farther down the road. Here I could meet the rest of the staff casually, as I encountered them in my comings and goings, without setting up formal interviews. Here I did not have to worry about outstaying my welcome. Moreover, I liked this district of Nairobi. I liked the nannies out walking with their charges. I liked the watchmen chattering with the passers-by at every entrance. I liked the groups of orderly well-dressed children wending their way through the municipal arboretum to and from the schools by its front gate. I liked what I saw of the university students who walked from their hostels on our hill to the lecture rooms on the other side of the valley. True, these were the children of the elite, but the less developed the country, the more significant the role of the elite, and here there was an atmosphere of vitality, hope, and improvement, which made me feel that this was an African country where things had to turn out all right.

It was with such optimistic preconceptions that I set out to discover what I could about the present state of the University of Nairobi and of Kenyatta University, which was its metropolitan partner. I called separately upon three of my oldest and most trusted academic friends, and I found that their testimony agreed that the hand of government had been heavy and was getting heavier. Government was interested in numbers and not in quality. Above all, it was concerned to push the build-up of a third university situated in President Moi's Kalenjin homeland and destined to bear his name. But three universities, all with burgeoning student numbers, were to run on the same budget as the existing two. Academic salaries had already been allowed to slide with inflation to about one-third of their value at the time of independence. With many students, few books, no travel grants, and little sabbatical leave, research had ceased to be possible and had lost its place among the criteria for promotion. The six top positions at the two universities were overtly filled by government nominees, while academic supporters of the government were rewarded with part-time directorships of state enterprises on a scale that made it impossible to prevent the taking of second jobs by others. One of my consultants shrewdly remarked that the use of taped lectures from outside Africa would cause an immediate crisis of expectations by students about the shortcomings of the Nairobi libraries, where no books at all had been purchased for two years. Another pointed out that the exchange of teaching materials would only be acceptable politically and psychologically if contributions from inside and outside Africa were roughly equal, and yet how could they be so, seeing that so little new work was being done at the African end? I called on Leonard Allinson at the British High Commission who amply confirmed the information I had been given. He said that two universities were being starved of cash— to the point that the payment of the next month's salaries was always uncertain—in order that a third could be built and staffed from scratch. He was specially concerned, since Nairobi University was receiving £1 million a year of British aid, while Kenyatta University had just been given a new library building at a cost of £900,000.

With such misgivings about the Kenyan universities, which had grown up against a background of peace and stability, it was naturally with increased apprehension that I set out the following week for Uganda. At Entebbe airport I was amazed to be met by Bernard Onyango, the long-serving registrar of Makerere and by my old friend and former student Sam Karugire who had recently returned from exile in Zambia to his post as head of the history department. Lacking any private transport, they had come in the university's only utility van, and as we drove towards Kampala, they broke it to me that it would not be possible to accommodate me at Makerere, since the guest house was fully occupied by newly appointed members of staff for whom no housing was available. We stopped at the Speke Hotel in town, where all the armchairs in the reception hall were occupied by uniformed servants, all fast asleep. I was shown to a miserable hole of a room, dirty and without a window that opened or a lightbulb that worked, or a plug for the basin or a lavatory seat. As I soon discovered, the better rooms in the place were all permanently occupied by the local prostitutes. My hosts departed crest-fallen, promising to return and rescue me on the morrow. Meantime, I occupied the remaining hours of daylight by watching the sparse traffic in the main road weaving its way cautiously around potholes two yards across and a foot deep and then walking over Nakasero Hill, observing what remained of the former houses of the colonial administration, their entrances chained up, their gardens stacked with refuse, while soldiers with machine-guns sat on stools at every crossroads.

Next day, to my vast relief, I was moved to the university guest-house where a tiny room had somehow been cleared for me. It was not luxurious. I washed and shaved in a bucket and tipped the residue down a loo unflushed for twenty-four hours. But at least it was in the right place, and I could begin to do my work of interviewing the heads of the arts and social sciences departments. Some of these were impressive people who had stayed at their posts through all or most of the terrible years of Amin's dictatorship, keeping their heads down so as to avoid denunciation and arrest, earning barely enough to feed themselves and their families, improvising the means to keep their subjects alive without access to new books and periodicals, sometimes without paper or typewriter ribbons. Their gravest problem, however, had been the recruitment of younger staff. Every department had been reduced to employing its own raw graduates, without higher degrees or foreign travel, who could do little more than reproduce as lectures the notes they had taken as students. I found great interest in my EC-inspired project for retraining fellowships, and we identified potential candidates and likely costs. In the vice chancellor's absence abroad, Bernard Onyango agreed to sign a request for funds that we would take to the EC delegate in Kampala. When we arrived there the delegate opened the proceedings by reminding Onyango that the delegate had been holding for several months the funds for the repair of Makerere's chemistry laboratories, which he could not release until he received a formal request for them, signed by the vice chancellor. The same would apply to our present proposal, which he would nevertheless begin to process. For whatever reason that all-important signature was to go missing for our present project also.

Meanwhile, at the guest-house a surprising invitation awaited me from Picho Owiny, the assistant minister for foreign affairs in President Obote's government. Picho had earlier been a student at the Lumumba Freedom University in Moscow, where he had earned a doctoral degree for a thesis on colonial Uganda of the limited kind that was all that was possible for an English speaker working from the printed materials available in the Soviet Union. He had then sought my help to see whether, during a few months in London, it could not be amplified into something more worthwhile. Now he wrote inviting me to dine with him the following evening, and I assumed that it would be a domestic occasion at his private house. At the appointed time, however, two cars full of armed soldiery drove up to the guest-house and whisked me off to the Uganda Club on Nakasero Hill, where I found myself the guest of honour at a splendid meal attended by four ministers, four permanent secretaries, the EC delegate, and some senior figures from Makerere. Television cameras rolled, while we drank toasts of champagne and listened to speeches of welcome. As we ate, Picho mentioned quietly that he had arranged to introduce me to the president the following afternoon.

Next day the two cars returned to pick me up, and we drove to the president's office on the top floor of a building adjoining the parliament house. There were armed men everywhere—at the door, in the corridors, even in the lift. I had assumed that it was to be a private meeting, but I was shown into a long room furnished with a huge U-shaped settee, the open end of which was filled by a television camera. Several ministers sat down one side, together with the Uganda high commissioner in London, Shafik Arayn. I was invited to sit opposite them, with a half-dozen senior staff from Makerere on my right. Obote entered, shook hands briefly, and took the central position facing the camera. He said he had heard of my presence on the radio, coupled with a statement that I was spending Lomé money, which made it *his* business. I explained my connection with the EC, which he accepted without trouble. We then talked about Makerere, and I stressed the lack of resources, which he endorsed. He said the problem was whether to include Makerere in general requests for international aid or leave it to cultivate its special constituency—he rather thought the latter. He then launched into a monologue on the record of his government. He spoke of seven thousand political prisoners he had released, as against only thirty still held in confinement. He spoke of the two wasted years following the fall of Amin and before his (Obote's) return. He spoke of the problems attending the restoration of discipline and morality in a society more full of criminal elements than it should be. The peroration was rather well done, and it was the only part of the proceedings to be shown on the television news that evening. After watching it, I took an evening stroll on Makerere Hill and was soon joined by a couple of students. It was the middle of the Christmas vacation, so I asked them why they were not on holiday. They said that their homes in central Buganda had been destroyed by the army and their families had disappeared. They said that there were many others in like case, and they thought the situation was getting worse rather than better. This was the most vivid of several indications I gleaned during my visit that the military repression of southern Uganda by a predominantly northern government was still very much a reality. Earlier that day Sam Karugire had organised a farewell lunch for me at a pleasant restaurant on the outskirts of Kampala. As we sat on the terrace, our conversation was interrupted by a prolonged burst of machine-gun fire somewhere close by. The restaurant loudspeaker responded by playing the truimphalist final movement of Beethoven's Choral Symphony. It seemed entirely appropriate to the occasion, and everyone laughed.

On my return to Nairobi I found Sarah already installed at the institute's guest cottage, having come to join me for a Christmas holiday on Mount Kenya. There was just time enough beforehand to pay a short visit to the excavation being conducted by the assistant director, Peter Robertshaw, at Lemek in the high hills to the west of the Rift Valley beyond Narok. It was five hours' drive from Nairobi, and the second half of it took us by rough trails across unfenced wilderness, occupied only by Masai pastoralists whose cattle grazed in small herds in peaceful company with those of zebra and various kinds of antelope that moved unconcernedly in and out among them. The Mara game reserve, with its constant flow of minibuses and camera-toting tourists, lay fifty miles farther west, but here we found the Robertshaws' tidy camp established on a bare hillside with no other habitation nearer than the village of Lemek, which had grown up round a mission station of the Mill Hill Fathers three miles away. When darkness fell, the fire burned brightly, and after supping off our nightly goat stews, ten of us would sit round it—two Robertshaws, two Olivers, a student volunteer from Cambridge, and five members of the institute's African staff—until one by one we crept exhausted to our tents.

Peter's project concerned the origins of pastoralism, which in this particular part of East Africa had been the earliest form of deliberate food production. Unlike their Iron Age successors these early pastoralists had made their sharp implements, skinning tools, scrapers, arrowheads, and spearblades from the natural volcanic glass known as obsidian, and it had been from the presence of obsidian microliths, in association with animal bones and pottery in surfaces exposed by erosion, that their settlement sites had been recognised. During two previous seasons Peter had collected more than enough tools and pottery for the study of the material culture. He had also taken carbon samples that had yielded dates from the second century B.C. until the first century A.D. His present concern was to reconstruct the pattern of the settlements by tracing the postholes of their houses and their boundary fences. The purpose of my visit was simply to listen and to learn and then to help the institute decide whether the expense of a third season of excavation here would be justified or whether Robertshaw and his team would be better advised to publish what they had done and then move on to another problem.[2]

Our 1984 Christmas house party took place at ten thousand feet above sea level on the northeastern slopes of Mount Kenya, where the Kenya Mountain Club maintained a circle of self-catering chalets built on a grassy ledge just above the belt of dense bamboo forest that encircles the central massif between eight and ten thousand feet. It was likewise above the cloud bank that, seen from below, seems to envelop the entire mountain for most of the daylight hours. Here we enjoyed ten glorious sun-drenched days with clear views of the high peaks from a natural parkland lit by splendid wildflowers and alive with hovering sunbirds and gorgeous butterflies. We were a party of ten, with John and Inez Sutton and their two daughters, Jim and Helen Armstrong from the Library of Congress, and Nick and Sheila Allen, he an Oxford anthropologist and an experienced mountaineer who soon set off alone to climb the peaks and descend on the other side. The rest of us climbed as high as we could manage. I found my ceiling at about twelve thousand feet, beyond which my progress became so slow as to be tedious. Sarah went to thirteen thousand and could, as she has since proved on Kilimanjaro, have gone much farther. But there were plenty of fine walks within the reach of all of us, and we would return in the late afternoons to find wood fires blazing in our chalets and an evening meal that we ate together. In the early mornings there would be frost on the grass and, often enough, elephant droppings within yards of the huts.

We descended the mountain reluctantly on January 3, 1985, and on the sixth Sarah departed for her visit to Uganda, to stay some days at Gayaza School, which had survived the country's time of troubles relatively unscathed. Next day John Sutton and I set off by Land Rover for a two-week two-thousand-mile journey in Tanzania; our main destination would be the University of Dar es Salaam. We decided, however, that it was a necessary part of my education to see the Leakeys' great palaeolithic site at Olduvai Gorge and also desirable for John to make a brief visit to Engaruka, the stone-terraced Iron Age farming site in the Rift Valley, that I had first visited with Neville Chittick in 1958. We therefore chose a little-frequented route passing down the western rim of the Rift Valley to Lolliondo and straight across the Serengeti Plain to Olduvai. Our first night was spent at Entsekera in the Loita Hills, where we camped beside a pioneer mission of the Mill Hill Fathers. The incumbent, Father Gogerty from County Kildare, lived there quite alone, save for one Masai servant. His parishioners consisted of some seven thousand highly mobile Loita Masai, of whom, as yet, only thirteen were baptised and only seven practising. He had worked for twenty-two years at other longer-established missions in Masailand, and he spoke the language fluently. At Entsekera his pastoral function consisted mainly of talking to elderly Masai who walked considerable distances to see him. Most came in the first instance because they were hungry, and he would feed them and offer them overnight accommodation, making it clear to them that, if they came again, he would assume it was for advice and not for food. Despite my early specialisation in missionary history, it was the first time that I had actually witnessed the first stage of mission work in a new area, and I found it fascinating that in a country already equipped with an indigenous hierarchy of clergy, bishops, and archbishops, it was still the man from County Kildare who was bringing the gospel to the Masai.

From Entsekera we drove along ever more vestigial tracks through noble scenery of forested hillsides and grassy valleys, backed by ridge upon ridge of blue volcanic peaks crowning the eastern rim of the Rift. We were happy to think of it as the Garden of Eden. "After all," as John remarked in a rare moment of flippancy, "you could put quite a decent country house almost anywhere here." The Tanzanian frontier was unmarked, and after reporting to a sleepy police post at Lolliondo, we continued across the Serengeti, soon abandoning the track altogether and steering towards Lemugurut Mountain, which was our landmark for Olduvai. Driving across country we came upon the famous gorge so suddenly that we understood how its first European discoverer, Professor Kattwinkel, nearly fell into it while chasing a rare butterfly. On arrival we drove cautiously around its head and made for the Leakeys' excavation house on its southern rim, where Mary Leakey had kindly invited us to camp. Although its wider setting is glorious, with Oltumi Mountain to the northeast and the crater of Ngorongoro to the south, the gorge itself struck me as a hellhole resembling the residue of some ghastly open-cast mining operation long since abandoned. We spent the whole of the next day walking and scrambling in the ancient riverbed at its base and observing the four geological beds laid down by volcanic action during the past two million years, from which the Leakeys had been able to reconstruct the sequence and chronology of its occupation by hominids and early humans. But to me, at least, the gorge lacks any attraction. It is one of those places I am glad to have seen but to which I have no ambition ever to return.

From Olduvai to Engaruka our route took us over Ngorongoro, and by making a long day of it we were able to spend the morning in the crater and to enjoy what must be the most beautiful and the best-stocked game park in the world. From the crater's edge at Windy Gap there was the magnificent view of the whole mountain circle, wonderfully reflected in the water of the lake at its centre. The grasslands in the basin went through every shade of colour, and from this distance they looked quite empty. Then, as we descended the steep and stony track that led down to it, our first animal companions were the thousands of cattle being led down to water by their Masai herdsmen. At the lakeside the cattle were roughly pushing aside the zebra gathered there to drink. We worked our way clockwise round the lake, passing groups of ostrich and gazelle, and stopped short of a river line, beyond which we could see elephant standing with a rhinoceros and calf in their midst. We crossed the river and turned up it to see a couple of lionesses sitting two hundred yards away from us on the other side; they saw us but did not move. Further on we had a good view of buffalo, and all this was within two hours, after which we climbed up again to the rim and looked for a snack at Wildlife Lodge, a hundred-bedroom tourist hotel splendidly situated, overhanging a forested section of the crater's edge. Such was the state of inaction and poverty to which the country as a whole had been reduced that only six rooms were let. As the Swiss manager explained to us, he could never be sure that he would be able to serve butter with the breakfast rolls or replace an electric lightbulb when one failed. It was sad to see that Tanzania, under the benevolent dictatorship of a Julius Nyerere, could be ruining itself nearly as effectively as the Uganda of Amin and Obote.

Descending from Ngorongoro we turned north up the Rift Valley floor to Engaruka and camped there for two nights, while John sprang fleetly up and down its steep slopes in search of the hydrological data that he needed. The next two days we spent uncomfortably on the crumbling surfaces of the main road leading southwards to Dar es Salaam. There we circulated for five days between the university, National Museum, British Council, EC delegacy, and the local Ministry of Labour. The academics with whom I spoke, who included some old and trusted friends, responded eagerly enough to my projects but warned me that the economic position of the university would impose a total barrier to any expenditure of foreign currency, including even the cost of tapes and players. They told me that the real impact of currency control had come with the Uganda Liberation War of 1978—the library had bought hardly anything since, and subscriptions even to the most basic scholarly periodicals had been discontinued. There were other factors at work to discourage enterprise. Academic salaries might look reasonable on paper in 1985, but the marginal tax rates rose to 80 percent for professors and 70 percent for lower-paid staff. This put a premium on the search for untaxable second incomes from small-scale farming and trading. Private cars could be bought only with money earned abroad, and few possessed them. Public transport no longer adhered to schedule and was therefore immensely time consuming to use, so that even visits to the national archives eight miles away in town were considered by most to be impracticable. There were difficulties about every kind of publication, so that the spirit of competition was fast disappearing and giving way to an entirely campus-based outlook that no longer sought improvement. None of this augured well for effective participation in exchanges of teaching materials or even opportunities for midcareer retraining. The difference from Obote's Makerere was simply that in Dar es Salaam there were more of the older and more experienced academics still around, whereas their Ugandan counterparts were mostly either in exile or else had taken up other occupations.

The Department of Antiquities in Dar es Salaam, which controlled excavation permits for the entire country, was housed in the National Museum, which, like the Uganda Museum in Kampala, was closed to the public. Custodial staff could no longer be afforded, and the exhibition halls stood bare and empty. The director was friendly and welcoming but made it clear that things had changed since the days when Neville Chittick had been allowed to conduct major expeditions year after year at famous sites like Kilwa and Mafia. There was now a feeling of cultural xenophobia in the ruling circles, and our institute would need to formulate small projects in out-of-the-way places for permits to be given. John sensibly agreed to follow the director's advice. We returned to Nairobi aware of the difficulties ahead but conscious that most were the result of the country's deepening poverty and the ineptitude of its well-meaning government. Within our profession we had found many friends still trying to do their best in increasingly difficult circumstances and grateful for our continuing interest and attempts to help. As for the current generation of East African students, it was remarkable that the seminar I gave in Dar es Salaam was so crowded that the overflow filled every doorway and window. Likewise, the public lecture I gave the following week in Nairobi had to be halted while the audience of several hundred was transferred to a larger theatre.

The last leg of my local travels was to Kisii, in the western province of Kenya, where Peter Robertshaw took me to see the important site he had begun to excavate at Gogo Falls. Here, where the foothills of the western highlands dropped into the Lake Victoria basin, the construction of a hydroelectric dam had exposed archaeological deposits, in places nine feet deep, with Late Stone Age ceramics of the Oltumi tradition at the bottom, obsidian artifacts of the Elementeitan tradition in the middle, and early Iron Age artifacts associated with Urewe pottery at the top. Here, as at Lemek, the question for the institute was whether to encourage Peter to publish what he had already done or to support another and larger round of expensive excavation.[3]

To get there from Nairobi we drove for nine hours (340 miles or so) across the Rift Valley, over the summit of the Mau, through the tea estates around Kericho, and thence down into Kisii, with its green hills and wide valleys all cultivated from top to bottom by a rural population denser than any I had seen. Every half-acre of the landscape seemed to have a house with a teeming family in occupation, and I wondered what would happen to all these people when their numbers doubled, as they were expected to do within twenty years. Our destination lay in much drier and stonier country, just sixteen miles from the eastern shores of Lake Victoria. We reached the dam and camped beside it through a rainy night. In the morning Peter showed me his site and explained what he had already done there and what might be done in the future. Then we proceeded on foot to examine the ruined remains of a stone settlement some two miles to the north, which was known as the *ohinga* of Timlich. It consisted of a walled enclosure 12 feet high and some 150 years in diameter, with some smaller extensions adjoining it on the side opposite the main entrance, the only access to which was through small low-roofed gateways from the great enclosure. The whole complex could be convincingly described as a rather grand kraal, which the proprietors had presumably shared with their cattle and small stock. The warden told us that there were several other ohingas on neighbouring hilltops and that the largest had been demolished for ballast by the builders of the Gogo Dam. Although the present-day inhabitants of the area were Luo who had arrived as conquering migrants during the nineteenth century, local traditions asserted that the ohingas had been built by the Bantu speakers who had preceded them, who were Luyia-speaking subjects of the Wanga kingdom, which had its centre at Kakamega. Clearly, there was a problem here that might have bearings upon the traditions of stone building in Zimbabwe and the Transvaal and

389

that deserved investigation by oral historians and archaeologists working together.

On our return journey we stopped for two nights at a little hotel on Homa Bay on the southern shores of the Kavirondo Gulf and from there visited Rusinga Island, where Louis Leakey had found the skull of Proconsul, a primate that he regarded as possibly a prehominid, in a deposit dated to seventeen million years ago. We also followed the lakeshore southwards to Sindi Bay in order to visit a small community of Bantu-speaking Suba people who lived almost entirely by fishing and salt boiling, though growing a few bananas in small scattered plantations. There were said to be pockets of Suba living all round the northern shores of Lake Victoria, and it seemed possible that they represented the surviving descendants of the first Iron Age settlers of the lakeshores during the early centuries A.D. Altogether, this little-frequented corner of Kenya seemed to be rife with problems of the kind that the institute existed to explore.

I stayed only two days in Nairobi before returning to England on January 31, 1985, but on one of them Derek Aspinall, who was the senior representative of the British Council in the East African countries, had kindly organised a working lunch for those most likely to help in carrying forward my projects for the exchange of teaching materials. They included representatives from the Kenya Ministry of Education, the EC delegacy, and French research organisation CREDU, and Allan Ogot, who spoke for the Kenya universities. It was Allan who took the lead, underlining again and again the importance of full reciprocity between the European and African participants and questioning whether it could be achieved. With rare outspokenness he observed that people who knew that they were behind in their subjects were prone to take refuge in ideologically inspired models of "what must have happened" in the past or of "what must be" the nature of social and economic phenomena in the present. As teaching material for international exchanges such contributions would not be viable for long. Much as I wished my project to succeed, I felt that he had put his finger on the most essential difficulty.

30

A Man of Letters

(1985–90)

In a matter of weeks after my return from East Africa in February 1985 I began to be aware that Sarah had found a partner, Michael Wilson, a microbiologist at the Eastman Dental Institute at the University of London, whom she would later marry. It took me some time to grasp the implications of this for my future life, but as I gradually did so, I realised that it must greatly affect the issue of when I should retire. I would reach the statutory age limit in three years in any case, but I could decide to go sooner, and the more I thought about it, the more attractive the prospect appeared. I did not really need to keep up two establishments just for myself, nor did I like the idea of daily commuting from Frilsham without a London base. Above all, I realised that I wanted as soon as possible to free myself from academic administration and to devote most of my working time to *The African Experience*. My presidency of the British Institute in Eastern Africa could go on and would provide me with the opportunities for further African travels. So could my chairmanship of the Minority Rights Group, which was beginning to acquire an international dimension with the formation of national groups in other countries. Above all, I was sure that I wanted to go on living at Frilsham. My books and papers were there. I loved my garden and my seasonally changing view of the Pang Valley. And, increasingly, I valued my proximity to Douai Abbey and the ecumenical values represented there. By November 1985 I felt sure enough of my decision to send in a letter of resignation, effective in September 1986.

Meanwhile, during 1985 and 1986 I spent the busiest two years of my academic career. It was in 1985 that the British government began the process of separating the funds granted to the universities for teaching and research. No longer was it accepted that all university teachers should engage equally in both activities. Henceforward, most funds would be for teaching and only a small part of them given selectively for excellence in research. In general the change was probably an inevitable consequence of the increase in the number of universities. For SOAS, however, it was of particularly crucial significance because of the small size of our student body. To survive we had to excel in research and to be seen to do so by the increasingly bureaucratic criteria by which excellence was to be judged. There were to be peer reviews of all research projects. Journals were to be recognised as "learned" only if their contents were "refereed." Publications were to be assessed on the basis of how often they had been cited in other publications. In fact, from now on almost everyone was going to have to spend a lot of time writing reports about everyone else. It was with a heavy heart that I accepted the chairmanship of the powerful committee that was set up to start moving SOAS in these directions, but it seemed that there was no alternative.

Again, during these two years I was still much involved with the EC Development Commission about my two projects. Professor Adebayo Adedeji, the respected head of the Economic Commission for Africa, had written to the heads of all the African universities about our proposed exchange of tapes, and several of them had replied positively. The matter had even appeared on the agenda of the committee of vice chancellors in East and Central Africa. To my mentors in Brussels the time seemed ripe for a further assault on their labyrinthine decision-making processes, and they suggested that our immediate target should be a grant of 30 to 50,000 *écus* (£25–30,000) to cover the expenses of "project identification" and that this could be achieved on the basis of an application by the committee of ambassadors of the associated states. During a three-day visit to Brussels in April I was taken to call on the Jamaican secretary general of the associated states, Edwin Carrington, who duly promised to place it before his committee of ambassadors. In an attempt to drum up some Francophone support we also called on the Ivoirian ambassador to the EC, who had been a former rector of Abidjan University. I think it was probably he who later caused Carrington to renege on his promise. At any rate, it was clear that our failure on this round was the result of Francophone opposition to the project, and the same was true of all our subsequent attempts. I concluded that it was small wonder that the unspent trillions of Lomé funds remained unspent.

The year 1985 was the centenary of the Berlin Congress, which is conventionally held to mark the start of the colonial partition of Africa. This brought me three attractive invitations to take part in conferences to celebrate the occasion. The first, appropriately, was in Berlin, where a delightful house party of some thirty guests assembled for three days under the auspices of the Deutsche Stiftung für internationale Entwicklung (German Foundation for International Development) at the Villa Borsig, which occupied a private peninsula jutting into the Tegelsee. They included may of my oldest and most intimate friends—Jacob Ajayi, Henri Brunschwig, Michael Crowder, John Flint, John Hargreaves, Suzanne Miers, Ronald Robinson, George Shepperson, and Jean Stengers. It was our German hosts who were the odd men out, for as diplomatic historians without any commitment to African history they seemed to think that the important question about the conference of 1885 was Bismarck's motive in calling it. For the rest of us 1885 was simply a landmark, and what mattered was the significance of colonial intervention in the history of a continent. Was colonialism a necessary gateway through which Africa had to pass in order to reach the modern world, or could it have got there more easily on its own? Each historian's answer to that question shaped his or her entire approach to the twentieth-century history of Africa. At Berlin it so happened that all of our five African members were from southern Nigeria, and it became obvious that to all of them the colonial partition of Africa was the great act of betrayal committed against an already-existing Westernised and Westernising elite of coastal West Africans who, left to themselves, would have become the pioneers of modernity among their hinterland neighbours. Instead, colonialism had intervened to block their growing influence, characterising them as "trousered blacks" who must be prevented by every means from exploiting their unlettered countrymen.

It was a difference of outlook that emerged again at the two succeeding conferences, at Uppsala in June 1985 and in Brussels in December. And it showed at its starkest in the seventh volume of the UNESCO *General History of Africa*, which was published that year and organised its entire treatment of the colonial period under the twin themes of resistance to colonialism and the rise of nationalism, without giving any space to the initiatives or achievements of the colonial powers during the seventy-odd years of their rule. This was precisely the kind of ideological gulf that John Fage and I had foreseen when we were planning the *Cambridge History* in the 1960s. During the 1970s it had still not been evident, except on the wilder shores of Marxist historiography in East Germany and the Soviet Union. Now in the 1980s it had arrived in force and was affecting much of the literature published, not only in Africa but in Western Europe and North America also. I addressed my contributions to the Uppsala and Brussels conferences to the differing perceptions of the partition of Africa held by historians of colonisation on the one hand and historians of Africa on the other.[1]

Early in 1986 I paid a three-week visit to the British Institute at what was, I believe, the most perilous moment of its history. Our all-important patrons at the British Academy had recently sent a visiting mission to inspect us, and it had reported that our institute, while doing some good research, was living too much unto itself and was failing to make its presence sufficiently felt in the host country. When I arrived on the scene, I found that the local representative of the British Council, at the behest of his masters in London, was busy drafting a scheme for the virtual takeover of our little organisation by his big one. There were voices in the university that held that we were not doing enough to help it, and Godfrey Muriuki gave me his opinion that the institute had an image problem, deriving partly from the worldwide fame of Richard and Mary Leakey, which caused many Kenyans to view archaeology as the last bastion of white imperialism in Kenya. British officialdom simply felt, with much justification, that the institute was doing nothing to attract a local public in and around Nairobi. It was not teaching. It was not organising conferences or sponsoring public lectures. It was not even offering simple entertainment as a means of advertising its whereabouts and its facilities.

Such were the problems that John Sutton and I had to resolve in discussion as we went about our routine business of inspecting the work in progress. He took me first into the Rift Valley, where he himself had been working on the abandoned occupation sites known as *Sirikwa holes,* erroneously described by earlier investigators as *pit dwellings,* which had proved on excavation to be partially sunken cattle pens, each with a human dwelling built on the surface and close to the stock entrance. There were thousands of these sites scattered across the floor of the Rift Valley and on its western slopes, and the carbon evidence suggested that the period of occupation had extended from about the tenth century until the seventeenth. Their abandonment could probably be attributed to the coming of the Masai who, according to their traditions, had expanded southwards down the Rift Valley from the Lake Turkana basin during the seventeenth and eighteenth centuries, seizing the cattle of the Kalenjin and forcing their herdsmen to retreat into the high hills to the west of the valley floor. It was John's great contribution to this outline scenario to perceive that the Sirikwa holes represented merely the pastoral outreach of the Kalenjin, who had always had their agricultural bases in the high hills, which had better rainfall and deeper soils than the Rift floor.

On our 1986 trip we visited the sites at Lanet and Hyrax Hill, both in the neighbourhood of Nakuru, and ended up at Pamela Scott's farm at Deloraine, just under the western wall of the Rift. The farm had both a fine collection of Sirikwa holes and an earlier but still Iron Age occupation site, with pottery distinct from that of the Sirikwa sites and dating to about the eighth century. A Sirikwa cattle pen had been superimposed on part of this earlier site, so there was the possibility of establishing a direct sequence of cultures. I therefore listened with some sympathy as John committed himself to spending a month at Deloraine later in the year but also noted in my diary that both of the institute's archaeologists would thus be working on pastoralism in the Rift Valley and western highlands of Kenya. Somehow we would have to find a means of broadening the perspective.

My next journey with John was to the coast, which I had last visited with Neville Chitick in 1982. Our talk then had been mainly of stone towns dating from the tenth century onwards, many of them sited on off-shore islands and inhabited, at least initially, by communities of immigrant traders from Arabia and the Persian Gulf, that had supposedly introduced the practice of Islam and gradually transmitted it to their African slaves and dependants. Now I was going to see the work of a young Cambridge archaeologist, Mark Horton, who had been excavating for two seasons with some help from the institute at the ruined town of Shanga on the southern shore of Pate Island. There he had uncovered the remains of a succession of three stone mosques, the earliest dating to the tenth century, and below them several more layers of smaller mosques built in mud-and-wattle and dating from the eighth century on. Not only had he added two centuries to the history of Islam on the East African coast, he had also undermined still further the old conception of Arab colonists implanting a vastly superior religious and material culture upon the coastal peoples. It was now apparent that the first Muslims to build mosques on the coast had been in material ways quite humble people who had gathered in buildings large enough to accommodate only ten or twenty worshippers. Their descendants had evidently built up their prosperity only gradually, and probably the process of acculturation with the local inhabitants had begun with the earliest contacts.

Mark came to meet us at Lamu one evening in the little dhow he used to fetch food and freshwater for his expedition, for neither were available at the site. We left at dawn, sailing in great style up the Mkanda Creek between Manda Island and the mainland, arguing furiously with each other about Swahili origins, with the three Swahili sailors nodding sagely, if uncomprehendingly, in the stern. When we emerged into the open bay north of Manda Island, however, we had to tack into a strong wind in quite rough water. For the first hour we were sailing close to the wind and pitching, after which we turned to the northwest, and the little ship's motion became a corkscrew one that soon left me lying flat on top of the ballast with a towel over my head. At last we grounded in Shanga Bay, but we were still a mile from the shore, and we had to finish the journey by wading on sharp and potholed coral with the tide swirling around our blundering feet and legs. It seemed like an endless torture, but we arrived at Mark's camp in time to snatch a quick meal and then to walk over the site before the workers went off duty. We inspected the Friday mosque, with its three levels of stone building, and Mark showed us how the two upper levels were built of coral rag quarried from ancient beaches above the shoreline, whereas the builders of the earliest stone mosque had used porites coral mined from the sea floor that could be cut with precision tools while still soft and then allowed to harden as it dried. The porites technique was much practised in the coastal towns of the Red Sea, whereas the use of coral rag was common in the Persian Gulf as well as in East Africa. In the earliest levels of all, built in mud and thatch, the only features requiring any external influence were the apselike *qiblas* on the northward-facing walls.

In camp that evening we made the acquaintance of Mark's three volunteer site supervisors. There was a classical archaeologist from Israel, a young graduate in classics and ancient history from University College, London, and an assistant from the Ironbridge Museum in Shrophire. They were living very hard, these people, eating mostly beans and rice with a little corned beef for relish. They washed in the sea, slept without pillows on improvised beds, and told horror stories about suppurating sores caused by mosquitoes and sand flies. From 7 A.M. until 4:30 P.M. they were out in the hot sun, each supervising the work of six or more locally recruited labourers whose language they scarcely understood. In the evenings they sorted the finds by the light of hurricane lamps. They earned nothing and seemed entirely happy. The next day being a Friday, when the Swahili workmen took their weekly holiday, we were able to make an unhurried inspection of the whole site and to see the Friday mosque in perspective with the area of close-built stone housing to the west of it, and larger area of mud-and-thatch housing on the northern landward side, and the area of large stone-walled gardens and plantations to the east. Mainly, we were considering the priorities for further work at this rather difficult and inaccessible site. Its situation so close to the northeastern limits of Bantu speech raised intriguing questions about the ethnic character of the indigenous population in early Islamic times, which might be answered by further excavation in the areas of domestic settlement. It seemed clear to me that the great achievement of Mark's work thus far had been to show that the spread of Islam had long preceded the use of stone for building and therefore that the first priority for coastal archaeology was to look again at some other sites that had so far been excavated only to the depth of the earliest stone structures in order to discover whether they too had experienced Islamic influence at an earlier period than had long been assumed. It was with such a broad programme in mind that we soon afterwards applied successfully to the Leverhulme Foundation for a three-year grant to enable Mark to pursue his research more generally on the origins of Islam in East Africa, including especially the islands of Zanzibar and Pemba.

Meanwhile, during our journeys by road, rail, and air John and I were taking every opportunity to work at the institute's image problem and to define the priorities for its future research. We decided that the existing overconcentration on western Kenya would soon be ended. Peter Robertshaw had almost finished writing up the results of his work there and would then be ready to tackle a new project in western Uganda, where the success of Yoweri Museveni's insurgency movement against the second Obote government had opened up the possibility of resuming the work begun by Eric Lanning and Merrick Posnansky in the 1950s and 1960s. John's interest in the Iron Age economy of the Rift Valley was about to take on a much wider scope, extending from the Nuba Hills and southern Ethiopia in the north to the Nyanga highlands in northeastern Zimbabwe in the south. It amounted to nothing less than the exploration of a whole strategy of food production practised for many centuries in the dry highlands between the eastern coastal region and that of the great lakes. The strategy depended upon the intensive cultivation of terraced hillside fields fertilised by the manure of penned and stall-fed cattle. Last, with the growing successes of the Tigre Peoples Liberation Front against the Mengistu regime in Ethiopia, it was beginning to look as though a return to the institute's largest project, at the ancient capital city of Aksum, which we had been forced to abandon in 1974, might before too long be once more possible.

At the end of all our talks I felt convinced that John Sutton had a more than adequate vision of where he should try to lead the institute in its future research. Above all, he understood that not even the most urgent tasks could be carried out by the institute's staff unaided. Mark Horton's work at the coast was an example of what could be achieved by offering ideas and encouragement to visiting scholars who could bring with them some additional funds from their home bases. There remained the much more intractable problem of involving the local universities in our research. Whereas in the 1960s Posnansky had been able to attract a small band of Makerere students to help him at Bigo by providing only their keep and their travelling expenses, the East African students of the 1980s were being educated in departments much less aware of the importance of research. Moreover, most of them needed to earn money during their vacations in order to supplement their scholarship grants. In this matter we had to accept that the times were against us and that most of our success would depend upon the help we could enlist from outside. As the vice chancellor of Nairobi said when I went to see him, we were filling a gap that East Africa could not for the time being fill for itself and that must be our defence, if we needed one. The high commissioner, Leonard Allinson, proved sympathetic to the idea that the institute would be wise to maintain a fairly low profile in Kenya and to keep reminding people that its interests were spread over as much of eastern Africa as political conditions in the various countries allowed.

On returning to London in February 1986 I was within a few months of my retirement from the university, and, as everyone who has shared that experience must know, a retirement once announced removes most of the scope for further initiatives and restricts one to performance of routine tasks. It is a time for reflection and gratitude, marked by some necessary and intensely moving acts of farewell. Among these I remember especially a party given by Cambridge University Press and held in the senior common room at SOAS to celebrate the completion of the *Cambridge Hisroty of Africa*. John Fage, my fellow general editor, was there. So were Richard Gray, Andrew Roberts, Michael Crowder, and Neville Sanderson, among the volume editors, and Humphrey Fisher, David Birmingham, Shula Marks, Anthony Atmore, and Michael Brett, who had all been major contributors. The eight substantial volumes were on display around the room, and our host, Michael Black, the publisher, did not fail to begin his speech of welcome with the Horatian tag, *Si monumentum requiris aere perennius, circumspice* (If you need for a monument, look around you.) Although it had no formal connection with my coming retirement, that gathering best symbolised what my academic career had most essentially been about. Most of those present had been at some time close colleagues at SOAS, and most had been in the business long enough to remember the pitifully inadequate state of the published literature when we had begun our teaching of the subject twenty-five or thirty years before. It was truly satisfying to think that we now had a full-scale work of reference, prepared entirely by professional scholars, with comprehensive bibliographies and careful evaluation of the main sources, which, without pretending to say the last word on any part of the subject, nevertheless offered a firm base on which others could build. I suppose that our largest regret was that so few of the university libraries in Africa would be able to afford it at its hugely inflated price of some £400 a set.

In May 1986 Sarah and Michael installed themselves in a house that they had bought together in Hackney, and I began to prepare for my departure from the London flat by making some structural changes at Frilsham that would enable me to keep the best of my London furniture and pictures. At the school I spent my final months winnowing the papers accumulated during thirty-eight years of continous employment. Retirement day found me happily at Frilsham with the opening pages of *The African Experience* already on my desk and the seedlings of next year's wallflowers ready to be planted out in the place of the past summer's petunias.

Although I worked on it most days, it took me four years to write *The African Experience*. It was to have twenty-one short chapters of some five thousand words apiece, and I found that each one took me two months, allowing four weeks to read, three to write, and one to tidy up. In public I pretended that I worked only when there was nothing better to do, but in fact I was away from home very little. I spent three weeks of each winter in East Africa on the business of the British Institute and a month of every summer on holiday, usually in Scandinavia where I greatly enjoyed the company of friends much younger than I. On these trips I would usually pick up Christopher Steed in Uppsala, and we would join Inger and Richard Marklund at their summer cabin near Skellefteå. From there we would make a round of family visits to the Aasas and the Marklunds scattered across the northern shores of the Baltic and then drive in convoy over the mountains into Norway and spend a week or two of perpetual daylight on one or other of the offshore islands—Lofoten, Vesterålen, and Senja—with their incomparable scenery of blue waters backed by the snow-capped conical mountains of the mainland between Narvik and Tromsø. For accommodation we would use the wooden cabins erected by earlier generations of southern Norwegian fishermen when following the annual migration of the codfish between January and April. Nowadays the fishing trawlers are so much more comfortable than the onshore cabins that the crews prefer to sleep on board, leaving the cabins to be converted for tourism of a modest kind, suited to the purses of the young and adventurous.

In 1987 my Scandinavian holiday coincided with Richard Marklund's ordination as a pastor in the Church of Sweden. At the ceremony in Luleå cathedral Inger, wearing the national dress of North Bothnia and carrying the cross, led the resplendent procession of bishop and clergy, moving at a smart pace up the nave and into the sanctuary, where the ordinands, six men and two women, awaited them. After the laying on of hands all donned eucharistic vestments and concelebrated with the presiding bishop, each then administering the Sacrament to their families and friends. Later in the day Christopher, Bengt, and I sat down to an afternoon meal with eighty members of the Marklund and Aasa families, after which speeches and toasts continued late into the summer evening. From Luleå on this occasion I drove about five hundred miles with Christopher northwards through Finland to the northeastern corner of Norway, where we stayed briefly at the little offshore island of Vardø, which looks across the Varanger Fjord towards Murmansk and the Barents Sea. Behind us to the west it was all moorland country, grazed by herds of small reindeer whose Saame owners maintained a low profile. Most of the human population was concentrated in a handful of fishing villages around the coasts. From Vardø we made our way slowly westwards to the Porsangenfjord and the North Cape, at the tip of the island of Magavoy, where we found accommodation at the home of a brave old fisherman who spent four nights of every week alone in a forty-foot trawler out on the Barents Sea.

He told us that often he returned with nothing but sometimes with as much as one thousand kilos of cod, which he sold to a processing factory on the island. His wife claimed to be the northernmost district nurse in the world, and the top floor of their house was fitted up as a little hospital, where she had beds for up to fourteen in-patients; serious cases were taken by helicopter to Hammerfest. We arrived there on July 7, which was described as the first warm day of the year. On the previous day the only road across to the island had been closed because of heavy snow, but we were able to climb the local mountian at midnight, in nearly full daylight and a comfortable temperature.

By the summer of 1988 Richard and Inger were settled in a vast rectory in the forest parish of Arvidsjaur. One of Richard's duties was to provide pastoral care for the Saame reindeer herdsmen in their summer encampments in the high mountians near the Norwegian frontier, and on this occasion Christopher and I accompanied them to a church weekend at a summer village, called Vejsaluokta in the upper valley of the Luleå River. There the parsonage consisted of a sunken rondavel with a roof of turf; the place was furnished only with birch boughs laid upon the floor and

Suzanne Miers at Frilsham in 1990

400

with a pair of long poles that ran from the entrance to the central fireplace, marking off the reception area from the private quarters to the left and right of it. When visitors came to discuss their spiritual or matrimonial problems, they would sit down on the end of a pole nearest to the door, and as their confidence grew, they would edge farther and farther along it, until finally they would venture to chop a small piece of kindling and place it gently on the fire. Meanwhile, smoke filled the entire chamber down to about knee height, causing those of us who were unaccustomed to it to lie rather than sit and to move around only by rolling. It was in these circumstances that the pastor wrote his Sunday sermon, passing it sheet by sheet to his wife for her approval and correction. Sunday morning was picturesque, with Saame dressed in their brightest clothes striding down the mountainside through the birchwoods to the church rondavel, which was somewhat bigger than the domestic ones and furnished, fortunately, with a metal stove and a chimney pipe. After the service a sandwich lunch was provided for all on trestle tables in a nearby birch copse.

As always, however, it was the travels that I made in East Africa that were chiefly significant and memorable. In 1988 I at last had an opportunity to visit Malawi, a country whose almost every corner I had long been familiar with on paper, both from *The Missionary Factor in East Africa* and from my biography of Harry Johnston, the founder of the British protectorate there during the 1890s. Now I had an invitation to visit the university at Zomba that had been founded following the breakup of the Central African Federation in 1965 and where three of my former research students—John Flint, Bertin Webster, and now Owen Kalinga—had succeeded each other as heads of the history department. Owen and his wife now invited me to be their houseguest, enabling me to see things much more from the inside than would have been possible otherwise.

I was fascinated by the contradictions of this small country, which had grown up under an elderly dictator who had accepted so much aid from the white government of South Africa and yet continued to express admiration for most things British. It was more obviously a police state than any other African country I had visited. In any public place people lowered their voices and leaned closer to one another, whatever the topic of their conversation. Midnight arrests of suspected critics of the government occurred frequently enough to inspire general unease among the educated. At the university such had recently been the fate of Jack Mapanje, a teacher of English literature and a poet in his own right who was considered by those who knew him best to have no strongly held political views of any kind. His family had been told by the secret police to forget him, as they would never see him again. (He reappeared three years later.) And yet, despite all this, it seemed to me that the morale in the academic community in Zomba was noticeably higher than in the other East African universities that I had visited. It was the only university on the continent that had never been closed on account of student unrest. Scholarship seemed to be more highly valued than elsewhere, and academic staff did not in general have second jobs. In the history department there was a fine tradition, implanted by Bertin Webster, of requiring honors candidates to contribute a long essay based on original research, either in the national archives or in the traditional history of their home districts. These were deposited in the university library, and I saw many that were of more than passing interest. There was also a flourishing master's programme, the keenest member of which was a captain in the Malawian army who was writing a thesis on the Nyasaland battalion of the King's African Rifles. He had so far absorbed the spirit of his sources that he would write with enthusiasm about the actions of his regiment against the "recalcitrant tribes" of his homeland. One day he took me to visit the barracks built by Harry Johnston to house the seventy Sikh soliders he had recruited in the Punjab as the nucleus of his "defence force." It was still in active use, and in the forecourt a large fig tree spread its shade over a circular bench, where retired soldiers gathered each morning to share their memories of past campaigns. They told us that life was altogether to easy for the young soldiers recruited these days. I could not help wondering whether they too, when left to themselves, talked to each other about recalcitrant tribes. They probably did.

When my work in Zomba was done, Owen escorted me in a borrowed Land Rover labelled "Save the Children" on a quick tour through the central province of the country. We made first for Lilongwe, the new capital built by Hastings Banda in his Chewa-speaking homeland to replace the old colonial capital at Blantyre. I called on the high commissioner, Dennis Osborne, who, remarkably, had begun his African career as a lecturer in physics at the University of Ghana, where he had suffered arrest and imprisonment by the government of Nkrumah. I found him well aware of the Mapanje case and actively disposed to help. The main purpose of our visit to Lilongwe was, however, to make contact with the Department of Antiquities, presided over by Gade Ngomezulu and Jusuf Juwayeye, both former students of Desmond Clark's at Berkeley, with whom we discussed the possibility of a joint research project with the historians of the university. We also sought some help from the British Institute for the identification of the precolonial capital sites of the main Chewa kingdoms. Full cooperation having been promised, we drove across the centre of Chewaland to our overnight lodging by the shore of Lake Malawi near Kota Kota, which during the nineteenth century had been the main refreshment station for the Swahili-Arab caravan trade from Kilwa on the Indian Ocean coast.

Southwards from Kota Kota lay a stretch of Chewa-speaking country where small kingdoms had emerged during the seventeenth and eighteenth centuries. Some of the capital sites were said to be well known to local people, and we spent an interesting day looking for likely leads that Owen's students might follow up later. We returned to Zomba by the Shire Valley, where the small town of Fort Johnston, its name unchanged, still dominates the outflow of the river from the lake. Dr. Banda was said to be on a speaking tour in the neighbourhood, and the police had set up a roadblock to divert the traffic. It was a hot day, but Owen reached for his jacket and necktie. "This should do the trick," he said. And it did.

In 1989 and 1990 my annual travels with John Sutton took us from Nairobi to Uganda, where the institute had restarted its work on the sites associated in oral tradition with the Chwezi (see Chapters 7, 8, 12, and 17). With Museveni's government now firmly in power it was possible to travel there by car without excessive risk of theft or hijacking. Indeed, the main road from the Kenya frontier to Kampala was already under active reconstruction with the help of international donors. One arrived there dusty but on time. At Makerere one wing of the guest-house was now once again able to provide accommodation for guests. In the history department, however, things now seemed worse than they had five years previously. Sam Karugire had left it for the chief commissionership of customs, and his younger colleagues, whom we met in a group, were not impressive. We hoped to discover what interest they might have in the work of our institute, but they spoke to us only of the difficulties they encountered in their teaching and especially in the shortage of books. Having arranged in 1986 for the donation of a complete set of the *Cambridge History* to the university library, I inquired whether they were finding it useful. It transpired that none of them was even aware of its existence, although the library had been displaying it prominently on its main reference shelves for more than two years. We were left wondering whether an institution that had slipped so far downhill could realistically be expected to recover, and yet the students whom we met as we moved around the campus seemed as bright, alert, and friendly as their predecessors during the great days of the place.

In 1989 our main destination was Ntusi, the subcounty headquarters nine miles from the great earthwork site at Bigo, where I had excavated with Merrick Posnansky in 1960. The place is today an outlying community of Ganda farmers who live mainly from their banana groves. All, however, are conscious that their land is littered with pottery shards easily distinguishable from the modern ones and with old querns and grindstones, the hallmarks of earlier grain-eating people who lived here before them. Moreover, a part of the little valley that drops away to the north of the village is marked by an artificially rounded basin flanked on three sides by large mounds that are no less obviously artificial. Though formerly described as dams, these are in reality nothing but the spoil from the original hollowing out of the basin, augmented by that from more recent cleanings of its floor. The basin was in fact a large drinking pond for the cattle of the grain eaters, who have now disappeared from the scene. John Sutton had been reexamining the whole area during the previous year with a visiting student from the University of Birmingham, Andrew Reid. Together they had excavated two large middens and the remains of an iron-smelting forge on opposite sides of the modern village and had formed the impression that the ancient site must have been that of a town rather than a village. Carbon samples had yielded dates as early as the tenth century and as late as the fifteenth. Ntusi had therefore predated Bigo by perhaps three centuries and had continued in occupation during Bigo's early period. There was some reason to think of it as the metropolis to which Bigo had been an adjunct, built to accommodate the king and his royal herds.[2]

At all events, it was clear that Ntusi held the potential to revolutionise existing conceptions of a Chwezi kingdom centred in the grasslands of western Uganda and situated astride the more recent ethnic frontiers between Buganda, Bunyoro, and Ankole. At the time of our visit Andrew Reid was back working there, now as a doctoral student at Cambridge University, on a surface survey of the smaller pastoral sites in the vicinity, linked to Ntusi and Bigo by a common configuration and by shards of identical pottery. He walked into our camp, a knapsack on his back, just as we were erecting our tents in the dark after a late arrival. As we ate our meal by the light of a hurricane lamp, he told us of his adventures as he had criss-crossed the country within a thirty-mile radius, walking as much as 120 miles a week and sleeping wherever he happened to be at nightfall. To add to his exertions he had been playing Saturday afternoon football for the local district team, which had greatly helped him in securing goodwill for his unusual mission. Just then he was temporarily supported by two more British students who had been cleaning and classifying his pottery samples, which were to be deposited at the Uganda Museum. Indeed, we took them all on board our Land Rover for our return journey to Kampala.

We spent a couple of days walking round the Ntusi and visiting some of the more accessible of Andrew Reid's pastoral outliers, and it became clear to me that, looked at in its entirety, the archaeology of Ntusi and its related Chwezi sites constituted a problem that could only be tackled in dribs and drabs by different investigators as opportunity offered. Most of the central site was under intensive cultivation by farmers who, for all their goodwill, would not brook a major disturbance to their livelihood. The only viable policy was that of nibbling, now here, now there, whenever outside help, like that of Andrew Reid and his friends, was available. John Sutton's role as academic sponsor and intermediary with the museum and antiquities authorities and as visiting consultant, logistical provider, and intermittent participant, seemed to make good sense.

Our next journey to Uganda, in 1990, had as its main objective the village of Kibiro by the northeastern shore of Lake Albert, where the Nyoro inhabitants were specialists in the mining and refining of the salt deposited by a natural spring that flowed into the lake at this point. The special archaeological significance of such a site was that, unlike most African village sites, the same spot had been continuously occupied for many centuries and therefore offered the possibility of recovering a complete sequence in the development of material culture, which could then be used as a guide for dating the more transitory occupation sites found in the surrounding country. More generally, however, we hoped that it could be used as a gateway to the study of lakeshore fishing cultures right up and down the line of the great lakes of the western Rift. The institute's current interest in the site was that it was providing logistical and other kinds of help to Graham Connah, a seasoned archaeologist with a distinguished record of work in Nigeria and now employed at the University of New England in New South Wales, which had granted him research leave for this project.

We drove there along fearsome roads, making a long detour by Masindi in order to avoid a collapsed bridge on the direct route from Kampala to Hoima, arriving late in the afternoon at Graham Connah's base camp, where the side road from Hoima turned into a footpath descending steeply to the lakeshore, a thousand feet below. We found Thaddeo, the institute's driver-mechanic, camped by the end of the road, along with our second Land Rover. He was a Luo from western Kenya, and he had been living here for the past two months, buying the supplies for the whole expedition and sending them down the escarpment with locally recruited porters. We pitched our tent beside his and next morning set off down the same footpath that I had last trodden with Caroline and a couple of White Fathers during our first visit to Bunyoro thirty-six years before. Soon we could see Kibiro village below us, with its salt pans decending in tiers to the lakeshore. The Connahs were accompanied by a research student from Australia and by two members of staff from the Uganda Department of Antiquities, and after spending the afternoon with them on the site, we joined them in their camp, which was set in a grove of trees on the edge of the village and close to the shore. It seemed an idyllic spot, but as we ate our dinner at a trestle table in the open air, thunder clouds gathered and lightning flashed all round us, soon followed by drenching rain, that sent us fleeing to our little tents. Unlike most tropical storms, it continued without pause for the whole night. Sleep was out of the question, and we emerged in the morning sodden, muddy, and bleary-eyed to climb the slippery path up the escarpment and make our getaway. I have never, since that episode, been able to think of Lake Albert with the same warm feeling as I had for it before.

In September 1989 I paid my first visit to Ethiopia since the revolution of 1974. John Sutton had been there once or twice for short trips and had quietly dropped hints that the institute would be ready, as soon as conditions permitted, to resume its work at Aksum. The Tigre Peoples Liberation Front was by this time clearly winning its war against the Mengistu regime, which was now being deprived of its arms supplies by the Soviet Union's general disengagement from African adventures. The fighting line was now only some sixty miles north of the capital, and our friends at the University of Addis Ababa and the National Museum thought the time ripe to organise a small international seminar at which scholars from Western countries could state their interests in future archaeological research in the country. The unspoken premise was that, although the central government was likely soon to change, the civil servants in charge of antiquities and research permits were likely to continue in office. They invited me to be one of the chairmen, and I attended, along with John Sutton, David Phillipson, and Stuart Munro-Hay, who had recently completed the memoir of Neville Chittick's two expeditions of 1972–73.[3] We duly presented a copy of the published volume to the minister of education and sport at a formal reception at the National Museum. Thus we prepared the way for the largest research project ever undertaken by the institute, which began operations under David Phillipson's direction in 1992. It was to be followed in 1993 by another project almost as large, to study the ancient economy of the Nyanga Mountains of northeastern Zimbabwe, where there existed a vast conglomeration of stone terraces and stock pens clearly designed for the manuring of the terraced fields (see Chapter 18). In both projects we were able to secure the full cooperation of the local universities and to contribute significantly in the training of their students in archaeological research.

Meanwhile, the American African Studies Association had done me the honour of choosing me as the recipient of its Distinguished Africanist Award for 1989, the formal presentation of which took place at the concluding banquet of the annual conference, held that year in Atlanta in November. I had the opportunity to make a short speech of thanks, and I used it to express the thought, which I had long been evolving, of America's role as the centre and guardian of African studies, at least until such a time as Africa itself had overcome its economic and political problems sufficiently to take the lead. Europe had played a big part in the

With Sue on our wedding day, July 6, 1990

A recent photograph of Roland Oliver

407

Roland Oliver and Suzanne Miers Oliver, 1994

initiation of African studies, but Europe seemed to be turning increasingly inwards and towards the problems created by the collapse of the Soviet empire along its eastern frontiers. It lacked the kind of built-in interest in Africa that the United States possessed in its significant minority of forty million African Americans. Increasingly, it was in American universities that the most gifted Africans now sought places, not merely as passing students but as mature scholars in search of the academic posts that would afford them the opportunities for research and publication that no longer existed in their home countries. There was here a spirit of openness and generosity towards would-be migrants that in Europe had been signally lacking and that must be to the advantage of America and Africa alike.

For me, however, the Atlanta conference had a momentous consequence, with which I must bring this autobiography to a close. From there I travelled with Suzanne Miers to Athens, Ohio, to give a public lecture at Ohio University, where, walking on the attractive golf course that faced her house, we began to discuss the possibility of marriage. We had known each other well since 1962. We were the same age and shared the same interests. She had been widowed for twenty-seven years and I for six. We both had happily married children with young families of their own. I had already taken retirement, and she was thinking of it. During the six months that followed we exchanged three more visits before taking the final leap in a nuptial mass at Douai on July 6, 1990; our life together since has been a dream too blissful to be externalised by the telling of it.

Notes

Index

Notes

CHAPTER 1. A CHILD OF THE RAJ (1923-30)

1. A. E. Housman, *A Shropshire Lad*, 1896.

CHAPTER 3. STOWE AND KING'S (1936-42)

1. N. G. Annan, *Our Age: Portrait of a Generation* (London: Weidenfeld and Nicolson, 1990), pp. 98–112.

CHAPTER 6. THE FIRST EXPOSURE (1948-49)

1. C. H. Philips, *The School of Oriental and African Studies. 1917 to 1967* (London: School of Oriental and African Studies, 1967); C. H. Philips, *Beyond the Ivory Tower* (London: Radcliffe Press, 1995), pp. 41–53, 152–78.

2. H. M. Stanley, *In Darkest Africa*, vol. 1 (London: Sampson Low, Marston, Searle, and Rivington, 1890), pp. 267–68.

CHAPTER 7. THREE KINGDOMS (1949)

1. In Bantu languages singular, plural, and other shades of meaning are conveyed by prefixes. Modern scholarly practice is to omit these prefixes as far as possible, writing the *Ganda* rather than the *Baganda* and the *Chwezi* rather than the *Bachwezi*. The local prefixes *U* and *Bu* are, however, generally retained: thus *Buganda* rather than "the Ganda country."

2. For the only autobiography of the principal of an African University see B. de Bunsen, *Adventures in Education* (Kendal, England: Titus Wilson, 1995), pp. 79–117.

3. A. Kagwa, *Basekabaka be Buganda* (The Kings of Buganda) (London: Macmillan, 1901, 1912, 1927, 1953); M. S. M. Kiwanuka, *The Kings of Buganda* (Nairobi: East African Literature Bureau, 1970); J. Roscoe, *The Baganda* (London: Macmillan, 1911) .

4. K. W. [pseud.], "The Kings of Bunyoro-Kitara," *Uganda Journal* 3 (1935): 155–60; 4 (1936): 75–83; 5 (1937): 53–69.

5. J. W. Nyakatura, *Abakama ba Bunyoro Kitara* (The Kings of Bunyoro-Kitara) (St. Justin, Quebec, 1948).

413

6. R. Oliver, "The Baganda and the Bakonjo," *Uganda Journal* 18 (1954): 31–33.

CHAPTER 8. PASTORAL PURSUITS (1950)

1. A. G. Katate and L. Kamugungunu, *Abagabe b'Ankole* (The Kings of Ankole) (Nairobi: East African Literature Bureau, 1955).

2. H. F. Morris, *The Heroic Recitations of the Bahima of Ankole* (Oxford, England: Clarendon, 1964).

3. S. R. Karugire, *A History of the Kingdom of Nkore in Western Uganda to 1896* (Oxford, England: Clarendon, 1971).

4. The 'red dean' (Hewlett Johnson) was an ultraleft cleric who was constantly visiting China at this time. Viktor Kravchenko defected to Canada from the NKVD (the Soviet secret police), exposing many of his former colleagues. He was tried in absentia in the USSR.

5. A. Kagame, *Inganji Karinga* (Songs of the Drum) (Kabgayi, Rwanda: 1943, 1947).

6. J. Vansina, *L'évolution du royaume rwanda des origines à 1900* (The Evolution of the Rwanda Kingdom from Its Origins to 1900) (Brussels: Académie Royale des Sciences d'Outremer, 1961).

CHAPTER 9. TO LAKE TANGANYIKA AND BACK (1950)

1. *Bakama*, the plural of *mukama*, is a royal title that means 'milkers', pastoral cattle owners.

2. E. Cézard, "Le Muhaya," *Anthropos* 30 (1935): 75–106; 31 (1936): 97–114, 489–508, 821–49; 32 (1937): 15–60.

CHAPTER 10. THE MARTIAL RACES (1950)

1. A. W. Southall, *Alur Society* (Cambridge, England: Cambridge University Press, 1956).

2. J. P. Crazzolara, *The Lwoo* (Verona, Italy: Missioni Africane, 1951–54).

3. J. Tosh, *Clan Leaders and Colonial Chiefs in Lango* (Oxford, England: Clarendon, 1978), pp. 17–34; John Lamphear, *The Traditional History of the Jie of Uganda* (Oxford, England: Clarendon, 1976).

CHAPTER 11. THE EAST AFRICAN HORIZON (1950)

1. John Gray, *History of Zanzibar from the Middle Ages to 1856* (London: Oxford University Press, 1962).

CHAPTER 12. TAKING STOCK (1950–53)

1. H. Trevor-Roper, "The Rise of Christian Europe," *Listener*, November 28, 1963, p. 871.

2. R. A. Hamilton (ed.), *History and Archaeology in Africa: Report of a Conference held in July 1953* (London: School of Oriental and African Studies, 1955).

3. Editorial, "Africa's Past," *Times* (London), July 18, 1953.
4. Ibid.

CHAPTER 13. THE POLITICAL KINGDOM (1953–55)

1. R. M. Slade, *English-Speaking Missions in the Congo Independent State, 1878–1908* (Brussels: Académie Royale des Sciences d'Outremer, 1959).
2. J. E. Flint, *Sir George Goldie and the Making of Nigeria* (London: Oxford University Press, 1960).
3. William Shakespeare, *Richard II* 3.2.55.

CHAPTER 14. A CHAIR DECLINED (1955–57)

1. The reference is to the south bank of the Thames, site of Lambeth Palace, official residence of the archbishop of Canterbury.
2. D. H. Jones (ed.), *History and Archaeology in Africa: Second Conference held in July 1957* (London: School of Oriental and African Studies, 1959).

CHAPTER 16. WEST TO EAST (1958)

1. The CFA franc was the currency used in all the French African colonies and convertible into French francs at Fr 2 to CFA 1.

CHAPTER 17. EAST AFRICA REVISITED (1958)

1. R. Oliver, "The Royal Tombs of Buganda," *Uganda Journal* 23 (1959): 124–33.
2. R. Oliver, "Ancient Capital Sites of Ankole," *Uganda Journal* 23 (1959): 51–63.

CHAPTER 18. EAST TO SOUTH (1958)

1. J. Vansina, *L'évolution du royaume rwanda des origines à 1900* (The Evolution of the Rwanda Kingdom from Its Origins to 1900) (Brussels: Académie Royale des Sciences d'Outremer, 1961).
2. R. Summers and K. R. Robinson, *Zimbabwe Excavations, 1958* (Bulawayo, South Africa: National Museums of Southern Rhodesia, 1961).

CHAPTER 19. FULL THROTTLE (1958–60)

1. B. A. Ogot, *History of the Southern Luo* (Nairobi: East African Institute Press, 1967).
2. *Historians in Tropical Africa* (Salisbury [now Harare], Rhodesia: University College of Rhodesia and Nyasaland, 1962).

CHAPTER 20. SPREADING THE WORD (1960–62)

1. D. Birmingham, *Trade and Conflict in Angola: The Mbundu and Their Neighbours Under the Influence of the Portuguese, 1483–1690* (Oxford, England: Clarendon, 1966).
2. S. Marks, *Reluctant Rebellion* (Oxford, England: Clarendon, 1970).

3. J. B. Webster, *The African Churches Among the Yoruba, 1888–1922* (Oxford, England: Clarendon, 1964).

4. I. A. Akinjogbin, *Dahoney and Its Neighbours, 1708–1818* (Cambridge, England: Cambridge University Press, 1967).

5. K. Y. Daaku, *Trade and Politics on the Gold Coast, 1600–1720* (Oxford, England: Clarendon, 1970).

6. J. K. Fynn, *Asante and Its Neighbors, 1700–1807* (London: Longman, 1973).

7. R. H. K. Darkwah, *Shewa, Menelik, and the Ethiopian Empire, 1815–1889* (London: Heineman, 1975).

8. W. Rodney's first book was *A History of the Upper Guinea Coast, 1545–1800* (Oxford, England: Clarendon, 1970).

9. G. L. Caplan, *The Elites of Barotseland, 1878–1969* (London: Christopher Hurst, 1970).

10. M. S. M. Kiwanuka, *A History of Buganda from the Foundation of the Kingdom to 1900* (New York: Africa Publishing, 1972).

11. S. Miers, *Britain and the Ending of the Slave Trade* (London: Longman, 1975).

12. R. Oliver and J. D. Fage (eds.), "Third Conference on African History and Archaeology," *Journal of African History* 3 (1962): 173–374.

13. J. Vansina, R. Mauny, and L. V. Thomas (eds.), *The Historian in Tropical Africa* (London: Oxford University Press, 1964).

CHAPTER 22. THE CREST OF THE WAVE (1962–63)

1. D. W. Cohen, *The Historical Tradition of Busoga* (Oxford, England: Clarendon, 1972).

2. N. Levtzion, *Muslims and Chiefs in West Africa: A Study of Islam in the Middle Volta Basin in the Precolonial Period* (Oxford, England: Clarendon, 1968).

3. G. Haliburton, *The Prophet Harris* (London: Longman, 1971).

4. M. Twaddle, *Kakungulu and the Creation of Uganda, 1868–1928* (London: James Currey, 1993).

5. T. Tamrat, *Church and State in Ethiopia, 1270–1527* (Oxford, England: Clarendon, 1972).

6. N. Chittick, *Kilwa: An Islamic Trading City on the East African Coast* (Nairobi: British Institute in Eastern Africa, 1974).

CHAPTER 23. THE START OF THE MARATHON (1964–65)

1. R. Oliver, *African History for the Outside World* (London: School of Oriental and African Studies, 1964).

2. D. H. Jones (ed.), "Problems of African Chronology," *Journal of African History* 11 (1970): 161–268.

3. J. Vansina, *Living with Africa* (Madison: University of Wisconsin Press, 1994), p. 116.

4. T. O. Ranger (ed.), *Emerging Themes of African History* (Nairobi: East African Publishing House, 1968).

5. Ibid.

CHAPTER 24. THE LIONS OF JUDAH (1965–66)

1. M. Twaddle, *Kakungulu and the Creation of Uganda, 1868–1928* (London: James Currey, 1993).

2. D. W. Cohen, *The Historical Tradition of Busoga* (Oxford, England: Clarendon, 1972).

3. A. I. Salim, *The Swahili-Speaking Peoples of Kenya's Coast* (Nairobi: East African Publishing House, 1973).

4. S. R. Karugire, *A History of the Kingdom of Nkore in Western Uganda to 1896* (Oxford, England: Clarendon, 1971).

5. G. Muriuki, *A History of the Kikuyu, 1500–1900* (London: Oxford University Press, 1974).

CHAPTER 25. SCHOLARLY WANDERINGS (1967–68)

1. E. A. Alpers, *Ivory and Slaves in East Central Africa* (London: Heineman, 1975).

2. R. Oliver, "The Problem of the Bantu Expansion," *Journal of African History* 7 (1966): 361–76.

3. M. Guthrie, *Comparative Bantu* (Farnborough, England: Gregg, 1967–70).

CHAPTER 26. REVOLTING STUDENTS (1968–72)

1. C. F. Oliver, "Richard Burton: The African Years," in Robert I. Rotberg (ed.), *Africa and Its Explorers* (Cambridge, Mass.: Harvard University Press, 1970); C. F. Oliver, *Western Women in Colonial Africa* (Westport, Conn.: Greenwood, 1982).

2. A. M. Fika, *The Kano Civil War and British Overrule, 1882–1940* (Ibadan, Nigeria: Oxford University Press, 1978).

CHAPTER 27. FILLING IN THE GAPS (1973–78)

1. Fundãcao Calouste Gulbenkian, *Colóquio sobre Educação e Ciências Humanas na Africa de Lingua Portuguesa* (Colloquium on Education and the Human Sciences in Portuguese-Speaking Africa) (Lisbon: Fundacão Calouste Gulbenkian, 1979).

CHAPTER 28. IN TENEBRIS LUX (1979–83)

1. H. N. Chittick, *Manda: Excavations at an Island Port on the Kenya Coast* (Nairobi: British Institute in Eastern Africa, 1984).

2. D. A. Welsby and C. M. Daniels, *Soba: Archaeological Research at a Medieval Capital on the Blue Nile* (London: British Institute in Eastern Africa, 1991).

CHAPTER 29. THE END OF THE MARATHON (1984–85)

1. Paris I and Paris VII are divisions of the Sorbonne, two of twelve autonomous units created after the student protests of 1968.

2. P. Robertshaw, *Early Pastoralists of Southwestern Kenya* (Nairobi: British Institute in Eastern Africa, 1990).

3. P. Robertshaw, "Gogo Falls: A Complex Site East of Lake Victoria," *Azania* 26 (1991): 63–195.

CHAPTER 30. A MAN OF LETTERS (1985–90)

1. R. Oliver, "The Partition of Africa: The European and the African Interpretations," in *Le centenaire de l'état indépendent du Congo* (The Centenary of the Congo Independent State) (Brussels: Académie Royale des Sciences d'Outremer, 1988).

2. J. E. G. Sutton, "The Antecedents of the Interlacustrine Kingdoms," *Journal of African History* 34 (1993): 33–64.

3. S. C. H. Munro-Hay, *Excavations at Aksum* (London: Faber, 1989).

Index

Aasa-Marklund, Inger & Richard, 359, 377–79, 399–401
Abdullahi Bayero University, Kano, 335–38
Abir, Mordechai, 270–71, 302
Abraham, Donald, 219–20, 256, 283
Académie Royale des Sciences d'Outremer, 247, 249
Achimota. *See* Ghana, University of
Adams, Walter, 78, 218, 235, 275, 283
Addis Ababa, University of, 235–37, 272, 302–3
Aderibigbe, Ade, 147, 239, 322-3
Africa Bureau, 162–64, 229, 231
Africa Educational Trust, 164, 229–30, 288
Africa in the Iron Age, 334–35
Africa Private Enterprise Group, 289
Africa since 1800, 292–93
African Experience, The, 374–75, 391, 398–99
African History for the Outside World, 284, 291–92
African Middle Ages 1400–1800, 361
African Studies Association of the U.K., 275–76, 288
African Studies Association of North America, 275, 406–7
Ahmadu Bello University, Zaria, 338
Ajayi, Jacob, 147, 256, 320, 322, 351, 353, 393
Akinjogbin, Isaac, 244, 320–22
Aksum, anciental capital city, Ethiopia, 367, 397, 406
Allinson, Leonard, 369, 382, 397
Alpers, Edward, 270, 314
Amin, Idi, 118, 302, 341

Anstey, Roger, 186, 231
Arden-Clarke, Charles, 276–82
Aregay, Merid, 343
Arkell, A. J., 141
Astor, David, 157, 309–11, 348–49
Athman, Adrian, 105–6
Atmore, Anthony, 269–70, 292–93, 326–27, 360–62
Austin, Dennis, 177
Axelson, Eric, 219, 222–23
Ayandele, Emanuel, 147

Baker, Kenneth, 80
Baker, William, 130–32
Ballhatchet, Kenneth, 58
Balme, David, 172–73
Banda, Hastings, 231, 401–3
Barns, John, 37–38
Barry, Boubakar, 256
Beasley, W. G., 58
Beecher, Leonard, 205
Belgian Congo: in 1949, 61–71; in 1958, 197–200; in 1959–60, 232. *See also* Zaire
Benin Historical Research Scheme, 167, 190
Benin, Oba Akenzua II of, 190–91
Bennett, Norman, 261
Berlin Congress, centenary conference, 392–93
Beves, Donald, 28, 32
Bigo, earthwork site, Uganda, 144, 202, 212; 1960 excavation of, 240–41
Bimanyu, Daniel, 344, 353–54
Bindoff, S. T., 243, 254

419

Index

Index

Index